The Ruin of Roman Britain

How did Roman Britain end? This new study draws on fresh archaeological discoveries to argue that the end of Roman Britain was not the product of either a violent cataclysm or an economic collapse. Instead, the structure of late antique society, based on the civilian ideology of *paideia*, was forced to change by the disappearance of the Roman state. By the fifth century elite power had shifted to the warband and the edges of their swords. In this book Dr Gerrard describes and explains that process of transformation and explores the role of the 'Anglo-Saxons' in this time of change. This profound ideological shift returned Britain to a series of 'small worlds', the existence of which had been hidden by the globalising structures of Roman imperialism. Highly illustrated, the book includes two appendices, which detail Roman cemetery sites and weapon trauma, and pottery assemblages from the period.

JAMES GERRARD is a Lecturer in Roman Archaeology at Newcastle University. He previously held a position at the McDonald Institute for Archaeological Research in Cambridge and worked extensively in commercial archaeology. His research focusses on the end of Roman Britain and particularly the impact of the fall of the Western Roman Empire on the use and production of material culture, and he has published widely on late Roman pottery, coins and hoarding, including the internationally significant hoard of metal vessels discovered at Drapers' Gardens in the City of London in 2007. His publications include *Debating Late Antiquity in Britain* AD *300–700* (with Rob Collins, 2004) and a major excavation monograph, *A Roman Settlement and Bathhouse at Shadwell* (with A. Douglas and B. Sudds, 2011). He is a member of the Institute for Archaeologists, the Study Group for Roman Pottery, and a Fellow of the Royal Numismatic Society.

The Ruin of Roman Britain

An Archaeological Perspective

JAMES GERRARD

CAMBRIDGE
UNIVERSITY PRESS

CAMBRIDGE
UNIVERSITY PRESS

University Printing House, Cambridge CB2 8BS, United Kingdom

Cambridge University Press is part of the University of Cambridge.

It furthers the University's mission by disseminating knowledge in the pursuit of education, learning and research at the highest international levels of excellence.

www.cambridge.org
Information on this title: www.cambridge.org/9781316625682

First published 2013
Reprinted 2014
First paperback edition 2016

A catalogue record for this publication is available from the British Library

Library of Congress Cataloguing in Publication data
Gerrard, James (James Frederick)
The ruin of Roman Britain : an archaeological perspective / James Gerrard.
    pages   cm
Includes bibliographical references and index.
ISBN 978-1-107-03863-9 (hardback)
1. Great Britain – History – Roman period, 55 B.C.–449 A.D.
2. Great Britain – Antiquities, Roman.   3. Romans – Great Britain.   I. Title.
DA145.G45   2013
936.104 – dc23   2013011222

ISBN 978-1-107-03863-9 Hardback
ISBN 978-1-316-62568-2 Paperback

R. F. G.
1923–1979
Dis Manibus

Contents

Figures

Acknowledgements

The seed of the present work was planted under the auspices of Dr (now Prof.) John Moreland at the University of Sheffield some fifteen years ago. It was nourished by Steve Roskam's supervision during my postgraduate research at the University of York. I owe a debt to both of these individuals neither of whom should underestimate their influence on my thinking.

The Mellon Foundation's Sawyer Seminar Series 'Crisis, what Crisis?' held in the McDonald Institute at Cambridge University in 2009 played an important role in crystallising my thinking about the end of Roman Britain and I remain grateful to Dr James Barrett and Prof. Martin Millett (Cambridge) for the opportunity to participate in that project. Prof. Millett's support and generous assistance encouraged me to begin this task and helped me to complete it. I also owe a specific debt to the Newton Trust for funding the period of post-doctoral research at Cambridge where much of the manuscript was drafted. Profs. Henry Hurst (Cambridge) and John Hines (Cardiff) were kind enough to support the funding application.

The manuscript was completed at Newcastle University in 2012. I'd like to record my thanks to the archaeology team at Newcastle who welcomed me into History, Classics and Archaeology and allowed me the time to finish the book: Prof. Ian Haynes, Dr Sam Turner, Dr Mark Jackson, Dr Jane Webster, Dr Chris Fowler, Dr Andrea Dolfini and Dr Jan Harding. The Stage 3 students of ARA3114 'Regionality and the Fall of Rome' also deserve a mention for having served as unknowing guinea pigs for some of the ideas contained within.

Over the course of writing this book I was humbled by the kindness and generosity of friends, colleagues and acquaintances who freely shared information, thoughts and data with me. Specific mention must be made of Gary Brown, Vicki Ridgeway and Mark Roughley, Cate Davies and Strephon Duckering (Pre-Construct Archaeology), who were generous beyond measure (as a glance at the picture credits will demonstrate) to their ex-colleague. I'd also like to thank in no particular order: Andrew Agate (Newcastle), Dr Sam Lucy (Cambridge), Dr Catherine Hills (Cambridge), Dr Helen Geake (Cambridge), David Klingle (Cambridge), Belinda Crerar (Cambridge), Lacey Wallace (Cambridge), Prof. Lotte Hedeager (University of

Oslo), Dr Philippa Walton (PAS), Sam Moorhead (PAS), Dr Rob Collins (PAS), Dr Clare Randall (Poole Museums), Paul Martin (Absolute Archaeology), Dr Peter Guest (Cardiff), Dr Alan Lane (Cardiff), Dr David Petts (Durham), Prof. Tony King (Winchester), Paul Booth (Oxford Archaeology) and Dr Malcolm Lyne (freelance). If I have omitted you from this list know that it is from forgetfulness rather than malice and please accept my thanks.

Michael Sharp, Fleur Jones and Beata Mako have been patient editors and the team at Cambridge University Press turned the manuscript into a publishable form with speed and efficiency. I'd like to thank Julene Knox for her meticulous copy-editing and Pam Scholefield for producing the index. The anonymous readers also deserve thanks for their guidance and thoughts, without which this book would be a poorer study.

Pre-Construct Archaeology, The British Museum, English Heritage, Heritage Technology Ltd, Dr Sam Turner, Absolute Archaeology, The Museum of London, Dr Clare Randall and Fern Archaeology all supplied images which are individually credited where appropriate.

Finally, some personal acknowledgements: it is to my wife Sally and daughter Min that I owe the greatest debt. They have suffered sharing their husband and daddy with this book for too long and I cannot express my gratitude at their patience. My Great Uncle Ken should also be mentioned for the kindness he showed to a nephew he'd never met.

1 | Introduction

This is a book about Britain during what might be described as the 'long fifth century'. During this time, which stretches a hundred years either side of the period 400–500, the inhabitants of the British Isles were confronted with a series of challenges – the end of Roman imperialism, barbarian immigration, conflict, economic transformations and social realignments – that are often seen as shaping the future course of insular and world history. The most dramatic example of this is the contemporary use of English as the *lingua franca* of global communication (e.g. Coates 2007), which can be traced to West Germanic dialects supplanting insular Celtic and Latin in lowland Britain during the fifth and sixth centuries. Similarly, the contemporary political geography of Britain – England, Wales and Scotland – is often thought of as originating in the collapse of the Western Roman Empire (Geary 2002). To historians and archaeologists these simplistic visions of the past are invented traditions but they have an enduring popularity (Hobsbawm and Ranger 1983; Howe 1989). For many the early medieval period remains the origin of our modern nation states (e.g. Starkey 2010).

Britain's experience of the fifth century was not unique and the fall of the Western Roman Empire allowed similar transformations to play out across Europe. The longevity of Classical civilisation, the impact of Germanic culture and scale of settlement (e.g. Mathisen 1993; Goffart 2006; Halsall 2007; Heather 2009) are all themes shared by scholars of the late antique west. Given this perspective, a book about the end of Roman Britain might be considered an introspective conceit, which emphasises the situation in what was one of Rome's most peripheral possessions at the expense of other more central regions (Esmonde-Cleary 2013). However, many recent works on the late Roman and early medieval west have only discussed Britain in passing.

This treatment of Britain in wider reviews of the late antique west is largely a consequence of their text-based approach. As a peripheral region Britain rarely featured in surviving documentary and historical sources and the sources that do survive are both problematic and mutable. It is thus impossible to write an account of fourth-, fifth- and sixth-century British history that would compare with the detailed discussions of the same period available for Gaul or Italy (Mathisen 1993; Heather 2005). The response has been either to discuss Britain in a pseudo-historical fashion, or to largely discount the written sources and treat the period from an archaeological perspective as essentially prehistoric.

The pseudo-historical discussion of Britain in the fifth century has largely collapsed under a deluge of informed theoretical criticism, which has come from both historians and archaeologists. The former have demolished narratives based on sources written many hundreds of years after the events they purport to describe and the latter have moved away from historical interpretations of material culture and archaeological sequences. Nevertheless, in a period in which problematic written sources tantalise, the temptation to produce pseudo-historical interpretations of the period remains.

This volume is an archaeological study of the past and its material culture, monuments and landscapes. However, the period is not treated as prehistoric. The existence of both insular and continental written sources cannot and should not be ignored or discarded. Nor should the physical remains of the past be treated as a poor proxy through which a 'history' can be written. The historical sources are used here to illuminate processes of change that can be read in the material culture of the period. The result is a work that largely avoids the pitfalls of pseudo-history but integrates Britain's unique experience of the fall of the Western Empire within a wider cultural context.

The other benefit of approaching Roman Britain's 'end' from an archaeological standpoint is that there is an ever increasing body of data available for study. Developer-funded archaeology has led to an exponential growth in high-quality data since the early 1990s and the creation of the Portable Antiquities Scheme has revolutionised our understanding of material culture during the Roman and early medieval periods. These empirical transformations have been coupled with new methodological approaches which are challenging long-held assumptions about both periods. One academic challenge is to synthesise this new material in a meaningful way and this volume is a modest contribution to achieving such a task.

The fall of Rome and the end of Roman Britain

It is a truism that those studying the past are largely condemned to write their contemporary concerns into their historical and archaeological analyses and interpretations. In the eighteenth century Gibbon's (1993) view of the decline and fall of the Roman Empire was intimately connected with the role of religion in secular society, which was an issue that exercised both him and his contemporaries (Pocock 1999). In the following century Britain's dialogue with the fall of the Roman Empire reflected its own fluctuating relationship with imperial power. Early in the nineteenth century English scholars were at pains to stress their Germanic roots and supposedly ancient democratic institutions (MacDougall 1982, 116) in contrast to the imperialist and tyrannical ambitions of the French (Hingley 2000, 19–20). However, by the end of the century Rome offered an obvious parallel for Britain's own supposed 'imperial destiny' (Hingley 2000, 22–25).

The study of the end of the Roman Empire during the twentieth century was clearly influenced by the experiences of two long and bitter global conflicts. The First and Second World Wars allowed Germanic barbarians to be recast as the enemies of civilisation (e.g. Haverfield and MacDonald 1924, 264) but other less clear-cut visions of the past were also promoted (Pirenne 1939; Delogu 1998). In the aftermath of conflict, a purely 'German' past founded on genocidal Anglo-Saxon invaders sweeping the hapless Britons into the mountains of Wales and Cumbria (Camden 1586, 43–44; Freeman 1867; Leeds 1913, 20; Stubbs 1926; Lennard 1933; Hodgkin 1935) became increasingly uncomfortable (Babcock 1916; Collingwood and Myres 1936, 426–427; Stenton 1971, 314–315; Higham 2007, 2). For European scholars the decades following the Second World War were also a time for re-evaluating models of the early Middle Ages. The concept of racially pure Germanic tribes invading and conquering parts of the Western Empire was discarded in a deconstruction of suspect historical methodologies associated with Nazism (Wenskus 1961). Thus the end of the Western Roman Empire and Roman Britain became a tale of migration and the partial assimilation of indigenous inhabitants.

In Britain the 1960s and 1970s saw the climax of a pseudo-historical school of research that sought to blend a seamless medley of late Roman and early medieval historical sources with a limited body of archaeological evidence (e.g. Evison 1965; Myres 1969). The resulting works, which included the final chapters of Frere's (1967) *Britannia* and Salway's (1981) *Roman Britain* as well as volumes such as Alcock's (1971) *Arthur's Britain* and Myres' (1986) *The English Settlements*, epitomise this essentially culture-historical approach. The narrative framework was provided by supposedly historical accounts and fleshed out with archaeological evidence. At its most extreme – exemplified by Morris' (1973) *The Age of Arthur* – this type of analysis could be used to produce a history of the early medieval period that approached fantasy (Kirby and Williams 1976).

By the end of the 1970s this paradigm was beginning to crumble in the face of a twin onslaught. Withering criticism of the written sources was spearheaded by historians such as Dumville (1977) and Sims-Williams (1983). They swiftly demolished the narrative framework by pointing out that many of the early medieval texts used in its construction were the product of later times. Ninth-century annals and twelfth-century saints' lives could no longer be trusted as witnesses to fifth- and sixth-century events. The second attack on the orthodoxy was driven by changes happening within archaeology. The adoption of the so-called 'New Archaeology' or processualism (Clarke 1978), which borrowed methodologies and approaches from allied disciplines such as geography and anthropology, opened up new avenues of research and prompted questions about the nature of society and its organisation, rather than just the geographical and chronological spread of material culture (e.g. Scull 1993; Arnold 1997, 14–15). At the same time, major projects to redevelop urban centres and the construction of infrastructure like motorways turned field archaeology from a well-meaning but often haphazard exercise, led by academics, museum curators and interested amateurs, into a profession funded first by the state and then later by the developer. The resulting upsurge in data changed our understanding of the landscape of Roman and early medieval Britain. The densities of sites, and thus ancient populations, increased many times (e.g. Millett 1990, Table 8.1); material culture was being assessed in a more rigorous fashion (e.g. Young 1977; Dickinson 1982) and new statistical and scientific approaches were beginning to unlock the complexity of the period.

The main interpretative issue to emerge from this debate concerned the mechanism or mechanisms that brought about the 'end' of Roman Britain. The old culture-historical model had promulgated to a greater or lesser degree the notion of invading Germanic barbarians as a cause of extra-systemic change. Yet the removal of many of the historical sources and the new archaeological data seemed to illustrate an alternative story. A Gildasian cataclysm of Anglo-Saxon raiding could no longer be held responsible for the destruction of late fourth-century towns (e.g. Leeds 1913, 20) when the archaeological evidence demonstrated that they crumbled into ruin. Equally, a more critical approach to claims of destruction at archaeological sites meant that villas that had previously been interpreted as burnt by Saxons, or forts sacked by Picts, were being reinterpreted as accidental fires or the residues of industrial processes. The barbarian 'Other' as a *deus ex machina* ushering in the new Germanic early Middle Ages was definitely out of favour and this perspective was also fashionable in broader analyses of the Western Empire (Goffart 1980).

The dominant paradigm suggested that Roman Britain underwent a socio-economic 'collapse' in the early fifth century. This left a power vacuum into which the 'Anglo-Saxons' could step during the middle of the fifth century (Esmonde-Cleary 1989). However, those Anglo-Saxons were no longer seen as tidal waves of invaders or migrants crashing against Britain's eastern shores (Moreland 2000). Developments in approaches to material culture and identity led to a questioning of the easy equation between Germanic style objects and architecture and Germanic origins (Lucy 2000, 155–186; 2002). It was now argued that a small Germanic elite offered an ideology and identity which the rudderless inhabitants of Britain, left bereft by the collapse of the Roman way of life, seized upon (Higham 1992; Hills 2003; Halsall 2007, 361).

There were, of course, individuals who did not subscribe to this hypothesis. Those working on the west of Britain pointed out that they were free of Anglo-Saxon material culture for much of the early medieval period. Clearly the societies in those regions followed a different path. The excavation of sites like Cadbury Castle (Alcock 1995) or Cadbury Congresbury, both in Somerset (Rahtz et al. 1993), revealed a society trading with the Mediterranean that could be interpreted either as traces of a 'Celtic' warrior elite, or as the remnants of late Roman power structures (Alcock 1995, 151). The discovery of an ephemeral, but large timber building of supposedly Classical plan at Wroxeter (Shropshire) added fuel to the notion of post-Roman communities perpetuating some elements of a Roman way of life (K. Dark 1994, 2000; Barker et al. 1997; White 2007). In the east some of those concerned with the Anglo-Saxons argued that the scale of the change seen in the fifth century and the impact on language and placenames could only have come about due to a significant movement of people from northern Germany (Welch 1993).

By the turn of the millennium the end of Roman Britain had become polarised between those who continued to argue for a short and sharp 'end' (Faulkner 2000, 2004) and those suggesting that *Romanitas* lingered on in some form in the west (K. Dark 1994, 2000). This discussion is sometimes referred to as the 'continuity–discontinuity debate' and it seemed particularly intractable because the two apparently diametrically opposed positions were argued from the same body of evidence. An attempt to reconcile these positions and the study of the east of Britain through the adoption of 'late antiquity' as an over-arching framework failed, because the term soon came to be both used and abused as a synonym for the 'continuity' approach (contrast Esmonde-Cleary 2001 with the use of 'late antiquity' by

Bowles 2007). The debate over the 'Anglo-Saxons' was also fractious as new scientific techniques, such as the analysis of mitochondrial DNA and isotopic data derived from human skeletal remains, were deployed in increasingly technical and specialist studies (e.g. Lucy 2002; Thomas, Stumpf and Härke 2006; Pattison 2008; Hills 2009).

These discussions did not exist in an insular vacuum but were part of a wider debate about how the Roman Empire ended in Western Europe. The starting points for this were Jones' (1964) magisterial *Later Roman Empire* and Brown's (1971) short survey *The World of Late Antiquity*, both of which argued that the post-Constantinian period was not just a time of decline, but worthy of study in its own right. This emphasis on late antiquity enabled scholars to approach the 'end' of Rome as a positive experience rather than the last gasp of Classical civilisation (Bowersock 1996). Ultimately, this new paradigm led to the fourth and fifth centuries being cast as a period of *transition* or *transformation*, in which the legacy of Rome was fused with new Germanic ideas and ideologies (Van Dam 1985; Mathisen 1993). This approach culminated in a European Science Foundation Project that ran between 1993 and 1998, titled: The Transformation of the Roman World, which brought historians, archaeologists, linguists, art-historians, numismatists and others together to examine the process of change that led to the origins of the modern European nation states.

Since 2000 this comfortable view of the fall of Rome in which provincials and their new Germanic overlords came to mutually beneficial accommodations has begun to be questioned. Ward-Perkins (2005) has forcefully restated that the fifth century in Europe was nasty and brutish, with epidemic violence and a catastrophic decline in living standards. Heather (2005, 2009), reacting against those that have sought to minimise the scale of barbarian migration, has presented a new history of the late Roman period dominated by warfare and large-scale migration. No single meta-narrative suffices for Wickham's (2005) view of the late Roman and early medieval world, in which a multiplicity of socio-economic and political processes occurred across Europe and the Mediterranean. The impact of these works (and others) on the historiography of the end of Roman Britain is beginning to be felt. Warfare and migration are re-emerging as causal agents and the pendulum of academic debate is beginning to swing again.

This shift in the parameters of academic debate about the 'end' of the Roman Empire and Britain reflects, as did earlier historiography, the time in which it was written. That violence, migration and collapses should be back in academic fashion is far from surprising. In a decade that has seen real-time televised conflict on an unprecedented scale, the rise of mass migration in a globalised world, increasing concern about the weakening of western political and economic hegemony (Ferguson 2011) and fear of environmental change (Diamond 2005), it is no surprise to find Rome being used as an example of the consequences of these factors. Ward-Perkins (2009) cautions in the *Financial Times* that at least the 'Credit Crunch' was not a new Dark Age; the spectre of mass migration on a fifth-century scale can be used by an admiral to justify defence spending (Almond 2006); the fall of Rome can be associated with climate change recorded in the dendrochronological record (Büntgen et al. 2011); and the end of Roman Britain might have been due to religious conflict (Dark 1994). Here is Rome's end as a mirror for princes, reflecting contemporary events on the distant past (e.g. Murphy 2007).

This volume is also a product of its time. Written during the early twenty-first century, it has been influenced by the historiographical tradition outlined above. Some of these influences are overt and deliberate and this is especially true of the first half of this work where the importance of violence and warfare and economic collapse as explanatory mechanisms is discussed. The second half of this volume is concerned primarily with worldviews, ideologies and identities. Contemporary concerns are discernible here as well and the shadow of globalisation, migration and integration can be easily detected. There are undoubtedly other contemporary themes that the reader may identify. Thus this is a statement of one view of the fourth-, fifth- and sixth-century past at a particular point in time. Other perspectives will emphasise alternative interpretations and this multivocality is to be welcomed. There is no explanation for the fall of Rome or the end of Roman Britain – just competing alternatives that in some configuration may, or may not, reflect the complexities and challenges that accompanied the end of the ancient world and the beginning of the Middle Ages.

Chronology and datasets

The period under study runs from *c.*300 to *c.*600 and this block of time can be defined in a number of ways. Historically the start date is approximately congruent with the accession of Diocletian in 286 and the foundation of the so-called Dominate (Corcoran 2000). The fall of the Western Empire occurred in the late fifth century (e.g. Cameron 1993; McGill 2010) and the terminal date for Roman Britain is usually either marked by the usurpation of Constantine III (*c.*407) or placed *c.*410 when the so-called Honorian Rescript is thought to have been written (Esmonde-Cleary 1989, 137–138).

The beginning of the 'Anglo-Saxon' period is usually dated to c.450 following Bede's calculation of the *adventus Saxonum*. The end date coincides with the establishment of St Augustine's mission to Kent in 597. Thus the period spans the transition between the late Roman period and the early Middle Ages: a time of profound political, social and economic change in the British Isles.

Archaeologically the late Roman period in Britain can be defined as starting c.250/270 and ending c.400. This is not significantly different to the historical periodisation and there is, of course, an important inter-relationship between the historical and archaeological chronologies. How-ever, these dates also mark significant shifts within Romano-British material culture. The ubiquitous and chronologically sensitive red-slipped pottery known as *terra sigillata* or samian is typical of the early Roman period but large-scale importation of this ware ceased in the middle of the third cen-tury (King 1981; Webster 1996). This occurred at the same time as the well-known monetary problems that followed the Severan dynasty (e.g. Casey 1994, 9–12). Some decades later new Romano-British pottery producers began to manufacture red-slipped samian imitations and other vessel forms (Fulford 1975; Young 1977). It is the products of these kilns and the new and relatively abundant copper-alloy coinage of the late third and fourth century that become the main archaeological indicators of the late Roman period. However, new coinage ceased to be imported into Britain (and large parts of northern Gaul) on any scale shortly after 402 and it is usually assumed that the 'end' of Roman Britain marks the end of the production of Roman period objects (Fulford 1979).

The appearance of 'Germanic style' objects in eastern Britain during the fifth century marks an important change in the use and role of material culture (Figure 1.1). Traditionally, this material was dated to no earlier than the middle of the fifth century. However, some forms of metalwork and assemblages of objects are likely on the basis of continental parallels to pre-date 450. Some cremation cemeteries also appear to be of primarily fifth-century date. From c.470 objects decorated in a new style, known as Salin's Style I, began to appear and inhumation became the dominant burial rite. By the seventh century new artistic styles (Salin's Style II), the process of conversion and other socio-economic transformations indicate the beginnings of the Middle Saxon period.

In the west of Britain there is relatively little material culture. Some forms of metalwork, especially penannular brooches, can be dated to the fifth and sixth centuries and there is also a small but important group of sites that yield imported pottery from the Mediterranean. These vessels, mainly amphorae

Fig. 1.1 A silver-gilt
brooch in the
fifth-century Nydam
style from Gillingham,
Kent. The appearance of
fifth-century metalwork
with parallels in
northern Germany and
southern Scandinavia
marks the beginnings of
the Anglo-Saxon period
(© Pre-Construct
Archaeology Ltd).

but also African and Phocaean Red Slipped Wares, have an apparently restricted date range of 475 to 550 and distribution in the south-western peninsula and around the Irish Sea (E. Campbell 2007). The other significant chronological indicators are absolute methods such as radiocarbon dating. Radiocarbon dating is usually undertaken on human remains and this has led to the increasing identification of fifth- and sixth-century cemeteries in western Britain (Cullen et al. 2006).

Clearly, the datasets for the late Roman and early medieval periods in Britain are very different. The archaeological definition of periods on the basis of material culture is also problematic. It is, for instance, extremely difficult to determine when a particular type of pottery was broken and discarded. One type of late Roman vessel, such as the Oxfordshire red-slipped bowl imitating the samian form Dr38 (Young 1977, C51), serves to illustrate the point. These bowls were common across much of southern Britain and have a date range of *c.*240–400+. The vessel may have been produced at any point within that range: in the middle of the third century; the late third century; the early, middle or late fourth century; or even the early fifth century. This is a far from trivial point because the chronology is 'smearing' the experiences of individuals who lived during the late Roman period. The date range of the particular vessel considered above encompasses eight twenty-year generations. To labour this point, it is inconceivable that the concerns of someone born in 240 were the same as those of an individual born in 400. Issues such as these mean that the association of archaeological 'events' with 'historical' events is very difficult to achieve.

These packages of material culture, as well as architectural traditions and burial rites, underline another important point: the archaeological traces for each period are very different and inspire different modes and methods of analysis (Esmonde-Cleary 1993). The study of late Roman Britain is dominated by the analysis of architectural forms (Perring 2002). Urban centres were surrounded by walls and contained townhouses, monumental public buildings, bathhouses, temples and a multitude of other buildings often constructed from stone. The countryside was densely studded with farmsteads and nucleated settlements of varying forms and also contained richly decorated and embellished elite residences and religious complexes (Taylor 2007). Associated artefact and ecofact assemblages are generally those produced by domestic or 'industrial' activities. This has led to a focus on the study of trade and exchange. In contrast, the study of the early Anglo-Saxon period is dominated by cemetery sites and assemblages of objects deposited in burials (Lucy 2000). There are relatively few excavated settlement sites and they were built from timber and rarely contain extensive finds assemblages (Hamerow 2011).

The fundamental difference in the datasets for the late Roman and early medieval periods means that comparing the two is extremely difficult. Two examples suffice to illustrate this point. First, in the late Roman period a study of elite architecture would discuss groundplans, bounded space and room decoration (Smith 1997); in the early Saxon period it is difficult to advance the discussion far beyond noting that one timber 'hall' is bigger than another (Marshall and Marshall 1991). Secondly, the detailed study of Anglo-Saxon burial rites has revealed the complex use of gravegoods to distinguish gender, status and identity (Stoodley 2000). Any study of late Roman cemeteries with the same aim would founder because relatively few fourth-century burials contain gravegoods (Philpott 1991). Thus it can often appear that late Roman Britain and early Anglo-Saxon England run on parallel tracks and the study of neither can be brought into line or focus with the other.

It can be argued that one of the reasons for this dislocation in the study of the two periods lies in the simple fact that a 'fourth-century' situation is being contrasted with a 'sixth-century' situation. One of the aims of this volume is to try and separate the fourth and sixth centuries from the fifth century. This enables the fifth century to become a pivotal hundred years in which life in Britain underwent a transformative process. The gap between late Roman and early medieval only looks impassable if we ignore the malleable and flexible years that separate the more stable societies of the fourth and sixth centuries.

New approaches

This volume intends to examine the fifth century in Britain as a time of change. It has been more than ten years since the last works that tackled this theme (K. Dark 2000; Faulkner 2000) and more than two decades since the publication of a volume that garnered something approaching academic consensus (Esmonde-Cleary 1989). The aim of this work is to synthesise some of the new archaeological data (Bradley 2006) and changes in interpretation that are of relevance to late Roman Britain. It is not a study of late Roman and early medieval dynamics on a pan-European scale (for which there are a number of recent overviews: Heather 2005, 2009; Wickham 2005; Halsall 2007; Christie 2011).

The geographical focus is lowland Britain and this reflects the fact that it was in the lowlands of Britain that the greatest changes were seen during the fifth century. It touches upon, but does not examine in any detail, the trajectories followed by late and early post-Roman communities in the northern frontier zone. Hadrian's Wall and its hinterland formed a distinct region with 'military communities' and has been recently discussed by Collins (2012). The frontier exerted an influence over the south of Britain but it is the transformations seen in the civilian regions in what is now southern England that provide the core of this study.

The analysis and discussion is broadly divided into two parts. The first part is essentially a critique of two major interpretative frameworks that are being deployed to explain the end of Roman Britain (and also the Roman Empire). The second half examines social structure and identity. Together these two halves form a whole that offers not only a deconstruction of developing orthodoxies but also presents a model and mechanism for explaining the transformation from Roman Britain to Anglo-Saxon England.

Since 2000 conflict has re-emerged from the obscurity of being academically unfashionable as an explanation for change. Work by scholars such as Heather (2005) and Ward-Perkins (2005) has placed violence and warfare firmly in the centre stage of late antique studies. This approach has in turn been picked up by archaeologists concerned with late Roman Britain. As was observed above, this approach partially reflects the increased emphasis on conflict in contemporary geo-politics. In Chapter 2 it is argued that the evidence for growing insecurity in late fourth-century Britain is a product of a particular approach to the historical sources. Elements from a diverse range of textual sources have been taken out of context and reworked to create a narrative of decline that conforms to teleological preconceptions about the end of the Roman Empire. Analysis of the context of these sources is well advanced in historical enquiry. However, the implications of this research have not always been followed through in archaeological narratives.

Deconstruction of the narrative of conflict derived from historical sources allows the archaeological evidence to be approached from new perspectives. Below in a review of defensive architecture it is suggested that late Roman 'defensive measures' in Britain differ significantly from those seen along the Rhine–Danube frontier and also in Gaul. This is then combined with a discussion of settlement patterns and phenomena such as hoarding to argue that there is very little evidence for fourth-century military instability in Britain. A review of the situation in the fifth and sixth centuries suggests that violence may have been slightly more common in the post-Roman period. This phenomenon accompanied an increased interest in some regions in material culture with military overtones but the evidence for conflict remains equivocal.

In Chapter 3 the idea of an 'economic collapse' is investigated. Many commentators have explained the end of Roman Britain as a product of a fundamental crisis that destroyed the late Roman economic system. This crisis, according to some, plunged Britain into a state not seen since the Bronze Age. However, under close examination this hypothesis can be questioned. Significant methodological issues relating to how relative chronologies are constructed for material culture have arguably created the impression of a 'collapse'. This impression is reinforced by uncritical comparisons between the extent and range of 'Roman' material culture and 'early medieval' material culture. A more sophisticated approach argues that the types of material culture available in late Roman Britain were already restricted before *c*.400. Furthermore, the emphasis on archaeologically visible material restricts our analyses to a minor part of the wider economy. Of greater importance was the almost invisible agricultural production. This is developed into a model that suggests that late Roman Britain was over-producing to fulfil the demands of the Roman state. Due to this the end of the Roman period saw an economic realignment to less efficient forms of agriculture (such as cattle rearing) because the need for intensive and extensive arable production had ceased. These changes, visible in the wider landscape, are often read as evidence of catastrophe but in fact may represent a more relaxed agricultural regime. The real economic powerhouse in late Roman Britain was not the elements (like pottery production) that can be argued to have collapsed but farming. This emphasis on farming lays the foundations for the second part of this volume where the control of agricultural surpluses features prominently.

Chapters 4 and 5 examine the elites that controlled society during the fourth, fifth and early sixth centuries. In Chapter 4 the position and role of the late Roman elite is discussed. A significant distinction is drawn between the civilian elites professing shared cultural values (*paideia*) and the 'militarised' apparatus of the late Roman state. It is suggested that the late Roman civilian elites formed from a range of allied and competing groups. Their use of an overtly civilian ideology was constructed to reinforce and maintain their social position while also ensuring their place within the imperial hierarchy. To this end, material culture such as dress accessories and personal adornment, as well as architectural complexes and decorative embellishments, were deployed to highlight social difference and status.

Chapter 5 extends the discussion of the elite into the fifth and sixth centuries. It is suggested that in the west of Britain a two-stage process can be determined. The first, dating mainly to the early and mid fifth century, represents the transformation of the Roman civilian ideology and the growth of a militarised outlook in the west of Britain. This was then followed by the development of an early medieval elite society in the late fifth century. These late fifth- and sixth-century societies drew inspiration from both the transformed Roman past and the reinvented ancient past to create a new society in which martial display was paramount.

In the east of Britain the new 'Germanic' cultural influences began during the fifth century as a military ideology that may have been not dissimilar to that displayed by late Roman 'soldiers'. The elites during this phase continued to reference the Roman past and display was focussed primarily on the person. During the later fifth and sixth centuries changes in material culture and the development of sites with some signs of architectural pretension may indicate the creation of more stable communities. These societies used, in contrast to the west, furnished inhumation as a burial rite that involved the deposition of weapons in male burials and suites of personal adornments in female graves. This suggests communities in which a martial ideology was an important component of male identity and female identity was regulated.

Chapter 6 examines the lower-status inhabitants of Britain. It begins by assessing the extent to which the population of late Roman and early post-Roman Britain can be studied as successors to earlier Iron Age 'tribes'. This approach is found to be problematic and in its place a vision of 'small worlds' that can be dimly discerned in the use of material culture and social practice is introduced. It is these small worlds that were controlled by the elites discussed in the preceding chapters. These small-scale societies formed a patchwork of communities that exploited the rural landscape. The extent, scale and impact of the exploitation of these communities by the elites was the foundation of rural power and an important element in the transformations that were to occur in the fifth century.

In 'The ruin of Roman Britain' (Chapter 7) a model of responses to the end of Roman power is presented. It suggests that the key fifth-century transformation was the adoption of a martial ideology that had previously been the preserve of the Roman state. In order to maintain position and status the indigenous elites adopted the trappings of martial display. Through the use of retinues (nascent warbands) that may have included Germanic warriors authority was maintained. However, the collapse of the Roman state meant that social trajectories were now available to Germanic migrants and lower-status indigenous communities. Over time this led to a process of ethnogenesis through which a 'British' west and 'Anglo-Saxon' east were created. Similar in social structure and economy, these groups were divided by their use of material culture, language and religion. Ultimately, these communities would crystallise into a new medieval order based on small kingdoms.

The ruin of Roman Britain was thus not an event but a process stretched out over two centuries and more. There was no sudden collapse or catastrophe but a series of changes that groups of people responded to in different ways. Eventually the Roman civilian lifestyle based on the shared values of *paideia* became an irrelevancy. The future lay in localised control and personal power backed by the point of a sword.

2 | Violence and warfare

Identifying a specific point or event in time at which the Western Roman Empire ended is a fruitless task. However, few would disagree with the suggestion that the key distinction between the late Roman and the emerging early medieval world was the Roman state's inability to impose its will effectively on barbarian groups through armed force. The inverse of this phenomenon was the growth of groups, like the Goths or Burgundians, within the empire who were capable of deploying armed force and violence to further their own ends. The continuing presence of such groups – even if the details and subtleties of each specific situation are open to debate – within the boundaries of the Roman state and the fact that such communities might serve the empire – but could also follow an independent path – remains the starkest distinction between 'before' and 'after' the fall.

What continues to be debatable is the scale and significance of violence and warfare. Recent works have offered opposing visions of the Germanic threat in the fourth and fifth centuries. Analysis of the late Roman administrative document known as the *Notitia Dignitatum* has led one historian to conclude that warfare in early fifth-century Gaul was the crucible of Rome's defeat, which drew the Western Empire's armies into brutal conflict from which they could not recover (Heather 2005, 246–248; 2009, 151–206). Others have concentrated on the experiences of those, like the nuns of Carthage (Ward-Perkins 2005, 13), who were subjected to barbarian invasion. Together this is a potent and emotive vision but it is not uncontested. Some see the 'barbarians' as little more than a convenient bogeyman, easily contained by Roman arms unless the state was distracted by other concerns (Drinkwater 2007).

The co-existence of these viewpoints reflects the course of historical analysis during the twentieth century. In the latter half of the nineteenth century the fall of the Western Empire was primarily seen as the destruction of a civilisation by external aggressors (Freeman 1867). Whether this was a 'good' or a 'bad' thing depended on one's point of view. For some, Rome was a decadent and corrupt Mediterranean civilisation overdue for replacement by a younger and more vigorous Germanic society, but for others it was a beacon of enlightenment about to be swamped by a rising tide of barbarism

(Halsall 2007, 10–11). In the aftermath of the Second World War academic consensus began to shift. The polarisation of barbarian and Roman started to weaken as attention focussed on continuities and the accommodations reached between Roman and barbarian groups. By 1980 Goffart could claim that 'what we call the fall of the Western Roman Empire was an imaginative experiment that got a little out of hand' (1980, 42). Recent works, such as those mentioned above, have reacted against these perspectives and attempt to re-establish the central place of conflict in our understanding of the end of the Roman Empire (Drake 2006).

The analysis of Roman Britain's end has followed a similar trajectory. Violence and conflict played an important role until the 1980s but by the end of that decade social, economic and environmental factors were being favoured as causal agents over barbarian invaders (Esmonde-Cleary 1989; Higham 1992; Jones 1996). However, in recent years the spectre of a violent end has returned: a peasants' revolt (Faulkner 2000), tribal warfare (Laycock 2008) and Christian fundamentalism (Dark 2005) have all been posited as 'explanations' for the disappearance of a Roman way of life in Britain.

Each of these explanations is drawn, not from any substantive analysis of the physical remains of the late fourth- and early fifth-century past, but from text-based narratives. The so-called 'peasants' revolt' (Faulkner 2000) is based on a particular characterisation (Thompson 1952) of a controversial late antique socio-political phenomenon known as the *Bagaudae* (Drinkwater 1992); tribal warfare is a hypothesis developed from a particular, and Classically derived (Mattingly 2007, 59), view of social structure in Roman Britain mixed with a probably inappropriate modern analogy (Laycock 2008, 7–14). Finally, the notion of Christian fundamentalism (Dark 1994, 55–57) is based on a very specific vision of early Christianity in the north-western provinces and may also reflect modern concerns about religious discord.

What each of these interpretations demonstrates is an unwillingness to develop models that are free of the textual sources. Archaeologists studying the end of the Roman Empire in Britain may be very comfortable with their own data – the pottery, structural plans and animal bones – but when it comes to the interpretative framework they remain reliant on a meta-narrative derived from the written word (Hume 1964; Moreland 2001, 2006). Of course, it would be ludicrous to suggest that the period could be approached without reference to the surviving sources, which are both rich and varied. However, given that Britain was only ever of marginal interest to late antique authors, it seems perverse that there has not been more confidence in divorcing ourselves from the historical narrative. Partially this is the result of a disciplinary boundary that has separated historical enquiry from archaeological analysis. Britain's place in some contemporary histories of the fall of the Western Empire is almost as marginal as its position in the ancient sources (e.g. Heather 2005, 437–438). The study of fourth- and fifth-century Britain remains the preserve of archaeologists.

The historical narrative

The creation of Romano-British archaeology as an academic subject grew out of the teaching of Classics at Oxford by Haverfield (Freeman 2007). The scholars that followed in his footsteps, individuals like Collingwood (1930), Rivet (1964) and Frere (1967), continued the tradition of having been first trained as Classicists and historians. This allowed them to bring to the new subject of 'Roman archaeology' a keen awareness and appreciation of the value and limitations of the written sources. Their fieldwork and its interpretation were guided and influenced by ancient historical accounts and, in the excavation of Roman urban centres and military sites, there was the sense that archaeology was placing flesh upon the bare bones of the historical narratives of first-century events (e.g. Webster 1980). The legionary fortress at Inchtuthil in Scotland became physical evidence of Tacitus' assertion that Britain (Pitts and St. Joseph 1985), 'once conquered was immediately let slip' (Tac. *Hist.* I.2). Frere's (1967) *Britannia: A History of Roman Britain* was the culmination of this approach.

Perhaps more importantly historically recorded events provided fixed points to which the artefactual and structural sequences of Roman Britain could be related. The destruction of London, St Albans and Colchester by the forces of Boudica in 60/61 was visible archaeologically and thus provided a dated horizon. So too did the construction of the two northern walls in the second century. An extension of this methodology argued that historically recorded events ought to be visible archaeologically in the later Roman period as well. The fortification of towns or the addition of projecting towers to their walls was argued to be the result of stimuli recorded in the historical sources and the study of Hadrian's Wall became wedded to a series of so-called 'Wall Periods'; the latest of which was argued to be a direct consequence of the *comes* Theodosius' restoration of Britain in the aftermath of the 'barbarian conspiracy' of 367 (Birley 1961, 262–265; Hodgson 2008).

During the 1970s the development of the so-called 'New Archaeology' opened the study of Roman Britain, albeit slowly, to scientific techniques and approaches borrowed from subjects as diverse as anthropology, sociology, geography and mathematics. This broke the link between the teaching of history and archaeology (Halsall 1997, 788–789). This dislocation has led many archaeologists to a point where they often reject the use of history to direct research agendas and as means of interpretation but remain reliant on it for the chronological structure of their period (e.g. Arnold 1984, 6). Furthermore, the separation of the two subjects (Halsall 1997) has left few students of fourth- and fifth-century Britain (who are by definition archaeologists) feeling comfortable dealing with the textual sources. This has led to recent archaeological works tabulating historically recorded late Roman events pertaining to Britain (Millett 1990, Table 9.2; Mattingly 2007, Table 6). Such summaries are undoubtedly useful and avoid the reader becoming bogged down in the complexities of historical argument that may be of only superficial interest. However, problems arise when this narrative, derived from snippets of ancient works taken out of context, equally weighted and hammered into time-line history, are accepted as fact.

The perpetuation and repetition of a constructed historical narrative provides a convenient explanation for a wide variety of social phenomena. Hoards of precious objects, city walls and settlement abandonment are all explained by reference to increasing insecurity and named barbarian groups. The historical 'facts' provide the common-sense interpretation but deny us the opportunity to explore alternatives. To put it bluntly: the historical tail is very much wagging the archaeological dog.

There are various ways in which those studying late Roman Britain could respond to this challenge. One would be to approach the period as if it were prehistoric in an attempt to interpret its remains without preconceptions drawn from the textual sources (Arnold 1984). Unfortunately such a counter-factual approach is doomed to failure. There are written sources, they colour our judgement and they cannot be unwritten, or more importantly unread. One of the challenges for archaeologists working on the period in Britain is to recognise that the accepted narrative of fourth-century history is manufactured from 'snippets' of text removed from their source and context and all too often forced to conform to a pre-conceived narrative of 'decline and fall'. In the following discussion the events listed in Table 2.1 are examined. Analysis of their context (Moreland 2001) should weaken our unthinking acceptance of them as events that conform to a pre-conceived narrative of increasing insecurity, violence and warfare. A 'new' or 'alternative' narrative cannot be constructed for Britain from these sources because the evidence is too mutable to allow a definitive reconstruction of Britain's history during the late fourth century.

Table 2.1 *Late fourth-century military events pertaining to Britain*

Date	Event
342/343	Winter visit to Britain by Constans – linked by some to issue with scouts (*areani*) of northern frontier.
360	Raids of Picti, Scotti, Saxones and Attacotti on Britain.
367–368	Barbarian conspiracy – Count of the Saxon Shore killed and *dux Britanniarum* 'ambushed'. Situation restored by land/naval campaigns of Count Theodosius in north and south Britain.
382/383	Magnus Maximus defeats Picti and Scotti.
396–398	Stilicho (or a subordinate) campaigns in Britain against Picti and Scotti.

This list, taken from a recent work on Roman Britain (Mattingly 2007, Table 6), portrays sixty years of conflict but fails to discuss the complexities and context of these events.

'Winter visit to Britain by Constans – linked by Ammianus to some issue with scouts (*areani*) of the northern frontier'

In the winter of 343 the Emperor Constans visited Britain. Modern works on Roman Britain usually cite an ancient account of this visit found in the late fourth-century *Res Gestae* of Ammianus, where a passing reference to the visit is juxtaposed with a description of the Emperor Julian's decision to send troops to Britain in the winter of 360. Further linkages are sometimes made with a group labelled by Ammianus as the *arcani* or *areani* and occasionally interpreted as 'frontier scouts'. The methodology employed can be unkindly termed 'Britain spotting', whereby a series of events in a historical source or sources are linked together to form a narrative: in this case a military or political crisis. The event that has been concocted by this process is a 'crisis' that has then been sought in changes to the fortifications of towns and frontier defences.

The military and political crisis of 343 can be quite easily deconstructed. The account of the *areani/arcani* that survives merely states that they were discussed in more detail in one of the lost books of Ammianus detailing the reign of Constans. This does not necessarily imply that the *areani/arcani* were the subject of the visit. The only other evidence for the crisis of 343 is the linking of Constans' visit with Julian's later difficulties (of which more below) in Ammianus' narrative. However, given that both events took place in the winter, is it possible that it was the season that was the focus of the comparison? Winter was a closed sailing season when few ancient seafarers would sail the waters of the Mediterranean, let alone dare to transport an emperor or an army across the tempestuous and unpredictable northern ocean (Portmann 1999, fn. 144). At first sight such an interpretation may appear as special pleading, but it gains force when two other accounts of Constans' visit, which are rarely mentioned in works on Roman Britain, are considered.

Both Firmicus Maternus (Firm. Mat. *Err. prof. rel.* 28.6) and Libanius (Lib. *Or.* 59) mention the event and concentrate on the crossing of the Ocean during winter. Of the two, Libanius' account is the fullest and most illuminating:

> It is not right to pass over in silence his [Constans'] voyage to the island of Britain, because many are ignorant about the island ... [O]thers, who actually believe that the Ocean exists somewhere, become dizzy at the name. But Constans was so far from suffering from such a condition that, if he did not investigate and launch a ship, embark and be conveyed and come to anchor in the harbours of Britain, he thought he would be neglecting the greatest of his duties ...

> The emperor considered none of these risks [in crossing the Ocean], or rather, despite being well aware of everything, he did not hesitate. The more he knew of the much vaunted danger, the more he hastened to put to sea. And what is even more remarkable, he did not sit and wait upon the beach until when the fair weather came the Ocean would calm the storm, but immediately just as things were, with the winter at its height and everything roused by the season to a peak of fury – clouds, icy chill and surf – without giving prior word to the cities there and without announcing the launch in advance, not wishing to be admired for his purpose before achieving his objective, he embarked a hundred men, so it is reported. He loosed the mooring cables and began cutting the Ocean ...

> There can be no dispute that this youthful undertaking was not without the blessing of God. If therefore after the island had rebelled, its inhabitants were holding an uprising, and the empire was being plundered, the news had arrived, and he had been seized with rage on hearing it and had thrown the die for the voyage, to report his act of daring would not have been to the credit of his resolve, but the crisis deriving from the rebels would have taken away the greater part of the glory. But in fact affairs in Britain were settled. He was completely free to enjoy the wonders of the Ocean from the land. There was no cause of anxiety compelling him to make the voyage. (Lib. *Or.* 59, 137–141; Lieu and Montserrat 1996, 196–197)

That the expedition was not prompted by a military crisis or rebellion seems clear. Given that the *Oration* was a panegyric (Lieu and Montserrat 1996, 161–162) it would seem implausible to suggest that a military event was being suppressed by Libanius for some reason. Military glory and victory was a precious commodity jealously guarded by the emperor (McCormick 1986). It would be expected that Libanius would mention such a victory in his panegyric if one had occurred.

It is possible to argue that the visit was a carefully planned piece of imperial bravado (Malosse 1999) that may also have included an out-of-season inspection of the British garrisons (Birley 2005, 415). Britain's location beyond the Ocean and its distance from the Mediterranean world gave it a long-standing mystique that may have made visiting the island an attractive option. Here a rare bronze medallion struck in Rome depicting Constans on a galley accompanied by standards, a victory and the legend BONONIA OCEANEN[SIS] (*RIC* VIII (Rome), 338) is of relevance. Boulogne was the usual embarkation point for Britain and *The Theodosian Code* records Constans at the city in January 343 (*Cod. Theod.* 11.16.5). The emperor is portrayed levelling a spear at a figure in the water, who is usually interpreted as Oceanus, and this medallion perhaps may depict Constans' metaphorical subjection of the Ocean rather than a defeat of distant barbarians (Portmann 1999, fn. 140). The medallion also shares similarities in design with the common FEL TEMP REPARATIO 'galley' coinage. The message of an emperor supreme on land and sea may thus have been intended for wide consumption.

'Raids of Picti, Scotti, Saxones and Attacotti on Britain'

The events of 343 were mentioned in connection with Julian's difficulties in the year 360. Ammianus recounts how the Caesar Julian sent his *magister equitum*, Lupicinus, to Britain to deal with an incursion of Picts and Scots (Birley 2005, 424–426) who 'were laying waste the regions near the frontiers, so that fear seized the provincials' (Amm. Marc. XX, 1.1). The general was accompanied by four units of Julian's field army and set sail mid-winter to tackle the barbarian incursion. Superficially this appears to be firm evidence of conflict prompted by barbarian invasion in fourth-century Britain.

In many respects the incursion of 360 neatly illustrates the dangers of mining ancient sources for snippets of information with which to construct a narrative history for late Roman Britain. To contemporaries 360 was an important year because it saw the usurpation of Julian and this event has a direct bearing on the interpretation of Lupicinus' expedition to Britain.

Ammianus is well-known as an apologist for Julian and his history goes to some lengths to portray the late emperor in a positive light. Thus the usurpation was described by Ammianus as an act forced upon a man cornered by circumstances beyond his control. Modern scholars have been divided between those who accept this view (Matthews 1989, 93–100) and those who see Julian's bid for the purple as the climax of carefully nurtured ambition (Drinkwater 1983, 370–383; Barnes 1998, 153–154).

Lupicinus' expedition to Britain and its aftermath incline one to the latter view.

The usurpation was supposedly prompted by Constantius II ordering his nephew to turn over to his command the 'Aeruli [Heruli] and Batavi and the Celts with the Petulantes, as well as 300 picked men from each of the other divisions of the army' (Amm. Marc. XX, 4.2) for service in the east. Significantly, these troops were to be placed under Lupicinus. From this it may be deduced that Lupicinus was an officer loyal to Constantius. It may be further supposed that if Constantius was seeking, at least in part, to weaken his nephew's position (Drinkwater 1983, 383–387) then the units selected for transfer may have been some of Julian's most loyal troops.

Taking these points together it can plausibly be suggested that Lupicinus' expedition to Britain was a convenient means of removing an officer loyal to Constantius II at a critical juncture. We might go further and suggest that any 'barbarian incursion' could have been prompted or encouraged by the western Caesar's court in order to provide a reasonable pretext for removing Lupicinus. On his return to the continent Lupicinus was arrested, which rather suggests the whole incident had been an imperial intrigue from the outset. This is not a new idea (Drinkwater 1983) and has been mentioned in at least one account of late Roman Britain (Esmonde-Cleary 1989, 44). Yet that same account was unwilling to discount the barbarian invasion on the grounds that Julian would not willingly send four of his *comitatensian* units to Britain unless there was a pressing need to do so. Of course, those same units involved at least some of the troops requested by Constantius II and also may have served to insulate Lupicinus and the soldiers in Britain from interfering in the imperial drama being planned in Paris.

'Barbarian conspiracy – Count of the Saxon Shore killed and *dux Britanniarum* "ambushed". Situation restored by land/naval campaigns of Count Theodosius in north and south Britain'

Early in the reign of Julian's eventual successor, the emperor Valentinian, another imperial intervention in Britain occurred. This was the so-called 'barbarian conspiracy' of 367 in which Picts, Scots and Saxons overwhelmed Roman Britain's defences, killed one senior military commander and besieged another. This dangerous situation was recovered by the *comes* Theodosius, who then set about restoring the cities and defences of Britain. For much of the twentieth century this event played a central role in how the end of the Roman period was characterised and understood. The barbarian conspiracy was supposedly visible in a widespread episode of destruction and rebuilding in the frontier zone, led to the erection of new 'signal stations' along the Yorkshire coast and was the cause of the abandonment of many villas in the south of Britain (Frere 1967, 358–359). Today few of these associations are accepted uncritically by archaeologists and the reinterpretation of many sites shows that there is no archaeological horizon that marks the events of 367. Nevertheless, the idea of the 'barbarian conspiracy' remains attractive to many and it is widely used as evidence of a deteriorating security situation in late Roman Britain (Faulkner 2000, 164–165; Mattingly 2007, 235–237).

The reinterpretation of the archaeological significance of the 'barbarian conspiracy' was partially driven by better archaeological methodologies and also data. However, it was also accepted that the events may have been exaggerated. Given that the *comes* Theodosius was the father of the ruling eastern emperor at the time Ammianus was composing his work, it is unlikely that he would downplay the achievements of his ruler's father. Thus it is widely recognised that his treatment of the *comes* Theodosius is essentially panegyrical (Barnes 1998, 182; Mratschek 2007). However, this is not the only issue that should be considered when discussing the significance of 367.

The text of the *Res Gestae* survives in a single Carolingian manuscript from which all later editions are ultimately derived. The manuscript is lacunose and suffers from a variety of scribal errors, which have been emended by modern editors since the early modern period (Barnes 1998, 201–208). In a controversial paper that has not received wide acceptance, Bartholomew (1984, 173–182) has argued that if certain passages were emended the barbarians could be removed from the 'barbarian conspiracy' and the event recast as a reaction to a military insurrection caused by a food shortage (see also Drinkwater 1999, 133–134). That such an argument can be made regarding our most important fourth-century written source should at the very least disturb our secure view of this 'factual event', regardless of whether Bartholomew's (1984) interpretation is accepted or not (e.g. Birley 2005, fn. 49).

Even accepting that Ammianus' account was probably coloured by a pro-Theodosian agenda, and recognising that the text is not unproblematic, there remains an important further point of analysis. Following his accession in 364 Valentinian divided the empire between himself and his brother Valens. The following year Valentinian spent his time at Milan and Paris presumably showing that he was a worthy successor to the late Gallic favourite Julian and concerning himself with the Alamanni. Late in 365 the new imperial house was shaken by the dangerous usurpation of Procopius, who had links to the Constantinian dynasty. The rebellion was not crushed by Valens until May 366. Then in 367 Valentinian fell ill at Amiens, an event that prompted jockeying for position in the western court and the elevation of Valentinian's young son Gratian to *Augustus* at the end of August. Thus the first years of Valentinian's reign were a dangerous time for the new post-Constantinian imperial regime.

The 'barbarian conspiracy' occurred during 367 but its exact chronology is uncertain (e.g. Demandt 1972, 84–85; Tomlin 1974). Ammianus records that Valentinian heard about the crisis *en route* from Amiens to Trier and this would place the conspiracy after Valentinian's illness (Drinkwater 2007, 279). However, Ammianus' chronology may be mistaken and it has been suggested that the emperor's itinerary (Rheims in June; Amiens in August; Rheims *en route* to Trier in October) suggests that news of trouble in Britain reached Valentinian in mid-summer, prompting a dash to Amiens where illness and court politics struck (Tomlin 1974; Blockley 1980). If this reconstruction of events is accepted then it follows that Valentinian intended to campaign in Britain (Tomlin 1974, 305). Such a campaign would have been intended to furnish the emperor with a much needed victory to demonstrate his military mettle (Drinkwater 2007, 279). This might explain the speed with which the senior officers Severus and Jovinus were sent to Britain and returned with negative reports. That barbarian threats were exaggerated in order to aggrandise the emperor's eventual victory, or to fulfil some other political purpose, has been suggested for other fourth-century accounts of military actions (e.g. Drinkwater 2007, 273–274). The carefully crafted lustre of the event, perhaps originally intended for Valentinian, was then reflected by Ammianus onto the father of Theodosius I.

An alternative reconstruction of events would see the visit of both Severus and Jovinus to Britain as a reaction to Valentinian's illness. Here it is worth noting that Severus was touted as a potential successor to Valentinian. Perhaps their visits were analogous to Julian's sleight of hand with Lupicinus in 360. At a point of political delicacy, in this case Valentinian's illness rather than Julian's usurpation, a senior general could be quarantined on the far side of the Channel.

This discussion has been based on a reconstruction of events that relies on the barbarian conspiracy prompting Valentinian's visit to Amiens. However, it is possible that this reconstruction is erroneous and that news of trouble in Britain reached the emperor after he left Amiens en route to Trier. If this were so, then the seriousness of the news was not enough to deflect Valentinian from his move towards the Rhine. This, given that one recent study has painted Valentinian as in desperate need of military glory at this point in his reign, undermines the gravity of the 'barbarian conspiracy'. The emperor still sought conflict with the Alamanni, arguably a traditional and suitable opponent (Drinkwater 2007), even when invasion threatened Britain.

Where does this leave the 'barbarian conspiracy' and the history of late Roman Britain? It may have been a non-event, little more than a few chance raids that were exaggerated to a great conspiracy to fulfil Roman political ends. Ultimately suppressed by a relatively junior general with a limited number of troops, it was probably no more than an over-reaction by the western imperial court. The despatch of generals and units of the emperor's field army may also have fulfilled one further imperial goal: a reminder to the garrison, provincials and would-be usurpers in Britain of Valentinian's reach in the aftermath of Procopius' usurpation.

'Magnus Maximus defeats Picti and Scotti'

In 383 Magnus Maximus, a general in Britain with close links to the eastern emperor, usurped the imperial throne, executed the western emperor Gratian and made himself master of the north-western provinces. Maximus was ultimately defeated by Theodosius I in 388 and his 'tyranny' remains an important and relatively well-recorded episode. The same cannot be said of the years preceding his bid for the purple. What he was doing in Britain remains unclear, as does his rank at the time, but it is usually argued that he was a disaffected army officer, perhaps the *dux Britanniarum* or *comes Britanniarum*. The only evidence for him campaigning against external foes in 382/383 is a single entry in the *Gallic Chronicle* of 452. This leads to a circular argument in which Maximus was present in Britain because of an external threat and the evidence for this threat is his victory recorded in the *Gallic Chronicle*.

Given that the *Gallic Chronicle* is the sole source for Maximus' campaign against the Picti and Scotti it may be unwise to read too much into this event. Composed in southern Gaul during the mid fifth century it is at pains to contrast Magnus Maximus as the last effective ruler of Gaul with the lackadaisical Theodosian dynasty (Muhlberger 1992, 34). The recorded event may have been little more than a sham concocted as a prerequisite for Maximus' usurpation. Such a victory would establish his credentials with the army and also the provincial elite. The core of his rebellion may have been units drawn from the so-called field army, but as we have seen, previous events might suggest that this force was relatively small. In the early days of the usurpation Maximus must have also required the support of the British garrisons who had long-standing links with their local communities (James 2011a). It is unlikely that such troops and the local elite would countenance a dash to the imperial core without first ensuring the local barbarians could not take advantage of the lowered troop levels.

'Stilicho (or a subordinate) campaigns in Britain against Picti and Scotti'

The source for this final event is a series of panegyrics by the poet Claudian (Schindler 2009, 59–172). These mention Britain, Saxons, Picts and Scots in a variety of bellicose situations but not in such a fashion as to enable a sound historical reconstruction of the type or scale of actions taken against these groups (*contra* Miller 1975). Here we might note that Claudian has Orkney running red with Saxon slaughter and tents being camped in Caledonian snows. These are motifs that owe more to Claudian's rhetorical style and Britain's perceived position as a frigid wilderness at the edge of the world than any late fourth-century reality.

Each of the episodes discussed above is open to interpretation. The continued recycling of these 'snippets' of late fourth-century history in archaeological works as evidence of military insecurity needs to be tempered by a better recognition of the context and limitations of the sources. Free of this unsatisfactory meta-narrative the defence of late Roman Britain can be approached in a less constrained fashion.

Defending late Roman Britain

The defence of fourth-century Britain rested on regiments of soldiers and a variety of fortifications. What might, perhaps anachronistically, be described as the 'late Roman army' is a substantial topic and it is impossible to discuss comprehensively the importance, role, equipment and capabilities of Britain's fourth-century garrison (Southern and Dixon 1996; James 2011a). It is also unnecessary as there are a variety of works that attempt detailed discussions of both the late Roman army and its presence in Britain. Nevertheless, some understanding of the situation is needed if only to counteract some long-held preconceptions.

Many works on Roman Britain use a document known as the *Notitia Dignitatum* to structure their analysis of the fourth-century military. This work, which is ostensibly a document listing army units and government officials in the Roman Empire, has a complex history and historiography.

The surviving version was revised in parts until *c*.428 but the British sections may not post-date *c*.390. It was probably created as an administrative text and it may also have functioned in either a complementary or alternative role as a piece of imperial propaganda that underlined the fictive unity of a fragmenting state (Kulikowski 2000a). Work on aspects of the *Notitia* is voluminous and growing (for a summary and references see Maier 2012).

The *Notitia* lists three commands in Britain (for a useful summary see Hassall 2004; Birley 2005, 401–403): that of the *comes Britanniarum*, an officer who seemingly had under his command a 'field army' of six cavalry units and three infantry units (*Not. Dig. Occ.* XXIX); that of the *dux Britanniarum*, whose troops are listed as occupying forts in northern Britain and *per lineam valli* (along the line of the wall) (*Not. Dig. Occ.* XL); and finally the *comes litoris Saxonici*, whose command covered a number of fortifications along Britain's south-eastern coast. This information has then been used to sketch the fourth-century military situation. Static garrisons in the north and south-east faced external aggressors and could be supported by a mobile reserve consisting of the *comes Britanniarum*'s field army (Hassall 2004).

For a long time archaeological research on the fourth century was focussed on relating material culture and structural remains to this document. Pieces of metalwork were identified as the accoutrements of the *comitatensian* troops stationed in urban centres (Hawkes and Dunning 1961); forts that were meant to be occupied in the late fourth century were found to be abandoned and fortifications absent from the *Notitia* produced evidence of activity. Clearly the problematic snapshot that this text provides cannot be reconciled with the surviving physical remnants of the past. Equally unsettling is the recognition that the only evidence for the existence of the *comes Britanniarum* is contained in the *Notitia*. Ammianus (Amm. Marc. XXVII 8.1) mentions the *dux Britanniarum* and a 'count of the maritime region' in his discussion of the events of 367 who may or may not be the same as the 'Count of the Saxon Shore' (White 2007, 58–59).

The challenges presented by the main documentary source would indicate that it is of limited utility in understanding the specifics of late Roman Britain's military organisation. Instead a broader view should be taken. The garrison of Britain was probably mainly composed of so-called *limitanei*, the frontier troops created by the reforms of the early fourth century (Jones 1964). These forces were occasionally bolstered by mobile *comitatensian* troops (Whitby 2004, 160) of the western field army (as in 360 and 367). There is no reason to subscribe to the old view of the *limitanei* as a static frontier militia formed of poorly trained, poorly equipped and ill-disciplined soldier-farmers (e.g. MacMullen 1963; Halsall 2007, 102). Nor is there any reason to believe that the fourth-century army was unreliable and barbarised by Germanic recruits (Halsall 2007, 102–105) who sought to hasten the empire's end (Ferrill 1986; Nicassie 1998). Such assumptions have been much over-stated (Elton 1996; Whitby 2004, 166–167) and serving barbarians often became loyal and capable soldiers and generals (Halsall 2007, 148). It has also been suggested that Roman units adopted 'barbarian' labels as unit identities and that this has been misinterpreted by modern scholars as 'barbarisation' of the army (Halsall 2003, 2007, 106–110).

The suggestion that fourth-century Britain's garrison was largely effective receives further support from the scale of the garrison. A figure in the region of 10,000–15,000 men (James 1984), half the size of the second-century garrison (for alternatives see Jones 1996, 166), has been suggested. If this is a true assessment of the situation, and the archaeological evidence would seem to indicate less intensive activity at many forts during the fourth century (Gardner 2007), then the late Roman garrison was perfectly capable of defending the diocese with a third to a quarter of the manpower needed in the early Roman period (Esmonde-Cleary 1989, 63). The troops also felt able to intervene in the wider empire, if their support for usurpers in 306, 350, 383 and 407 is anything to go by.

This review of the late Roman army in Britain largely complements the critique of the historical narrative for growing external pressure advanced earlier in this chapter. Fewer troops continued to effectively maintain security and the notion of a strategic defensive response by the Roman state to barbarian threats has been shown to be a modern construct. These conclusions can be carried forward to the analysis of late Roman defensive architecture in Britain and beyond.

The architecture of 'defence'

Some of the most impressive surviving structural remains from late antiquity in Britain and the north-western provinces are stone-built defences. These fortifications can be divided into two broad categories: those that served military functions and those that surrounded urban centres. These categories may have resonated with their ancient builders and users, who seem to have distinguished between military and civil defences. Both types of fortification have been traditionally interpreted as symptoms of the developing insecurity supposedly revealed by the textual sources. However, closer analysis of the biographies of late Roman forts and city walls reveals a less certain story.

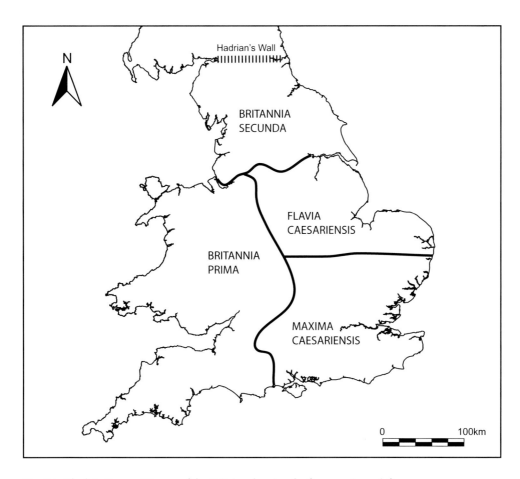

Fig. 2.1 The late Roman Diocese of the Britains showing the four provinces (after White 2007, Fig. 17).

Military fortifications

The late Roman army seemingly occupied a number of fortifications on the periphery of the late Roman diocese (Figure 2.1). These fortifications included frontier works in the north of Britain, and defensive installations around the south-eastern coast and around the Welsh coastline (Gardner 2007). These defences seem arranged to counter threats from *barbaricum*: Pictish raiders from what is now Scotland, and seaborne raiders from Ireland and northern Germany. Together with documents like the *Notitia* the presence of these dramatic monuments seems to reinforce the self-evident explanation that there was a military threat to fourth-century Britain. The construction and maintenance of fortifications was costly, in terms of both money and resources, and it could be argued that they would only be constructed and garrisoned in response to a real or perceived threat. The number and scale of these fortifications serve to underline how seriously the late Roman state took this threat. This interpretation can be questioned by briefly considering the fourth-century tradition of military architecture along the Rhine–Danube frontier.

The Tetrarchic fort of Kellmünz on the Iller, a tributary of the Upper Danube, provides a useful starting point (Mackensen 1994, 1995, 1999, 207–213). The walls, some 3.6 m thick, were constructed to enclose a polygonal area set on a spur overlooking the river. The walled circuit was provided with twelve projecting towers and a single monumental gateway, flanked by two projecting towers. This was a considerable deviation from the 'playing card' type plan of the early imperial fort and represents a shift in the nature of defensive architecture.

Kellmünz was a new foundation *c.*297. Elsewhere the army of the fourth century modified earlier structures by adding projecting towers to earlier wall circuits (Kandler and Vetters 1986, 130–146). However, the most dramatic modification of an early Roman fort can be seen at Eining where an auxiliary fort of the Flavian/Trajanic period (Johnson 1983a, 173–174; Mackensen 1999, 214–216) received a tiny fort utilising one corner of its defences in the fourth century. A similar modification occurred to the fort of Azaum in Pannonia (Johnson 1983a, 182). Other late modifications in Raetia included the provision of a large number of fortified granaries (Mackensen 1999, 234–238) and watchtowers, many of which date to the Valentinianic period (Garbsch 1967; Johnson 1983a, 257–258).

The reign of Valentinian was important in the fourth-century development of the Rhine–Danube frontier. Ammianus (Amm. Marc. XXVIII, 2) noted in positive terms Valentinian's drive to fortify the frontiers of the empire and modern authors have been equally keen on asserting this emperor's prowess as a builder (Schönberger 1969, 182; von Petrikovits 1971, 184; Johnson 1983a, 257). At least sixteen sites along the Rhine–Danube frontier have literary and epigraphic evidence indicating their construction or modification under Valentinian (Lenski 2002, 376–378). Archaeology suggests that many more sites should be added to this tally, even allowing for the imprecision of the dating evidence at some sites (e.g. von Petrikovits 1971, 184; Lander 1984, 270–276).

In the Rhineland two of the many known or presumed Valentinianic fortifications provide useful case studies. The first is Oedenburg, located approximately 48 km south of Strasbourg (Nuber and Reddé 2002). At this site a large rectangular fortification with square projecting towers was probably constructed during the Valentinianic period. Accommodation for the

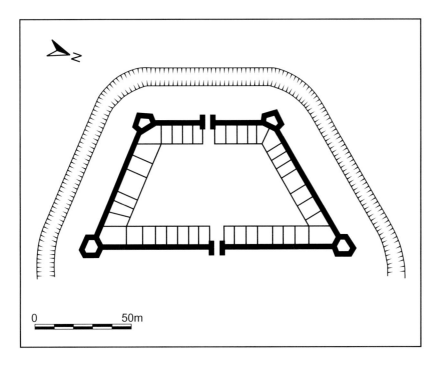

Fig. 2.2 Plan of the Valentinianic fortification at Altrip (Germany) (after von Schnurbein and Köhler 1989, Abb. 6).

garrison was provided by ranges of rooms built internally around the walled circuit – a situation also found at Alzey, where the arrangement may also be of Valentinianic date (Johnson 1983a, 153). Interestingly, the groundplan of Oedenburg finds a parallel at Pfalzel, near Trier (Nuber and Reddé 2002, Fig. 42). The second fortification is Altrip (von Schnurbein and Köhler 1989) where a combination of historical and dendrochronological evidence suggests that a new fortification was constructed in 369 (Figure 2.2). The walled circuit encloses a polygonal area and is backed by ranges of buildings similar to those at Oedenburg and Alzey. The fortification was further enhanced by the provision of four polygonal corner towers.

The brevity of this discussion underlines that it is not and cannot be a comprehensive review of late Roman fortifications along the Rhine and Danube (for which see Johnson 1983a; Lander 1984). Instead it offers an introduction to something of the rich variety of fourth-century defensive plans in this region, as well as the imperial interest and investment attested by them. The British evidence – the forts of the 'Saxon Shore', the defences of Wales and Hadrian's Wall – offers a contrast to this continental picture.

The 'Saxon Shore' is a term found only in the *Notitia* (*Not. Dig. Occ.* XXVIII) but it is often used anachronistically as shorthand to describe a series of third- and fourth-century coastal fortifications located on harbours and estuaries stretching from the Wash to Portchester (Hampshire) (Johnson 1976; Pearson 2002, 2005) (Figure 2.3). These fortifications include sites that are not listed in the *Notitia* but which are of comparable form (such as Bitterne, Southampton; Caister-on-Sea, Norfolk; and Walton Castle, Suffolk). Traditionally these fortifications (and others on the shores of northern Gaul) have been viewed as coastal defences erected against the Saxon menace. Elaborate scenarios involving fleets and signal towers have been created to describe how such a defensive system might have worked (Hassall 2004). However, the evidence for the ships to carry out coastal patrols (Cotterill 1993, 232; Rankov 2002) and the signal towers (Douglas, Gerrard and Sudds 2011, 165–166) is virtually non-existent. Due to this, more recent scholarship has emphasised the role of the forts as transit points and secure compounds for the temporary storage of supplies destined for Gaul (Cotterill 1993; Pearson 2002, 2005).

The forts of the 'Saxon Shore' show a development through time that is reasonably well understood (Pearson 2002). The earliest in the sequence are Brancaster (Norfolk) (Figure 2.4), Reculver (Kent) and possibly Caister-on-Sea, all of which might date to the first half of the third century (Hinchcliffe and Sparey Green 1985, 187; Philp 2005, 207; Darling and Gurney 1993, 11). They are of square 'playing card' plan, with stone walls backed by an earth rampart and lack external towers. These contrast with other forts at Richborough (Kent) (Figure 2.5), Portchester (Figure 2.6 and Figure 2.7) and Bradwell where freestanding walls and square plans were wedded with projecting towers. Finally, there are forts at Dover (Kent) and Pevensey (East Sussex) (Figure 2.8) that have irregular groundplans and projecting towers. The only fortifications once considered as fourth-century foundations are Pevensey and Bitterne. However, both of these sites are now known to have been constructed in the late third century (Fulford and Tyers 1995; King 1991; Fulford and Rippon 2011). There is thus no evidence for the late fourth-century construction or serious modification of any of the fortifications, but Richborough has produced coins of Constantine III (*r*. 407–411), and Portchester, Bradwell-on-Sea and Brancaster (Johnson 1976, Fig. 63) have yielded coins of the House of Theodosius suggesting that activity at these sites continued until the early fifth century.

In the west of Britain a number of fortifications constructed or used in the late Roman period can be identified. The most important from an early Roman perspective were the two legionary fortresses at Caerleon (Newport)

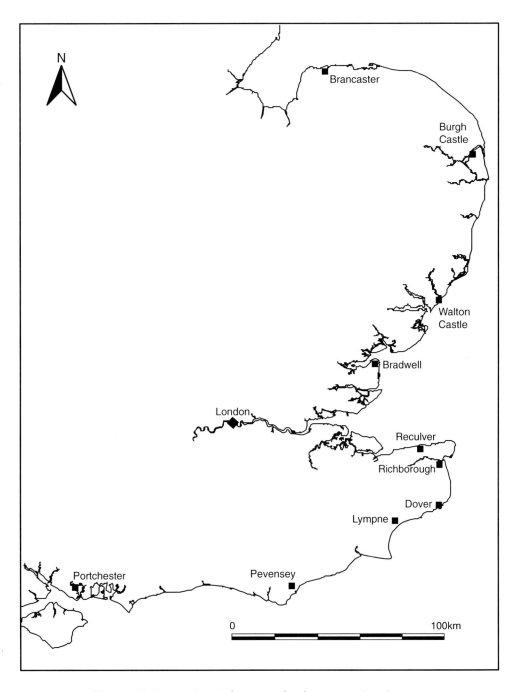

Fig. 2.3 Map of the so-called Saxon Shore (after Esmonde-Cleary 1989, Fig. 11).

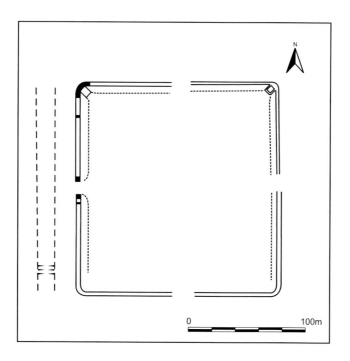

Fig. 2.4 Plan of the Roman fort at Brancaster (after Johnson 1976, Fig. 20).

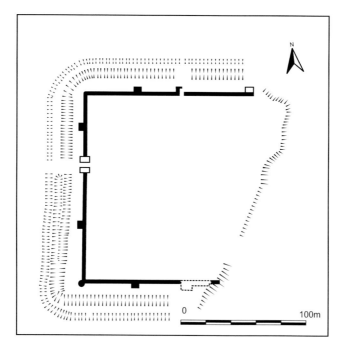

Fig. 2.5 Plan of the Roman fort at Richborough (after Johnson 1976, Fig. 30).

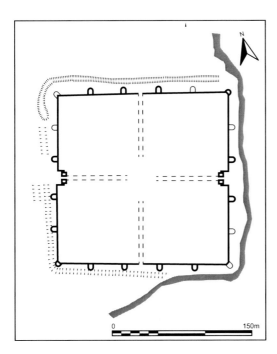

Fig. 2.6 Plan of the Roman fort at Portchester (after Johnson 1976, Fig. 38).

and Chester (Cheshire). Both have produced evidence of fourth-century activity and both have traditionally been interpreted as given over to civilian uses at this date (Boon 1987, 43; McPeake 1978). Gardner (2007) has shown how problematic distinguishing military from civilian can be in the fourth century and the two legionary fortresses may both have continued to fulfil some military role (Gardner 2007, 176–177; Seaman 2010, 43–44). However, neither of the sites received substantial late Roman modifications to their defences (such as projecting towers, or projecting corner or gate towers). The same can be said of the fort at Caernarfon (Segontium, Gywnedd) (Casey, Davies and Evans 1993), which was occupied until the end of the fourth century.

   In contrast to sites such as Segontium and Caerleon, new forts at Cardiff (South Glamorgan) and Lancaster (Lancashire; the latter arguably better discussed here than as part of the northern frontier) were constructed in the so-called 'Saxon Shore' style with freestanding walls and projecting towers. Unfortunately neither is precisely dated. A late third- or fourth-century date seems appropriate for Cardiff (Evans 2003) and Lancaster may have

Fig. 2.7 Reconstruction drawing of the shore fort at Portchester. Note the imposing projecting towers and high walls (© English Heritage).

been constructed as late as *c.*326 on the evidence of a single stratified coin (Jones and Shotter 1988, 80). The three-sided fortified landing place at Caer Gybi, which is strikingly similar to some of the late Roman fortifications on the right bank of the Rhine (Johnson 1976, 137), and the 'watchtower' on Holyhead Mountain (both on Môn, Anglesey), are also probably fourth-century foundations (Davies 1991, 56). However, the chronology for both of these sites is far from certain. Nevertheless, these fortifications represent an otherwise rare attempt to replicate the types of defences seen on the Rhine–Danube frontier.

Lancaster brings this discussion to the only land frontier in Britain: Hadrian's Wall. Running from the Tyne to the Solway, Hadrian's Wall was constructed in the early second century and, apart from short oscillations

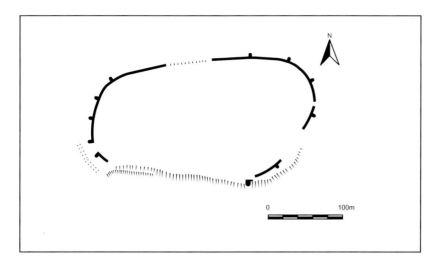

Fig. 2.8 Plan of the Roman fort at Pevensey (after Johnson 1976, Fig. 36).

northwards in the Antonine and Severan periods, marked the northernmost limit of the Roman Empire. To the south of the wall was a militarised zone formed of forts positioned astride roads at key geographical locations, such as fords, passes and road junctions (Figure 2.9). The southernmost limit of this zone is usually seen as being marked by the legionary fortresses at York and Chester. The *Notitia* (*Not. Dig. Occ.* XL) lists forts and garrisons in this area as the command of the *dux Britanniarum*. However, many forts, such as Piercebridge, Binchester, Lancaster, Brougham and others are not listed in the *Notitia* but contain evidence for fourth-century activity (Esmonde-Cleary 1989, Fig. 10).

Some thirty years ago one commentator on the northern frontier remarked that '[l]ittle can be said of the last days of Hadrian's Wall' (Breeze 1982, 159). Today an enormous body of work has illustrated that the period from *c.*300 to 500 in the north of Britain was an extremely complex time (e.g. Dark 1992; Wilmott 1997, 195–232; Collins 2007; Collins and Allason-Jones 2010). However, the significant changes that occurred in the frontier zone during the late Roman period are not reflected in the region's defensive architecture, which remained outmoded, if not old-fashioned.

The outmoded nature of fort defences in the north of Britain is manifested in the almost complete absence of projecting towers (Figure 2.10). This form of augmentation, so familiar from the towns and 'shore' forts of Roman Britain and the fortifications on the Rhine–Danube frontier, is lacking from all sites in the north (including 'urban' centres such as Catterick,

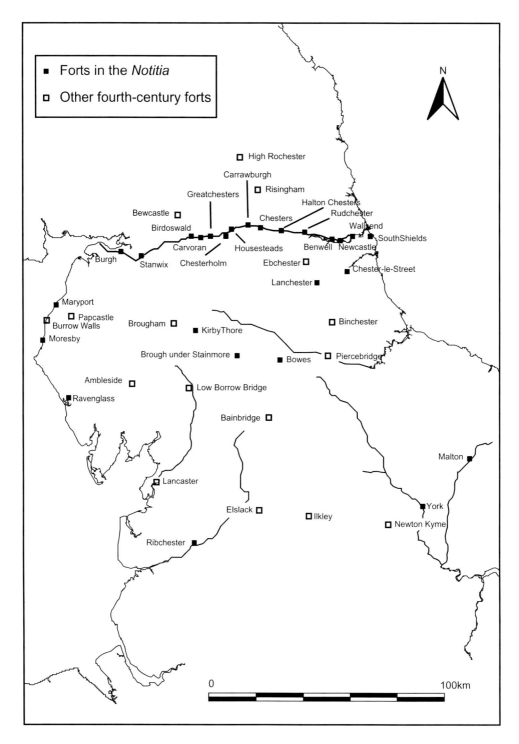

Fig. 2.9 Map of northern Britain showing fourth-century fortifications (after Esmonde-Cleary 1989, Fig. 10).

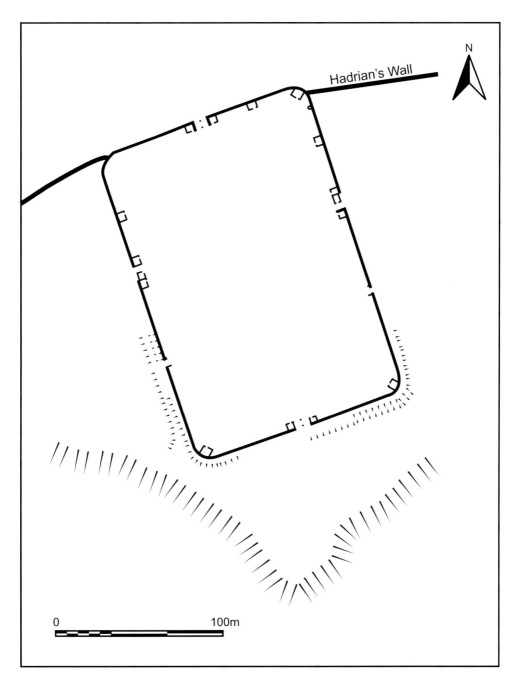

Fig. 2.10 Plan of the fort at Birdoswald on Hadrian's Wall (after Wilmott 1997, Fig. 8). Note the 'old-fashioned' playing card shape and lack of projecting towers.

North Yorkshire). The only exceptions to this rule are Lancaster (discussed above) and York, where the legionary fortress received projecting towers to its riverside wall. These are usually interpreted as a symbol of status associated with the importance of the fortress as an occasional imperial residence and presumed headquarters of the *dux Britanniarum* (Hassall 2004, 182). Even forts founded *de novo* during the third century, such as Carlisle (Cumbria) (Zant 2009, 267) and Piercebridge (Co. Durham) (Cool and Mason 2008, 306), were constructed without projecting towers. This is particularly significant because Piercebridge with its 3m-thick wall (but lacking projecting towers) is argued to have been constructed *c.*260–280, at a time when the 'shore' forts and many towns (below) were being built with projecting towers (Cool and Mason 2008, 306).

As noted above, the lack of projecting towers, which were added to earlier forts on other imperial frontiers (Kandler and Vetters 1986, 130–146), is a peculiar phenomenon. Even more unusual is the absence of any major modifications to fort defences, as at Eining, and the lack of new fourth-century forts, which are relatively common on other frontiers. This pattern is reinforced by the comparative lack of fourth-century epigraphic evidence from the frontier zone. On other frontiers fourth-century building programmes produced inscriptions. In Britain the latest inscription from Hadrian's Wall was found at Birdoswald (Cumbria) and is dated to the Tetrarchic period (Donaldson 1990). The general decline in the use of inscriptions in Britain and the empire can be invoked to explain this phenomenon (MacMullen 1982). However, it might be expected that the army, where literacy was particularly concentrated, would continue to create monumental inscriptions.

This discussion of inscriptions leads to the so-called signal-towers on the Yorkshire coast. One of these installations, formed of a tall tower surrounded by a curtain wall with projecting corner towers, produced an inscription recording that it had been created by a certain Justinianus and Vindicianus, *praepositus* and *magister* respectively (*RIB* I 721). These towers are traditionally thought to have been constructed in the aftermath of the so-called 'barbarian conspiracy' in 367, although some current thinking favours construction during the reign of Magnus Maximus (383–388) (Ottaway 1997, 139). The historical context is largely irrelevant, but what seems certain from the coin and pottery evidence is that these fortifications date to the reign of Valentinian or later and they are well paralleled by similar kinds of fortifications on the Rhine and Danube (Ottaway 2000, 94). In terms of function these towers have been seen as a part of a coastal chain defending

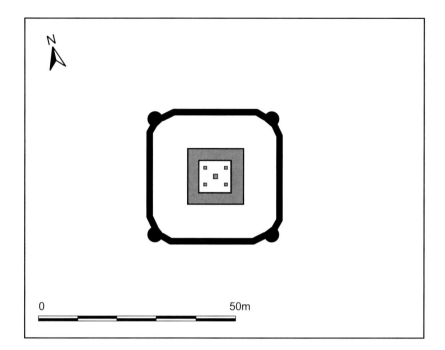

N

0   50m

Fig. 2.11 Plan of the late fourth-century 'signal station' at Filey (after Ottaway 1997, Fig. 1.57). Note the position of the projecting corner towers, which are so placed as to make enfilading the walls impossible.

the eastern flank of Hadrian's Wall from seaborne Pictish raiders (Johnson 1983a, 212; Wilson 1991). Certainly, they could have functioned to observe movement along the north-east coast, police small harbours and provide refuges in times of trouble (Wilson 1991). Whether this in turn implies a primarily defensive function is less certain. They are very small installations and, despite appearances, are not particularly defensible: the projecting corner towers are so situated that they cannot enfilade the curtain wall (Wilson 1991, Fig. 23.3) (Figure 2.11). An alternative interpretation would see these fortifications as a means of physically defining the limit of empire.

The review of the evidence for fourth-century military architecture on the Rhine–Danube frontier demonstrated that the Roman army was capable of building new fortifications. These included substantial new forts like Kellmünz or Oedenburg and smaller establishments like Eining, or the watchtowers of the Danube frontier. It is usual to see these defences, with their projecting towers and thick walls, as a response to the Germanic threat. The scale and nature of this threat is a matter of debate. Some have argued that barbarian groups on the far side of the Rhine and Danube were credible foes (Heather 2005). Others have suggested that the threat was over-hyped by a Roman state keen to emphasise its necessity to the provincial populations (e.g. Drinkwater 1999, 2007; Halsall 2007). What the evidence of fortifications demonstrates is that, whatever the scale and nature of the threat to the Rhine–Danube frontier, the Roman state expended resources and manpower investing in defensive architecture. The emperor's interest in promulgating an ideology of military defence against the barbarian other was being written on the ground in the physical form of major defensive works. In Britain the story was very different.

In the aftermath of the so-called 'barbarian conspiracy' the *comes* Theodosius was replaced by a senior army officer called Dulcitius (nothing else is known of him or his position: Birley 2005, 440). This individual, transferred from the continental armies, would have sailed to Britain and, like Theodosius, Julian and probably Constans, would have landed at Richborough. The thick walls, square plan and projecting towers would have made that fort instantly recognisable from his experience of defensive architecture on the empire's other frontiers. Its form may have been somewhat outmoded compared to the new fort at Alta Ripa (the modern Altrip, near Ludwigshafen) but it was a reasonably up-to-date fortification. The fortress at York, where Dulcitius may, if he was *dux Britanniarum*, have had his headquarters, would appear as a venerable and ancient seat of Roman power. The site of two emperors' deaths and the elevation of Constantine, its status was proclaimed by the polygonal projecting towers along its riverside wall (Ottaway 1993). An old fortification remodelled, like so many others, to reflect a new age (Elton 1996, 165–167).

As he rode north to inspect his troops on the wall Dulcitius would have passed the fort of Piercebridge, standing guard over a ford through the Tees. Here was a fort, perhaps only a century old, but lacking Richborough's familiar attributes. Finally, he would have reached the wall and perhaps progressed along its length, from Wallsend to Carlisle. What Dulcitius would have seen were occupied forts garrisoned by *limitanei*. However, nowhere were there signs of imperial interest. The walls of South Shields (Tyne and Wear), no doubt maintained, were still largely those erected by Legio VI in the Antonine period (Bidwell and Speak 1994, 18–19) and this was a pattern repeated along the length of the frontier. Not a single surviving building inscription proclaimed the activities of Constantine and his dynasty, not a single fort received projecting towers. Even the names of the units and the titles of their officers were those of an earlier age (Hodgson 1991) and the soldiers may have dressed differently to other units in the Roman army, if the lack of zoomorphic belt fittings from the frontier is any guide (Coulston 2010, 52–56; *contra* the interpretation offered by Halsall 2007, 196–197). In modern archaeological parlance this could be glossed as being 'regionally distinct', but it might be more accurately described as a backwater. If this view is correct and reflects an attitude of 'if it isn't broken, don't fix it' on the part of the imperial administration, then it follows that the northern frontier was not perceived to be under any kind of threat that required a substantial response during the fourth century (Collins 2009, 194). The 'relentless Pictish threat to Britannia' – to quote from one recent Scottish history (Fraser 2009, 61) – was nothing more than a bogeyman easily contained by Roman arms.

Urban fortifications

The civilian fortifications of Roman Britain present an alternative process of development. By the end of the fourth century virtually every urban centre in Britain (including so-called 'small' towns) had been girt with walled circuits of varying types and designs (Esmonde-Cleary 2007). The process of development, in general terms, is well understood. Earthen defences, usually erected in the later second century, were supplemented by walls inserted into the faces of ramparts during the course of the third century. Finally, in the fourth century many towns received the addition of projecting towers (which are often referred to anachronistically as 'bastions') that are so absent along the northern frontier.

The interpretation of the significance of this phenomenon has divided quite sharply along two separate lines. The first, typical of most work until the 1980s, attempted to connect campaigns of wall construction and the augmentation of urban defences with known historical events (Casey 1983, 121): invasions, usurpations and imperial visits (e.g. Corder 1956; Wacher 1964, 1998; Frere 1984). This approach was firmly based on the notion that the function of city walls was primarily defensive (Rivet 1964, 96; Myres 1969, 65; Webster 1983; Bachrach 2000, 195–196; Lyon 2007, 46) and that the costly construction programmes needed to build them would only be undertaken 'in the hour of bitter need' (Haverfield 1904, 628) or at imperial urging. The second line of enquiry, influenced by concerns over how to define a Roman town and an academic fashion that emphasised the ideological importance of material culture, suggested that town walls had less to do with defence than prestige (Guest 2002; Wilson 2006; Esmonde-Cleary 2007).

The fourth century, shackled to the narrative of threat discussed above, has largely been bypassed by these debates. The late Roman provision of projecting towers is still linked to the supposedly declining security situation (Johnson 1983a, 115–116; Mattingly 2007, 225–252), or the increasing militarisation of the late Roman world (Faulkner 2000, 126–137). Far rarer are attempts to link the construction of projecting towers to ideological explanations, or to changes in the fashions of urban defensive architecture and civic pride (Esmonde-Cleary 2003, 2007). Of course, any attempt to impose an explanation or interpretative framework on a phenomenon that was far from homogeneous must be doomed to failure. Nevertheless, situating the Romano-British evidence in a wider context highlights the contrast between Britain and other regions of the empire and this weakens the defensive argument.

It has long been recognised that the trajectory followed by Romano-British cities in the late fourth century differs considerably from that seen in Gaul. Many cities in Gaul and the Germanies did receive walls in the late Roman period but these often enclosed a tiny fraction of the area occupied in the early Roman period (Roblin 1951, 1961; Maurin 1992). Paris is one of the most famous examples. An extensive townscape on the south bank of the Seine that contained the forum, amphitheatre and baths was left undefended while the Île de la Cité in the Seine was defended (Roblin 1951; Johnson 1983a, 103 and Fig. 34). Tongres (Raepsaet-Charlier and Vanderhoeven 2004), Kaiseraugst (Schwarz 2004), Xanten (Johnson 1983a, 146) and a host of other sites display a similar pattern (e.g Johnson 1983a, 82–114): the creation of small fortified enceintes enclosing only a fraction of previously (or even contemporary) occupied urban space (Figure 2.12).

Attempts to replicate the Gallic pattern in Britain have never been convincing. The late fourth-century walls at Cunetio (Mildenhall, Wiltshire) (Corney 1997) are well paralleled by Gallic fortifications, and a handful of other defensive circuits appear to have been constructed in a similar tradition. However, these are sites that are poorly understood (Johnson 1983a, 132). At London a fortified late Roman enceinte within the circuit of the earlier walls has been hypothesised (Merrifield 1983, 246; Reece 2008, 47), but the suggestion is almost certainly erroneous. A recent study of the distribution of late fourth-century material culture in the City shows no patterning that would support such a hypothesis (Gerrard 2012). Explanations for this difference between Britain and Gaul have been sought in the different nature of urbanism between the two regions. Gallic towns, it was argued, suffered seriously during the third-century crisis while Britain did not. This meant that the contrast in the length of walled circuits between Britain

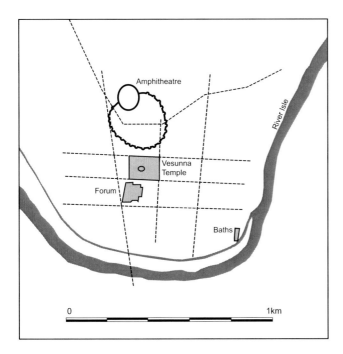

Fig. 2.12 Plan of the walls of Périgueux (France) (after Johnson 1983b, Fig. 78).

and Gaul was simply reflecting the greater urban population and vitality of British towns (Esmonde-Cleary 2003, 84; 2007; Loseby 2000, 322–324). An alternative view of this phenomenon has emphasised that British city wall building occurred earlier than in Gaul (Esmonde-Cleary 2007). Thus the inhabitants of fourth-century towns merely inherited that which had been built to secure an earlier townscape. This interpretation needs to be situated within an academic orthodoxy that suggests that fourth-century towns in Britain were sparsely populated (Reece 1980, 1992). The implication is that the towns were so run down that they were not worthy of being defended along the lines of Gallic cities.

The contrast between urban fortifications in Britain and Gaul is marked. However, the British situation does find some parallels in third- and fourth-century defences erected in Spain where a number of cities, including Astorga, Lugo and Gijón, have late Roman walls that enclose large areas (Johnson 1983a, 124–131; Fernández-Ochoa and Morillo 2005). They differ from Romano-British fortifications in sometimes having very closely set projecting towers (Fernández-Ochoa and Morillo 2005, 314) but nevertheless reflect a significant departure from the Gallic pattern (Esmonde-Cleary 2007).

Fig. 2.13 A fragment of a projecting tower under excavation at Chichester. The chronology and development of many urban defensive circuits have been established from small excavations (© Pre-Construct Archaeology Ltd).

Two final ingredients, the blocking of gates and the addition of projecting towers to city walls, need to be added to these contradictory and conflicting interpretations (Figure 2.13). At some sites, most famously Caerwent (Monmouthshire), but also at Silchester (Hampshire) (Fulford 1984) and Kenchester (Herefordshire) (Burnham and Wacher 1990, 76) town gates were blocked. This is a phenomenon that also occurs at some forts on Hadrian's Wall and elsewhere in the empire (Christie 2000, 279). As gateways are the weakest point on a defensive circuit (Elton 1996, 170) this pattern would appear to indicate that the security situation in fourth-century Britain was deteriorating. The projecting towers can also be seen as a reflection of a society under military pressure. They serve to augment the defences of a town or fort and enable the defenders to cover the bases of the walls with enfilading fire (Elton 1996, 163). The provision of a wide 'U' shaped ditch (in contrast to the narrow 'V' shaped ditches of the early Roman period) in conjunction with the projecting towers supposedly produced a killing zone for archers mounted on the defences. Projecting towers are also often linked to the increased use of artillery. However, the significance of this should not be over-emphasised. Artillery, as Elton notes (1996, 165), could only increase the effectiveness of a garrison and, in an urban context, would seemingly require specialist troops to operate and maintain what were, for the time, technically complex weapons (Baatz 1983, 139; Elton 1996, 171; Southern and Dixon 1996, 158).

As a package the walled circuits and their modifications can be, and have been, understood as illustrating the defensive measures being taken by the inhabitants of late Roman Britain. The substantial differences between the Gallic and British situations have been highlighted here, but all too often are explained away or ignored in the grand narrative of late Roman military decline. This narrative soon struggles if one reviews the individual histories of wall circuits at different urban sites. To this end three cities and their walls are discussed here: London (Londinium Augusta), Caerwent (Venta Silurum) and Mildenhall (Cunetio).

London was the centre of the late Roman Diocese of the Britains, the seat of the *vicarius* and, at various points in the fourth century, an imperial mint and treasury (Esmonde-Cleary 1989, 48). Its Roman walls formed, as with most European cities, the basis of its later medieval defences but little survives above ground today. However, a long history of archaeological exploration means that the construction of the defences is relatively well understood.

The first major defensive work in London was the 'Cripplegate' fort constructed in the second century for soldiers seconded to the governor's staff (Howe and Lakin 2004). The landward wall was constructed *c.*200 (Maloney 1983, 104; Butler 2001, 47–52) but left the riverside with its docks and wharves undefended. By the later third century the city wall had been constructed along the riverside and this included *spolia* from demolished early Roman monuments and structures (Maloney 1983, 111–112; Williams 1993, 13–14) (Figure 2.14).

The Cripplegate fort seems to have lost its military function by the fourth century (Howe and Lakin 2004, 46–47) and the next major alteration to the defences occurred *c.*350 when projecting towers were added to the landward defences on the eastern side (Maloney 1979, 295; Marsden 1980, 170; Sankey and Stephenson 1991; Lyon 2007, 46–47). A wide 'U' shaped ditch was also dug at some point during the fourth century and is usually linked to the construction of the projecting towers (Bishop 2000, 182; Butler 2001, 51). Finally, the city walls at the south-east corner of the City (near the Tower of London) were modified *c.*390 (Parnell 1985).

The history of Roman London's defences can be seen as challenging the idea that they represent a response to a military threat. In their earliest incarnation the lack of a riverside wall meant that the defences were only

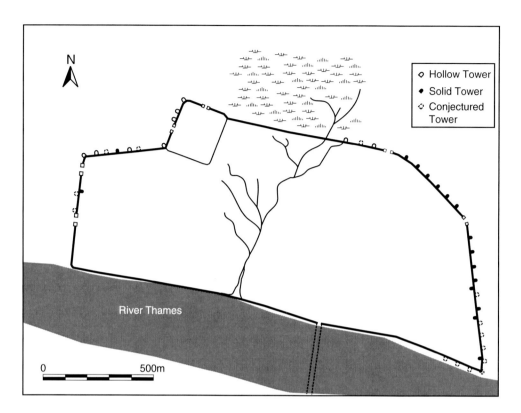

Fig. 2.14 Plan of the walls of London (after Maloney 1983, Fig. 100). Note the absence of projecting towers along the riverside wall. The projecting towers in the west are likely to be of medieval date.

of use against a land-based force. It is also interesting to note that the construction of the riverside wall seems to have occurred after changes in the river level forced the abandonment of the Thameside wharves and docks (Miller, Schofield and Rhodes 1986; Brigham 1990a). In this context the construction of the riverside wall could be linked to the changes that overtook the riverside in the late third century. These alterations included the construction of a monumental complex of buildings in the south-west corner of the city (Williams 1993; Bradley and Butler 2008). It is also worth considering the length of the walled circuit: almost 5 km. Walls lose much of their utility as defences if they are unmanned (Elton 1996, 173) and by analogy with the figures used in the tenth century *Burghal Hidage* (Radford 1970, 83) the walls of late Roman London would have required almost 2,700 men to defend them. This is a high figure for the fourth century, even allowing for the conscription of the civilian population, given that the population of the city is likely to have been considerably smaller than in the early Roman period (Marsden and West 1992).

The mid fourth-century projecting towers are also more problematic than they first appear. There are no riverside projecting towers known and, more disturbingly, the projecting towers that do exist fall into two distinct groups (Maloney 1983, 105–107). The first (eastern) group have solid bases that contain much *spolia* and run from what is now the Tower of London to where the Walbrook entered the Roman city west of Bishopsgate. The second (western) group of projecting towers runs from Ludgate to Crip-plegate. Morphologically they differ from the eastern projecting towers in that they are, with a single exception, hollow and none has yet (despite archaeological investigation) been proven to be of Roman date (Maloney 1983, 105). It seems reasonable to suggest that the fourth-century project-ing towers ran from the south-east corner of the city to the marshy area around Moorgate (Butler 2006). The lack of projecting towers along the riverside and apparently west of Walbrook would in turn imply that defence was not the primary function of these structures. One difficulty with this interpretation is that the wide ditch has been detected in the west as well as the east of the City (Butler 2001, 50–51; Watson 1992, 377). However, the connection of the ditch with the projecting towers is assumed, not proven, and rests on archaeological assumptions about the function of projecting towers (Magilton 2003, 165). The presence of the ditch in the western sector does not preclude the absence of projecting towers.

In contrast to the diocesan capital of London, Caerwent (Venta Silurum) in south-east Wales was a *civitas* capital in the fourth century (Figure 2.15). Like Silchester and Wroxeter it was not reborn as a medieval town and the absence of modern urban sprawl has encouraged a series of extensive campaigns of excavations (Wacher 1990, 378–391). These have revealed much of the town's topography and the more modern of these interventions is beginning to unravel the detail and chronology of the urban sequence (Dr Peter Guest *pers. comm.*). Caerwent's walls, which are some of the finest surviving Roman urban defences in Britain, have also received much scrutiny and this has been driven in part by their apparently late construction date and the provision of projecting towers and so-called 'counterforts' to the defences (Casey 1983; Manning 2003). All of these changes have been, and continue to be, associated with the threat of Irish raiding in the Bristol Channel (Manning 2003, 177).

The most recent discussion of the defences of Caerwent presents a care-fully argued review of their history and development. Manning (2003) hypothesises that the first set of defences were earthworks and monumental

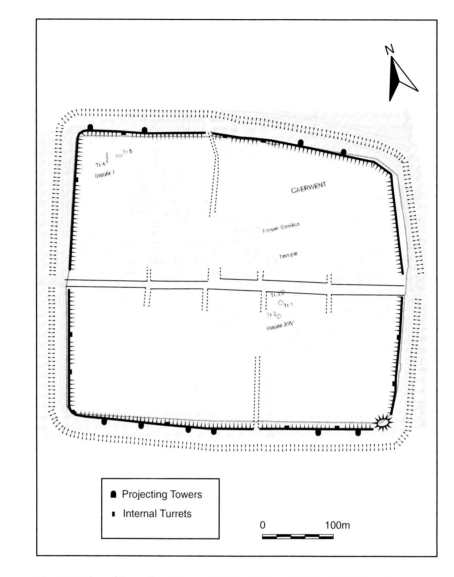

Fig. 2.15 Plan of the walls of Caerwent (after Wacher 1990, Fig. 170). Note the absence of bastions on the eastern and western walls.

stone gateways erected in the second century. The stone wall, he suggests, was not built in the 330s (as others have argued) but in the late third century and, as much depends on the ambiguous stratigraphic position of a single coin from early excavations, this seems a reasonable conclusion. The southern and northern gates may also have been blocked at this time, although this is uncertain (Manning 2003, 180). During or soon after the construction of the city wall the so-called 'counterforts' were added on the interior. These rectangular expansions are known from all four sides of the defences and are variously interpreted as either a means of accessing the rampart walk or as settings for *ballistae* (Manning 2003, 181). In the middle of the fourth century the defences were further augmented by the addition of projecting towers at irregular intervals on the northern and southern walls. These are also interpreted as linked to the provision of artillery.

The absence of projecting towers on the eastern and western sides of the walled circuit is clearly significant and Manning (2003, 182) goes to some lengths to explain this peculiarity. He suggests that the projecting towers and counterforts should be seen as operating in tandem and that this produces a more coherent system, albeit one with 'a rather *ad hoc* appearance which may indicate that it was a compromise of some type' (Manning 2003, 182). He further asserts that the surviving gate towers (which slightly project forward of the wall's line) on the eastern and western walls would have sufficed as locations of enfilading artillery, supported by *ballistae* positioned on the counterforts. The logic behind this reconstruction of events, which is forced by the desire to interpret these pieces of architecture as primarily defensive in function, is counter-intuitive.

The presence of projecting towers on the southern and northern walls would suggest that the greatest care was being undertaken to defend these sides of the walled circuit. However, if Manning's (2003) suggestion that both gates were blocked *before* the construction of the projecting towers is correct (and there is no meaningful evidence to date the gate blockings one way or the other) then the southern and northern walls were the most secure. Furthermore, the idea that *ballistae* mounted in the eastern and western gate towers would suffice, in conjunction with the counterforts, to defend the walls would surely undermine any reason to construct projecting towers on the southern and northern walls. Why not just mount the *ballistae* in the redundant gate towers and carry on using the counterforts? Alternatively, it could be suggested that the original intention had been to provide projecting towers along the walls' entire length but that the will or resources to do so had failed (Hobley 1983, 81). However, if this were so why start building the projecting towers on the sides of the defences that (possibly) lacked gateways?

The defences of Caerwent offer no easy solutions. It seems difficult to believe that they were constructed solely for defensive purposes and any explanation of the absence of projecting towers on the eastern and western walls in defensive terms sounds like special pleading. Yet the alternative, that the projecting towers were constructed for prestige and display, seems

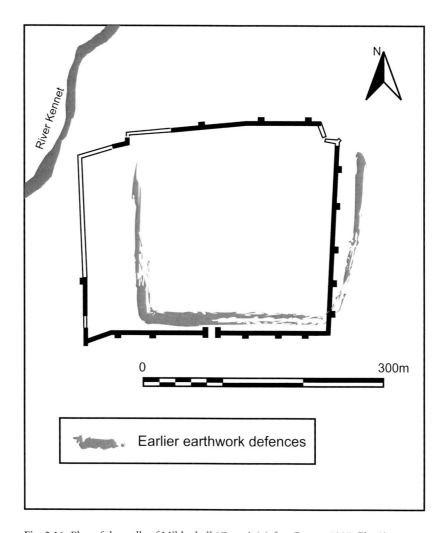

Fig. 2.16 Plan of the walls of Mildenhall (Cunetio) (after Corney 1997, Fig. 3).

equally difficult to fathom as the towers did not overlook the sides of
the town which most (if not all) travellers would have approached during
the fourth century. Guest's (2002) suggestion that the projecting towers
were constructed to project an image of deterrence to the hill dwellers to the
north and the coast to the south is at least an explanation for this unusual
situation.

The final site stands in sharp contrast to both Caerwent and London.
Cunetio (Mildenhall) is a poorly understood 'small' town in Wiltshire
(Burnham and Wacher 1990, 148–152; Corney 1997) (Figure 2.16). From
uncertain beginnings in the early Roman period the site was first enclosed

by a substantial set of earthwork defences, which probably originated in the second century. These were replaced by a substantial freestanding masonry wall, some 5–6 m thick and enclosing a roughly rectangular area of 7.5 ha. Projecting towers are known on three of the wall's four sides and are likely to have existed on the fourth side but are masked in aerial photographs by a modern road. A monumental gateway is known on the southern side and other gates are suspected in the other three sides of the walled circuit. The date of the defences has been established as *c*.360 on the basis of stratified coins and this makes Cunetio's walls among the latest civil fortifications in Roman Britain (Corney 1997, 344–345). Little excavation has been under-taken within the walls and what has been undertaken has struggled to elucidate the nature of the site's occupation (e.g. Brooke 1920; Moorhead 1997; Cooke 2003). However, aerial photographs and a recent geophysical survey (GSB 2009) show the interior to have been occupied with enclosures, stone buildings and a formal street grid.

Cunetio's fourth-century defences are best paralleled, as Corney (1997, 348) observes, by Valentinianic fortifications at Alzey and Bad Kreuznach near Mainz (Johnson 1983a, Fig. 57). Out of all of late Roman Britain's fortified sites it represents a tradition of fortification best exemplified by sites in Gaul and the Rhineland: an extremely thick wall enclosing a small area and heavily defended by projecting towers along its entire length. Here, we might suggest, is a site that gained an easily defensible walled circuit – unlike London, Caerwent or many of Roman Britain's other towns.

The defences of Cunetio are an exception that proves a rule: town walls in Britain seem poorly designed as purely defensive installations. The situation in Gaul, where many short, defensible circuits similar to that at Cunetio exist, suggests a different response to fourth-century conditions. The failure of Romano-British wall circuits to be modified to reflect those conditions further weakens the notion that there was a substantial military threat to late Roman Britain. The only exception that might be raised to this is the augmentation of old defences with bastions or projecting towers in the fourth century.

The addition of projecting towers to existing wall circuits is another phenomenon that has arguably been misunderstood. The desire to link these architectural changes to the provision of artillery is surely an error. It seems unlikely that the late Roman army could ever have provided enough trained men or machines to man these projecting towers (Guest 2002). Furthermore, it is difficult to see what use these towers would have been if they were not constructed around the entirety of a town's walled circuit (as at Caerwent and probably London). It is better to view them as architectural embellishment that brought the defences 'up to date': a case of style being more important than function.

The interpretation of these defensive works or architectural embellishments depends largely on who authorised or commissioned them. Britain, unlike other parts of the empire (e.g. *CIL* 3.14149), lacks the epigraphic and documentary evidence that would illuminate this issue. Due to this, discussion has tended to polarise between two viewpoints. City walls and projecting towers were either constructed by the state, or they were built by local initiative. In the former case the construction campaigns are seen as an imperial response to military threat, whereas the latter perspective emphasises the importance of walls and projecting towers as statements of civic status and power (Kulikowski 2004, 107–109). The artistic depiction of cities in late antiquity as walled and turreted suggests that such accoutrements were vital in defining a town's status (Millett 1990, 141).

State and local involvement were not mutually exclusive and thus the distinction is not particularly helpful in considering who commissioned civic defences. Parallels from other parts of the empire might suggest a more symbiotic relationship between the local elite and the state or its agents. The elite of a city might want to add projecting towers to their city walls in the spirit of competitive emulation with another nearby town. To this end, they might choose to use a portion of the tax revenue (*Cod. Theod.* 15.1.18) and allocate some of their own wealth to fund such a project (Slootjes 2006, 82–83). The local governor, of whom there were four or five in fourth-century Britain (*Not. Dig. Occ.* XXIII), might also be interested in supporting the construction as he was expected to be a benefactor of public works (Slootjes 2006, 84–85). Finally, imperial contributions are not unheard of. In 505 the emperor gave to the governor and bishop of Edessa 200 Roman pounds and 20 Roman pounds of gold respectively, to aid in the restoration of the city and its walls after a period of famine, plague and warfare (Joshua the Stylite, *Chronicon* 87). Imperial largesse might be prompted by the impoverishment of a community (as at Edessa), or be a product of (real or imagined) military concerns (Drinkwater 1999), or simply reflect the emperor's role in late antique society as the pre-eminent gift-giver.

The contradictory motives of those involved in supporting wall construction – a local elite competing with a neighbouring town, a governor interested in self-aggrandisement and an emperor promulgating an ideology of defence – allow for a more nuanced view of this pattern. A military threat or explanation is unnecessary and an explanation for the phenomenon can be found in a broader understanding of late antique society.

Rural settlements

The study of defensive architecture usually confines itself to the walled centres like towns and forts. One of the ironies of this approach is that it ignores the locations where arguably nine-tenths of Roman Britain's population lived: rural settlements. These rural dwellers, living in villas, small settlements and isolated farmsteads (Taylor 2007), have been marginalised in many studies of the period. Yet they formed the majority of a population estimated at three to five million (Millett 1990, 181–186), a figure that is close to that suggested for the fourteenth-century population maximum (Broadberry, Campbell and van Leuwen 2010). It was presumably the rural population and their homes, possessions, crops and herds that were most vulnerable to the depredations of bandits, exploitative landlords and roving warbands and armies. If urban populations were supposedly driven to defend themselves then it may be assumed that the rural population would also have taken steps to protect their lives and livelihoods. This might be visible archaeologically in the nucleation of settlements and the creation of earthworks that, if not true defences, would at least enable a community to hold off bands of brigands and warriors.

The study of late Romano-British settlements and their morphology is a significant undertaking (Taylor 2007) and only a number of case studies can be discussed here. Many sites were small dispersed farmsteads associated with field systems and trackways. Sites of this type, such as those excavated ahead of the construction of the Cotswold Water Park (Miles, Smith and Perpetua-Jones 2007), or at Great Holts Farm in Essex (Germany 2003), Kilverston in Norfolk (Garrow, Lucy and Gibson 2006) or Bradley Hill in Somerset (Leech 1981), are typical (Figure 2.17). Often formed of individual structures, or two or three buildings, associated with ditched fields and wells, they represent the bulk of the late Roman rural population's dwelling places (Taylor 2007, Figs. 4.1 and 5.2). Little work has been undertaken on the social structure linked to this type of site but it seems reasonable to assume that they are the habitations of extended families or kin groups. None of these sites in the lowlands of England show any sign of enclosure or defensive form. Given that their

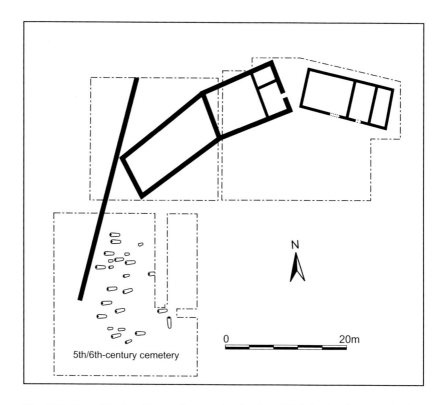

Fig. 2.17 Plan of the late Roman farmstead at Bradley Hill (after Leech 1981, Fig. 2).

location indicates small groups leading relatively isolated lives it is difficult to imagine communities that could be more vulnerable to 'raiders' than these.

In contrast to the dispersed farmsteads late Roman Britain also had a seemingly bewildering variety of more or less nucleated settlements that are sometimes referred to as 'villages'. Three such sites provide useful introductions to this form of settlement: Old Ford, Higham Ferrers and Catsgore.

The Roman road from London to Colchester crosses the River Lea at Old Ford not far from the Olympic Park. Here a community lived and worked from the late third until the early fifth century and excavation over the last forty years has pieced its history and landscape together (Brown et al. in press). It is by necessity a fragmentary picture, but what is clear is that the settlement was formed of dispersed clay and timber buildings set within enclosures and fields either side of the road. Burials in stone coffins and accompanied by rich gravegoods indicate that some of the settlement's inhabitants were of high status. A single stone building has been excavated under very difficult circumstances close to the fording place. Large numbers of late fourth-century coins and deposits of specialised butchery waste suggest an economically vibrant settlement. There is little at this site to suggest a community living in fear. None of the enclosures would offer any means of defence and the inhabitants were seemingly thinly distributed across a reasonably large area. What makes Old Ford particularly interesting is that it is a site that would appear to be vulnerable to coastal raiding. In the ninth century the Vikings were able to sail up the River Lea (*ASC(A)* sa896) and one might assume that raiding Saxons would have been just as capable of making the late Roman community's life equally uncomfortable.

The sites of Higham Ferrers (Northamptonshire) (Figure 2.18) and Catsgore (Somerset) offer something of a contrast to Old Ford. Stone buildings lined a roadside forming a nucleated community with associated property boundaries and enclosures. Both were occupied until the end of the fourth century and both produced a wealth of artefactual and ecofactual evidence. Despite their nucleation neither site looks particularly defensible. Access to the buildings was easy and unhindered and there are no structures that can be seen as refuges. The excavators of Higham Ferrers (Lawrence and Smith 2009, 322) and Catsgore (Leech 1982, 7) suggest that the decline in quantities of late fourth-century material at the sites suggests that they were shrinking and gradually being abandoned. If so, the destination of the emigrating population remains a mystery.

Finally, it seems worth considering the wealthy rural establishments, so-called villas. These high-status buildings are assumed to be the seats of the local elite and are usually seen as vulnerable targets. They would, we presume, be either easy sources of plunder, or the homes of those against whom violence might be directed. It is therefore striking that there is no archaeological evidence for fortified villas in Britain and precious few examples in Gaul (Percival 1992, 158–159; Smith 1997, 215–216) even with Sidonius' description of such a residence (Sid. Apoll. *Carm.* 22). Of course, villas may be more defensible than their groundplans indicate, but even so it seems prudent to agree with Elton's conclusion that 'the literary mentions have given these sites an artificially high profile' (1996, 172).

If the population of late Roman Britain largely lived in isolated and undefended settlements then it is reasonable to ask what happened to these settlements once the protective shield of the Roman state had disappeared. A violent end can arguably be seen in some parts of the empire. At Nicopolis in Moesia (the Balkans), intensive survey has identified more than thirty villas, all of which appear to have been destroyed by fire *c.*400 – a set of events presumably reflecting the period of conflict following the Battle of

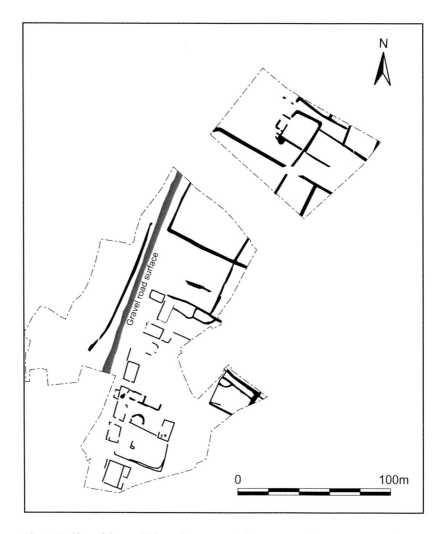

Fig. 2.18 Plan of the roadside settlement at Higham Ferrers (after Lawrence and Smith 2009, Fig. 2.18).

Adrianople (Poulter 2004, 2009, 234). Occasionally archaeologists working in Britain are exhorted to find similar evidence (e.g. Pearson 2006, 329). However, the end of virtually every fourth-century structure appears peaceful: a story of gradual decay, abandonment and stone robbing. This is not to say that there are no destroyed buildings: the occasional example can be found, such as the burnt structure at Uley in Gloucestershire whose destruction deposits contained a fourth-century or later sword (Woodward and Leach 1993, 59–60 and 135), but these are the exceptions that prove the rule.

Moving beyond the 'end' of Roman Britain and into the fifth and sixth centuries the story is much the same. In the 'Anglo-Saxon' regions of Britain settlement sites are, without exception, undefended (Hamerow 2004). The best examples of this type of settlement morphology remain Mucking (Essex) (Hamerow 1993) and West Heslerton (East Yorkshire) (Powlesland 1998). This does not indicate that people felt particularly vulnerable at their settlement sites. In the west of Britain the picture is rather different. Here the settlement record for the fifth and sixth centuries is dominated by fortified or refortified hilltop sites like Cadbury Castle (Alcock 1995), Cadbury Congresbury (Rahtz et al. 1993) and Dinas Powys (Glamorgan) (Alcock 1963). Sites such as these are usually seen as being high-status central places. Lower-order settlements either reflect earlier architectural traditions (such as 'rounds' in Cornwall: Quinnell 2004) that appear more defensible than Roman period or Anglo-Saxon types of settlement, or remain frustratingly archaeologically invisible. This very invisibility suggests that these sites lacked substantial earthwork barriers as such features would make them visible to the fieldworker.

The distribution and morphology of these settlements and many hundreds like them indicate a society in which the majority of the population felt secure in undefended and unenclosed settlements. That these small communities could live in isolation, or dwell next to busy routeways or close to coasts and estuaries, demonstrates that fourth-century Roman Britain was not only secure but also confident in that security. Whether this confidence was derived from a standing army and the rule of law, or from a genuine absence of threat, is less easily discerned. Together with the nature of both civilian and military fortification in Britain this evidence presents a strong counter to the argument that the fourth century became increasingly insecure.

Plunder, subsidies and treasure

After fortifications there are few ancient finds that lend themselves better to being interpreted as evidence of insecurity than hoards of precious objects (Figures 2.19 and 2.20). Within the Roman Empire maps of such finds have often been used not only as evidence of insecurity but also to track the course of invasions (Johnson 1983a, Fig. 24; Künzl 1993; Martin 1997; Hobbs 2006, 128–130; Drinkwater 2007, 201). However, this approach has received sustained criticism from two directions. First, it is impossible to know why hoards were not recovered: non-recovery might be due to the violent

Fig. 2.19 A hoard of the late third century radiates under excavation at Chichester. The careful excavation of hoards can often reveal details about their deposition (© Pre-Construct Archaeology Ltd).

death of the hoard's owner, or down to purely mundane factors (Reece 1988a). Secondly, prehistoric and anthropological parallels suggest that the deposition of precious objects could be caused by economic factors or 'religious' reasons (Millett 1994; see also Johns 1996b). The latter suggestion is beginning to receive support from the controlled excavation of some groups of objects (e.g. Gerrard 2009, 2011b; Moorhead, Booth and Bland 2010, 36).

Hoarding is an important phenomenon because late fourth- and early fifth-century Britain has produced a very large number of such finds (Hobbs 2006, Fig. 28). Interestingly, it has been argued (Guest 1993) that the distribution of the hoards does not reflect the direction of the supposed military threats to the diocese. A similar conclusion can also be reached by studying hoarding in a wider European perspective (Hobbs 2006). The routes of some 'barbarian' groups, such as the Goths, are reasonably well known but their progress is not marked by clusters of hoards.

Finds from beyond the imperial frontiers may offer different insights into the hoarding phenomenon. At Szikáncski in southern Hungary a hoard of almost 1,500 mid fifth-century gold *solidi*, weighing 20 Roman pounds, was discovered. The scale of this hoard and the presence of large numbers of freshly minted and heavily die-linked coins may suggest that this hoard is part of the vast subsidies paid to Attila and the

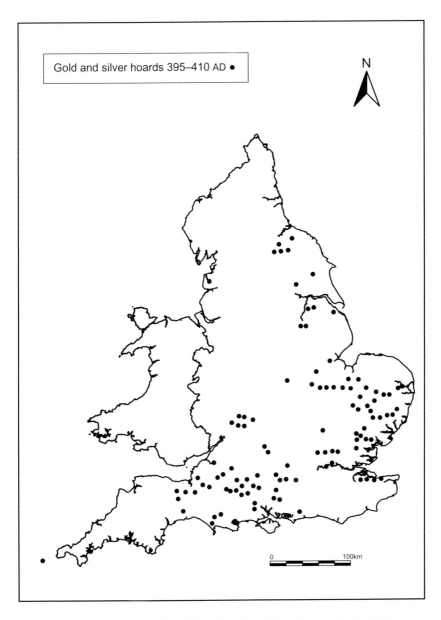

Gold and silver hoards 395–410 AD ●

N

0   100km

Fig. 2.20 Map of hoards of gold and silver in Britain 395–410 (after Hobbs 2006, Fig. 15).

Huns (Heather 2005, 307; Guest 2008, 295–296). This is graphic evidence of the power of external foes to extort wealth from the late Roman state.

There are few comparable finds from beyond the frontiers of Roman Britain. Scotland has produced a variety of precious objects, including an inscribed gold crossbow brooch from the Moray Firth (Robertson 1970, 212) and the hoard of hacksilver from Traprain Law (East Lothian) (Curle 1923). Ireland has also produced similar material including silver ingots and coins from Coleraine (Co. Londonderry) and Newgrange (Co. Meath) (Mattingly, Pearce and Kendrick 1937; Bland and Loriet 2010, 334–335). This material has been interpreted as booty or diplomatic gifts/subsidies (Freeman 1995; Hunter 2007). However, these caches of wealth sit alongside more humble objects, and trade across the *limes* with *barbaricum* could also account for these items.

If some of the Irish and Scottish material could be interpreted as plunder then similar groups of objects might be expected in northern Germany, Denmark and southern Scandinavia – the regions where the later Anglo-Saxons are supposed to have originated (Hines 1984; Yorke 1990, 5–6). By analogy with the areas discussed above we might presume to begin by looking for quantities of gold and silver coins and plate. Considerable numbers of gold *solidi* are known from Sweden and Denmark and in particular from the islands of Öland, Bornholm and Gotland in the Baltic (e.g. Fagerlie 1967; Herschend 1979; Horsnaes 2002). However, almost all of these coins post-date the reign of Honorius and are thus extremely unlikely to have originated in Britain (Bland and Loriet 2010, Figs. 25 and 46). There are also finds of late Roman silver coins from southern Scandinavia, which include issues struck at eastern mints and also a small number of clipped *siliquae* (Guest 2013, 103). These coins probably made their way from Britain across the North Sea because clipping appears to have been a peculiarly British phenomenon *c.*400 (Guest 2005, 110). The number of coins is, however, small and other objects associated with these *siliquae* are usually dated on stylistic grounds to *c.*500 so it is difficult to accept them as evidence of significant raiding during the late Roman period.

Other forms of Roman material culture are common in Germany beyond the Rhine (e.g. Eggers 1951; Hedeager 1992). However, with the exception of a zoomorphic belt fitting of Hawkes and Dunning's (1961) Type I from near Cuxhaven (Böhme 1986, Abb. 30), it is noticeable that there is not a single object of demonstrably Romano-British manufacture from southern Scandinavia (I am grateful to Profs. John Hines and Lotte Hedeager for confirmation of this point). In a recent paper (Pearson 2006, 347) it was suggested that slaves may have formed a major part of the plunder taken by North German raiders. If this were so, it is striking that not one single personal adornment of Romano-British type is known from the region. The later Viking raids on Anglo-Saxon England have produced a widespread distribution of insular metalwork, including dress accessories, in Scandinavia (e.g. Wamers 1983; Harbison 2004).

Hoards may have been buried for a variety of reasons and, just as is the case with city and fort walls, cannot be uncritically accepted as evidence of a deteriorating security situation. Recognising that hoarding varied across time and space (Hobbs 2006) suggests that it was a varied social response to differing stimuli, which may have been economic, political or religious. However, the occurrence of such finds beyond the frontiers of the Roman world remains an important reminder of the contacts between different regions. This in turn might suggest that had barbarian groups been plundering late Roman Britain some other forms of material culture might have made it back to their homelands, as happened in the Viking period. The absence of Romano-British material culture from northern Germany and southern Scandinavia is remarkable and suggests that raiding from this area may have been less significant than is usually thought.

Violence to the body: blade trauma on late Roman and early medieval skeletons

Architecture and material culture offer two related avenues of investigation in this attempt to assess the scale of violence and warfare in the fourth and fifth centuries. A third line of enquiry is offered by the osteological analysis of human skeletal remains. Furthermore, the richness of the funerary evidence allows the late Roman period (Philpott 1991) to be compared with the early post-Roman situation of the fifth and sixth centuries (Lucy 2000).

The so-called 'warrior graves' of eastern England have usually loomed large in discussions of early medieval warfare and violence. These burials are generally those of men inhumed with a variety of warlike paraphernalia including swords, spears and shields (e.g. Härke 1992) and this rite is part of a wider phenomenon of funerary display that occurs across Europe during the fourth to sixth centuries (Halsall 1992). It is an obvious interpretative leap to move from the burial rite to social structure. This in turn has led to the assumption that the deceased individuals buried with these weapons were the barbarian warriors whose exploits are seemingly recorded in such sources as *The Anglo-Saxon Chronicle* (Alcock 1971). The historically derived picture of rampaging Germanic warbands was thus confirmed by the contents of graves from across England and Europe.

More recent scholarship has emphasised the importance of weapon burials as a means of social display, status differentiation and religious belief (e.g. Härke 1990; Halsall 1992; Crawford 2004; Williams 2005). This led Härke to conclude that:

The Anglo-Saxon weapon burial rite was independent of the intensity of warfare; it did not always reflect functional fighting equipment; it was not determined by the individual ability to fight; nor by the actual participation in combat. (Härke 1990, 42)

The weapon burial has therefore moved from being evidence of a warlike society and been recast as an abstract means of investigating social structure and ideology.

In late Roman Britain and the early post-Roman west the absence of gravegoods in the majority of cemeteries has meant that the search for the warrior aristocracy supposedly visible in sources such as *Y Gododdin* (Jarman 1988) has remained stubbornly elusive, much to the frustration of those who sought to illustrate their quasi-historical accounts of the fourth to sixth centuries with the armaments of the Britons (Alcock 1971). Instead, the burial evidence was mobilised in an attempt to discover the victims of Germanic barbarian aggression.

An approach that explicitly sought so-called 'massacre' deposits appeared to be a sensible methodology. The Roman invasion in the first century was associated with deposits of human skeletal material at Iron Age sites, such as Maiden Castle (Dorset) (Sharples 1991, 124–125) and this apparent correlation between dead people and historical accounts appeared sound. Furthermore, at sites such as Dura-Europos (Syria) (James 2011b), Visby (Sweden) (Ingelmark 1939), Towton (North Yorkshire, England) (Fiorato, Boylston and Knusel 2007), Aljubarrota (Portugal) (Cunha and Silva 1997) and Vadum Iacob (Israel) (Mitchell, Nagar and Ellenblum 2006) the victims of Roman and medieval warfare have been clearly identified. In Roman Britain the search for similar deposits from the end of the Roman period has been fruitless. The oft-quoted 'massacre' deposit excavated by Atkinson (1932) at Caister-by-Norwich (Norfolk) has been successfully reinterpreted as a post-Roman inhumation cemetery (Darling 1987). In short there are no indisputable deposits of human remains associated with warfare and conflict from late Roman or early post-Roman Britain.

In the absence of 'massacre' deposits the osteoarchaeological studies of human remains from inhumation cemeteries offer one means of establishing the levels of violence within society. Unfortunately, this is not a straightforward undertaking. Across large swathes of Britain bone preservation is

Table 2.2 *Weapon trauma on late Roman and early medieval skeletons*

	Number of burials	Number of blade injuries	Percentage with blade injuries
Late Roman *c.*250–*c.*450	4,977	18	0.36
Western post-Roman *c.*450–*c.*700	854	2	0.23
Anglo-Saxon *c.*450–*c.*700	3,020	40	1.3

extremely poor due to the effects of acidic soils (e.g. Murphy 1992; Campbell and MacDonald 1993; Webster and Brunning 2004; Weddell 2000). Furthermore, even when skeletal remains do survive they are not always subjected to detailed osteoarchaeological analysis and this difficulty is particularly acute with cemeteries excavated before *c.*1980. The results of osteoarchaeological analysis can also be equivocal. Only those injuries that have left marks on the bone can be studied and many individuals could have suffered from violent, conflict-related injuries that leave no traces on the skeleton (Roberts 2000). Of visible pathologies, many, such as fractured bones in the forearms or crush injuries, may be due to accidents or domestic violence and brawls as much as warfare. Given these caveats it is unsurprising that osteoarchaeologists have concentrated on discussing unequivocal weapon injuries because of their intrinsic interest (e.g. Wenham 1989; Anderson 1996; Boylston 2000).

Only in the field of Anglo-Saxon studies has there been any serious attempt to assess the prevalence of weapon injuries in order to understand the social impact of violence (Härke 1992, 211–214; Stoodley 1997, 124). The conclusion of such studies has been that weapon injuries are uncommon in an Anglo-Saxon context. However, this is a problematic observation as the samples used include old excavation reports with poor reporting of the human remains. More importantly, the failure to qualify what 'uncommon' means in comparison to other periods yields a meaningless conclusion. As we have seen, the vagaries of preservation and the need for the injury to produce pathology visible on the skeleton means that weapon injuries will always be 'uncommon'. The question is: how prevalent are such injuries in the Roman period or the Anglo-Saxon period?

The simplest way of tackling this question is to examine the osteological reports that accompany most modern publications of ancient cemeteries (Figure 2.21, Table 2.2 and Appendix A). Such reports only include information on a tiny fraction of the population who lived during the period

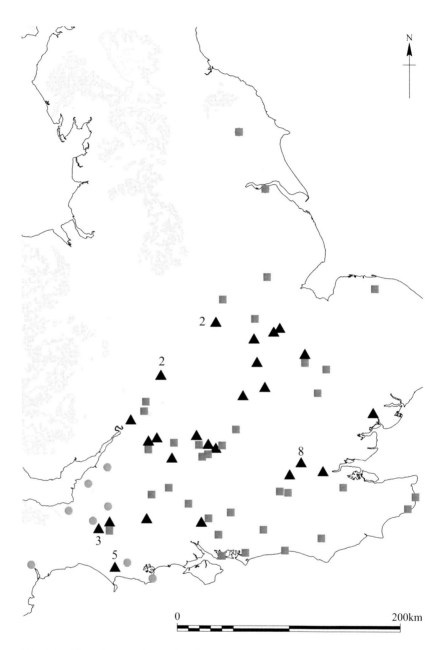

Fig. 2.21 Map of cemeteries used in this study. Triangles = Roman cemeteries, squares = Anglo-Saxon cemeteries, circles = western British cemeteries. Numbers indicate multiple cemeteries in the same location (drawn by Mark Roughley, source the author).

Fig. 2.22 A typical late Roman inhumation unaccompanied by any gravegoods. Iron fittings from the coffin are visible at the feet and above the head (© Pre-Construct Archaeology Ltd).

under consideration but data is available from a myriad of sites dating to the late Roman period (*c.*250–*c.*450) and the early Middle Ages (*c.*450–*c.*700). At each site only blade trauma was considered to be adequate as evidence of weapon injuries (Lewis 2008) and all burials were included in the analysis, irrespective of age or gender. This may have an impact on the percentages discussed below as there is some evidence that men were more likely to be the victims of blade trauma than women and children (Stoodley 1997, 124).

The late Roman dataset is formed of forty-one inhumation cemeteries containing 4,977 burials (Figure 2.22). The sites examined are to some degree biased towards urban cemeteries, such as Poundbury (Dorset) (Farwell and Molleson 1993) and Cirencester (Gloucestershire) (McWhirr, Viner and Wells 1982), and those sites that are familiar to the author personally. However, an effort was made to include smaller rural cemeteries (e.g. Jones 1975) and the so-called 'dispersed dead', found in small numbers on many rural sites (Pearce 1999). It is important to note that some of these so-called 'late Roman' cemeteries probably continue into the first half of the fifth century (Hills and O'Connell 2009). Therefore this sample should include not just individuals who lived under the protection of the Roman state but also individuals who lived through the supposed 'end' of the Roman diocese between 407 and 411.

The post-Roman dataset is divided between the inhabitants of western Britain during the fifth to seventh centuries and the contemporary 'Anglo-Saxon' cemeteries in the east. It is logical to start with the western cemeteries as they appear to have been derived from the late Roman burial tradition. Unfortunately the sample is much smaller than that for the Roman period. This is because the absence of gravegoods makes post-Roman cemeteries difficult to identify in the west and many, such as the recently excavated cemetery at Filton (Gloucestershire) (Cullen et al. 2006), are only discovered through serendipity. Furthermore, acidic ground conditions in many areas mean that skeletal preservation is extremely poor (e.g. Campbell and MacDonald 1993; Webster and Brunning 2004). Nevertheless, 854 burials from nine sites could be included in the dataset, although the sample is dominated by the large cemetery at Cannington (Somerset) (Rahtz, Hirst and Wright 2000). The equally large early medieval cemetery at Llandough (Glamorgan) has been excluded because of its wide date range from the fifth to eleventh century (Holbrook and Alan 2005).

Finally, the Anglo-Saxon dataset includes 3,020 burials from some thirty-six sites. This sample is to a certain extent derived from the gazetteer of sites used by Stoodley (1997). However, it excludes many of the older excavation reports utilised by Stoodley and includes new data published since his study. Obviously, the sample is biased in much the same way as for the other periods. Burials from sites with acidic ground conditions, such as Spong Hill (Norfolk) (Hills, Penn and Rickett 1984), must be excluded and the sample is further constrained by the fact that cremation was more common in the fifth century and in the so-called 'Anglian' regions (Lucy 2000, 119).

What is immediately apparent from the results of this analysis (Table 2.2) is that blade injuries are extremely uncommon in all three datasets. During the late Roman period fewer than one in two hundred inhumations includes an individual harmed with an edged weapon. The Anglo-Saxon dataset shows an increase to approximately four blade injuries per three hundred inhumations. The contemporary early medieval cemeteries from the west of Britain have produced only two blade injuries, both from Portbury (Somerset) (Aston 2011, 188). This limited evidence for conflict is confirmed by 'battle damage' apparent on some Anglo-Saxon shields (Härke and Dickinson 1992, 56).

The implication of these conclusions is that an individual was more likely to be wounded by a blade during the fifth century in the east of Britain, than in the fourth century or in the fifth- to seventh-century west. Of course, this conclusion could be countered by the suggestion that victims of violence in late Roman Britain and the early medieval west were disposed of differently to the rest of society, or that the heavy and largely unavoidable dominance of urban data in the sample means that those most vulnerable to warfare are under-represented. The first criticism is based on an argument from silence and the second fails to recognise that violence in Roman urban contexts was endemic. Crime, riots (e.g. Africa 1971; Brown 1992, 81) and the victims of gladiatorial contests (Kanz and Grossschmidt 2006) could all potentially contribute to an urban cemetery's population. It is thus possible to conclude that an individual was three times more likely to be wounded with an edged weapon in early Anglo-Saxon England than in fourth-century Britain.

Violence and society

This discussion has focussed on the role of 'external' groups, or so-called barbarians, as agents of conflict and violence in fourth- and fifth-century Britain. It has moved from specific issues of historical cause and effect to a more general review of violence as a social phenomenon. The final part of this chapter briefly examines the casting and recasting of the so-called *Bagaudae* as enemies within the Roman state and concludes by developing a model of violence as a means of social control.

So far this work has been at pains to distance itself from historically driven narrative interpretations of violence and warfare. The *Bagaudae* offer another textually attested group who take the place of violent agents of change. Originally a late third-century phenomenon, the term returns to prominence in fifth-century Gaul and Spain. The details of how the term developed and was used have been discussed elsewhere and need not detain us further here (Drinkwater 1992; Sánchez León 1996). However, it is worth noting that there are no references to the existence of this group in late Roman Britain.

The *Bagaudae* have been variously interpreted as rebellious peasants engaged in class conflict (Thompson 1952; see also Faulkner 2000, 174–178) or as local elites consolidating their position in the power vacuum left by the weakening of the state (Van Dam 1985, 25–58). They have also been seen as well-organised bandits (Kulikowski 2004, 182). Other subtleties and nuances to these three positions have also been suggested (Drinkwater 1992). That the term is mutable is unsurprising. It was ultimately a label, much like 'barbarian' or an ethnic appellation like 'Frank' or 'Goth', applied to others that describes a 'Roman' view of their social and political position. Simply put, it was a means of Othering by the state that labelled groups with diverse agendas as non-conforming outsiders and justified action against them. Here the term 'insurgent' – a modern piece of Newspeak – might provide a useful analogy. It is a label applied indiscriminately in modern parlance to those driven by ideology, wages, criminal profiteering or a need for community security (Paul 2010, 490–500). A scholar in a thousand years may be just as vexed in an attempt to reconstruct the motives and social position of contemporary 'insurgents' as we are by the motives and social position of the *Bagaudae*.

The importance of the *Bagaudae* for this study lies in what they reveal about the role and position of violence in late Roman society. Violence and conflict were not simply confined to polarised opponents – the barbarians and the army – but involved a variety of different actors in a number of different situations (MacGeorge 2002; Halsall 2003). The army could be used against individuals within the state; the local elite could take up arms against the barbarians and be branded as bandits; communities could prey on one another and rebel against their overlords. The key to understanding the role of violence and warfare lies in understanding it as a form of social practice.

Violence can be simply defined as the 'intentional rendering of physical hurt on another human being' (Riches 1986, 4). Specific acts of violence and whether they are viewed as legitimate or illegitimate depends largely on cultural context (Gaddis 2005, 3–8). What is seen as violent in one society or situation may not necessarily be viewed as violent in another (Das et al. 2000). Violence and the threat of violence are, of course, ultimately a means of control: a means of 'securing practical advantage over one's opponents in the short term through forestalling their activities' (Riches 1986, 5). It is a means of enabling individuals and communities to subjugate or resist the will of others.

The use of legitimate violence is usually held to be a monopoly of the state (Weber 2004) and this was the case in the late Roman world. The emperor used the ability to project force *via* the army as a means of controlling those who threatened (or were perceived as threatening) the structures of the state (James 2011a). These threats included barbarians from beyond the empire's frontiers, as well as internal malcontents such as bandits, brigands, *Bagaudae* and other forms of criminal. The legal system (Harries 1999), as the strictures in the *Codex Theodosianus* reveal (Pharr 1952), also used legitimate violence to enforce the state's will on its citizens (Harries 2007, 59–85). The nature of that system, often labelled anachronistically as 'corrupt' (Kelly 2004, 3–5), ensured that punishment was geared towards the social status of the condemned (Garnsey 1970). The lowest social orders, the *humiliores*, often received severe physical punishments (Humfrers 2006, 201; Harries 2007, 36). In contrast, the wealthy strata in society (the *honestiores*), who could use their money and influence to manipulate the legal system (Jones 1964, 496–497; Brown 1992, 52–53), were treated differently, often suffering financial penalties in the place of physical punishment.

Legitimate violence can be assumed to have occurred in other spheres of social interaction. The carrying of arms by the civilian population appears not to have been proscribed (although see *Cod. Theod.* 15.15.I.; Pharr 1952, 439); however, their use in specific circumstances was. Thus arms could be carried and used for self-defence, although their use against the state and its agents was illegal (Brunt 1975). It can also be assumed that, given the nature of the late Roman legal system, parallel systems of dispute resolution based on local law and custom existed. As the lower social orders in the late Roman world appear to have been increasingly tied to their overlords (Sirks 2001) it may be that many disputes would have been resolved at a local level (Harries 1999, 67). The complexity of how this occurred is impossible to reconstruct in the absence of documentary evidence. However, analogies with elsewhere in the Roman Empire (Kehoe 2007) or even the medieval period in Britain (e.g. Bonfield 1989) suggest some possible scenarios, and violent coercion would have been one available sanction. Indeed, the ability of the wealthy to behave violently towards the poor seems to have been commonplace in late antiquity (Harries 2007, 116; James 2011a, 165). In contrast to this it might be expected that conflict between wealthy peers would have been resolved using the Roman legal system (Liebeschuetz 2006, 40). However, the *humiliores*, to whom appeal to the law courts was theoretically possible (Honoré 2004, 114) but in practice nearly impossible (Humfrers 2006), may have resolved disputes between peers *via* their patrons or so-called 'rough justice' (as happens in other societies) (Harries 1999, 79). Social context can be seen as legitimating most of these actions, although those who suffered as a result of them may have held a different view.

The use of illegitimate violence can only be determined from the position of those who believe that they monopolise legitimate violence. From a Roman perspective, barbarian violence, whether raiding or warfare, was illegitimate. It was a product of the barbarians' supposed irrational nature coupled with their insatiable desire to acquire Rome's wealth or land (Pohl 2006, 21–22). From a barbarian perspective the violence they unleashed against Rome was undoubtedly legitimate, or legitimated as a means of responding to Roman aggression, or enforcing an agenda on their unwilling Roman neighbours (Halsall 2007, 150–152).

Other forms of illegitimate violence were used by those who fell outside of Roman law. These others included the *latrones*, a term usually translated as brigands or bandits, but in reality a label that was applied to a variety of individuals engaged in violent activity to achieve disparate aims (Grünewald

2004). The *Bagaudae* discussed above can also be placed under the umbrella of 'banditry' (Drinkwater 1992, 208; Kulikowski 2004, 182). Clearly, any individual or community resisting tax collection, the power of an overlord or the state was probably criminalised but their resistance could be justified within and sometimes beyond their immediate communities. Religious violence represented a particularly grey area in that the state could legitimate violence against pagans or heretics (Gaddis 2005). However, violence not sanctioned by the state could be justified in the name of religion and claimed as legitimated by an authority greater than that of the emperor. This was clearly problematic as it undermined the state's monopoly of violence.

The use of violence by the Roman state and its agents as a means of control is one of the defining features of the Roman world. Rebellion and intransigence were usually punished. The appearance of para-state actors, be they barbarian warbands, a warlord's retainers or *Bagaudae*, challenged the ideology of the emperor's monopoly of violence. The weakening of imperial power in the western provinces also allowed the trappings of military power, which had previously been denied to the civilian elite and provincial population (Sivonen 2006, 115–117), to be reclaimed. It is this process, not the confirmation of historical events, that the physical remains of the past describe. Archaeological analysis, freed of the meta-narrative of insecurity and conflict, can then begin to examine and interpret this phenomenon and what it means for the end of Roman Britain (Chapter 7).

3 | Economic collapse

The publication of two important works – *Framing the Early Middle Ages* (Wickham 2005) and *Origins of the European Economy* (McCormick 2002) – on late Roman and early medieval economic trajectories have both placed renewed emphasis on the importance of economic history in understanding the developments that accompanied the fall of Rome. Britain is a relatively marginal component in these magisterial pan-European syntheses but Wickham (2005, 806) feels secure enough to claim that the disappearance of Roman political structures in Britain rapidly brought about an almost unparalleled economic collapse. In a recent work on the end of the Roman Empire Britain's situation in the fifth and sixth centuries was even used as the yardstick by which economic collapse could be measured (Ward-Perkins 2005). Coin use, pottery production, construction in stone: all this and more ceased in the fifth century – a situation seen nowhere else in the Roman Empire, with the possible exception of northern Gaul (Halsall 2007, 348–350).

A brief outline of society and economy in Britain in *c*.300 and *c*.600 serves to underline the contrast that Wickham, Ward-Perkins and others find so striking. In *c*.300 Britain south of the Tyne–Solway line was part of a Mediterranean empire with a taxation, currency and legal system that linked the province to the imperial core, long-distance and inter-regional exchange and perhaps two widely spoken languages (Salway 1981; Millett 1990; Mattingly 2007). In *c*.600 the same region was a patchwork of polyglot communities, some smaller than a modern county, many of whom looked, not to the Mediterranean but the lands around the North Sea as their cultural, if not genetic, homeland (Bassett 1989; Yorke 1990). The structures of the Roman state – taxation, currency, literacy – were gone, urbanism was dead. Political, social and economic complexity had disappeared only to tentatively re-emerge in the seventh century and even then on nothing like the scale that had gone before.

Archaeology and history are both rearward looking disciplines. Their practitioners have the benefit (usually) of knowing what happened and when and often convince themselves that they understand the linkages between events that would have eluded contemporaries. Hindsight is, of course, perfect vision. The mistakes, errors and shrewd moves are always obvious after the fact but were rarely so clear-cut when decisions were being made. The danger for archaeologists and historians is that the gift of hindsight bestowed upon them becomes a set of blinkers blinding them to all but a teleological view of the past. In this scenario Britain's situation in *c.*600 must be the product of an economic collapse, the cause of which was the fall of Rome.

It is argued here that understanding the fall of Rome lies, not in taking two points in time and listing the similarities and differences between them, but in trying to grasp the complexities of the period and its social, economic and political changes. It is not enough to be able to *describe* two situations. They must be *explained*. What follows is an attempt to free the fifth century from the shackles of the teleology of Rome's fall.

The Roman economy

In order to explore the collapse of the systems that the Romano-British economy comprised it is necessary to define the nature of those interlinked systems and their economics. This is a far from simple task. For generations archaeologists and historians have been engaged in a titanic struggle. Like many opposed positions taken in historical analysis the pieces in this struggle are battling over the extent to which the past was essentially the same as, or differed from, the present world (Polanyi 1957). In the study of the Roman economy the argument revolves around the extent and significance of trade and market-based exchange *versus* the role of the state and socially embedded economic networks. Examining this argument in detail would go far beyond the remit of this work (for a recent discussion see Bang 2007a, and 2007b, 17–60). However, the general trends of the formalist *versus* substantivist debate are crystallised in the works of Rostovtzeff (1926) and Finley (1985).

Rostovtzeff (1926) argued that the Roman period had seen laissez-faire capitalism during the Principate, but that this economic golden age had been brought low by state intervention under the Dominate. In contrast, Finley (1985) suggested that the Classical world was formed of fundamentally agrarian societies, which were bound by social relations to their elites, and constrained by primitive methods of transportation that restricted widespread trade and exchange. Since the publication of these works, research has concentrated to a greater or lesser extent on demonstrating or modifying one view, or the other. Important papers have explored the role the taxation system played in stimulating trade (Hopkins 1980) and the significance of taxation and tribute (Wickham 1984). Nevertheless, the pendulum is currently tending towards a 'modernising' view of the Roman economy (e.g. Ward-Perkins 2005, 87–102) and this conclusion has been driven by the exponential increase in archaeological data over recent decades. The small and restricted worlds envisaged by Finley (1985) seem difficult to reconcile with the evidence for the long-distance exchange of commodities as diverse as marble (Hirt 2010) and olive oil (Funari 1996).

In Britain the debate on the Romano-British economy has rarely, if ever, been fully articulated. Indeed, Romano-British archaeology's love affair with Romanisation, identity and post-colonial theory means that the study of economics has been sadly neglected. This has moved one specialist in the analysis of Romano-British finds to caution that students are now more likely to interpret the distribution of a class of object as a reflection of the user's 'identity' than the economic reach of a workshop (Johns 2007, 32). There are, of course, significant exceptions to this state of affairs (Swift 2000), but it remains fair to say that the study of the Romano-British economy is not receiving the attention it should deserve (Greene 2005) even within syntheses that subsume economics within the discussion of other elements of social practice.

The mainstream view of Roman Britain's economic course can be easily summarised. In the early Roman period (and to a lesser extent the Late Iron Age) an indigenous society was exposed to new economic systems (Millett 1990; Cunliffe 2005). These included taxation, coin use and urban markets. These elements of the Roman economic world were imposed on a local economic system that was based on socially embedded relationships, such as gift-exchange. At first the new order was confined to major urban and military sites, but over time other types of site became increasingly bound into this disembedded money-using economy. By the late Roman period the province's reliance on imported goods, such as samian, had been replaced with the indigenous production, such as red colour-coated imitations manufactured in Oxfordshire, the New Forest and elsewhere. Coin use had penetrated to the very base of the settlement hierarchy, and market exchange is considered to have been the primary means by which the economy functioned (Mattingly 2007, 506).

The dominance of the market came about through the tax–pay cycle operated by the state. The modelling of the tax–pay system is far from certain but the broad outlines run along these lines: the state had a finite quantity of bullion with which it paid its servants (primarily the army and administration). Much of this bullion was distributed as high-value coins (*solidi* and *siliquae*) which, if they were to be spent, had to be changed into many low-value copper-alloy coins. These could then be used to buy goods and services from the civilian population. The civilians were required to pay their taxes in gold and silver and were thus drawn into market exchange. They needed to sell their produce to acquire copper-alloy coins that could be exchanged for the *solidi* needed to pay taxes (Bang 2007a, 35). Thus the gold and silver flowed in a (hypothetically at least) closed loop from state to the army, and back to the state as tax, ready to be disbursed again as wages (Reece 1984, 144–146; Millett 1990, 178–180).

When the defeat of Constantine III and Honorius' problems in Gaul combined to separate Britain from the rest of the Western Empire in the early fifth century, the tax–pay cycle was broken. Without gold and silver coins to guarantee the value of the base metal currency (Burnett 1984; Moorhead 2006, 104) the system of market exchange broke down and the economy quickly collapsed (Fulford 1979; Mattingly 2007, 497) – hastened on its way, in some interpretations, by plague (Wacher 1975, 414–416, restated 1990, 411–415), famine (Jones 1996) and war (Laycock 2008). What follows the Roman collapse is the story of the early Middle Ages: a slow climbing out of an economic trough characterised by the simplicity of primitive socially embedded exchange, back towards the heights of economic complexity: coins, markets, towns, long-distance exchange and, eventually, capitalism (Hodges 1982, 1989; McCormick 2002).

Exploring the collapse

It is impossible to argue that there was not a reduction in economic complexity in Britain between c.300 and c.500. Coin use almost ceased and there was no significant insular production to make up the shortfall. Proxy records, such as ice cores from Greenland (A. Wilson 2002, 25–27) or lake sediments in Sweden (Bindler et al. 2009), demonstrate that atmospheric lead pollution peaked during the Roman period before declining substantially in the fifth and sixth centuries. This is a pattern that suggests that widespread lead mining and smelting significantly declined in the post-Roman centuries. Other forms of industrial production are likely to have ceased or significantly declined too. In Britain there is not a single late Roman pottery producer that can be shown to have been still producing ceramics c.500 and no mortared buildings were constructed. Urbanism appears to have failed almost completely. This is demonstrated in a comprehensive fashion by London. In a recent study the distribution of three types of late

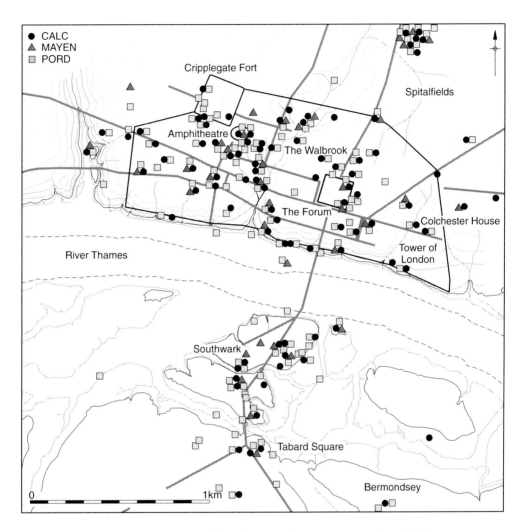

Fig. 3.1 The distribution of three types of fourth-century (CALC, PORD and MAYEN) pottery in London and Southwark (the author).

fourth-century pottery and coins later than AD 364 were plotted and the contrast between these finds and the handful of early Anglo-Saxon finds could not be more striking (Gerrard 2012) (Figures 3.1, 3.2 and 3.3). Even Wroxeter (Barker et al. 1997), a site where there is reasonable evidence for post-Roman activity (although some dispute this – Dr Alan Lane *pers. comm.*), cannot be categorically claimed as representing 'urbanism'. A fundamental change had occurred.

This fundamental shift from a seemingly complex economy to something simpler poses a number of questions. What was the nature of the collapse?

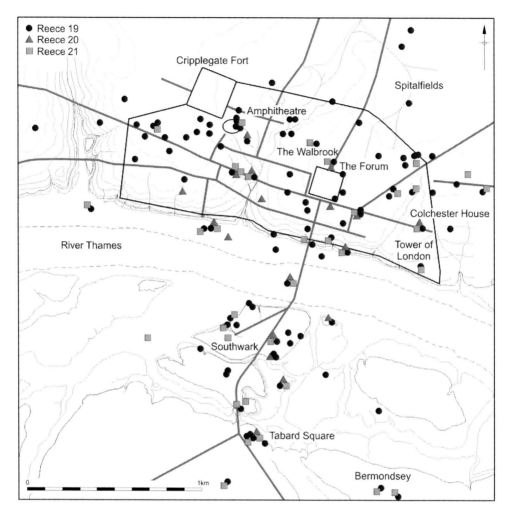

Fig. 3.2 The distribution of coins of Reece Periods 19–21 (364–378, 378–388 and 388–402) in London and Southwark (the author).

Was it a heart-stopping systemic shock that took place over no more than two decades? Was it a slide followed by a bump, a period of readjustment followed by a less severe collapse? Or was the 'collapse' a soft landing, a readjustment of economic realities that took place over two centuries or more?

Model 1: systemic shock

The 'systemic shock' model often includes some extra process or event to provide added impact. Warfare, plague and climate change are commonly

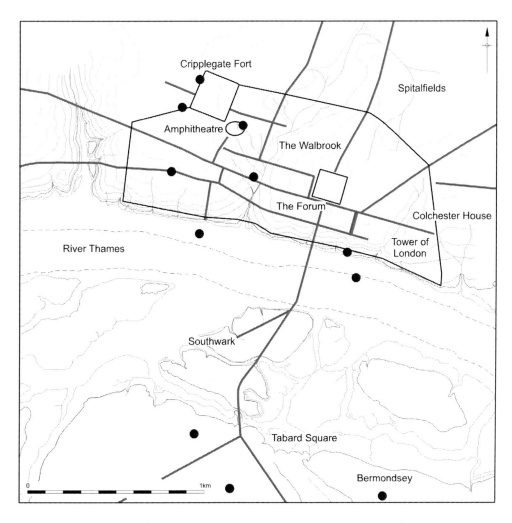

Fig. 3.3 The distribution of early Anglo-Saxon (450–600) material culture in London and Southwark. The rarity of this material demonstrates a significant change in the availability and use of material culture in London between the fourth and sixth centuries (the author).

hypothesised and it seems relevant to devote a little attention to each of these factors before tackling the main issue. Warfare and violence are discussed more fully in Chapter 2 and need not detain us further here. Plague was most famously touted as an explanatory mechanism by Wacher (1975, 1990) and soundly rebutted by Todd (1977). Epidemics could have had a significant impact on ancient populations. However, the best attested 'Roman' plagues are those that struck in the Antonine period (Brunn 2003; Greenberg 2003) and during the reign of Justinian and after (Russell 1968; Maddicott 1997;

Sarris 2002). These plagues are respectively too early and too late to be of significance to the problems of the fifth century. The impact of climate change is also equivocal (Jones 1996, 186–243). There is good European evidence for significant fluctuations in temperature and precipitation levels between *c.*300 and *c.*500 (Büntgen et al. 2011). However, the social and economic impact of these changes is far from straightforward. The fifth century may have been wetter than the fourth but it also appears to have been a little warmer (Büntgen et al. 2011, Fig. 4). In climate terms the downturn that preceded the Justinianic plague appears more significant (Larsen et al. 2008; Baillie 2010) but, like the plague, it is a century and more too late.

Removing the primacy of major extra-systemic shocks, such as plague and climate change, suggests that the fifth-century crisis is likely to have been the product of the interplay of a multitude of social, political, economic and environmental factors. However, in Britain the historical end of the Roman period and the disappearance of its material culture occur with a synchronicity that is striking. At no other point in history or prehistory does the material culture of one period disappear with such rapidity. This, of course, could be interpreted as signifying the catastrophic nature of the economic collapse (Mattingly 2007, 497). However, it seems far more likely that a major methodological issue is having a severe effect on how the period and the economic collapse are perceived.

During the first and second centuries Romano-British material culture can be dated with some accuracy. This is especially true of assemblages of pottery. These can be dated by association with other types of chronologically sensitive material culture such as samian or coins, known historical events like the Boudican revolt or the construction of Hadrian's Wall, and also by association with coins in grave groups or dendrochronological dates derived from wooden structures such as quays, revetments and wells. In the fourth century there are very few historical events that have left unequivocal traces in the archaeological record, the pottery is not particularly sensitive to chronological changes (e.g. Young 1977), burials accompanied by grave-goods are rare (Philpott 1991) and dendrochronology is lacking (Tyers, Hillam and Groves 1994, 18–19). In fact the only advantage that the student of late Roman Britain has over the student of the early Roman period is that coins are extremely common in the late third and fourth centuries. The implication of this is that all of our late Roman artefactual chronologies ultimately depend on associations with coins.

In 403 the mint of Rome struck a coin bearing the reverse legend VRBS ROMA FELIX. This coin did not reach Britain in any meaningful quantities

Fig. 3.4 A *Gloria Romanorum nummus*
struck between 406 and 408 (© British
Museum).

(Brickstock 2000, 35; Abdy 2006) and, with the exception of the occasional gold or silver coin and very occasional later bronze (Casey 1974; Collins 2008) (Figure 3.4), the latest coins that are likely to be encountered are issues struck for the House of Theodosius between 388 and 402. Interestingly, these coins appear to have not been copied (as copper-alloy coinage had been earlier in the fourth century). This is usually taken as indicating the total collapse of the monetary economy. However, work by Wells (Nick Wells *pers. comm.*) suggests that copies of these coins may be more common than is often thought. The coins are small and poorly struck and this can lead to the misidentification of copies as regular issues. Furthermore, the Portable Antiquities Scheme dataset (Walton 2011) indicates just how patchy coin use was during the fourth century. This would suggest that the lack of bronze coinage need not indicate a catastrophic economic collapse. However, the impact of this phenomenon on archaeological interpretation is significant because it means that the latest Roman assemblages can only be dated 388+ or *c*.400. This is then followed by an assumption that the 'economic collapse' means that no new Romano-British objects were produced later than *c*.410. Thus the disappearance of coinage and the model of collapse become a circular argument. No Romano-British objects indicate a collapse and the collapse means that there are no objects.

The issue of coins and their relationship to how material culture is dated is even more problematic than this outline suggests. The distribution of coins in late Roman Britain, particularly in the late fourth century, was far from even. So although a technical *terminus post quem* of 388+ could be expected, in reality the odds of finding a coin as late as this are quite low (Walton 2011, 72). Thus many groups of objects that could have been deposited in the fifth century are possibly associated with coins struck perhaps thirty to fifty years earlier. The key point is that a coin can only ever provide the *terminus post quem* derived from the date at which it was struck (Barker 1993, 224–229); it can never provide the date at which the coin was lost.

Recourse might be made to early fifth-century 'Germanic' material culture in an attempt to resolve these chronological difficulties. However, our continuing inability to discover sites where late Roman and early Anglo-Saxon activity overlap suggests that there is a real hiatus between the two suites of material culture (e.g. Millett 1987). Furthermore, the foundations of Anglo-Saxon typologies rest on the fifth century as a watershed. As a gross generalisation objects found exclusively in northern Germany are considered as fourth-century artefacts, items found exclusively in Britain are of sixth-century date and items common to both regions can be dated to the fifth century (Brugmann 2011). Furthermore, most Anglo-Saxon typologies use 450 as their starting point (Lucy 2000, 17). This is an approximation to the date of 449 given by Bede (*Hist. Eccl.* I.15) to the *adventus Saxonum*, which is itself suspect as an event (Hills 1999), in much the same way that 410 is a suspect event marking the 'end' of Roman Britain (Bartholomew 1982, 262). This is a convoluted way of saying that it is extremely difficult to find any Anglo-Saxon objects that pre-date 450 and even late fifth-century objects are rare (e.g. Böhme 1986; Suzuki 2000). Often when we are discussing the early Anglo-Saxon period we are looking at the residues of the sixth, rather than the fifth century. Another significant issue is that Germanic material culture is restricted to particular southern and eastern regions. Much of the Midlands and western Britain lacks any Germanic material culture before the seventh century.

This methodological problem is of great importance because it means that any attempt to assess whether the collapse was a 'crash' is doomed to failure. The chronological resolution that would show whether the end of Roman Britain occurred with great rapidity, perhaps over as little as a decade, does not exist. Even absolute dating techniques, such as radiocarbon dating, are problematic (Booth et al. 2010, 449–452). When we talk of the end of Roman Britain we are discussing an archaeological period with blurred edges. It could start as early as 350 and finish in 450–500, or it might have occurred within a shorter period of time bracketed by those dates. It is impossible to tell.

A development of the crash model suggests that the collapse of the Romano-British economy was preceded by a period of economic decline.

The origins of this model probably stem from the adoption by archaeology of so-called 'New Archaeology', which sought to distance the discipline from the events of the 'culture-history' paradigm and contextualise human behaviour in terms of processes over the *longue durée*. It may also be suspected that such an approach, preceding a collapse with a period of decline, was intellectually satisfying because it echoed the Gibbonian view of decline and fall (Gibbon 1993).

The evidence for a period of decline in the late fourth century is far from straightforward. In many urban centres it seems clear that there was contraction during the fourth century with major buildings falling into disrepair or being converted to new uses (Rogers 2005, 2011). Large areas of some towns were also being blanketed in so-called 'dark earth'. These deposits of homogeneous sediment contain abraded Roman material culture and are the subject of intense debate (Yule 1990; Watson 1998; Macphail, Galinie and Verhaeghe 2002). Generalisations are probably inadvisable but in some circumstances these deposits may have originated as dumped waste that then underwent biological reworking. This suggests the abandonment of some areas of urban cores.

Other evidence of economic decline includes the abandonment, or the adoption, of villas and other sites for new purposes during the fourth century, although such claims need to be based on extensive and modern excavations. It is sometimes suggested that the fourth century saw a decline in the quantity and quality of pottery being manufactured (Faulkner 2000, 148). The handmade grog-tempered wares of Hampshire and Kent (Tyers 1996, 191) and the calcite-gritted wares of East Yorkshire (Whyman 2001) are often held up as examples of this phenomenon. Arguments such as these seem to say more about modern prejudices towards thick and unattractive handmade pottery than the Roman past. However, it is clear that these new or revanchist pottery traditions represent a new approach to manufacturing ceramics in some regions. Finally, there is the argument derived from historical sources such as *The Theodosian Code*, and rooted in the historical analysis of Rostovtzeff (1926), that any economy faced with the burdens imposed upon it by the oppressive late Roman state must have been struggling (Faulkner 2000, 142–143).

Model 2: slide and bump

The 'slide and bump' view of the fourth-century economy suffers from the same issues of chronological resolution that the economic crash model does. It is difficult to ascertain when events such as the conversion of a forum-basilica into a metalworking establishment (e.g. Brewer 1993) or a villa into a grain-processing building (George 1999) occurred. Perhaps more importantly the interpretations of these phenomena are often tightly bound up with cultural prejudices (Gardner 2007). An oven dug through a mosaic of the four seasons looks like a decline in living standards because we are biased towards the aesthetics of the mosaic (Lewit 2003). To the inhabitant of the site the oven may simply have signified that the building was being used in a new and more productive way. Even the abandonment of a site is a social and economic strategy (Wilcox 2010, 137). Decline is a difficult phenomenon to quantify objectively.

Model 3: soft landing

The final model can be described as a 'soft landing' approach to the end of the Roman economy. This is a controversial interpretation and one that is presented here as a counter-weight to the 'crash' and 'slide and bump' models. The starting point for this discussion must be a consideration of the nature of the late Roman economy.

The fifth-century economic collapse in Britain is usually argued to have been a consequence of the disappearance of the structures of the Roman state and the tax–pay cycle. This prompted, to consciously borrow the jargon of contemporary economics, a crisis of confidence followed by a crisis of liquidity. The small copper-alloy coins, seemingly used in everyday transactions, were a token currency guaranteed to be exchanged by the state for gold and silver. By analogy with provinces such as Egypt, the exchange rate between copper and gold may have fluctuated on an almost daily basis (Bang 2007b, Table 3.2), but theoretically the Roman state stood behind its copper-alloy coins with bullion. Once the state stopped paying its servants in gold and silver, which probably occurred in the aftermath of Constantine III's defeat, that guarantee was broken.

The severing of the link between the gold and copper-alloy sections of the currency would have had a serious and, it is often assumed, almost immediate effect on confidence. The value of the extant gold and silver would have dramatically increased as there was now a finite pool of precious metal. This would imply that few individuals would have had the confidence to exchange it for the valueless copper-alloy coinage. This in turn would have prompted a crisis of liquidity as those with surpluses were no longer able to convert those surpluses into money. Those surpluses would have, in essence, become illiquid assets. The result would have been an economic collapse in which any form of exchange based on coin use, and any form of economic activity based around the state's requirements would grind to a halt.

This attempt to characterise the nature of the breakdown of the tax–pay cycle is obviously predicated on Roman Britain having a fragile and highly integrated monetary economy of a 'modern' character. The existence of such an economy appears self-evident. Coins are incredibly widespread and found right the way through the settlement hierarchy in the fourth century (Walton 2011). Pottery is ubiquitous and its presence or absence from different sites is being charted in ever increasing detail. This reveals that some late Roman 'finewares', such as the colour-coated wares produced in Oxfordshire (Young 1977), the New Forest (Fulford 1975) and the Nene Valley (Howe et al. 1980; Perrin 1999), could be distributed over many tens or even hundreds of kilometres. Even seemingly coarse and utilitarian 'kitchenwares', like the Black Burnished products of south-east Dorset (Allen and Fulford 1996) or the greywares produced in the Alice Holt/Farnham (Lyne and Jefferies 1979) area achieved substantial distributions. In London, for instance, fourth-century pottery supply was almost completely dominated by the Oxfordshire and Alice Holt kilns (Symonds and Tomber 1991), which were located 80 km and 60 km away (Young 1977; Lyne and Jefferies 1979).

The production of these types of pottery, and by extension other types of commodities, appears well-organised and is rarely, if ever, seen as anything other than proto-industrial production for a complex system of late Roman markets. When sherds of Oxfordshire Ware are found on a rural site in Kent, Somerset or Gloucestershire they are seen as the product of trade. The inhabitants produced an agricultural surplus – grain, cattle, wool or some other commodity – and took it to the market at the local town, or nucleated settlement. There the surplus was sold and the pottery bought, perhaps from a middleman or merchant who had acquired the goods direct from the kilns or another intermediary (Peacock 1982, 108). Occasionally the slim epigraphic evidence from the province, such as the Vindolanda tablets (Bowman 1993) or inscriptions mentioning 'traders' (Hassall 1978), is mobilised to affirm this model of Roman economics.

Such a characterisation of the economy is, as was observed in the introduction to this chapter, one that has much in common with formalist approaches. However, there have always been those who have regarded this vision of fourth-century economics with scepticism. Long-standing economic networks based on tribal divisions (Millett 1990, 157–180), the hand of the state (Gerrard 2008), as well as a recognition that most economic activity took place within the context of elite control (Whittaker 1983), rather than the freedom of a laissez-faire marketplace, have all been used to counter this view. The implication of this is that if the foundations of the modernising model can be undermined, the close connection between the end of the tax–pay cycle and the fifth-century economic collapse can be questioned.

The opposition of the 'primitive' and 'modernising' approaches has polarised the nature of the debate in far from helpful ways. No one can seriously argue that the use of money to facilitate market-based exchange on a large scale did not take place. Nor can it be realistically argued that the economy of the Roman Empire was dominated by commerce and proto-industrial production. Even in the most heavily urbanised and developed Roman provinces the vast majority of the population were rural dwellers engaged in agricultural production (Scheidel and Friesen 2009, 62). If the Romano-British economy and the fifth-century economic collapse are to be fully understood these polarised positions need to be reconciled.

A recent contribution to this debate – *The Roman Bazaar* (Bang 2007b) – has proposed an alternative model of the Roman economy and it is one worth considering here. Bang (2007b, 10–11) argues that the Roman Empire was an agrarianate society and a tributary empire. Both are useful terms. The first emphasises the co-existence of an agrarian society with urbanism and literary 'high culture', while the second addresses the importance of imperial surplus extraction from localised economic and social systems. Finally, the concept of the bazaar is introduced to describe an imperfect trading world 'characterised by chronic imbalances and asymmetries in the supply of available information and goods' (Bang 2007b, 139).

An imperfect trading world

Bang's (2007b) imperfect trading world seems a useful point at which to continue the discussion of the fifth-century economic collapse in Britain. The discussions of that collapse fetishise material culture that is archaeologically visible. Pottery, jewellery, tools, structural fittings as well as building techniques are the types of things whose disappearance is used as evidence of the economic collapse (Ward-Perkins 2005). There is a danger in this type of approach that the transition from Roman to early medieval is treated as a balance in which a plethora of 'Roman' things weigh down one side of the scales and are barely offset by a handful of early medieval objects in the other pan. However, it seems likely that a smaller range of material culture was available in the fourth century than, say, the second century. The analysis of pottery assemblages provides some useful examples of this phenomenon.

The study of Romano-British pottery is a specialised field of research which has more than its fair share of technical jargon. Traditionally, pottery analysis has been seen as a means of dating sites and studying exchange networks (Orton, Tyers and Vince 1993). However, if assemblages are quantified in the correct way then they can also be used to study the functional composition of groups (e.g. Evans 2001). To achieve this aim, individual fragments of pottery need to be quantified using measures that allow one sherd to be compared directly with another. The most commonly used quantification measure for this type of analysis in Britain is the Estimated Vessel Equivalent (EVE), which is derived from measuring the percentages of rim circumferences surviving in an assemblage. These measurements are directly comparable with one another and allow inter-site comparisons to be undertaken (Orton et al. 1993, 166–181). Unfortunately, quantifying an assemblage by EVEs is a time-consuming and therefore expensive business, so relatively few groups are quantified in this fashion. The technique also has a tendency to over-represent some forms (such as flagons, which have small and robust rims) and under-represent others (particularly amphorae). Nevertheless, using EVE quantified groups allows analysis of the functional composition of assemblages to be undertaken. The interpretative benefits of such analyses are only just beginning to be unlocked (e.g. Cool 2006, 172–180; Pitts 2008).

By using EVEs and broad functional categories (such as flagon, bowl, dish, mortaria and so forth) the types of pottery available in the early Roman period and the late Roman period can be compared. To this end a group of large (>5 EVEs, usually >10 EVEs) early Roman assemblages and late Roman assemblages, quantified by EVE and arranged by nine functional categories, have been brought together. London and assemblages from other urban and military centres feature prominently in this dataset. However, a significant number of additional sites have been included and the major source for these is Lyne's (1994, Appendix 3) thesis. Nevertheless, some important methodological issues remain. First, urban and military sites tend to have a wider range of forms than rural sites (Evans 2001). Secondly, residual pottery (sherds of early date that have been redeposited in later contexts) is often included in quantifications and, thirdly, specific groups of pottery (especially samian and amphorae) within an assemblage occasionally are quantified differently due to alternative intellectual traditions.

The raw data for the assemblages is provided in Appendix B. However, the simplest way of illustrating the broad patterning is to produce a combined percentage for each of the functional categories for the early and late

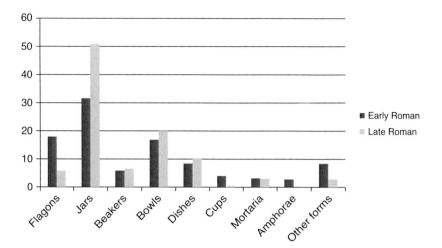

Fig. 3.5 The use of different vessel forms in the early and late Roman periods based on an average derived from the data presented in Appendix B (the author).

Fig. 3.6 Two early Roman flagons (© Pre-Construct Archaeology Ltd).

Roman periods (Figure 3.5). This demonstrates that flagons, drinking vessels, amphorae and 'other' forms are all more common in the early Roman period. The later Roman period is dominated by jars, bowls and dishes. This interesting pattern requires some explanation. The lack of amphorae is readily explicable as a consequence of the decline in amphora importation in the third and fourth centuries (Peacock and Williams 1986). However, other aspects are not so easily explained. The decline in flagons (Figure 3.6), which had been produced in some quantity during the early Roman period

Fig. 3.7 An early Roman triple vase
(© Pre-Construct Archaeology Ltd).

and continued to feature in the repertoire of late Roman pottery producers
(e.g. Tyers 1996), is quite striking and might be linked to increased consumption of beer instead of imported wine. The disappearance of cups,
primarily the samian form Dr33, is an odd phenomenon. Why this form
was not copied in any meaningful way by any of the late Roman fineware
producers (e.g. Fulford 1975, 60; Young 1977, 170) is a mystery. Finally,
'other forms' (mainly lids and unusual and miscellaneous vessels such as
triple vases (Figure 3.7) and tazza) almost disappear.

The significance of this pattern in the composition of ceramic assemblages
is difficult to establish. However, the fact remains that after the variety of
early Roman vessel forms, which includes sub-categories within groups
such as 'jars', communities in the third and fourth centuries were happy to
live their lives using a more restricted range of vessels. This is not, as some
might argue, an indicator of economic decline or barbarisation. Instead it
represents a return to a more comfortable order. For much of late prehistory
jars and bowls had sufficed for people's needs (Woodward and Hill 2002)

and these forms also dominate early medieval assemblages (McCarthy and Brooks 1988, 102).

A similar trend can be discerned for other classes of object. In the early Roman period glassware was used for a variety of functions but by the fourth century it was mainly associated with drinking (Cool 2006, 224–225). Copper-alloy brooches (Figure 3.8), a completely different type of object, see a similar restriction in the number of types available (e.g. Hattatt 2000; Bayley and Butcher 2004). Of the 34,000 Roman objects (excluding coins) recorded on the Portable Antiquities Scheme database in January 2011 (www.finds.org.uk) almost 12,000 were Roman period brooches. Of those brooches the vast majority were of first-, second- and third-century date – a mere 124 examples were fourth-century crossbow brooches. Even construction materials like ceramic tiles conform to a similar pattern. A late Roman building in London was typically constructed out of reused materials with any newly fired tiles reserved for the roof (Sudds 2011, 104). The great diversity and richness of Romano-British material culture trumpeted by those talking up the severity of the fifth-century economic collapse had ceased in the third century. What was available in the fourth century was a far more restricted range of items.

The production of late Roman material culture is imperfectly understood. Distributions of particular types or sub-types of object have been apparent for many decades and these distributions are becoming increasingly clear as data continues to accrue. However, there has been little interest shown in modelling how these distributions have come about. With items such as hairpins (Cool 1990), belt fittings (Swift 2000) and nail cleaners (Eckardt and Crummy 2006) there are definite regional patterns that are all too often explained in terms of 'identity'. There has been little work to understand whether particular classes of object were the product of a single urban workshop or peripatetic metalworkers and few attempts to understand the socio-economic context of their production.

Late Romano-British pottery production is somewhat better understood because a large number of kiln sites have been excavated (Swan 1984; Taylor 2007, Fig. 4.13). There have been some interesting discussions of the possible organisation and scope of Romano-British pottery producers (e.g. Buckland, Hartley and Vigby 2001, 87). Peacock (1982) argued that the manufacture of pottery could be described as household, workshop or nucleated production and this remains a widely cited model. Work on south-east Dorset Black Burnished Ware (BB1) has attempted to demonstrate the great scale at which it must have been produced (Allen and Fulford 1996) and this too is widely cited. Unfortunately, there has been little work

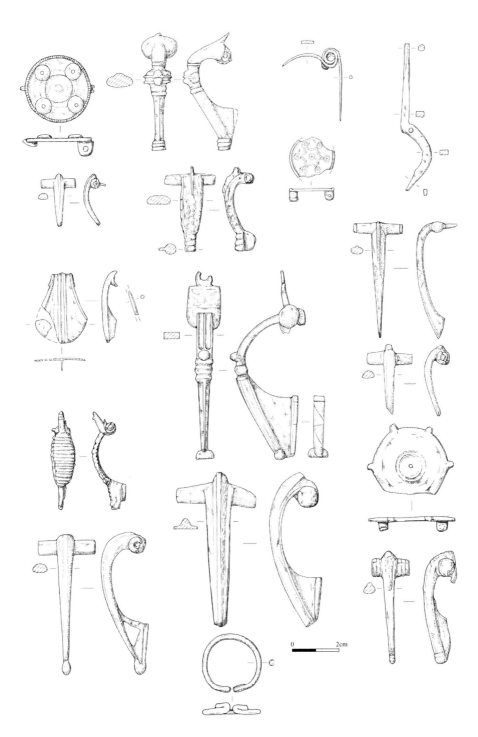

Fig. 3.8 A selection of early Roman brooches (© Pre-Construct Archaeology Ltd).

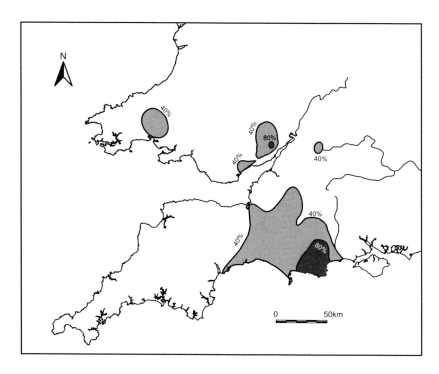

Fig. 3.9 Distribution map of BB1 pottery in south-western England (after Allen and Fulford 1996, Fig. 1).

on understanding how such material was distributed. The detailed distribution of BB1 mapped by Allen and Fulford (1996) shows an irregular fall off in the quantity of pottery used with distance from the kiln sites (Figure 3.9). There is also some evidence that roads and rivers were significant in distributing pottery (Fulford and Hodder 1975). Complex supply mechanisms that go beyond simple market-orientated economic models seem a probable explanation for this pattern (Gerrard 2008).

An unfortunate consequence of distribution maps is that they mislead the observer into believing that the mechanics of the pottery (or other artefact) distribution can be mapped. This is a fallacy underpinned by the belief that distribution maps are somehow analogous to a splash of ink on a piece of blotting paper. The ink spreads outwards from a core becoming paler with distance and putting out tendrils across the paper. In reality cargoes of pottery must have been shipped from the kiln sites to different points in the landscape and then redistributed. Early attempts to tackle the complexities of this suggested that urban markets may have been key in these networks (Hodder 1974), but more complex models are needed (Taylor 2004). Some of the major late Roman producers, like BB1 or the

Oxfordshire kilns, have major supra-regional distributions that cannot be explained by simple market economics (Allen and Fulford 1996; Gerrard 2008). It may also be noted that the archaeologist is condemned to study the places where pottery was used and not the locations where it was bought, sold or otherwise traded and exchanged.

Even more importantly it should be recognised that the supply of many of the items excavated from archaeological sites cannot have been consistent. To illustrate this let us consider southern Somerset and North Dorset. In the late Roman period the local walled urban centre was the town of Ilchester. The area was located far from the major centres of late Roman pottery production, located in Oxfordshire, south-east Dorset and the New Forest, and localised pottery production was on a small and seemingly insignificant scale. Could an inhabitant of a site like Bradley Hill, a late Roman farmstead located just north of Ilchester (Leech 1981; Gerrard 2005), really have acquired a red-slipped bowl from Oxfordshire whenever they chose? It seems unlikely. Even major pottery producers like the BB1 kilns or the Oxfordshire potters probably worked on a seasonal basis because it is difficult to dry and fire pottery successfully in the damp and cold British winter (Rice 1987, 189). Furthermore, for much of the year the roads were probably impassable to all but the most determined of travellers (Casson 1974; Bowman 1993, 146), let alone ox-carts and donkey trains carrying bulky goods like pottery. When goods did arrive at the local market or fayre they may have arrived as a glut that quickly evaporated, or in parsimonious quantities (Going 1992). The economy was far from the highly integrated beast imagined by some.

It is also necessary to consider the nature of Romano-British landholding and tenurial arrangements. Neither has been the subject of a detailed modern analysis and this is largely due to the fact that little meaningful documentary evidence survives that would allow investigation of these topics (Millett 1990, 198). Instead it is often assumed that a crude and simplistic settlement hierarchy can be reconstructed with villa sites at its pinnacle. These seemingly high-status dwellings are often viewed as the centre of familial estates with nearby settlements of non-villa type forming the dwelling places of the estate's tenants (Smith 1997). The broad outlines of such a system are undoubtedly true. However, what this model fails to emphasise is the fact that large swathes of land will have been owned by large landlords. Many villa buildings may represent the dwellings of tenants or bailiffs occupying land owned by large absentee landlords (Clark 1984). It is perfectly plausible to envisage some members of the elite in Roman Britain owning or renting hundreds of hectares of land across several modern counties (Todd 1988). Under such arrangements goods and commodities produced on one parcel of land could be distributed over long distances, in order to fulfil a demand at other estates owned or controlled by the same individual or groups of individuals. The Oxfordshire potters, for instance, could represent individual workshops producing large quantities of pottery not only for sale on the 'open' market but also for distribution to their owners' properties. It is also worth noting the close connections between a number of Romano-British pottery producers and sites producing salt (Gerrard 2005, 121; Taylor 2007, Figs. 4.13 and 4.14). Salt is, of course, a commodity vital to the agricultural economy and the distribution of salt may well have played an important role in facilitating the distribution of pottery like BB1 (Gerrard 2008) or the calcite-gritted wares of East Yorkshire (Whyman 2001, 253).

The idea of production tied, at least partially, into exchange networks built on estate economics and patronage is also of use when interpreting artefact classes other than pottery. Take two superficially very different classes of material culture: iron objects and mosaic pavements. The mining and smelting of iron ore occurred on an enormous scale in regions such as the Weald, the Forest of Dean, the East Midlands and possibly Exmoor during the Roman period (Taylor 2007). However, it also occurred on a much smaller and localised scale (Taylor 2007, Fig. 4.12). The manufacture of iron objects such as knives, nails, cart- and structural-fittings appears to have taken place on an equally localised level. Virtually every excavated Romano-British site produces some evidence of iron smithing waste. The smiths undertaking that work are, in a society where people could be owned or kept in other forms of 'servile' status (Samson 1992), unlikely to have been working solely within a market. Production and repair of tools and fittings for the immediate requirements of the estate must have been the dominant mode of production.

Mosaic pavements appear to be a radically different type of object when compared with the utilitarian knives produced by a local blacksmith. The art-historical study of mosaics and their iconography has allowed them to be classified into different stylistic and regional groupings (e.g. Johnson 1993; Neal and Cosh 2009). It has long been recognised that many of these groupings appear to correspond to what are often imagined to be *civitas* territories, which are supposedly earlier Iron Age 'tribal' units (Millett 1990, Fig. 76; Perring 2002, 131) (Figure 3.10). Mosaics have thus become a symbol of the heterogeneity of Roman Britain. However, the social context of the production of these high-status floors remains opaque. Particular stylistic groupings are often attributed to schools of mosaicists working in major

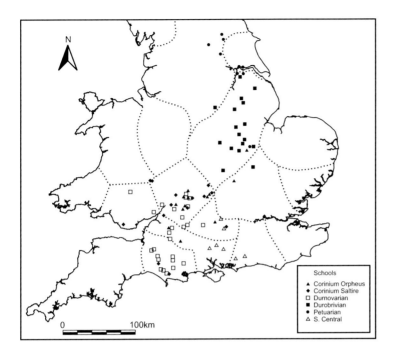

Schools
▲ Corinium Orpheus
◆ Corinium Saltire
□ Durnovarian
■ Durobrivian
● Petuarian
△ S. Central

0   100km

Fig. 3.10 The distribution of mosaics from different workshops in later
Roman Britain (after Millett 1990, Fig. 72).

towns. So there are postulated Corinian and Durnovarian schools producing
mosaics for the Dobunnic and Durnovarian *civitates* respectively (Johnson
1993; Scott 2000, 13–14). It is sometimes suggested that urban workshops
produced the mosaics for wealthy clients who chose the design from a
pattern book (Toynbee 1983). This though seems unduly modernising in
its approach. Mosaicists could easily have been peripatetic, or employed (or
owned) by a patron to carry out multiple commissions. The reproduction
of mosaic styles at different sites could be dimly revealing the webs of
patronage that existed between members of the late Roman elite in certain
regions (Scott 2000, 75–76; Perring 2002, 131). This puts a rather different
slant on mosaics than simply seeing them as the contemporary equivalent
of expensive, bespoke hand-printed wallpaper.

So far this discussion has concentrated on archaeologically visible material culture and it has attempted to show that the production of that material
culture need not be completely reliant on an integrated market economy.
This concentration on, or even fetishisation of, surviving material culture
is understandable. Archaeology is, after all, the study of the surviving remnants and residues of the past. Unfortunately, it means that we focus unduly

on relatively insignificant segments of the Romano-British economy. If, as the excavated evidence seems to suggest, 90 per cent of the population lived in settlements that practised a mixed arable-pastoral economy then the bulk of economic production in fourth-century Britain occurred in the agricultural sector. The production of grain, meat, timber and secondary products such as wool, leather and cheese, not pottery, iron, mosaics and other visible commodities, is the significant economic indicator and late Roman Britain can be seen as an agrarianate society.

The rural economy

The exploitation of the countryside has often been neglected in accounts of Roman Britain in favour of the more visible and 'Romanised' settlements like towns and villas. However, since the early 1990s fieldwork has been focussed not on sites selected for excavation but on those that happen to be in the way of modern development. An enormous volume of data regarding the fields and rural settlements of Roman Britain has been generated and the Herculean task of interpreting this ever expanding dataset has only just begun (Taylor 2007). The products of these fields were animals, grain and other crops (Fowler 2002, 127–160) and although it is often difficult to elucidate their chronology and development over large tracts of landscape these fields stand as a testament to the scale of Romano-British agricultural production.

The animals and foodstuffs produced by these fields and their farmers are, like the field boundaries, recovered on a routine basis. Faunal remains generally survive outside of the regions where acidic soils are present and their study has allowed some quite complex discussions of how different types of species were exploited (e.g. King 1988, 2005). The survival of grains, seeds, timber and leather is a much rarer occurrence as their preservation depends on charring or waterlogging (van der Veen, Lavarda and Hill 2007). Nevertheless, they provide some insights into the agricultural economy, which can be supplemented by indirect techniques such as pollen analysis (P. Dark 2000). One of the main difficulties with this type of data is that virtually all of it is derived from the consumption of the commodities and tells us little about the conditions under which it was produced. The bones of a cow excavated from a site will be those discarded by the butcher, smashed by the glue maker and dumped along with other waste to consolidate the ground. The information yielded by such data lacks fine detail and there is nothing from Roman Britain to compare with the detail contained in, say, later medieval documents regarding annual grain yields (Dodds 2004). Due

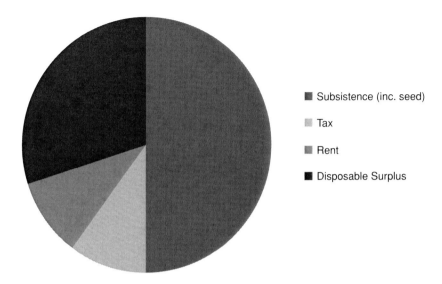

Fig. 3.11 Hypothetical reconstruction of the division of agricultural production between subsistence, tax, rent and disposable surplus (the author).

to this it is impossible to reconstruct the rural economy in anything like the detail that would be both desirable and necessary.

The absence of meaningful statistical data relating to agricultural production in late Roman Britain means that the agrarian economy can only be modelled along lines proposed for the Roman Empire in its entirety (Hopkins 1980, 1995/6; Bang 2007a; Scheidel and Friesen 2009). The agrarian economy can be divided between the resources needed for subsistence and what was left above this level: the surplus. The level of surplus production will have fluctuated with the harvest. However, we can, for argument's sake, model surplus as equal to that consumed as subsistence (Bang 2007b, Fig. 2.2). From the surplus any tax, rent or tribute would have to be taken. Much has been written on late Roman taxation (e.g. Jones 1964, 462–469, 820–823) but, in contrast to the reasonably abundant imperial legislation on taxation avoidance and remission (e.g. *Cod. Theod.* XI), there are few documents that provide any details of what tax rates were and how they were applied, and certainly none pertaining to Britain. In the second century state expenditure has been estimated as 15 per cent of the empire-wide disposable surplus (Bang 2007b, Table 2.1) and this would give a gross tax rate of 7.5 per cent. It is unlikely that the late Roman taxation rates were any lower than this and 10 per cent of gross production (20% of surplus) might seem appropriate and a similar figure might be envisioned as 'rent' (Figure 3.11).

Table 3.1 *A model of good and bad years in the*
agricultural economy

	Bad year (−25)	Average year	Good year (+25)
Subsistence (inc. seed)	50	50	50
Tax	10	10	10
Rent	10	10	10
Disposable surplus	5	30	55
Total gross production	*75*	*100*	*125*

In this model an average year in the agricultural economy
is given a notional value of 100. Good and bad years are
modelled as +/− 25 notional.

Modelling the rates of tax and rent as percentages of gross yields is
convenient for the purposes of this analysis. However, it may not reflect the
contemporary reality. If taxation or rent rates were fixed in quantities (of
solidi, cattle or grain) rather than percentages then the system of surplus
extraction by the state and landowners becomes more problematic. If the
rates of 10 per cent of gross yield for tax and rent are assumed for the
average year then what might happen in a good or bad year? In Table 3.1
gross production has been decreased and increased by 25 per cent to model
these scenarios. This demonstrates that in an average or good year the
agricultural producer will have few or no concerns. In a year with a poor
harvest there is a slender buffer between the producer, the demands for tax
and rent and his subsistence needs. If the state were to raise the tax rate over
the short term in response to a particular event (such as war), and if such
a rise were to coincide with a poor harvest, then the agricultural producer
would feel hard pressed. Equally if the state were less than conscientious
in assessing and collecting its dues (P. R. Brown 1971, 36), or distributed
the burden of taxation unevenly then paying taxes could quickly become
ruinous for some parts of society.

This model is only a heuristic device. Nevertheless, it can be taken one
step further. Estimates of the bare minimum subsistence requirements for
peasant cultivators have been suggested to be in the region of 250 kg wheat
equivalent *per annum* (Clark and Haswell 1970, 57–73). Grain yields are
problematic but a figure in the region of four times seed would be an
appropriate yield on slim Roman period (Evans 1981; Mayerson 1984; Bang
2007b, 89) and rather better medieval evidence (B. Campbell 2007). This
would add another 83 kg to the subsistence figure as the seed required for

the next season's planting. A family of four would need to grow 1.3 tonnes of wheat equivalent each year to meet their bare minimum subsistence needs. The population of late Roman Britain is uncertain but likely to lie between the figure for Domesday (*c.*1.71 million) and the medieval maximum of the mid fourteenth century (*c.*4.81 million) (Broadberry et al. 2010). The density of sites known from Roman Britain is impressive (Taylor 2007), and led Millett (1990, 181–186) to suggest a figure of 3.67 million people. This would mean that just over 1.2 million tonnes of wheat equivalent foodstuffs would need to be produced just to maintain the population at the minimum level necessary for subsistence each year.

If surplus production was a similar figure then it places the one piece of dubious information we have about the Roman state's view of late Roman Britain's economy into context. In 358–359 the Caesar Julian supplied the Rhine garrisons with grain from Britain transported, according to one source, in 800 ships (Zos. III.5). This may have been an extremely unusual event but it provides a figure to work from. If each of the 800 ships was similar to the Romano-British Blackfriars I vessel from London, which had a capacity of 50 tonnes (Marsden 1994, 89) and was relatively small (Marsden 1994, Table 9), then 40,000 tonnes of grain may have been transported across the North Sea. This total, with a tax rate of 10 per cent of gross yield, would equate to approximately one-sixth of the diocese's annual tax yield.

This discussion of the agrarian economy and surplus extraction has attempted to demonstrate that the academic focus on archaeologically recoverable items, such as pottery, jewellery and other forms of material culture, is misplaced. The late Romano-British economy was almost completely orientated towards agrarian production. In comparison, the production of goods and services formed a relatively minor component of economic activity. The notion of economic collapse, whether crash or bump, emphasises this minor element in the economy and fails to problematise or even discuss agrarian production. In addition to this it has been argued that the theoretical foundations of the crash and bump models are rooted in a modernising view of the Roman economy. This approach has been shown to be overly simplistic and ignores significant components of our knowledge regarding the material world in fourth-century Britain. The disappearance of coins, a money-using economy and the apparatus of the Roman state need not have led to a sudden and catastrophic economic collapse.

In the concluding half of this chapter the concept of an agrarianate economy will be combined with an acknowledgement of the theoretical and methodological ambiguities discussed above. This allows for a new and more open understanding of the transition from the fourth to the fifth century to be entertained. It is one that does not slavishly follow the notion of economic collapse or decline. Instead it sees the transformation as part of a long-term process, exacerbated, perhaps, by the fall of Rome.

Soft landing?

Our study of the economics of the fifth century can begin where our study of the fourth century stopped: the economic surplus. It was estimated that a fifth of gross production was consumed by the state and the elite as taxation and rent. Of course, to a greater or lesser extent the state was the elite as the elite served as the state's agents. It has sometimes been argued that with the disappearance of the structures of the state the taxation system would have ceased and that the peasantry would have benefited from such a move (Esmonde-Cleary 1989, 145). This is probably wishful thinking because the local elite would have found itself able to feed, jackal like, on the state's corpse, appropriating its economic and political potential for its own end. Such a process is unlikely to have been pretty or straightforward. Nevertheless, those landowners who had extracted from their tenants and peasants rent and tax (and the distinction to the peasantry may have been meaningless anyway) (Wickham 1984, 2005, 529) now found themselves able to keep not only the rent but also the tax revenues.

Superficially the Romano-British elite, far from feeling the pinch, may have found themselves the recipients of a greater portion of their peasants' surplus than they had ever dreamt possible. The problem was what to do with a surplus primarily formed of agricultural commodities. Meat could be salted down, wheat stored, barley malted into beer and kept for a season or two. However, what had previously been possible – the conversion of an agricultural surplus to gold and silver – was becoming increasingly difficult as the value of the bullion pool increased as it became ever scarcer. Some of these foodstuffs and other goods could be redistributed among a patron's tenants, retainers and clients. Some might even have been destined to pay for mercenaries and warriors. Dim echoes of such a system might be sought in Gildas' (*De Excidio* 23.4–5, Winterbottom 1978, 26) account of the *superbus tyrannus*' dealings with the Anglo-Saxons (Snyder 1998, 111–112). However, eventually it must have become clear that much of this surplus was simply wasted. There was only so much bread that could be eaten, beef that could be salted and beer that could be brewed. The various elite groupings and the peasantry must have come to realise that they could get by on far less than they had needed to produce under Rome's rule. The implications of this are that, perhaps, 10 per cent of land could fall from cultivation and the elite could still extract the same level of surplus that they had under Rome. Alternatively, the land could be worked in different ways.

In archaeological terms identifying early post-Roman material culture in many parts of Britain is challenging and this means that it is difficult to chart the development of the agricultural landscape in detail. Proxy records, such as pollen cores, offer one means of assessing how much land remained under cultivation. Unfortunately, their coverage is not even and palynological studies are generally restricted to the uplands where peat bogs and other suitable micro-environments have preserved ancient pollen grains. Where such studies have been undertaken and related to an absolute chronology determined by radiocarbon dating the picture revealed is complex. In some regions (particularly the northern frontier zone) there appears to be some evidence of a decline in agricultural land use, but in other areas the pattern is constant or even indicates an increase in land under cultivation (P. Dark 1996, 2000; Dark and Dark 1997, 143–144; Fyfe and Rippon 2004).

A more direct means of assessing the agricultural economy can be sought in the boundaries and ditches that divided the British landscape into field systems. For much of the twentieth century the study of such ancient landscapes was the preserve of aerial photographers. However, large-scale developer-funded excavations have begun to add a chronological dimension to many of the systems known from aerial photography. They have also demonstrated the presence of such systems in areas where the earthworks of field systems have been denuded by ploughing, or where the geological conditions are not conducive to crop or soil marks. This vast dataset is only just beginning to be synthesised but already the evidence points to a very heavily exploited Romano-British landscape (Taylor 2007, 55–72).

How the changes of the fifth century impacted on that landscape remains a hotly contested topic (Rippon 1991, 2006; Oosthuizen 1998, 2011a; Baker 2002; Upex 2002). Even with excavation it is difficult to date the abandonment or reorientation of field boundaries during the early Middle Ages. A demonstrably medieval field system reusing elements of Roman period boundaries might indicate long-term exploitation of the land, but not continuity of agricultural practice. The abandoned earthworks of a relict field system can be reused much later without implying continuous use. Nevertheless, some patterns can be discerned even if those patterns are often open to diverging interpretations.

During the Roman period some so-called marginal regions, like wetlands, were intensively managed and farmed. The pattern is not straightforward. However, in the Thames estuary a marine inundation appears to have occurred by the late Roman period, whereas around the Bristol Channel, Poole Harbour, the Fens and the Humber estuary all appear to have been inundated after *c*.400 (Rippon 2000, 138–142; 2006, 80–81; Edwards 2001). The causes of this inundation remain unknown (Rippon 2000, 142–149). Previously maintained sea defences may have been neglected because the resources to repair them were no longer available, or because it was pointless to repair them in the face of a rising sea level, or even because the land was no longer needed. Similarly some 'marginal' inland regions such as Exmoor (Rippon, Fyfe and Brown 2006, 49) were also abandoned and covered by woodland. Nevertheless, these examples appear to have been the exceptions rather than the rule (Oosthuizen 2011a).

It is difficult to generalise about what was surely a finely nuanced and complex situation that differed from valley to valley. However, there seems to be increasing evidence for the survival of landscape divisions from prehistory, through the Roman period and into the Middle Ages. The interpretation of this phenomenon is complex and it need not indicate either tenurial stability, or a continuity of agricultural regimes (Oosthuizen 2011a, 379–385). Infield-Outfield agriculture, where land close to the settlement was used intensively for arable agriculture and land further away managed less intensively as pasture (Fowler 2002, 216–217), seems to have been common in both the Roman and early medieval periods.

The biggest change that occurred in the agricultural landscape between *c*.400 and *c*.700 appears to have been a shift away from large-scale arable production towards less intensive pastoral farming (Oosthuizen 2011a, 383 and 2011b). Evidence of this process has been deduced from the organisation of field boundaries at a number of sites (e.g. Tabor and Johnson 2000, 324; Davey 2005, 79–80; Oosthuizen 2011a, 383). Such a transformation would fit the general model of the 'end' of the Romano-British economy well. The disappearance of the tax burden might lead to less intensive arable exploitation that would be conducive to an increase in grazing land. Furthermore, the end of the Roman monetary system might mean that animals (especially cattle) took on a heightened importance as a measure of wealth (Hamerow 2002, 129). This interpretation could be supported by the etymology of the Old English word *feoh*, which meant cattle, moveable goods, property and money (Bosworth 1838, 109).

This seeming shift towards a pastoral economy ought to be detectable in assemblages of faunal remains and plant macro-fossils. Unfortunately, few such assemblages have been excavated or published (Hamerow 2002, 127–154). A recent review was unable to marshal more than two dozen early Saxon faunal assemblages; within that sample only West Stow (Suffolk) and West Heslerton were considered to be both large enough and suitably studied to provide truly meaningful data (Crabtree 2010, 123). The situation in the west of Britain is if anything worse. None of the reoccupied hillfort sites has produced meaningful animal bone assemblages and this leaves just the faunal remains from Wroxeter (Hammon 2011). This slender evidence does suggest an emphasis on cattle rearing (Crabtree 2010, Fig. 1). There are equally few fifth- and sixth-century assemblages of preserved plant remains and those that do exist do not allow generalisations to be made (Sparey-Green 1987, 135–137; Hamerow 2002, 152–155).

The combination of palynological evidence, the study of field boundaries and the analysis of animal remains would appear to suggest that, from a rural perspective, the difference between the fourth and fifth centuries was a shift from arable agriculture to an increasing emphasis on pastoralism. This is significant because arable agriculture is more efficient than the production of meat and the secondary products of animals. Without the Roman tax burden agricultural production did not need to be as intensive as it had been in the fourth century. This process may have been speeded along by a climatic deterioration and the adoption of cattle as symbols of wealth. Nevertheless, it represents a major transformation rather than an economic collapse. For the most productive part of the fourth-century economy the fifth century was not a crisis but a far from catastrophic change.

The rest of the economy

The remainder of the economy, a minor component over-emphasised by the archaeological visibility of its products, also needs to be discussed if the idea of a 'soft landing' can be truly entertained. In this final section the possible trajectories of manufactured goods, like pottery vessels and personal adornments, are explored.

This discussion begins with a humble class of artefact: hairpins (Figure 3.12). In Roman Britain hairpins were manufactured from a variety of materials, including metal (Cool 1990), jet (Allason-Jones 1996, 38) and bone (Crummy 1983, 19–25). Hairpins are common finds on Romano-British sites and, as might be expected, bone examples are the most ubiquitous. An examination of the finds reports from hilltop sites such as Cadbury Castle (Alcock 1995), Cadbury Congresbury (Rahtz et al. 1993), Glastonbury Tor (Somerset) (Rahtz 1971) or Dinas Powys (Alcock 1967) reveals only a few dubious examples of objects that could be termed hairpins. A similar phenomenon is visible in post-Roman cemeteries (e.g. Rahtz et al. 2000),

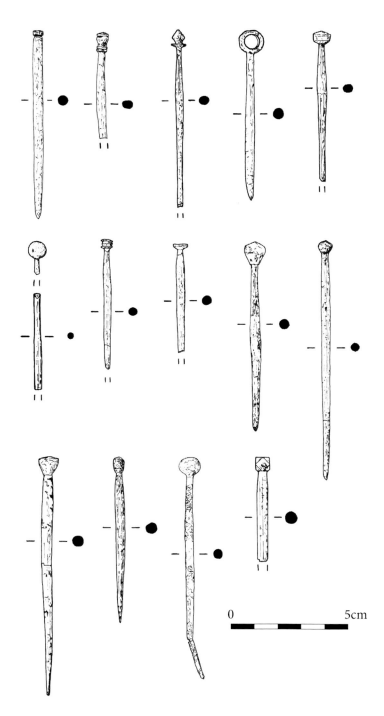

Fig. 3.12 A selection of late Roman bone hairpins (© Pre-Construct Archaeology Ltd).

although this might be related to a burial tradition that was intolerant of gravegoods or personal ornamentation.

Under the economic collapse model this absence of hairpins would be taken as evidence of the dire economic straits to which Britain had been reduced in the fifth century. Superficially this is logical. Getting access to Whitby jet or even bronze might, in a time of crisis, be difficult in many parts of the British Isles. However, the same cannot be said of animal bone. Whenever and wherever a cow was slaughtered bones were available for the manufacture of objects. Indeed, the late fourth century and the early Middle Ages saw the utilisation of bone for many objects, not least of which were hair-combs (e.g. Dunlevy 1988; Riddler 1988; Cool 2010, 272–274). Of course, it could be suggested that bone working was a specialist occupation and that those skills ceased with the end of an urban market economy. This, however, is clearly untrue; many late Roman hairpins were quite capable of being produced by someone who was relatively unskilled in bone working and some are argued to have been produced in a domestic setting (Crummy 1983, 20).

The decline in hairpin use is a phenomenon that has attracted some attention. Cool has argued that the use of hairpins was declining in the late fourth century, at much the same time as other bone objects (such as combs and bracelets) were becoming much more popular (Cool 2000a). This pattern was interpreted as a social choice. Some early Christian teachings insisted that female hair needed to be covered and thus elaborate hairstyles and the combs were no longer required once the population had adopted Christianity (Cool 2000b, 2006, 240). Whether this interpretation is correct or not need not concern us here. What is important is that this change in material culture was not the product of a systemic shock but a shift in social practice.

This pattern of a shift in social practice being reflected in material culture is echoed in the study of other artefact classes. Brooches have been discussed earlier in this chapter and it seems clear that the wearing of brooches had declined substantially by the end of the fourth century. However, some specific types, particularly penannular brooches and perhaps also crossbow brooches (Cool 2010, 279; Collins 2010), appear to have continued in production into the fifth century. Other types of personal adornments, such as bracelets, seem to have followed a similar trajectory. Copper-alloy bracelets appear to have fallen out of fashion in the late fourth century and may have been 'replaced' by bone and ivory examples. The famous late Roman zoomorphic belt fittings, long erroneously associated with Germanic *foederati* (Hawkes and Dunning 1961), appear to have been in production during the last decades of the fourth century and continued

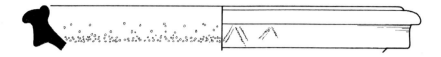

Fig. 3.13 A Crambeck Type 8 mortarium of ? fifth-century date (after Swan et al. 2009, 658).

to be used and possibly produced well into the first half of the fifth century (Cool 2010, 286; Coulston 2010, 52). They represent a strange late fourth- and fifth-century phenomenon that is poorly understood. This situation is not helped by the continuing lack of a comprehensive and up-to-date typological study of this material and its simplistic interpretation in some quarters as 'military' equipment for sub-Roman militias (Laycock 2008).

Pottery production is another industry that is often argued to have fallen victim to the economic collapse of the early fifth century (Fulford 1979). Of late this has begun to be questioned. Cool (2006, 227–235) has discussed the composition of late fourth-century pottery assemblages and suggested that changes in the types of vessel available reflect a transformation in the way food and drink were prepared, presented and consumed. These patterns, she argues, can be seen continuing into the fifth century. Work along more traditional typological lines has begun to produce indications that in some regions Romano-British pottery production continued for a time into the fifth century. Research on the pottery assemblages from York has demonstrated that the late fourth-century Romano-British pottery known as 'calcite-gritted ware' continued to be produced into the first half of the fifth century (Whyman 2001). In the south-west of Britain the Black Burnished potters of Dorset were manufacturing new vessel forms and pottery fabrics late in the fourth century and they appear to have continued producing such vessels into the first half of the fifth century (Gerrard 2004, 2010). Other studies have identified unusual vessel forms in Crambeck Ware (Figure 3.13) (Swan, McBride and Hartley 2009, 658), Hampshire grog-tempered ware (Lyne 1999) and atypical 'Romano-British' vessels from the Anglo-Saxon cemetery at Cleatham (Lincolnshire) (Figure 3.14) that seem likely to be of fifth-century date (Leahy 2007a, 126–127). In short, there is a growing body of evidence for the continued production and use, albeit on a small scale, of Romano-British pottery after *c*.400.

Metal vessels provide another illuminating case study. During the Roman period a wide variety of vessels were manufactured from silver, iron and copper- and lead-alloys. The metal content of these vessels meant that they had some value even when broken beyond repair and as such were

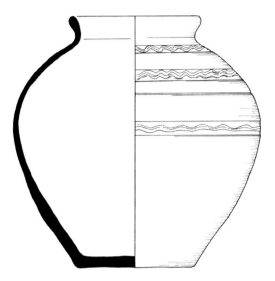

Fig. 3.14 A wheel-thrown 'Romano-British' jar from the Anglo-Saxon cemetery at Cleatham (after Leahy 2007a, 126–127).

conscientiously recycled. Due to this they are only rarely encountered during the excavation of settlement sites and rather more examples are known from hoards and other special deposits.

In 2007 one such hoard was recovered from the fill of a late Roman well in the heart of the City of London's financial district at a site called Drapers' Gardens (Gerrard 2009). Twenty vessels of bronze, iron and pewter were discovered, and associated coins clearly show that the hoard could not have been deposited any earlier than 375. Within the hoard are a number of vessels that must have been heirlooms by the late fourth century, but there are also four types of vessels of late Roman or early medieval form: a hanging basin, a Westland cauldron, *perlrandbecken* and *bassins à bord godronné*.

Early medieval hanging basins have long been seen as a vessel form that originated in the late Roman period and they are sometimes seen as the product of 'Celtic' smiths working for Anglo-Saxon patrons (Brenan 1991, 5–26). However, this view has been challenged by Geake (1999), who has argued that because they are only found in Anglo-Saxon graves of seventh- and eighth-century date they must date to this period. Their 'Roman' style, she argues, was part of an ideological movement attempting to 'recreate the power of Rome' in the seventh century (Geake 1999, 17). The strength of this analysis was the emphasis on occurrences in dateable contexts, which are graves almost without exception. However, this emphasis is also a weakness.

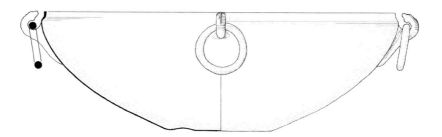

Fig. 3.15 Bronze hanging bowl from the Drapers' Gardens hoard (© Pre-Construct Archaeology Ltd).

Many hanging bowls and fragments such as individual escutcheons are, as Geake (1999) acknowledges, stray finds from undated contexts and the danger is that by ignoring these the date of a particular phenomenon (the deposition of hanging bowls in Anglo-Saxon graves) becomes the date of a type of vessel.

The Drapers' Gardens vessel with its form reminiscent of a late Roman vessel known as an 'Irchester' bowl and a *terminus post quem* of 375 represents a point that helps to link the early medieval sequence of hanging bowls with the Roman period examples (Gerrard 2009, 169) (Figure 3.15). Furthermore, it is similar to an undated vessel from Newham (Northumberland), which is usually considered to be of fifth-century date on typological grounds (Bruce-Mitford and Raven 2005, 11).

The Westland cauldron (Figure 3.16) is a type of vessel commonly found in fifth- and sixth-century Scandinavian and, to a lesser extent, Anglo-Saxon graves in Britain (Hauken 2005; Richards 1980, Appendix III). Hauken's (2005) typology of these vessels would classify the Drapers' Gardens example as a Type 2C, a form associated with objects of the Late Roman Iron Age (300–375/400) and Early Migration period (375/400–450/475) in Scandinavia (see Künzl 1993, 234 and Hoeper 1999 for an alternative view). Besides the Drapers' Gardens example the only other Romano-British examples are a possible fragment from the late fourth-century infilling of the theatre at Verulamium (Kennett 1971, 146) and the three undated examples from an antiquarian hoard find at Halkyn Mountain in North Wales (Knight 2007, 161–162).

The two varieties of bowls – the *bassin à bord godronné* and *perlrandbecken* – are both late Roman types. In Britain *bassins à bord godronné* are known from a number of 'late Roman' hoards in Britain and Gaul (Kennett 1971, Fig. 13; Gregory 1977) and they are occasionally found in continental graves associated with coins of late fourth- or fifth-century date. Similarly,

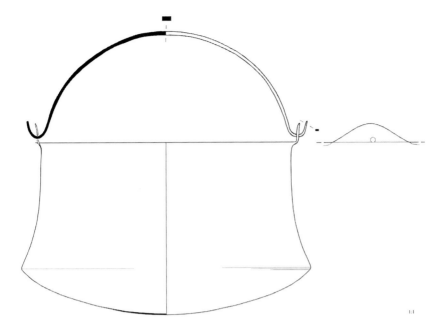

Fig. 3.16 Bronze Westland cauldron from the Drapers' Gardens hoard (© Pre-Construct Archaeology Ltd).

perlrandbecken (Figure 3.17) appear in Gallic graves associated with coins of Arcadius and Honorius (Kennett 1971, 123–141) but are more common as Anglo-Saxon or Merovingian gravegoods (Richards 1980, 15–18; Grunwald 1998, 37–38). The Drapers' Gardens examples appear to be the only such vessels from late Roman Britain.

The Drapers' Gardens hoard neatly encapsulates the chronological difficulties encountered in the late fourth century. The coins provide only a *terminus post quem* of 375 and this could be combined with a traditional depiction of the end of Roman Britain and the hoard dated to *c.*375–400/420. However, we have already explored the reasons why this might be fallacious. The metal vessels in this collection could easily stand for the type of vessels available in fifth-century Britain: some new forms sitting alongside patched and repaired antique vessels, that might be 200 or more years old.

This recent find is but one example of a wider phenomenon. However, very few such 'late Roman' hoards are associated with dating evidence. A handful of examples suffice to illustrate this point. At Amersham (Buckinghamshire) six copper-alloy vessels, including so-called Irchester bowls, are loosely associated with late Roman finds but are otherwise undated (Farley, Henig and Taylor 1988). A pewter hoard from Appleford (Oxfordshire) is

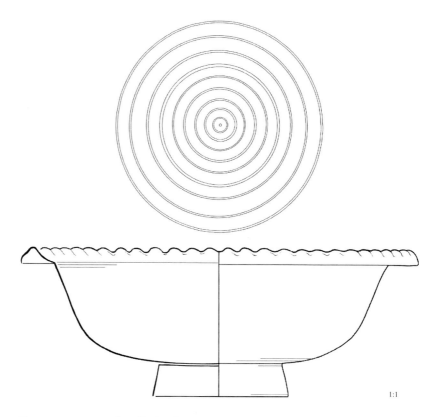

Fig. 3.17 Bronze *perlrandbecken* from the Drapers' Gardens hoard (© Pre-Construct Archaeology Ltd).

again considered to be typologically late Roman but is otherwise undated (Brown 1973) and another pewter hoard from Appleshaw (Hampshire) was found in a pit cut through a villa. On the basis of a coin list ending with issues of Decentius the excavator suggested that the hoard had been deposited *c.*350 (Engleheart 1898). However, this flimsy evidence allows a much later date to be entertained. This list could be extended but to do so would be to labour the point. These hoards can only be dated to the end of the fourth century if it is assumed that the economic collapse at the end of Roman Britain led to the cessation of metal vessel production in the fifth century.

Late Roman pewter production provides one example of an industry that might have continued after the 'end' of Roman Britain and some reasonable evidence can be marshalled to argue that this was in fact the case. Lead and tin ores were both mined extensively during the Roman period in Cornwall, the Mendips, Wales and Derbyshire. There seems no reason why the mining of these ores should have ceased in the fifth century. In fact the presence of Cornish tin and Mendip lead is often argued to be a factor influencing the distribution of imported Mediterranean ceramics in the late fifth and early sixth centuries (Thomas 1993; E. Campbell 2007, 129–130). Of the three excavated late Roman sites that have produced evidence of pewter manufacture, one (Lansdown, Somerset) was so badly dug as to defy interpretation (Lee 2009) and two (Camerton and Nettleton, Somerset) have produced, not only coin lists terminating with Honorius, but also so-called 'squatter' activity (Wedlake 1958 and 1982). By analogy with Shepton Mallet (Somerset), a local site excavated with modern techniques (Leach and Evans 2001), some of this activity is likely to be of fifth- or sixth-century date. Finally, there is a stone mould from a fifth-century building in the reoccupied hillfort of Crickley Hill (Gloucestershire) that might also suggest post-Roman pewter production (Jarrett 2011).

Given that the chronology of pewter vessels is poorly understood (Peal 1967; Beagrie 1989; Lee 2009) and, at the end of the fourth century, is heavily influenced by the economic collapse model it might appear fruitless to seek fifth-century pewter objects. However, this assessment can be questioned as a number of pewter objects appear to have been deposited in the fifth century. Near Shapwick (Somerset) peat cutting in the early twentieth century uncovered four small hoards of pewter objects. One of the hoards was associated with silver *siliquae* terminating with issues of Honorius, another had silver coins ending with issues of Arcadius and a third was associated with copper-alloy *nummi*, the latest of which was a coin of Magnus Maximus (Robertson 2000, Nos. 1,475, 1,497 and 1,584). All of these vessels can thus be shown to have been circulating at the very end of the fourth century.

Another potentially fifth-century pewter find was encountered during the nineteenth-century excavations at Silchester. At the base of a fourth-century well a stone column was found bearing an Ogham inscription. This column sat on top of a crushed pewter flagon, which is paralleled by one of the Shapwick finds. The dating of these events, given the circumstances of their excavation, is not as firm as might be wished for but a date after *c.*400 seems likely (Fulford, Handley and Clarke 2000).

The hot spring at Bath (Somerset) is also relevant. Many objects were recovered by antiquarian and modern excavators from the spring head and other objects remain buried *in situ*. These include a significant collection of pewter items, among which pride of place must go to a unique pewter candlestick. However, there is also a small pewter jug that is similar to the example from Drapers' Gardens and also a vessel in the Appleford hoard (Sunter and Brown 1988, Figs. 7.20–21). Usually this vessel is assigned a fourth-century date but such a date can be questioned on a number of grounds. The temple complex at Bath appears not to have fallen out of use until the end of the first third of the fifth century (Gerrard 2007a) and even after the temple was demolished the hot spring may still have been venerated. The presence in the spring of an enamelled penannular brooch, dated 450–550, would seem to confirm this point (Youngs 1995, 129).

There are no pewter objects from post-Roman sites and cemeteries in either the east or west of Britain and this could indicate that production of this material did indeed cease *c.*400. However, even in the Roman period pewter objects are rarely encountered outside of hoards. This suggests that any broken vessels were quickly recycled and would not normally enter domestic refuse. The same would be true of the fifth and sixth centuries. Secondly, metal vessels were never a common gravegood in either the Roman or Anglo-Saxon period and thus their absence from cemeteries is not significant.

Many of the issues surrounding the study of copper-alloy and pewter vessels also apply to silver tableware. It seems likely that some of the 'late Roman' hoards of silver (Hobbs 2006) actually date to the fifth century. Such groups of objects often include either complete or fragmentary vessels alongside other objects such as ingots and silver spoons. A fragment of silver vessel was found at the fifth- and sixth-century site of Longbury Bank (Dyfed) (Campbell and Lane 1993, 30) and seventh-century silver spoons in Anglo-Saxon contexts are argued to be derived from late Roman prototypes (Speake 1989, 43–47). However, these spoons may reflect imported continental or Byzantine progenitors (Harris 2003) as much as any continuing indigenous tradition of silver smithing. Occasional hints of silver vessels in early medieval literary sources (*Y Gododdin* 626; Jarman 1988, 42) may also be noted.

Less glamorous everyday iron objects such as knives, nails and structural fittings are also worthy of consideration (Manning 1985). During the Roman period it is clear that the use of iron penetrated to the bottom of the settlement hierarchy, except in upland regions like Wales and Cumbria where acidic soils make any assessment problematic. The ubiquity of iron objects and the substantial evidence for Roman period iron extraction in areas such as the Weald and the Forest of Dean are clear evidence of large-scale production. In the fifth century there are few sites that produce comparable assemblages of objects. The fifth-century refortification of Cadbury Castle appears not to have involved the use of nails (Alcock 1982, 364) and many Anglo-Saxon sites display a similar paucity of iron objects. There are dangers in extrapolating a general lack of iron objects from such observations. The presence of swords, spears and shield bosses in Anglo-Saxon graves suggests that iron must have been in wider use than it might otherwise appear. Thus part of the reason for the seeming disparity in numbers of iron objects in the late Roman period and the early Middle Ages might lie in differences in the treatment of 'rubbish' (Lucy, Tipper and Dickens 2009, 244). Nevertheless, it is difficult to believe that nails were profligately discarded on many Roman sites but carefully recycled (which is also technically difficult) in the fifth century.

That fewer iron objects were available in the fifth century than in the fourth century seems certain (Fleming 2012). Nevertheless, it would be wrong to see this as evidence of an economic collapse. The production of swords, of which many are known from Anglo-Saxon England but virtually none from late Roman Britain or the post-Roman west, demonstrates the presence of technically accomplished smiths (Gilmour 2007; Ottaway 2011, 7). Even greater skills are exhibited in the spectacular cauldron chain from the seventh-century burial at Sutton Hoo (Bruce-Mitford 1975; Manning 1983, 150). This chain is linked typologically to late Roman examples (Manning 1983) and suggests that such objects were more common than their rarity in the archaeological record suggests. This may be confirmed by the assemblage of sixth- and seventh-century iron tools at the 'Anglo-Saxon' site of Bloodmoor Hill (Suffolk). Some of the objects were indistinguishable from earlier Roman examples (Lucy et al. 2009, 265–267). Even knives have their own story to tell. The small number of post-Roman knives from the fifth- and sixth-century settlement at Poundbury were technically more accomplished than Roman period blades (Sparey-Green 1987, 98–99). Where structural fittings survive they display a stability of form that suggests smithing skills were maintained to the end of the Roman Empire. It seems possible that the end of the Romano-British economy forced iron smithing into two extreme positions. On the one hand much smithing probably went on (as it had in the Roman period) as a localised and low-intensity activity. On the other hand it may also have become an extremely specialist skill creating a group of technically very accomplished smiths producing high-quality ironwork (such as swords) for the upper echelons of society.

Finally, archaeologically invisible commodities should be considered. Late Roman Britain must have produced considerable quantities of textiles and leather goods. Small finds, such as spindle whorls and needles, suggest textile working and this artefactual evidence is supplemented by documentary references to *gynaecaea* (so-called imperial weaving factories) (*Not. Dig. Occ.* XI.60; Booth et al. 2010, 527–529). The study of faunal remains can indicate the exploitation of flocks of sheep for wool and, where waterlogged conditions prevail, leather items occasionally survive. Much of this evidence is lacking for the fifth and sixth centuries but textile production and leatherworking must have continued even if not on the same scale as Roman period production. The continued production of some 'Romano-British' fabric weaves in Anglo-Saxon contexts is noteworthy here (Walton Rogers 2007, 230–232). Similarly, there is very little evidence for the fifth- or sixth-century production of salt. However, it is noticeable that areas where salt had been produced during the Roman period, particularly Poole Harbour in Dorset and the area around Droitwich (Worcestershire), are both significant salt-producing sites once written documents appear in the seventh century and later (Keen 1988; Maddicott 2005). It thus seems likely that production of this commodity, which would have been extremely important as a preservative of foodstuffs like meat and dairy products, continued into the post-Roman period.

Fifth-century economics

If our visualisation of the Romano-British economy moves away from an over-fixation with archaeologically visible artefacts then the characterisation of the end of Roman Britain as an economic collapse falters. Grain, meat, dairy products, wool, leather, timber and a myriad of other commodities formed the bulk of late Romano-British production. Pottery, metalwork and stone and other archaeologically visible commodities will have formed only a small part of the economy by comparison. Thus the end of the Romano-British economy must be evaluated first and foremost from the perspective of agricultural production. The modelling of the Romano-British economy undertaken above is crude but provides some measure of the impact of Roman taxation. The removal of that tax burden as well as the decline of urban centres will have led to a reduction in the level of production. This appears to have manifested itself as a shift away from arable agriculture in favour of an emphasis on pastoralism.

The apparently catastrophic decline in the availability of archaeologically visible material culture has been seen as a product of the collapse of a market-based monetary economy. That the coin-using economy disappeared in the first few decades of the fifth century seems certain. However, for our purposes more significant is the recognition that much economic activity took place outside of the marketplace. Alternative socially embedded economies enabled the production and transportation of goods even in the absence of that supposed economic lubricant: coinage. This fixation on market-based exchange has been combined with views of Romano-British material culture that are, to all intents and purposes, ahistorical. These have lumped artefacts together without care for chronology to produce a 'Roman' cultural package which can be contrasted with the general paucity of fifth-century material culture. A more sensitive approach recognises that substantial changes were already occurring during the third and fourth centuries. Such an approach towards the dating of the latest 'Romano-British' artefact assemblages also allows that trajectory to continue into the fifth century for some time, perhaps fifty or so years.

The appearance of imported pottery and glassware during the late fifth century allows a relatively small number of high-status sites (such as Tintagel, Cornwall, and Cadbury Castle) to be identified in the west of Britain (E. Campbell 2007). These sites have often been denigrated as the refuges of the new post-Roman elite eking out an existence in the shadow of Rome. One commentator was moved to note that in this region 'it does not seem to have taken much to make an elite' (Wickham 2005, 327). Another author has characterised these sites as those of 'warlords starting from scratch, building small surpluses' (Faulkner 2000, 178). In this final section the economic significance of one of these sites, Cadbury Castle, is explored.

The multivallate hillfort of Cadbury Castle occupies a freestanding hill east of the Roman town of Lindinis (Ilchester) close to the Somerset–Dorset border. Excavations by Alcock (1972, 1995) in the 1960s demonstrated that the hill had been first fortified in the Bronze Age and continued in occupation during the Iron Age, reaching its zenith in the first century AD (Barrett, Freeman and Woodward 2000). It appears to have been forcibly captured by the Roman army during the latter half of the first century and then abandoned, except for a poorly defined late Roman reuse. Then in the late fifth century the hillfort was refortified and some major timber buildings, including a timber 'feasting hall', were built within its ramparts. This phase lasted into the sixth century.

The excavated finds – a few items of metalwork and the imported Mediterranean pottery – look far from impressive. However, this measure of the site's economic significance is a poor one. The inner rampart of the defences, which was refurbished in the fifth century, is 1,100 m long and 5 m wide. Its height is uncertain but 2 m might be a reasonable estimate (Alcock 1982, Fig. 1; 1995, Fig. 2.8). This suggests that 11,000 m^3 of rubble and earth would be needed to form the core of this rampart. Some of this will have been provided from recutting the Iron Age defensive ditches or scalping the surface of the hill. However, the rampart also included Roman building materials and the nearest known Romano-British structures are located at the foot of the hill beneath the modern village of South Cadbury (Randall 2010). Thus some of the material must have come from Roman period buildings that were being demolished and then carted to the summit of a hill 153 m high.

The core of the rampart needed to be retained by walls on either side. These proved to be of drystone walling and at least 2,200 m of walling approximately 2 m high was required for this task. Each of the slabs for this wall had to be quarried and, even given the local stone's tendency to split into slabs, roughly dressed and laid. The discovery of beamslots running through the rampart indicates that it was held together by a timber framework or lacing. Alcock (1982, 364) suggested that this framework would have required almost 20,000 m of timber beams, each of which would be 0.2 m^2. The absence of nails in the excavated beamslots suggested that these timbers were held together by joints alone (Alcock 1982, 364). If trees 25 m high were used with a diameter of 0.5 m then each tree might yield 100 m of timber. This would suggest that 200 mature trees needed to be felled, split or sawn into beams, furnished with joints and moved into position. In addition to this the top of the rampart may have been furnished with a breastwork, gate towers and perhaps interval towers.

To dig the ditch, build the rampart and cut the timber labour was needed. Where did this labour come from? In the fifth century the only available labour had to be drawn from the subsistence farmers who made up virtually the entirety of the population. Presumably this pool of labour was only available seasonally, when their subsistence regime and the agricultural cycle allowed it. Thus the individual or community who instigated the refurbishment of this hillfort had to be able to convince, or have the power to compel, a number of individuals to work on this task (Fulford 2006; Costen 2011, 23). Furthermore, the instigators would have not only had to bring the labour together but also feed and shelter it during the duration of the work. Draught animals, carts and tools would have been needed and locating suitable timber may have been no mean task. The absence of local palynological data means that it is difficult to estimate the scale of local forest cover but the ancient forest of Selwood, some 10 km to the north-east (Costen 2011, 109–112), might have been one source.

This discussion has attempted to illustrate the scale of the economic pull needed to refortify a hillfort. It is not something to be dismissed lightly and at the very least suggests societies on a scale equivalent to that of the Late Iron Age. Of course, it could be argued that Cadbury Castle is the pre-eminent fortified site in south-western Britain during the fifth and sixth century (Alcock 1995; E. Campbell 2007, 118). This is superficially true. However, we lack the extensive excavation of hillforts in the region that would demonstrate whether Cadbury is really unique or not. Cadbury Congresbury in North Somerset contains undoubted evidence for fifth- and sixth-century activity within its ramparts but was dug in such a way that we know next to nothing about its defensive sequence (Rahtz et al. 1993). It too could have been refortified on a like scale. Furthermore, the Wansdyke, a major linear earthwork, may also be of fifth-century date (Fowler 2001; see also Reynolds and Langlands 2006). If so, then this would also be an important statement of the economic power of the local communities in the immediately post-Roman period.

Conclusion

The fifth century can only be seen as an economic collapse if it is viewed from a perspective that emphasises the importance of items that are archaeologically visible. By inverting this perspective and focussing on archaeologically invisible commodities like agricultural surpluses the fifth-century collapse can be viewed quite differently. Furthermore, the disappearance of the tax system removed one of the most significant drivers of production. Once localised power structures became emboldened by the decline of Roman political and military power and authority, the production of a surplus for taxation was no longer necessary. Production could decline but this was spare capacity that was no longer necessary. This in turn drove significant shifts in the way the landscape was organised and structured with a move away from arable agriculture towards a pastoral economy.

The end of Roman Britain was not an economic collapse, but it was a significant economic readjustment. This transformation can be traced in other aspects of life and these are discussed further in the next chapter.

4 | Elite display in the fourth century

Earlier chapters of this book have discussed violence and warfare and economic collapse. These themes have been used as mechanisms to explain the 'end' of Roman Britain but both have been found wanting (Chapters 2 and 3). The intention of this chapter is to introduce a number of transformations in elite display visible across lowland Britain during the fourth century. In the following chapter this discussion is extended to include the fifth and sixth centuries. The focus of these two chapters is on material culture in its widest sense – artefacts, architecture and the altered landscape – and what it may reveal about society in the fourth and fifth to sixth centuries. Together they serve to set the scene for a new model of Roman Britain's end that is presented in Chapter 7.

Archaeology is the study of material culture and since its earliest days the subject has been concerned with wringing significance from the physical remains of the past. The work of the German scholar Kossinna (1928) in the inter-war period argued that recurring groups of objects and styles of material culture indicated ancient political, social and linguistic groups that could be traced into the prehistoric past. This approach was borrowed by Childe (1929, v–vi) and applied to Anglophone scholarship where it became the theoretical basis for understanding the past during the 'culture-history' phase of archaeological thought (Trigger 1989, 148–205).

The interpretation of material culture as a signifier of ethnic identity continues to exert influence over archaeological research (Jones 1997). After the Second World War the idea of primordial ethnic groups, whose existence in the distant past supposedly prefigured modern 'races' and nation states, fell from favour, tainted as it was by its association with the horrors of Nazism. One influential reaction to the traditional view of ancient ethnic identity was Wenskus' (1961) *Stammesbildung und Verfassung*. It suggested that ancient Germanic social and political groups were far more malleable than earlier models had allowed. Early medieval migrations were recast, not as the movements of primordial peoples or tribes, but of noble bands. These bands were responsible for maintaining and propagating a core of tradition (*Traditionskern*) that included origin myths and religious beliefs. The political or military success of individual bands attracted new members who subscribed to the *Traditionskern*. In time this led to the formation of an ethnic unit or a 'people' and this process has become known as 'ethnogenesis' (Callender Murray 2002, 49–59).

The concept of ethnogenesis has been deployed in many discussions of the early Middle Ages and this is a theme to which we will return in Chapter 7 (Wolfram 1988 and 1997; Pohl 1998a and 1998b; Geary 2002). From an archaeological perspective ethnogenesis has played an important part in the interpretation of material culture. No longer are artefacts a passive reflection of ancient identities. Instead they are now seen as active symbols used to fashion, construct and signify belonging (Jones 1997).

For the study of the Roman Empire these theoretical developments have been largely deployed in relation to the early Roman period and the vexed issue of 'Romanisation' (e.g. Freeman 1993; Barrett 1997; Woolf 1998). There is not space to discuss this topic in detail here. However, considerable work has, over the last quarter of a century, been concentrated on the extent to which the adoption of 'Roman' material culture can be seen as indicating the acceptance of, or resistance to, or reinterpretation of, a 'Roman' way of life (e.g. Webster 2001; Mattingly 2011). For the later Roman period there has been less interest in this issue and it is worth noting that works on the end of Roman Britain often simply sidestep indigenous group identity. At best there is a search for surviving 'Roman' traits and at worst indigenous identities are seen as being simply over-written by incoming Germanic groups (e.g. Esmonde-Cleary 1989, 200–203; Higham 1992, 224; Arnold 1996, 30–31; Heather 2009, 302–304). Furthermore, the notion of fixed and inherited ethnic identities still percolates through some work on the late Roman period and the early Middle Ages.

The search for ancient identities is an important theme. Unfortunately, identity is a complex and multifaceted topic (for a recent review see Halsall 2007, 35–62). A family dwelling in a fourth-century villa may have been using that villa to indicate their identity as 'Romans'. An individual cremated and buried in a particular style of pottery in northern Germany may have used that pottery style to indicate their 'Saxon-ness'. Yet they may also have had a series of other identities nested within this over-arching identity. Their belonging to a local community and position within it, their kin group and religious affiliation may have been of equal or greater importance than their 'Roman-ness' or 'Saxon-ness'. Understanding these nested and overlapping plural 'identities' is problematic and in some cases cannot be reconstructed from material culture alone (Jones 1997; Insoll 2007). There is also the danger that we impose identities on the past and interpret patterning within the use and style of material culture to indicate differences that did not exist (e.g. Bowles 2007).

In this chapter and the next the use of the term 'identity' is largely avoided because it is potentially misleading. Instead, it is argued that material culture can be used to construct and display complex worldviews or ideologies (Hodder and Hutso 2003) that may or may not be synonymous with past 'identities'.

Defining elites

Archaeology in historic periods has often been championed as giving voices to the voiceless (e.g. Deetz 1991, 6). History, written by literate elites, records a biased story focussed on a small minority. In contrast archaeology supposedly enables the stories of the majority to be told. There is some truth in this proposition but it is also true that archaeology is best at finding those who are most visible. By definition this is usually the elite. Even in the Roman period, when archaeologically recoverable material culture penetrates far down the settlement hierarchy, the sites which are most often dug remain forts, towns and villas. The smaller, less visible lower-status settlements that were often constructed in timber remain, if not elusive, then relatively difficult to identify (Taylor 2007).

This means that the elites of the late Roman and early medieval period remain those about whom we know most (Millett 1990; Woolf 2000; Halsall 2007; Mattingly 2007). It is also probably fair to say that it was the elites in these periods that controlled and directed society and provided its main characteristics. From the Late Iron Age onwards until the end of the first millennium AD the lot of subsistence cultivators may have been broadly similar and their wider social role restricted (Fowler 2002). This is not to say that they were unimportant but it is the elite and their responses to significant social, economic, political and religious changes that are most easily observed.

Understanding elite groups is not as straightforward as their potential visibility might imply. All too often the term is used loosely without definition and in the field of Mesoamerican archaeology it has been said that '[i]f anything is foreign, elaborate or unexplained it often was/is termed "elite" ' (Chase and Chase 1992, xi). This statement could be equally applicable to the late Roman and early medieval periods. Archaeologists sometimes interpret any seemingly 'rich' find as that of the elite, and historians occasionally divide society into the elite and 'the masses' (Slootjes 2006; see also

Hillner 2007, 380). To avoid this type of difficulty a robust definition is needed.

There are few who would argue with Chase and Chase's definition that the elite were the 'rich, powerful and privileged . . . who run society's institutions' (1992, 3). This is what makes elite groups the focus of study. Analysis of textual sources indicates that the inhabitants of the late Roman Empire in the west were part of a complex, hierarchical and highly stratified society (e.g. van Dam 1985; Mathisen 1993; Sivonen 2006). At its pinnacle stood the emperor, beneath the imperial family were the senatorial orders and senior military officers, lower still were individuals we might term 'local notables', the *curiales* and soldiers. At the bottom of the heap were the *humiliores* (Garnsey 1970): some 'free' peasants and artisans, freed slaves and 'unfree' groups such as *coloni*, *laeti* and slaves. The boundaries between these broad social groups were not hard and fast. Movement between them was difficult but not impossible (Sivonen 2006, 28–29) and within each division were a multiplicity of grades and distinctions. These distinctions were formalised for the senatorial order by grading individuals as *vir perfectissimus, vir clarissimus, vir spectabilis* and *vir illustris* (Jones 1964, 528–529; Näf 1995, 20–21; Mathisen 2001).

In fourth-century Britain these gradations of status were used to indicate the position of individuals such as L. Septimius, a *praeses*, who described himself on an inscription from Cirencester as *vir perfectissimus* (*RIB* 103; *PLRE* I, L. Septimius 3; Birley 2005, 426–427), or the various *vicarii*, one of whom became a bishop in Constantinople (*PLRE* I, Chrysanthus), and senior military officers (*duces* and *comites*) that the *Notitia* (*Not. Dig. Occ.* XXIII.8, XXVIII.12, XXIX.4 and XL.17) tells us held the rank of *vir spectabilis*.

Informal gradations of status are likely to have existed for other social groups below the senatorial order. Displaying social status was thus important as a means of confirming and reinforcing position within the social hierarchy (Sivonen 2006). Nor was this an abstract exercise. Social position was power: the power to intimidate tenants; the power to avoid paying the tax collector; the power to avoid the law and the power to avoid physical punishment if found guilty of wrongdoing (Kelly 2004).

The archaeological identification of elite groups and gradations of status within them is more difficult when based solely on archaeological evidence. Sites such as the extensive late Roman villa at Woodchester (Oxfordshire) (Lysons 1797; Clarke et al. 1982) (Figure 4.1) are likely to be the residences of the elite and groups of late fourth-century or early fifth-century precious objects (such as the Hoxne hoard, Suffolk) (Guest 2005) from Britain

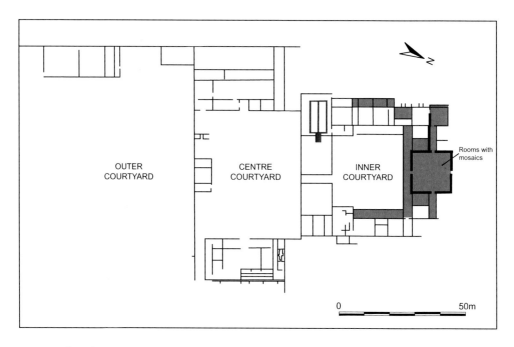

Fig. 4.1 Plan of the Roman villa at Woodchester (after Clarke et al. 1982).

must have belonged to important individuals. However, the interpretation of these finds is not straightforward and the Hoxne hoard provides an apposite case study.

The Hoxne hoard is one of the largest hoards of gold and silver objects from anywhere in the late Roman Empire (Hobbs 2006, Table 73). It contained nearly 600 gold *solidi* and almost 15,000 silver coins that indicate the owner's wealth (Guest 2005) (Figure 4.2). Gold jewellery included bracelets, finger-rings, necklaces and a body chain that was possibly intended as a bridal piece. All of these objects were intended to display wealth and this message was reinforced by the presence of silver spoons, bowls and pepper-pots (Johns 2010) that hint at elaborate dining (Dunbabin 2003). Clearly this was the treasure of a late Roman magnate, perhaps the Aurelius Ursicinus and the Lady Juliana mentioned in inscriptions on some of the objects (Johns 2010, 165–174).

Notwithstanding the size of the hoard, it lacked certain elements (in particular silver plate), which suggests that it represents only a fraction of its owner's wealth (Johns 2010, 204–205). Nevertheless, it is a salutary lesson to contemplate the value of the hoard. Using Hobbs' (2006, 18–24) measure of Equivalent Gold Weight the Hoxne hoard weighs in

Fig. 4.2 The late Roman gold and silver coins from the Hoxne treasure (© Trustees of the British Museum).

at 5,234.8 g of gold and this equates to a little over 16 Roman pounds. By anyone's standards this represents a considerable sum and for the purposes of comparison we might note that it would have been more than enough in the fourth century to qualify as a member of the municipal council in Timgad (Algeria), or to pay the tax bill of the Thebaid (Egypt) (Kelly 2004, 145–150). However, when compared with 1,000–1,500 lbs of gold, the annual income of a middle-ranking senator in the late fourth century (Jones 1964, 554), the Hoxne hoard begins to look parsimonious. Thus the hoard presents something of a contradiction. On the one hand it represents a store of wealth that must have been beyond the imagining of most of late Roman Britain's population, but at the same time it represents a mere fraction of the annual income of the highest echelons of late Roman society.

One conclusion that can be drawn from the Hoxne hoard is that the elite in late Roman Britain were not a homogeneous group. Within the stratum of population that formed the 'elite' there were thinner layers of smaller groups with different agendas who cannot be easily defined (Sivonen 2006, 28). All of these individuals were likely to be rich, powerful, privileged and capable of running their own affairs. However, understanding the context for their activities is critical. The *vicarius*, his subordinate governors and the military commanders were all members of an elite that operated on a pan-provincial scale. In contrast the local notables were undoubtedly powerful in their own local regions but may have been of far less consequence at a provincial, let alone diocesan, level (van Dam 1985, 25–56; Mathisen 1993, 10–13). Thus the 'elite' cannot just be seen as the controlling minority. The elite were not only stratified but, as their interests and allegiances coalesced and split apart, will have been further nested or subdivided.

This conceptualisation of late Roman elites as a heterogeneous series of shifting interests and alliances allows us to move away from characterising fourth-century social dynamics as stark binary oppositions. The networks that linked these groupings are, by analogy with other regions of the empire, likely to have been articulated through the operation of patronage (e.g. Wallace-Hadrill 1989), which shaped late antique social life (Brown 1992). To take one example: the *vicarius* and his subordinate governors were officials appointed by the emperor in an act of patronage. In exchange for this the emperor expected to receive their loyalty and diligence. They may have been deliberately appointed to positions far from their places of origin and this, superficially at least, made such office-holders immune to the intricacies of local politics. Yet they will have been the clients of individuals who were either at court or well situated within the imperial bureaucracy. This will have meant that the patronage of the *vicarius, praeses* and *consulares* will have been an important source of power to the diocesan elite. Equally the success of his tenure depended on the cooperation of the local notables (Slootjes 2006).

The relationship of the elites to the rest of society was probably governed largely by economic relationships. It was the elite groups who will have been the landlords and tax collectors and the foundation of their social position rested on their ability to extract an economic surplus from the lower social orders. The control and use of these surpluses were then deployed to signify and reinforce social standing and power. At the crudest level distinctions had to be drawn between the *humiliores* ('them') and the *honestiores* ('us'). This could be achieved through *paideia*: education, speech and worldview. However, subtler distinctions needed to be signalled in order to display the differences and gradations that defined position within each intricate web of patronage and at each social level.

Material culture and the built environment were critical components used in the construction and maintenance of late Roman social position and economic power. The surpluses deployed by the elite were expended on the built environment and material culture in a sweeping ostentatious display.

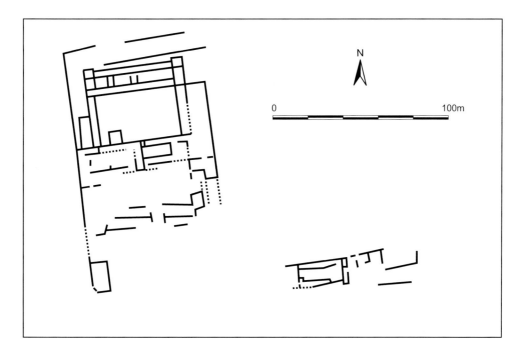

Fig. 4.3 Plan of the Roman villa at Turkdean (after Holbrook 2004, Fig. 4).

Displaying difference in fourth-century Britain

The social divisions and relationships that existed in fourth-century Britain would have been articulated in a variety of settings. To this end material culture and the built environment were critical components used in the construction of a social discourse that framed and highlighted the unequal power relations. By exploring these themes the use and significance of fourth-century elite display can be understood.

The built environment is used here in a broad sense to describe architecture, decoration and landscape features such as burial mounds and field boundaries. Of these categories 'architecture' is the most familiar and provides a convenient starting point. Late Roman Britain was endowed with a great variety of buildings (Haynes and Johnson 1996) ranging from humble timber structures to large stone buildings. Some of the latter, such as the Temple of Sulis-Minerva at Bath (Cunliffe and Davenport 1985), were by the fourth century of some antiquity, while others, such as the latest phases of villas like Turkdean (Gloucestershire) (Holbrook 2004) (Figure 4.3), or the fragments of a major building uncovered at Colchester House (City of

Fig. 4.4 The late Roman bathhouse at Shadwell in East London under excavation. This is one of a limited number of late Roman monumental 'new builds'.(© Pre-Construct Archaeology Ltd).

London) (Sankey 1998) or the bathhouse at Shadwell (East London) (Douglas et al. 2011) were new builds (Figure 4.4). These few examples serve to highlight the great wealth of evidence held in the physical remains of the built environment.

The greatest source of patronage in the Roman Empire was, of course, the emperor and the imperial court. As has been touched upon in Chapter 2 the emperor visited Britain on a number of occasions during the fourth century. However, these visits were so infrequent that there was little need for specific buildings to house the imperial person and court. The hypothesised imperial palace at Eburacum has never been discovered and imperial visits were most likely to have been hosted in buildings such as the fortress *principia* at York, or extant public buildings (Bidwell 2006). Elsewhere imperial patronage existed *in absentia*, channelled through the military and civilian administration and manifested in defensive works like those discussed in an earlier chapter (Chapter 2).

The three senior military positions in late fourth-century Britain, that of the *dux Britanniarum* and the *comes litoris Saxonici* and *Britanniarum*, are all listed in the *Notitia* as being held by individuals ranked as *vir spectabilis* and thus held a significant social position. The *dux Britanniarum* is thought to have been based at York and the *comes litoris*

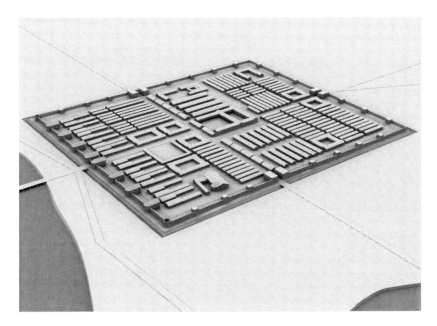

Fig. 4.5 A reconstruction of the legionary fortress at York (© Heritage Technology Ltd).

Saxonici at Richborough. If these locations are correct (and this is uncertain) then the architecture of these sites ought to allow some conclusions to be reached about how power relationships were articulated through the built environment.

At York one of the key locations is surely the *principia*, which lies deeply buried beneath the medieval cathedral. Partially excavated under extremely difficult conditions in the late 1960s and early 1970s (Phillips and Heywood 1995) the *principia* was a large monumental structure, built during the second century as the headquarters building of Legio VI. It appears to have been reconstructed in the early fourth century and stood at the heart of the legionary fortress (Phillips and Heywood 1995, 47; Bidwell 2006, 35). The fortress itself stood on the north bank of the Ouse and was linked to a walled civilian settlement on the opposite bank by a bridge (Ottaway 1993). The riverside wall had received projecting towers in the early fourth century, which served in part to emphasise the riverside approach to the fortress (Roskams 1996, 176).

Anyone approaching the fortress from the south would have passed from the bustle of the civilian settlement, itself ringed by walls, onto the bridge over the river (Figure 4.5). Ahead would have been one of the fortress's four gateways, flanked by projecting towers and probably adorned with

Fig. 4.6 A reconstruction of the legionary fortress and *principia* at York seen from the riverside gate (© Heritage Technology Ltd).

an imposing building inscription recording imperial titles and the unit responsible for the construction (see *RIB* 665) (Figure 4.6). Beyond this a broad street ran past barrack blocks and other structures to the front of the *principia*, where a range of buildings almost enclosed a gravelled courtyard. At the rear of this courtyard was the great *basilica principiorum* (Phillips and Heywood 1995, Fig. 81). This building may well have been adorned by further inscriptions and probably statues of imperial personages, as suggested by the surviving life-size marble head usually identified as Constantine (RCHM 1962, 112).

The arrangement of the fortress and its architectural embellishments were clearly designed to emphasise the separateness of the garrison. The *dux*, if he did receive visitors in the *principia*, was even more separated from the community (Figure 4.7). Access to the fortress and *principia* was probably controlled and this will have highlighted the power and position of the *dux*. Perhaps more importantly the adornment of the buildings with statuary and inscriptions will have further emphasised the links between the *dux* and other high-ranking officers with the emperor and the state. Finally, the weight of history may also have been significant. The fortress at York had seen the death of two emperors and the elevation of their successors

Fig. 4.7 A reconstruction of the interior of the *principia* at York (© Heritage Technology Ltd).

and this is unlikely to have been seen as inconsequential by its inhabitants and the wider community (Ottaway 1993).

Far to the south in Kent the *comes litoris Saxonici* may have been based in the fort at Rutupiae (Richborough). Much of what has been described for York can be adopted for this site. Clearly the fortress walls separated the inhabitants from any inhabitants of the extra-mural settlement known from geophysical survey (Millett and Wilmott 2003). Within the walls the story is less clear. Excavations in the early twentieth century (e.g. Bushe-Fox 1926; Cunliffe 1968) failed to identify many structures and it seems likely that they were perhaps heavily robbed (or of timber) and went unrecognised, although some structural remnants have been identified as a Christian church and baptismal font (P. D. Brown 1971). This may be significant as it suggests a connection between the inhabitants and the new state-favoured religion, evidence of which is rare in Britain (Petts 2003).

Richborough was also probably adorned with inscriptions and other embellishments to link the site with the emperor and the state but little of this evidence survives. Nevertheless, the location controlled the safe harbour of the Wantsum Channel and was the entrance-way to Britain, known to some ancient authors as the 'Rutupine land' (Rivet and Smith 1979, 449). For much of the early Roman period Rutupiae had been the site of a first-century triumphal monument (demolished by the fourth century) and a settlement of uncertain nature (Millett and Wilmott 2003). By the fourth century the fort had taken the place of this earlier monument but the practical and symbolic significance of the place could hardly have been lessened by this. Contact with the *comes* would have thus involved travel to the very edge of the diocese where he sat astride the communications routes with the continent and the imperial court.

The military architecture associated with the probable locations of the *dux* and *comes* ensured that their connections to the imperial core were clear and undeniable. To a certain extent this architecture was replicated at every fortification in late Roman Britain and every local garrison commander would have benefited from a similar visual statement about his power. However, this was only one facet of an army officer's identity. Beyond the walls of the fort, the *dux, comes* or *tribunus* would exercise power in other arenas (Sivonen 2006, 28–29). Most probably these would be in residences indistinguishable from high-status civilian dwellings. Here the commanding officer's house at South Shields on Hadrian's Wall is instructive. Located within the walls of the fort it was, to all intents and purposes, a Mediterranean peristyle house imitating civilian architectural preferences (Hodgson 1996). Further afield, the late Roman villa recently excavated at Ingleby Barwick (Stockton-on-Tees) has been interpreted as the civilian residence of a high-ranking military officer (David Petts *pers. comm.*). The role of these buildings in the articulation of elite power will be investigated further below. However, they serve as a reminder that there were different forms of power that were exercised in different ways.

The other side of the late Roman administration was the civilian hierarchy at the top of which sat the *vicarius* and his subordinate *praeses* and *consulares* (governors). These individuals were responsible for the administration of the diocese including the collection of taxes and dispensing justice. We know the names and careers of few of these late Roman governors of Britain. They appear to have been appointed from outside of the province and some at least were individuals of importance (*PLRE* I, Chrysanthus). As with the military commanders, locating the seats of these governors is problematic. The *vicarius* was based in London along with the *consularis* of Maxima Caesarensis and various financial and administrative staffs. The location of the *consularis* of Valentia is unknown but the three *praesides* of Britannia Prima, Britannia Secunda and Flavia Caesarensis are likely to have been located at Cirencester (where an inscription dedicated by a *praeses* has been found: *RIB* 103), York and Lincoln.

It might be assumed that provincial governors would have had access to buildings specifically constructed for their needs. These structures are, in the late antique world, often described in textual sources as *praetoria*.

However, their archaeological identification is problematic (Lavan 2001) and the search for a standard building plan probably misguided. The structures near Cannon Street Station in London, often referred to as 'the governor's palace', are nothing of the sort, as was demonstrated many years ago (Milne 1996).

Lavan (2001, 50–55) has suggested that the identifiable functions of *praetoria* include the hosting of public ceremonies as well as law courts, prisons, administrative offices and storage space. These, he argues, make such buildings distinguishable from the residences of the powerful. However, Britain during the fourth century saw relatively little investment in public buildings and the situation Lavan describes pertains to a fully developed late antique phenomenon visible in the cities of the Eastern Empire. For these reasons it seems sensible to suggest that in Britain governors probably utilised extant public buildings and residences that were largely indistinguishable from well-appointed private dwellings.

If the governor used a 'private' dwelling and a 'public' building to articulate his power then this would appear to be little more than the replication of how power was articulated at lower levels. The fourth-century 'elite' will have used their residences in their relationships with their clients as well as institutionalised power channelled through organisations such as the local *ordo* (town council). The study of the physical remains of these juxtaposed arenas of elite display and power is illuminating and poses fundamental questions regarding the nature of power in the fourth century (Rogers 2011).

Venta Silurum (Caerwent, South Wales) is, by walled area, one of the smallest *civitas* capitals in Britain. These towns, of which there were twenty or so, were urban settlements that had been structured in the early Roman period along Mediterranean lines as a means of regulating and controlling pre-existing 'tribal' units. At the heart of each stood a forum-basilica where the *ordo* met. At Caerwent excavation of the forum-basilica revealed that it was constructed in the Hadrianic period and heavily refurbished at the end of the third century (Brewer 1993). A large rectangular room was identified as the *curia* (council chamber) and surviving features demonstrated the internal arrangements. At one end of the room was a raised dais for the chief magistrates to sit upon; along the long walls were timber benches for the councillors with the space between floored with mosaic panels. Here was an arrangement depicted on a third-century coin struck in the eastern Mediterranean (Brewer 1993, Fig. 8) and presumably repeated in towns and cities across the empire: a room in which the local notables met to decide the issues of the day.

The forum-basilica functioned as the heart of local administrative power where petitions, legal cases and decisions about building projects (such as the construction of town walls) and taxation were made. As such it represents the architectural framework for institutionalised local power. To this end they were highly decorated with imported marbles and other types of stone and adorned with statues and inscriptions. Many of these recorded the construction of buildings and dedicated the works to the reigning emperor (e.g. *RIB* 3,123) or recorded the influence of a local benefactor (e.g. *RIB* 311). Virtually none of these adornments relate to the late Roman period when the epigraphic habit in Britain had, in any case, declined and there is nothing to compare with the late antique statues of magistrates and governors from sites like Aphrodisias (Turkey) (Smith 1999). Nevertheless, they would have lent an air of antiquity and prestige to many of these structures in the late third and early fourth century.

At Caerwent the main hall was used for metalworking from *c.*300 until *c.*360, when it was demolished. However, other rooms within the complex continued to be used and at least one room received a hypocaust and mosaic as late as *c.*370 (Dr Peter Guest *pers. comm.*). Similar patterns of use, alteration and demolition occur at a number of other Romano-British urban centres. London (Marsden 1987, 67; Brigham 1990b, 77; Dunwoodie 2004, 34), Cirencester (Holbrook 1998, 121), Lincoln (Jones and Gilmour 1980) and Silchester (Fulford and Timby 2000, 576–581). Traditionally, these types of activities have been seen as reflecting the decline of the urban centres (Rogers 2005, 31), and occasionally the evidence for metalworking is linked to the increased role of the state in urban life (Fulford and Timby 2000, 579). This interpretation connects the decline of local power to the increased autocracy exercised by the state and its agents during the fourth century. However, a wider consideration of these sites suggests that such a narrative is too simplistic.

In London it has been suggested that part of the basilica, including an elaborately decorated apse, continued in use during the fourth century and there are hints of similar practices at Cirencester (Holbrook 1998, 121), Lincoln (Jones and Gilmour 1980, 68; Jones 1994, Fig. 5), Silchester (Fulford and Timby 2000, 580–581) and other sites (Rogers 2005, Fig. 1; 2011). If parts of these structures were retained then it is possible that they continued, despite the noisome industrial activities, to function as places of power. However, the scale of activity was clearly very different. This has traditionally been seen as reflecting either a decline in the wealth of individual urban communities or a decline in public-spirited euergetism. In contrast, Rogers (2005, 2011) has argued that the reuse of major public buildings for metalworking was a conscious and positive social choice that referenced earlier Iron Age practices and symbolic narratives. Either interpretation is possible, but it is also possible that the diminishing or transformed significance of these public structures in the fourth century reflects the growing importance of other forms of elite display and arenas of power.

Villas

The transformations that can be seen in public buildings in towns are balanced by a growth in private residences. The modern terminology for these private dwellings is divided between so-called townhouses and rural villas for which the ancient terms *domus* and *villae* might be appropriate labels (Bowes 2010, 17). This discussion concentrates on the late Roman villas of Britain but is equally applicable to the townhouses of London (e.g. Brigham, Nielsen and Bluer 2006; Birbeck and Schuster 2009) (Figure 4.8), Cirencester (McWhirr 1986) or Verulamium (Frere 1972). These private houses, which were often lavishly decorated, have long been seen as the dwelling places of the late antique elite. From Woodchester in Gloucestershire (Lysons 1797) (Figure 4.1) to the Villa di Casale (Piazza Armerina, Sicily) (Gentili 1999) these buildings appear to speak of shared values displayed in an ostentatious fashion.

In Britain the most recent survey of villas has suggested that perhaps 1,500 sites deserve the appellation (Scott 1994). Whatever the true figure (and many villas surely remain undiscovered) it seems clear that sites like Bignor (West Sussex), Turkdean (Holbrook 2004), Dewlish (Dorset) (Putnam 2007, 97–106), Beadlam (North Yorkshire) (Neal 1996) or Wharram Grange (East Yorkshire) (Rahtz, Hayfield and Bateman 1986) are rare and their prominence in the archaeological literature is largely due to their visibility in field survey. Work on other forms of rural settlement shows that villas were the dwelling place of a true minority (Taylor 2007). This group's rural dwellings were constructed in a number of varying forms. Much effort has been expended in discussing these sites as 'farms' and many of them certainly had agricultural overtones (Branigan and Miles 1988). However, it is difficult to see these sites primarily as economically productive units. Even allowing for the bias in excavation towards the higher-status parts of the structures it seems improbable that they functioned simply as farm estates. Their primary function appears to have been as centres for display and conspicuous consumption and it is these themes that are investigated here.

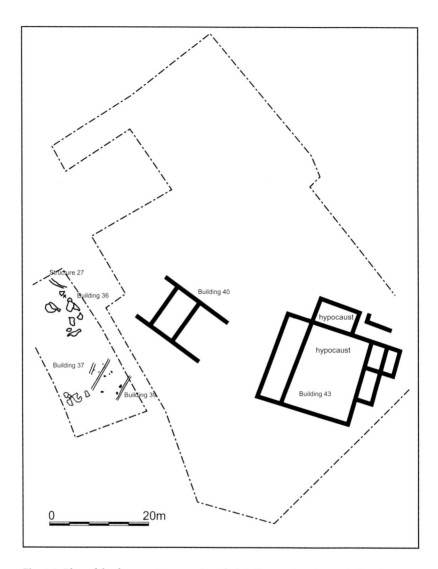

Fig. 4.8 Plan of the fragmentary remains of a late Roman townhouse in London (after Brigham with Nielsen and Bluer 2006, Fig. 46).

Various schemes have been developed for classifying villas and their architectural form. They range from the simple (Collingwood 1930, 113–134) to the fantastically complex (Smith 1997) and, as is the case with all such typologies, they all represent a conflation of reality that normalises and smooths over the differences between each individual site (Figures 4.9, 4.10 and 4.11). A corridor house may appear to be a simple structure, but examples were embellished with rooms, bath suites and other accoutrements

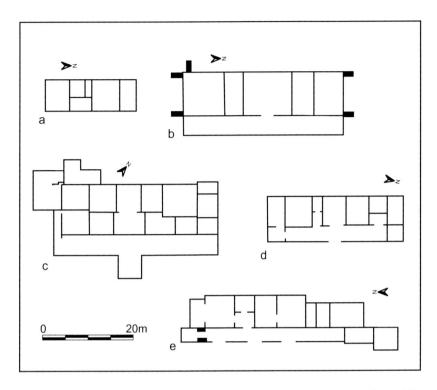

Fig. 4.9 Cottage and corridor villas: a) Park Street, Hertfordshire, b) Feltwell, Norfolk, c) Ashstead, Surrey d) Sparsholt, Hampshire, e) Pitney, Somerset (after Perring 2002, Fig. 24).

to diversify what, at first sight, appears to be a straightforward plan. This uniqueness means that each individual site functions as an interpretation of an ideal. The language of the late Roman villa was the same from Sicily to Yorkshire, but the script differed from region to region and the words from site to site.

The easiest way to view these late Roman villas is to compare them with non-elite buildings. The majority of the non-elite structures were rectangular buildings constructed from timber or stone. The most common form is relatively small and sometimes divided into two or three rooms internally with a communal hearth (e.g. Leech 1981; Leary 1994). Other types of non-elite building include the so-called aisled halls, which tend to be larger timber buildings divided into three aisles by two rows of roof-supporting posts running longitudinally. These often contain hearths and may have been used in some cases as communal dwellings.

In contrast, the various types of villa show strikingly different layouts. A corridor villa would, as the name suggests, be fronted by the corridor,

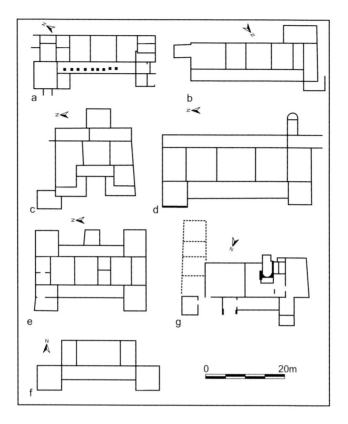

Fig. 4.10 Winged corridor villas: a) Lockleys Wood, Hertfordshire,
b) Cobham Park, Kent, c) Ely, Glamorgan d) Walton-on-the-Hill,
Surrey, e) Hambledon, South Buckinghamshire, f) Great
Staughton, Cambridgeshire, g) Barnsley Park, Gloucestershire
(after Perring 2002, Fig. 25).

which was often colonnaded and adorned with a mosaic floor (Perring 2002,
157–158). Off of this corridor were rooms with various functions. Some will
have served as reception rooms, others as bedrooms and living quarters and
more still as kitchen areas and bathing suites (Perring 2002). Courtyard
villas represent an increase in complexity. A site such as Dinnington (Somerset) had three ranges laid out around a courtyard (Gaffney and Gater
2002). These were fronted by a colonnade which granted access to rooms of
varying functions and decoration. Finally, there are more complex sites like
Chedworth (Gloucestershire) (National Trust 2010), Turkdean (Holbrook
2004), Bradford on Avon (Somerset) (Corney 2002, 2003) and Cotterstock
(East Northamptonshire) (Upex 2001). At Chedworth a completely enclosed
courtyard fronted another 'courtyard area' flanked by a range of buildings

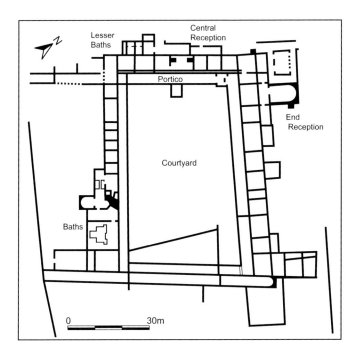

Fig. 4.11 Courtyard villa at Bignor (after Perring 2002, Fig. 28).

on one side. Turkdean was formed of a complex arranged around three courtyards set one behind the other. Bradford on Avon and Cotterstock had a similar arrangement but with the two courtyards laid out side by side. The interpretation of the function of these structures is, of course, debatable and not all of the buildings at these sites and other similar villas functioned as elite residences. At some sites more than one 'family unit' may have lived together in separate but architecturally linked complexes (Smith 1997). However, these observations do not detract from the main point: the complexity of the groundplans of these sites indicates a very different ordering and structuring of space to that seen on non-elite sites (Perring 2002, 155–156).

The structuring of space at many of these sites would seem, at least in part, to be about creating permeable spaces to which access was also constrained, or controlled (Perring 2002, 154–157). Turkdean would offer an extreme example where each courtyard might (depending on the location of entrance-ways at this largely unexcavated site) represent increasing privacy. Even if this were not the case the juxtaposition of rooms with smaller entrance vestibules at a number of sites (Smith 1997, 72) suggests the presence of private rooms. Such rooms contrast with other spaces within

Fig. 4.12 Simple geometric mosaic under excavation at
Butleigh villa (© Absolute Archaeology).

these buildings that are best interpreted as grand reception and dining
rooms.

Complementing the architecture of these buildings were decorative
embellishments and other trappings (Hales 2003; Swift 2009). The mosaic
floors are the most obvious of these decorative elements. The recent publication of a corpus of British mosaics has done much to shed light on
this body of data (e.g. Neal and Cosh 2006). There are clearly a number of
regional styles but the scenes depicted on many mosaics betray a sophisticated understanding of Classical culture and history (Scott 2000, 142). The
depiction of Dido and Aeneas on a mosaic from Low Ham (Somerset), or
the abduction of Europa by Zeus disguised as a bull at Lullingstone (Kent),
or the Orpheus mosaic from Woodchester (Gloucestershire) all support the
'idea of an educated pagan aristocracy who defined themselves through
Romanitas' (Scott 2000, 143) (Figure 4.12).

The mosaics were only a part of a wider array of decorative elements
deployed in these buildings. The walls were adorned with painted plaster.
This rarely survives to be reconstructed in detail but figural schemes and

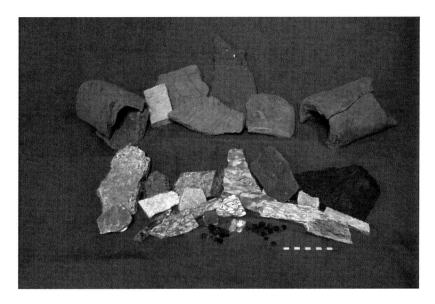

Fig. 4.13 A collection of ceramic building material, wall plaster and imported marbles. Materials such as these were used extensively in late Roman Britain to embellish high-status buildings. However, they were often reused from earlier Roman structures (© Pre-Construct Archaeology Ltd).

panels imitating marble, richly coloured with paints derived from rare and imported minerals, served to decorate the walls of these rooms (Ling 1991). Internally, these rooms would have been furnished with a variety of materials. Stone tables made from polished marbles (Figure 4.13) or Kimmeridge shale sometimes survive to be recovered archaeologically. Equally impressive furniture made from polished wood, inlaid with cedar, ebony and bone or ivory, is likely but rarely survives (Croom 2007) (Figures 4.14 and 4.15). On this furniture silver (Guggisberg and Kaufmann-Heinimann 2003) and glass vessels (Isings 1957) would have been displayed and the rooms lit by glass lamps and metal candlesticks (Eckardt 2002).

This expenditure on decoration and furnishing served as a means of articulating social discourse. Traditionally, these buildings have been seen as reflecting the increased concentration of power in the hands of the elite during the later Roman period and this is a perspective subscribed to here. Nevertheless, this is not the whole story (Bowes 2010). The use of villa architecture represents a multifaceted response to a number of complementary and conflicting demands.

The first of these demands has already been touched upon. The effort expended on villas and their embellishment was in part driven by a desire to

Fig. 4.14 A detail of a piece of Roman furniture found preserved in a well at Hayton (East Yorkshire). Note the use of bone inlay for decorative effect (reproduced by the kind permission of Martin Millett, Durham University and The Hayton Project).

Fig. 4.15 A reconstruction of the Hayton cupboard (drawn by Mark Faulkner and reproduced by the kind permission of Martin Millett, Durham University and The Hayton Project. © The Hayton Project).

Fig. 4.16 Reconstruction drawing of the apsidal dining room at Lullingstone
(© English Heritage).

display the identity of the buildings' inhabitant(s) (Hales 2003). The mosaics and furnishing signified that the owner was a member of the empire-wide educated civilian elite, a body of individuals who shared a culture, heritage and value system (Wickham 2005, 157; Halsall 2007, 66–67). It demonstrated his commitment to *paideia* (Brown 1992, 34–41) and to *otium* (leisure) (Matthews 1975, 1–12; Halsall 2007, 78).

This commitment to the ideals of *Romanitas* was designed to impress a group of varied audiences. One key group were the villa owners' peers. For Bowes (2010, 95–98) these dwellings were 'machines for competition' designed to enhance the owners' status and demonstrate their belonging to the late antique elite. By adopting this form of display the villa owner reinforced and enhanced his social position, even if that position was newly won or fictive. The messages encoded in the buildings and their furnishings were read at banquets and dinner parties to which the *dominus* (lord) had invited his friends, neighbours and supposed equals in power and *paideia* (Ellis 1991, 119) (Figure 4.16). However, *paideia* was, as Brown (1992, 39) notes, also a means of 'expressing social distance'. It separated the participants from those who were perceived as being uneducated and boorish (Brown 1992, 45) and it was to these classes that the architecture of the villa was also orientated.

Social relations and power in the Roman world were articulated through patronage (Wallace-Hadrill 1989) and this remained as true of the late empire as it was of the early imperial period. The social changes that accompanied the creation of the Dominate ensured, in Brown's (1971, 37) words, that 'all attempts to secure protection and redress of grievances had to pass through a great man – a *patronus*' (see also Cameron 1993, 121). The villa became the stage upon which the patron played his part (Ellis 1997), interceding on behalf of his clients with the state and its agents, manipulating the legal process (Harries 1999, 79) and subverting the bureaucracy (Kelly 2004). This intercession was driven by motives that were far from altruistic. In exchange for the protection of the *dominus* the clients undertook reciprocal obligations. What those obligations were remain opaque but we might expect that control of aspects of the individuals' lives, their loyalty and a portion of their economic surplus all passed to the patron.

The importance of the *patronus/dominus* was carefully emphasised through the use of the villa architecture and its decoration. One of the most obvious elements in this scheme was the apse, which proliferated in late antique domestic settings. Designed as a focus to exalt whatever it enclosed (Ellis 1991, 119–120) the apse was used for a variety of functions (Bowes 2010, 54–60) but it occurred in dining contexts (sometimes as *triclinia*), as in the so-called 'summer' and 'winter' dining rooms at Dewlish (Cosh 2001, 197), and in audience chambers (Ellis 1991, 120). In the context of dining the apse may have served as the setting for a *stibadium*, or semi-circular couch (Ellis 1995, 169; 1997, 41) and in an audience hall as the seat of the *dominus* where the elite were able to 'emulate the solemnity and transcendent remoteness of emperors' (Scott 1997, 54).

The mosaics also had a part to play in this drama. Ellis (1991, 126) has argued that the common choice of heroic scenes was driven in part by a desire to associate the patron with the *virtus* of the hero. The choice of themes such as Bellerophon slaying the chimera or Orpheus charming the beasts perhaps reflected the desire of the *dominus* to be associated with similar virtues: good overcoming evil, victory over adversity and order from chaos (Ellis 1991, 126; Scott 2000, 134).

The villa (or townhouse) created a backdrop against which the late antique patron could behave as an emperor (Ellis 1991, 126–127). It was here that the decisions could be made, rents raised or lowered, patronage extended or withdrawn. The buildings, often located in dominant topographical positions, were a part of the rural landscape but their architecture separated their inhabitants from their surroundings. Even accepting, as Smith (1997) and Reece (1997, 475) have argued, that some villa sites were the dwelling places of mixed communities, it is clear that those communities were divided. To the inhabitant of a small rural settlement, like Bradley Hill (Leech 1981) (Figure 2.17) or Shiptonthorpe (East Yorkshire) (Millett, Allason-Jones and Barclay 2006), entering a villa like Dinnington (Prof. T. King *pers. comm.*), or Wharram Grange (Rahtz et al. 1986), would have been equivalent to stepping into another world, which was dominated by colour, light and the trappings of power. The ostentatious display separated the elite from their lower-status clients and defined their role in society. This distinction was further emphasised by the ways in which the elite dressed (below). However, the built environment did not stop at the walls of the villas and the power of the elite can be found manifesting itself in humbler ways in the wider landscape.

Landscape divisions

The final component of the built environment that needs to be considered here are 'landscape divisions'. From at least the Bronze Age, communities in Britain had been formalising the landscape using various types of territorial markers. These markers, such as ditched field systems and boundary stones, were created to regulate farming practices as well as define grazing rights and land ownership (Figure 4.17). The Roman Conquest rarely appears to have led to substantial changes to the extant Iron Age field systems. Nevertheless, it seems clear that the imposition of Roman power will have changed attitudes towards land ownership and control. Land that had previously been an inalienable resource exploited by a long tradition of communal use had its nature transformed. It could now be defined as property that could now be bought and sold, rented and taxed in ways that would have been inconceivable in late prehistoric Britain. Ownership now depended not on long-standing custom but on the demonstrable ownership of title, which was written down using the formulas of Roman law (Turner 1956; Tomlin 1996).

The impact of these changes is difficult to assess on the ground and it would be wrong to suggest that every realignment of field boundaries in Roman Britain was the result of elite control imposing itself on the landscape. However, it is noticeable that in some regions wholesale shifts in how the agricultural landscape was divided occurred during the Roman period.

Fig. 4.17 A Roman ditch under excavation. Features such as these
are commonly encountered in commercial excavations. They range
in size from modest ditches (like this example) to significant
boundaries. Ditched field and property boundaries served to divide
and control the Romano-British landscape (© Pre-Construct
Archaeology Ltd).

In south-eastern Somerset arguments have been advanced suggesting that
field systems were realigned over quite large areas in the third century
(Davey 2005). Similar patterns are visible at Monkston Park (near Milton
Keynes) where field boundaries and enclosures were reorganised at the end
of the second century and adjusted in the late third century (Bull and Davis
2006). At Haddon (near Peterborough) early Roman field systems had silted
up by the third century and were replaced by new landscape divisions and
trackways that continued with modifications until the end of the Roman
period (Hinman 2003, 47–57). It seems reasonable to suggest that in at least
some cases this phenomenon was the product of elite-imposed change. The
impact of such changes would have been greater control over the rural
population and economic production.

This emphasis on the definition of boundaries is repeated in other contexts. At the Romano-British settlement of Catsgore a number of buildings aligned along a street were set within ditched enclosures in the early Roman period (Leech 1982, Fig. 5). These property boundaries were maintained until the fourth century when they were replaced with stone walls. The long-term maintenance of property boundaries within settlements occurs at other sites, like Higham Ferrers (Lawrence and Smith 2009, Figs. 4.10 and 4.32). This appears to be indicative of the continuous use of particular plots of land within settlements and suggests that methods existed to pass them from generation to generation, or owner to owner and tenant to tenant over hundreds of years. This suggests that there was relatively tight control of how property was used and maintained within nucleated settlements.

It is impossible to demonstrate that in any of the cases discussed above the excavated field and property boundaries were the product of the redesign or ownership of parcels of land by the elite. However, it would be naive to suggest that in a hierarchical society the elite were not a factor in organising the landscape. In some cases they must have been and the implications of this are significant. For the lower orders in society – the slaves, unfree and free peasants – the very geography of their existence and relationship with the land they worked was created by their social 'betters'. The juxtaposition of their dwellings and fields with those of the landlord, his peers and contemporary (e.g. villas, mausolea, temples) and 'ancient' monuments (e.g. barrows, hillforts) in the landscape were all part of this narrative of power.

Dress accessories

Dress and bodily adornment formed one of the most effective tools deployed by the late Roman elite to emphasise their status and position. However, the evidence for the clothing of individuals is limited (Croom 2000). Art-historical depictions of high-status individuals are not uncommon and include sources as diverse as the diptych of Stilicho (Kampen 2009, 133–137), the mosaics at the Piazza Armerina (Pace 1955) and the wall paintings at Lullingstone (Meates 1987). Yet the extent to which items like these reflect reality or regional diversity remains a subject for debate. Furthermore, the bias of many of these depictions towards the elite makes comparisons with the rest of society difficult. The everyday dress of peasants was a subject rarely thought suitable for artistic depiction or literary comment.

The archaeological evidence for clothing is even more problematic. In the north-western provinces ground conditions are rarely conducive to the preservation of organic materials like textiles. In Anglo-Saxon contexts, funerary rituals that included the burial of large metal objects (such as brooches and belt buckles) have helped to preserve fragments of cloth, which were mineralised by corrosion deposits (Walton Rogers 2007, 49). However, few Roman burials have such items and therefore fragments of clothing rarely survive. Even on waterlogged sites items of clothing are rare and often poorly preserved (Wild 1973, 2002). Nevertheless, this fragmentary evidence, which includes gilded leather shoe fragments from London (PCA 2009, 34), Chinese silk from York (MacGregor 1976, 14–15) and cloth dyed with 'Tyrian' purple from near Dorchester (Dorset) (Walton Rogers 2002), offers tantalising hints of how the elite sought to use their clothes to emphasise their status.

Dress accessories, by which personal adornments, jewellery and other items are meant, provide a better insight into elite display during the late Roman period because they survive in greater numbers. Fashioned from metal, bone, antler, glass and workable stones these items are often encountered during archaeological excavations and discovered by chance. Many objects can be shown to have been exclusive to one gender or another, although these associations should not blind us to the exceptions, such as a male buried at Catterick with a rich assemblage of female artefacts (P. Wilson 2002, 176–178; Cool 2011, 300–301), that prove the general rule.

The importance of dress accessories in emphasising the power and status of the elite is thrown into sharp relief by late Roman hoards of gold and silver. These often contain dress accessories and personal adornments and good examples are the large groups of objects from the Hoxne hoard (Johns 2010), or Thetford treasure (Norfolk) (Johns and Potter 1983) and smaller assemblages, such as the collection of finger-rings from near Silchester (Fulford et al. 1989).

These precious metal hoards are composed of gold and silver items that seem most appropriate to female dress. Hoxne, for instance, included nineteen gold bracelets (Figure 4.18), some of which had ownership inscriptions naming females (Johns 2010, 35–54). There was also an extremely rare gold body chain, plausibly interpreted as a wedding piece and of a size suitable for a young woman (Johns 2010, 23–39). Other items include necklaces and finger-rings, which are less gender specific. The smaller Thetford hoard also includes a range of gold bracelets, necklaces and finger-rings, as well as ear-rings and a belt buckle (Johns and Potter 1983).

Fig. 4.18 Late Roman gold bracelets from the Hoxne treasure (© Trustees of the British Museum).

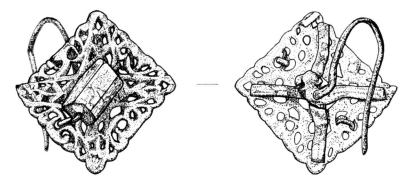

Fig. 4.19 Late Roman gold ear-ring with glass bead (© Pre-Construct Archaeology Ltd).

The apparent emphasis on female adornment in these hoards (Johns 2010, 56) is noteworthy because objects that ought to be associated with high-status males are known. These include gold and silver crossbow brooches, examples of which are known from Segontium (Hemp 1918), the Moray Firth (Kent and Painter 1977, No. 22) and a number of Portable Antiquities Scheme finds (e.g. LEIC-9C94D1). Belt sets in precious metals might also be expected. However, with the exception of the Thetford example with its religious iconography, such items are rare. A few fragments from silver belt sets are known (Cool 2010, 288–290) and Hoxne includes a fragment from what may be a silver scabbard fitting (Johns 2010, 145–147).

The picture that can be drawn from the precious metal finds is thus far from straightforward. The emphasis on female objects (Figures 4.19 and 4.20) in hoards may reflect the importance of jewellery as a store of female personal wealth. The significance of personal adornments as components of dowries and bride wealth is known from a variety of historic and cross-cultural situations. However, it seems clear that a female member of the

Fig. 4.20 Fragment of a late Roman gold and bead necklace (© Pre-Construct Archaeology Ltd).

elite would be marked out, at least some of the time, by her dress accessories and the explicit display of wealth that they entailed (Stout 1994). The male personal adornments appear less frequently but it seems likely that finger-rings and perhaps neck chains were important components in masculine elite display. The use of finger-rings by both males and females is particularly significant as these were often set with stones or other devices that display particular symbolic motifs. Occasionally, as with rings displaying Chi-Rho symbols (Johns 1996a, 66–67), these motifs are suggestive that the wearer subscribed to particular ideological viewpoints. Finally, it ought to be noted that these finger-rings would have been used for sealing documents and thus hint at the control of the written word and the delegation of power.

Objects of gold and silver are rare finds outside of hoards. There are many stray finds, usually recovered by metal detectorists, but these lack any archaeological context. Finds such as the gold finger-ring from the bedding for a mosaic in the villa at Littlecote (Wiltshire) (Walters 1985) or the gold ring on the finger of a young woman from Old Ford are rare (Brown et al. in press) (Figures 4.21 and Figures 4.22). The unfortunate fact that gold and silver objects are all too often divorced from the locations of their use is problematic, although not unexpected given the nature of archaeological evidence.

The Old Ford burial is significant for another reason. The individual was buried with not only a gold finger-ring but also a collection of copper-alloy bracelets. Such items are extremely common and include a number of types of bracelet (Swift 2000), hairpins (Crummy 1983, 19–25; Cool 1990), earrings (Allason-Jones 1989), finger-rings (Henig 1978; Guiraud 1989), belt fittings (Hawkes and Dunning 1961) and the like. Items such as these bring this discussion back to a point made at the beginning of this chapter: how do we define the elite and the gradations within that group archaeologically?

In general terms the items of personal adornment manufactured from base metals and their alloys can be seen as similar in nature to the precious metal objects discussed above. The great majority of late Roman personal adornments recovered from sites, be they urban or rural, are appropriate as items of female dress and this is a conclusion supported by the evidence of

Fig. 4.21 Close up of a female inhumation from Old Ford buried wearing a copper-alloy bracelet and a gold finger-ring (Figure 4.22) (© Pre-Construct Archaeology Ltd).

gravegoods (Philpott 1991). Further consideration of the cemetery evidence indicates that the presence of personal adornments in the grave depends on aspects of the identity of the deceased. Thus, there is evidence that personal adornments are more common in the graves of young women than children or more mature females (Cool 2011, 310). Of course, these dimly discernible patterns may not be reflective of how the objects were used and perceived in everyday life, but the phenomenon demonstrates that their use was structured and context dependent.

The wearing of these personal adornments presumably signalled a variety of information about the wearer's 'identity', including perhaps age, gender, social status and, in some cases, 'ethnic' origins (Swift 2000). An individual wearing, for instance, a cogwheel bracelet (Figure 4.23) in northern Gaul would almost certainly be identified as a woman of Romano-British origin (Swift 2010, 252) and the presence of the bracelet may also have conveyed some additional information. The use of these items allowed gradations of status to be advertised. The elite material culture exemplified by the Hoxne and Thetford hoards would be the pinnacle of this social stratification but there seems no reason to believe that the base metal bracelets and rings, many of which were manufactured from copper-alloy and (when polished) would

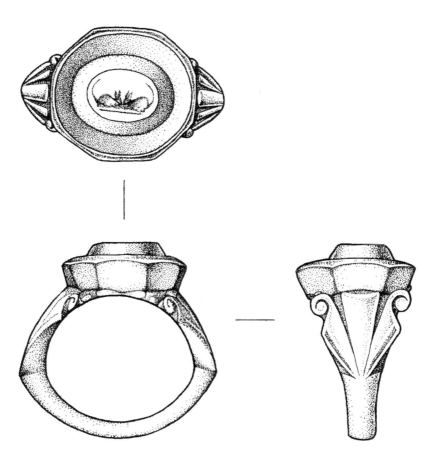

Fig. 4.22 Gold keeled finger-ring of late Roman type with an intaglio showing two mice. From a late Roman burial at Old Ford (© Pre-Construct Archaeology Ltd).

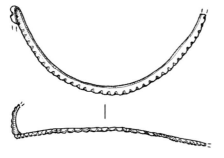

Fig. 4.23 A copper-alloy 'cogwheel' type bracelet. This form of jewellery was distinctive to Britain in the late Roman period (© Pre-Construct Archaeology Ltd).

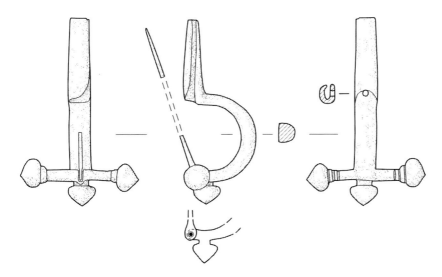

Fig. 4.24 A copper-alloy crossbow brooch from Norfolk. Brooches like these were symbols of status and 'military' identity (© Pre-Construct Archaeology Ltd).

have superficially resembled gold, were not signifying lower gradations of social status (Swift 2003).

The production of base metal versions of objects known in precious metals is a phenomenon replicated in items that might be seen as predominantly male adornments. The most obvious of these are the crossbow brooches that sometimes occur in gold and silver (Swift 2000, Fig. 15), but are more commonly found in gilt copper-alloy or simply copper-alloy. Various typological schemes have been suggested to classify these objects (e.g. Keller 1971). However, local production in different regions often makes these schemes difficult to apply in practice. They are important because a number of art-historical sources show high-ranking members of the late Roman army wearing this type of object (Janes 1996). Archaeological finds confirm a close correlation between the crossbow brooch and members of the late Roman state (Swift 2000, 24). This suggests that the wearing of such a brooch was a significant statement about the wearer's position and affiliations within society.

The crossbow brooch (Figure 4.24) was joined by ostentatious belts as symbols of the wearer's association with the Roman state (Sommer 1984a). The belt fittings are found across the Western Roman Empire in a wide variety of styles described in a number of typological schemes (Böhme 1974; Sommer 1984a; Swift 2000, 185–204). In Britain these objects were first classified by Hawkes and Dunning (1961), who divided them into Types I

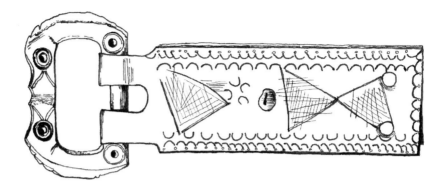

Fig. 4.25 A belt fitting of Hawkes and Dunning Type 1B (after Hawkes and Dunning 1961, Fig. 15).

Fig. 4.26 A belt fitting of Hawkes and Dunning Type 1A (after Hawkes and Dunning 1961, Fig. 15).

to VI. They recognised that some of their material, such as the elaborately chip-carved examples, was of continental origin and that their Types I and II were insular developments. Types IA and IB were small buckles decorated with confronted dolphins or horses' heads respectively and attached to a narrow decorated belt plate (Figures 4.25 and 4.26). Types IIA and IIB were defined as having a buckle in the form of confronted dolphins but with openwork plate. Hawkes and Dunning concluded by interpreting the belt fittings as evidence of the movement and settlement of barbarian units serving in the Roman army. This interpretation is no longer held to be valid and these objects are now simply seen as one form of personal adornment in late Roman society (Hills 1979; Leahy 2007b).

Many of the belt sets, particularly elaborately chip-carved examples of Hawkes and Dunning's (1961) Type IV (Sommer 1984a, Sorte 1 Form E), are well known from the continental *limes* (Böhme 1974, 90; Swift 2000, Fig. 246) and are likely to have been viewed as 'military' dress fittings – they are depicted as such in the *Notitia Dignitatum* (Böhme 1974, 97) (Figure 4.27). However, the associations of belts of Hawkes and Dunning's (1961)

Fig. 4.27 A chip-carved belt set from a late fourth-century burial in London. Elaborate items like these are uncommon in Britain but appear in some numbers along the continental *limes*. They are likely to indicate that the wearer had a close connection with the late Roman army or state (© Museum of London).

Types I, IIA and IIB are less clear-cut. They are rare in the north, a fact noted in Chapter 2 above (Coulston 2010, 52–56), and many come from seemingly civilian sites in the south with particular concentrations in the lower Severn Valley. Interpreting this pattern is difficult. Laycock (2008) has argued from finds recorded by the Portable Antiquities Scheme that these belt fittings are the accoutrements of late and sub-Roman militias. He develops this hypothesis by suggesting that certain sub-types can be associated with particular *civitates* or tribal units. This is an interesting suggestion but seeing these objects as markers of military and ethnic affiliation seems too simplistic.

What seems clear is that the Hawkes and Dunning Type I and II belt fittings developed from a fashion for wearing decorated belts that denoted service to the late Roman state (Speidel 2006) and was particularly prevalent within the late Roman army. That these belts originally marked status, rank and membership of a social group (the 'army') seems certain (Sommer 1984a). The Type I and II belt fittings may have appropriated these connotations within the late Roman elite in particular regions. Here it is interesting to note that this is one form of object that occurs in late fourth-century contexts and also appears in early Anglo-Saxon graves (White 1988). Further work is needed to refine their date and chronology but these belt fittings are one of the clearest phenomena associated with the end of Roman Britain and it is interesting to note the close connection between identifiable items of male dress and 'military' associations (Swift 2000, 230).

The final component of dress that needs to be considered here pertains to how the body was styled (Eckardt and Crummy 2008). Strap ends in the form of nail cleaners are associated with some of the Hawkes and Dunning (1961) belt fittings. They are a reminder that toilet instruments – tweezers, spoon probes and other items – are an extremely common and

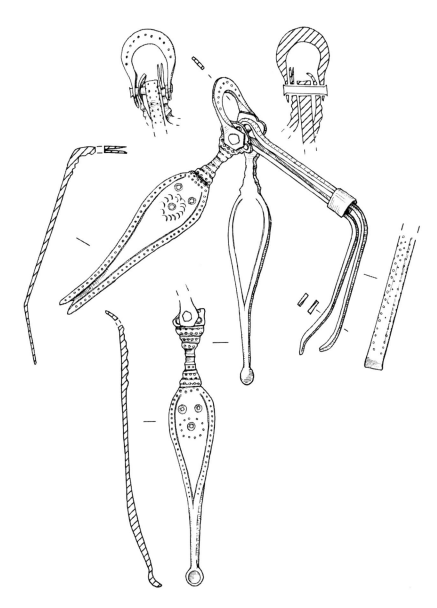

Fig. 4.28 Romano-British copper-alloy toilet set comprising a nail cleaner, spoon probe and tweezers (© Pre-Construct Archaeology Ltd).

important component in many Romano-British finds assemblages (Eckardt and Crummy 2008) (Figure 4.28). Items such as cosmetic palettes and hair-combs, the latter of which seem more common in the late Roman period (Chapter 3), further reinforce the significance of styling the body. The use of cosmetics, perfumes and the cutting and styling of hair may all have served as a means of defining and highlighting status alongside dress accessories like jewellery and belt fittings.

This brief discussion of dress accessories has demonstrated that the appearance of the late Roman elite was constructed and modified through the use of clothing, jewellery and cosmetics. This was undertaken to emphasise particular aspects of an individual's wealth, status or identity and served, like the architecture of villas and townhouses, to emphasise the elite's position within society.

Taken together the dress accessories, built environment and the social discourse that can be extrapolated from this evidence enable the construction of a fourth-century worldview. Rank, status and difference were critical and marked by a range of symbols that indicate membership of different groups. Crucial to elite display was the explicit advertising of an individual's *paideia* and occasionally their relationship with the Roman state. This in turn shows a society that was mainly concerned with demonstrating acceptance of a civilian ideology. Whether this acceptance was the product of a genuine aversion to more martial symbols of display, or the restricted opportunities to adopt such symbols, remains a moot point. However, in the following century it is the accoutrements of the soldier and warrior that come to dominate elite display and it is the development and construction of this alternative worldview that is explored in the next chapter.

5 | Elite display in the fifth and sixth centuries

The study of fourth-century material culture and architecture has demon-strated that late Roman elites in Britain used these media to display a specifically civilian and sometimes state-centric ideology. Running con-currently with this message were other important narratives. In particular there is clear evidence that forms of artefacts, dress accessories and the conceptualisation of built space were designed to indicate, maintain and reinforce hierarchies of power within provincial society. By the end of the fourth century there are also indications that this elite concern with advertising their *paideia* was beginning to shift as arguably 'para-military' dress accessories began to make their appearance felt. The intention of this chapter is to develop this theme and to examine how the elites of fifth- and early sixth-century Britain used material culture to promote a new ideological outlook based on symbols of individual and martial power.

The relationship between material culture and ethnic identity is an impor-tant theme in most discussions of the fifth and sixth centuries. This chapter is less concerned with trying to find 'Britons' and 'Saxons' than attempting to assess how the societies of early post-Roman Britain conceptualised their position in the world. As noted in the previous chapter, to this end the ter-minology of 'elite display' is retained in preference to 'identity' in order to avoid becoming embroiled at this point in complex and intractable debates (Pitts 2007). However, the significant differences between the west and east of Britain, which are often cast in 'ethnic' terms, remain a very real facet of the period. In fact this broad division of Britain is used to structure this chapter.

Elite display in the west of Britain during the fifth and sixth centuries

The late Roman diocese of Britannia stretched from Hadrian's Wall in the north to the south coast and included most of what is today England and Wales. In the fifth century the superficial coherence of this geographical area was shattered by the end of Roman political and administrative systems (Esmonde-Cleary 1989). From the early to mid fifth century onwards south-eastern Britain and much of the eastern seaboard fell within what is usually termed the orbit of Germanic cultural influence and settlement (Yorke 1990). However, Wales, south-western Britain, much of the Midlands and northern Britain, including areas beyond Rome's writ between Hadrian's Wall and the Forth–Clyde line, remained free of this influence (Alcock 1971; K. Dark 2000; Pearce 2004; White 2007). It is an area that is often described using terms such as 'the Celtic West' (Evans 1990), 'British', or occasionally – in a misappropriation of the term – as 'late antique' (Bowles 2007). Here the more neutral term 'western Britain' is used as a convenient shorthand to describe this region, even though it includes substantial tracts of land in the north.

Traditionally, the inhabitants of western Britain were defined in opposition to the newly arrived 'Anglo-Saxons'. They were simply the 'Other'; the 'sub-Roman' residue of the Romano-British population and a Celtic dead end (Hodgkin 1935, 182) on the progressive and teleological march towards the Anglo-Saxon achievement (Hodges 1989). Over recent decades these narratives have been criticised and revised, meaning that this region is now the focus of considerable academic research. It is tempting to draw together the disparate fragments of evidence from the west and use them to formulate a model of, for want of a better term, 'Dark Age' society (Alcock 1971; K. Dark 2000). Such a model can then be studied in opposition to fourth-century Britain and early Anglo-Saxon England. Continuities or discontinuities, similarities and differences can then be studied. Unfortunately this approach merely produces a simulacrum, an ersatz view of the period that denies its temporal and spatial heterogeneity.

The study of the fifth and sixth centuries has always been coloured by the historical end of Roman Britain, which marks the start of the period. However, it is becoming increasingly clear that the archaeological end of Roman Britain is not as clearly defined. In some places it may have occurred before *c*.400 and in others after. Finally, there are archaeological events that happen contemporaneously with the importation of pottery from the Eastern Roman, or Byzantine, Empire in the late fifth and early sixth century (E. Campbell 2007) (Figure 5.1). Any attempt to pick and choose specific elements from within this medley to create an overarching whole is doomed to failure. Instead, it is argued here that the study of the fifth century requires a more nuanced approach. We might study a period of time running from 350/370 until 430/470 and another period that begins in 430/470 and runs until 550/600.

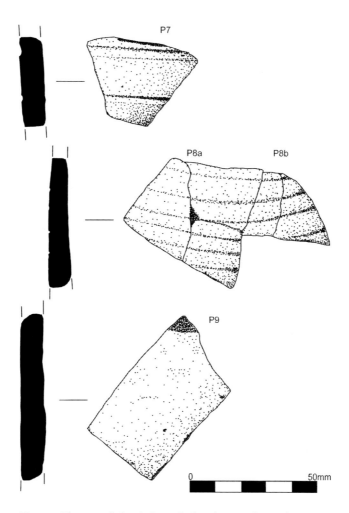

Fig. 5.1 These small sherds from the beach at Mothecombe are evidence of long-distance exchange with the eastern Mediterranean in the fifth and sixth centuries AD (drawn by Maria Duggan © Sam Turner).

The period from 350/370 until 430/470 might be characterised by so-called 'squatting activity'. This is a pejorative term often used to describe the change in function apparent in many late Roman buildings in their latest phases (Lewit 2003). These changes were often messy and industrial in nature; usually they overlie and damage 'high-status' embellishments such as mosaic floors (Figure 5.2). To early excavators this 'decline in standards' was the product of so-called 'squatters' taking over abandoned elite residences. The period from 430/470 to 550/600 encompasses a time in the west when hillfort refortification and hilltop settlements appear to have been the

Fig. 5.2 A paved floor overlying an earlier mosaic floor at the Butleigh villa. Such changes in use are often characteristic of so-called squatter occupation (© Absolute Archaeology).

dominant form of elite settlement. In many respects this period is based solely on the presence of imported pottery from the Eastern Roman Empire, which allows sites to be identified and dated. The dating largely depends on the presence of fragments of Phocaean and African Red Slipped Ware (PRSW and ARSW) (Fulford 1989; E. Campbell 2007, 14–26).

The historical sources for the fifth century in Britain are few in number and highly contentious, with there being little consensus about the authors' dates, aims or locations. However, they might be taken as broadly supporting the chronological subdivisions outlined above. The earliest insular sources are the works of St Patrick, who is usually considered to have been writing in the early to mid fifth century (Dumville 1993). In his *Confessio* and *Epistola* he describes how his father was a decurion (*Epistola* 10) and a deacon and that he grew up on an estate (*villula*) close to a settlement bearing a Romano-British name (*Confessio* 1). Then there is the *Life of St Germanus*, composed in Gaul during the late fifth century by Constantius, which purports to describe a functioning Romano-British community at a location usually equated with St Albans. Great interpretative edifices about the continuity of Romano-British life have been erected on these flimsy foundations, but these should be treated with scepticism (Thompson 1984; Wood 1984). Instead, we can conclude that some members of the elite in early fifth-century Britain still set some store by Roman power structures. Even so, Patrick's letter (*Epistola*) to the slave-raiding Coroticus demonstrates that new avenues of power were available and being utilised.

At some point in the early sixth century a British cleric Gildas, produced in accomplished Latin (Lapidge 1984; Breeze 2010) a vitriolic tract lambasting contemporary rulers and charting the moral decline of society (*De Excidio*). As the preface to this work he penned a historical introduction that has been the subject of countless interpretations and speculations that frustratingly produce no, or very little, academic consensus (Lapidge and Dumville 1984; Woolf 2003; Halsall 2007, 519–526; George 2009). What is significant is that Gildas describes an appeal to 'Aëtius, thrice consul' (usually equated with the *Magister Militum per Gallias* of the same name and thus dated to *c.*446) by the Britons (*De Excidio* 20.1). This suggests that two generations after the formal 'end' of Roman Britain some communities within Britain still believed that they could benefit from Roman intervention. The failure of this appeal led to an individual described as *superbus* and *infaustus tyrannus* (proud and ill-fated tyrant) recruiting Saxon mercenaries (*De Excidio* 23.1 and 23.4). Some of the language used to describe this alliance, such as *annonae*, *epimenia* and *hospites* (*De Excidio* 23.5), was used as late Roman technical terms for military supplies (Winterbottom 1978, 150; Wolfram 1998, 243) and may suggest a pattern similar to the settling of federate troops within other parts of the fifth-century Western Empire (Welch 1993). Finally, when the Saxons rebelled they were opposed by an indigenous leader with a thoroughly Roman name – Ambrosius Aurelianus – whose parents 'had worn the purple' (*De Excidio* 25.3).

When Gildas describes the contemporary early sixth-century situation the world appears to be a different place. There are tyrannical rulers described as 'kings' and 'judges'; a recent attempt to see these as the respective overlords of the upland zone and a sub-Roman lowland zone (Woolf 2003, 366), while interesting, seems too specific a reading to fit the rhetorical tone of Gildas' work. The tyrants (Snyder 1998) bear Latinised Celtic names (*De Excidio* 28–36) and are depicted as surrounded by militarised retinues whom they 'exalt to the stars' (*De Excidio* 27). Towns are long-abandoned and the Roman frontier works were becoming mythologised (*De Excidio* 15–19 and 24.3). Fortified hilltops appear as refuges (*De Excidio* 25.1) and this reference has been linked to the archaeologically attested reoccupation of hillforts (Dark 1993; see also Higham 1994). Of course, the contrast between Gildas' view of the immediate past and the contemporary situation was engineered. It fitted the moral purpose of the work. Nevertheless, it is difficult to believe that this moral purpose could be achieved if it could be shown to be untrue by the lived experiences of its readers. This suggests that elements of Gildas' account can be accepted as a reflection of contemporary reality.

This picture, drawn as it is from the few useful historical sources that have a bearing on the insular situation, seems to show a fifth-century world in which Rome was still significant and a later situation where Roman power had become replaced by local and largely indigenous networks of power. What follows is an attempt to show that these broad outlines can also be discerned in archaeological evidence from the fifth- and sixth-century west.

350/370–430/470

In the discussion of elite display during the fourth century considerable emphasis was laid on the use of architecture to frame, channel and control power. All too often it is assumed that these buildings were abandoned at the end of the fourth century and rapidly decayed. This view is erroneous. Buildings can be deliberately demolished and any demolition events need to be dated and explained. Unless demolition occurs many buildings will stand as ruins for decades if not hundreds of years. At Ravenglass (Cumbria) the walls of a Roman military bathhouse stand to roof height, the excavations of the temple at Pagans Hill (Somerset) showed that the roof collapse sealed green-glazed pottery of high medieval character (Rahtz 1951) and at any number of sites Roman structures can be shown to have been robbed out as late as the twelfth century (e.g. Woodward, Davies and Graham 1993, 99–101; Howell 2000). Thus in the fifth century the landscape will have been studded with Romano-British structures. Each of those structures will have its own individual biography of use and abandonment. Some sites will have been abandoned at the end of the fourth century. Others may have continued in use, but with a change of function. Some may have been abandoned and reused, either as dwellings or for other purposes.

The headquarters building of the legionary fortress at York has already been introduced (above) (Phillips and Heywood 1995). During the fourth century it was a focus of military and imperial power and a stage upon which the military elite of late Roman Britain could demonstrate their influence and importance. The building's demise was marked by a scree of tumbled roofing slates, rubble and collapsed stone columns. The date of this event is unknown. However, the rubble sealed layers that in turn overlay the latest 'Roman' flooring. These layers contained noisome waste like animal bones and industrial residues such as metalworking slag and appeared to have accumulated episodically. A few sherds of pottery suggested that this activity could be dated to the ninth century. However, other commentators have argued that these sherds are intrusive and that these 'squatter' deposits could be dated to the fifth century. This early date receives some support from a radiocarbon date on one of the animal bones (Phillips and Heywood 1995, 189).

So what do these messy activities within the former headquarters building of Legio VI tell us about life in the fifth century? Interestingly, the animal bones mainly comprised the remnants of juvenile pigs and sheep and this led to these deposits being dubbed 'the small pig horizon' (Carver 1994, 4). The animal bone specialist, clearly under the influence of the meta-narrative of decline and economic collapse (Chapter 3), interpreted the assemblage as the residues of a community eking out an existence among the ruins of the Roman fortress (Rackham 1995, 554–555). However, other interpretations seem more plausible. Pigs are animals that, unlike sheep, cattle or chickens, are kept solely for their meat. Furthermore, the consumption of juvenile (and thus underweight) pigs is a remarkably inefficient economic strategy. This suggests that the consumption of these animals ought to be seen as reflecting choice and power (Gerrard 2007b).

A group of individuals clearly had the power to consume juvenile pigs and animals on an apparently episodic basis within the basilica. This suggests that they had some control over the local agricultural production. More importantly, the choice of young pigs can be seen as reflecting Roman dietary preference. Pork consumption has long been associated with high-status and highly 'Romanised' sites and this is particularly true of suckling pigs (Gerrard 2007b). Interestingly, at Wroxeter pig consumption also increased during the fifth century (Hammon 2011). What may have been happening within the *principia* during the fifth century was a process whereby the local elite highlighted their power and importance by feasting within the echoing building on a seasonal basis. Their choice of this site and the menu was probably influenced by its connotations of Roman power (Gerrard 2007b).

The evidence from the sites of other late Roman fortifications is less clear-cut. Birdoswald (on Hadrian's Wall) provides one of the best examples. A late Roman granary was demolished and replaced by a timber hall-like building, which was associated with some high-status objects (Wilmott 1997, 201–231). This suggests that the walls of the fort were now sheltering a settlement where new forms of communal living were being exercised. Elsewhere on the Wall, a gateway at South Shields (Bidwell and Speak 1994, 45) was blocked at the end of the fourth century and new defensive ditches dug. To the south, in the hinterland of the old frontier, the fort at Piercebridge (Cool and Mason 2008, 308–309) has also produced a series of post-Roman defensive ditches as well as some post-Roman metalwork and an imported fifth-century amphora.

The continued use of some forts in the Hadrian's Wall area and the recovery of stray finds of fifth- and sixth-century material culture from other sites is a fascinating phenomenon. Dark (1992) interpreted it in quasi-historical terms as a sub-Roman re-defence of the frontier. What seems more likely is that each fort and the remnants of its garrison and attendant community reinvented themselves in the fifth century as tiny polities. The tradition of Roman military power and individual unit identities may have allowed these to function in concert with each other and exert control over a local hinterland (Collins 2012).

It seems impossible to avoid the conclusion that towns had ceased to exist by, or during, the fifth century. This is not to say that they ceased to be occupied, because there is evidence from a number of sites for fifth-century activity, but this was 'life in towns' as opposed to 'town life' (Wacher 1990, 408). However, it seems certain that the old urban centres continued to be significant places. The upstanding remains of their walls and buildings would have ensured this, as would their geographical positions on key road junctions. Furthermore, few lost their Roman names completely and this suggests that knowledge of these sites survived to become Old English toponyms (Table 5.1).

Of fifth-century life in towns we have few and faint traces. At some sites occupation probably continued, although its status remains elusive. The pits and other features at Silchester taken as indicating an extended post-Roman sequence do little to elucidate the character of activity (Fulford, Clarke and Eckardt 2006, 278–280). At Wroxeter serious arguments have been presented suggesting that the city continued to be an urban centre into the fifth century and later (Barker et al. 1997). This may well be the case, although questions have been raised regarding the interpretation of the archaeological sequence (Dr Alan Lane *pers. comm.*). Equally possible is that the baths-basilica site may have been a single, arguably elite residence (Halsall 2007, 359). More common are slight hints of activity. Typically these might include a length of ditch, a pit or burials dug through a Roman building.

Burials within the walls of Roman towns were probably not confined to the early fifth century and are part of a phenomenon that continued

Table 5.1 *Towns and their names*

Roman name	Intermediate name	Current name
Londinium	Lundonia	London
Lindum Colonia	Lindocolinae	Lincoln
Glevum	Gleawcaester	Gloucester
Eboracum	Eoforwic/Jorvik	York
Durovernum Cantiacorum	Cantwaraburg/Dorwiccaestre	Canterbury
Caesaromagus	Celmeresfort	Chelmsford
Verulamium	Werlame-ceaster	St Albans
Venta Icenorum	Castra	Caister-by-Norwich
Noviomagus Reginorum	Cisseceastre	Chichester
Calleva Atrebatum	Silcestre/Cilcestre	Silchester
Venta Belgarum	Vintancaestir	Winchester
Corinium Dobunnorum	Cirrenceastre/Cair Ceri	Cirencester
Durnovaria	Dornwaraceaster	Dorchester
Isca Dumnoniorum	Exanceaster	Exeter
Ratae Coritanorum	Ligera Ceaster	Leicester
Viroconium Cornoviorum	Rochecestre	Wroxeter
Venta Silurum	Cair Guent	Caerwent
Moridunum	Caerfyddin	Carmarthen
Petuaria	Burg	Brough-on-Humber
Isurium Brigantum	Aldeburg	Aldborough

After Millett 1990, Table 9.1 with amendments.

into the sixth century (Bidwell 1979, 110; Jones 1994). They represent a significant ideological shift because prior to the fifth century the burial of adults within the walls of urban centres appears to have been prohibited. This changing relationship with the dead can be linked to the use of extra-mural cemeteries. The role of such inhumation cemeteries was well established in the fourth century and there is a tendency to use these burial grounds as a proxy for the vitality of the urban population. However, the possibility that urban burial grounds were used by surrounding rural populations needs to be considered. They are of importance here because it seems likely that burial at a number of sites continued into the fifth century. Extra-mural cemeteries at Poundbury, Dorchester (Farwell and Molleson 1993), Cirencester (McWhirr et al. 1982), London (Barber and Bowsher 2000), Winchester (Hampshire) (Booth et al. 2010), St Albans (Hertfordshire) (Biddle and Kjølbye-Biddle 2001) and other sites may have all continued to attract burials after *c.*400. The extent of this phenomenon is unquantifiable given the failure to routinely radiocarbon date inhumation burials from 'Roman' urban cemeteries (Hills and O'Connell 2009, 1,106).

Poundbury adds another layer of complexity to the importance of late Roman cemeteries in the fifth century. The date at which burial ceased is unknown but in the fifth century the cemetery also became a settlement site (Sparey-Green 1987, 1996 and 2004). A number of irregular enclosures contained small structures with irregular plans and the fourth-century mausolea were also utilised during this phase. The earliest buildings contained Romano-British material culture but later structures seem to have been associated with few artefacts: a few iron tools and bone combs. However, grain-drying features yielded fifth- and sixth-century radiocarbon dates. The status of Poundbury remains problematic. Is it, as Esmonde-Cleary (1989, 178–179) would have us believe, a rare example of a non-elite fifth-century settlement? Or should it be linked to the continued significance of the burial ground? The importance of mausolea and cemeteries as Christian foci in the fifth century provides an interesting parallel and the movement of the living into the land of the dead represents a significant change. However, at present the Poundbury sequence remains unparalleled at any other urban cemetery site.

Finally, there are villas. These pinnacles of fourth-century elite display often contain evidence in their final phases for 'messy' activities labelled as 'squatting'. At the villa of Lufton (Somerset) these activities included digging a metalworking furnace into the floor of a room, subdividing other rooms with partition walls and leaving deposits of animal bone and oyster shells strewn over mosaic floors (Hayward 1952 and 1972). At Dinnington recent excavations have shown how a room within a late Roman villa had been converted into a granary (Prof. A. King *pers. comm.*). Dewlish saw a 'decline in living standards' (Putnam 2007) and at Chedworth a grain-drier was inserted into a room (George 1999). These examples could be expanded but demonstrate the range of activities and features that might be associated with so-called 'squatter activity'.

The interpretation of squatter activity is a matter for debate. Esmonde-Cleary (1989, 134) has wisely cautioned against it being seen as a purely fifth-century phenomenon and this is a useful reminder that it is a process that begins in the fourth century. Some argue that 'squatting' represents a very real decline in standards. However, others argue that it is a part of a wider late antique pattern of the reorganisation of social space within domestic settings (Ellis 1988; Petts 1997; Ripoll and Arce 2000). In a development of this argument Lewit (2003, 268) has suggested that 'squatter activity' represents the changed priorities of the late antique elite. Instead of investing resources in an increasingly irrelevant Roman style domestic architecture the elite chose to direct their wealth at new social arenas like the church.

The continued significance of Roman places suggests that such sites continued to be of relevance to the early fifth-century elite. That the semi-ruinous forts, townscapes and heavily modified villas continued to fulfil a role is paralleled by supposedly 'late Roman' material culture. The continued use of Romano-British pottery has been touched on in Chapter 3, but other types of late Roman material culture continued in use into the fifth century. It is this material that forms the focus of the following discussion.

The review of fourth-century 'elite' material culture in the preceding chapter paid particular attention to late antique silver plate. As we have seen, one of the functions of this plate was to display the owner's wealth. There has been a tendency to see this plate as belonging solely to the fourth century and ignoring its potential role in the fifth century. The discovery of the Patching hoard (West Sussex) should change this (White et al. 1999). The hoard was composed of gold and silver objects of British and continental manufacture, with the coins suggesting a date of deposition later than *c.*461. The hoard also included fragments of hacksilver derived from late Roman silver vessels and spoons. Other fifth-century precious metal hoards, such as Hoxne, Coleraine and Traprain, also include silver vessels, or hacksilver derived from vessels, and a piece of silver offcut from Longbury Bank is thought to be derived from a silver bowl (Campbell and Lane 1993, 30). Finds such as these clearly demonstrate that some of the late antique silver that circulated in Roman Britain continued to do so into the fifth century (see Chapter 3).

Accepting the existence of silver plate in the fifth century allows us to consider its significance. In the fourth century it seems clear that such plate functioned as prestige items, used on the table and displayed to illustrate an individual's wealth. It seems equally clear that some of these items were exchanged between members of the elite as gifts. These gifts may have been tightly structured between patrons and clients as largesse (Leader-Newby 2004; Guest 2005, 24–26). The presence of hacksilver in various fifth-century hoards indicates that this plate was still valued as a form of wealth and may also indicate the continuing role of largesse and gift-giving. Here the fact that the silver in the Patching hoard comes to almost one Roman pound may be significant, although this should not blind us to the possibility that silver plate continued to be used as tableware.

The continued use of silver plate might be associated with the probable production of bronze and pewter vessels hypothesised in Chapter 3. This evidence and the recent recognition that spoons with chip-carved handle junctions may be diagnostic of the late fourth and fifth centuries (Crummy 2006, Table 7) might suggest that some 'Roman' dining practices continued.

Unfortunately, there are very few meaningful reports on ecofactual evidence that relate to this period. The assemblages of faunal remains from York and Wroxeter (above) are exceptions that prove the rule. This makes testing any changes in dietary preference problematic. Nevertheless, the consumption of high-status foodstuffs, like the suckling pigs from York (Gerrard 2007b) or the game species at Wroxeter (Hammon 2011), might be an expected part of elite display during the early fifth century.

Personal adornment also formed an important part of the elite displaying their social status. As has been discussed, the wearing of gold finger-rings seems to have been relatively common among the fourth-century elite. Some 'late Roman' types, such as so-called 'Brancaster rings' (Johns 1996a, 53–55), may have continued to be worn and used in the fifth century and there are simple gold rings, like those from Patching (White et al. 1999, 310–311), which appear to continue this tradition. Finds such as the gold ear-ring from Birdoswald (Wilmott 1997, 217) suggest that this is another type of personal adornment that may have continued in use.

Other items of 'late Roman' personal adornment can also be seen as continuing into the fifth century. Work on penannular brooches has demonstrated the existence of a late fourth- and fifth-century type known as a 'Fowler D7' (Snape 1992) and Cool (2000a) has shown that glass beads, which are difficult to fit into the standard typology (Guido 1978), and bone bracelets often occur in fifth-century deposits. Crummy (2006, 129) has also recently argued that the terminal dates of *c*.400 for many late Roman categories of 'small find', such as multiple motif bracelets, is likely to be too early, and bone bracelets (Cool 2000a, 49) have been suggested to be a late fourth- or fifth-century phenomenon. These studies may, by extension, imply that many types of Romano-British object could have been used during the fifth century.

Both the Patching (White et al. 1999, 312) and Traprain (Curle 1932, No. 147) hoards contain fragments of silver belt sets and these serve as a useful reminder that examples in precious metal must have existed. Copper-alloy belt sets with zoomorphic decoration are known in a great variety of forms (see Chapter 3) and Cool's (2010, 286–287) recent review of their dating has highlighted a number of examples that come from fifth-century contexts. They are also found in a number of Anglo-Saxon graves and this would seem to confirm their use during the fifth century (White 1988).

Some of the belt fittings are typologically and functionally associated with decorated strap ends. Occasionally these are in the form of nail cleaners suggesting a continued interest in personal grooming (Eckardt and Crummy

2006, 2008). The importance of 'styling the body' seems to be confirmed by finds of bone combs from sites like Bath (Cunliffe and Davenport 1985, Fig. 79), Winchester (Cool 2010, 272–274), Cirencester (McWhirr 1986, Fig. 84.228), York (Ottaway 1993, Pl. 70) and London (Riddler 1988). Many of these combs are decorated with zoomorphic designs similar to those displayed by the belt sets. Nevertheless, the use of hairpins clearly declined and this suggests changes in the way female hair was being displayed.

Elite display from *c*.350/370 to *c*.430/470 cannot be easily characterised as representing a society that was the same as that which had existed in the early fourth century. There were, for instance, substantial changes in the way elite architecture was being used. Similarly, there may have been strong continuities in the use of personal adornment. However, these continuities were not clear-cut. The end of the fourth and the beginning of the fifth century was not a time of fossilised reproduction of the society of the preceding decades. Instead it was dynamic, undergoing change, developing and innovating from the fourth-century situation.

430/470–550/600

Defining when the 'latest Roman' activity ended and when the new early medieval order characterised by hillfort reoccupation began is far from straightforward. First, it is conceivable that stratigraphic sequences at a number of sites could represent activity for a generation or two after the loss of the latest Roman coinage. This, assuming that low-value coins fell out of circulation between 410 and 430, suggests a date of between 450 and 470. On many sites it would appear inconceivable that the stratigraphy can be stretched any further. Secondly, Anglo-Saxon material culture becomes more common during the later fifth century. Therefore, if those build-ings continued to be occupied one might expect their inhabitants to have some access to the new 'Germanic' style material culture. The absence of such material could be explained by ethnic antipathy, but the presence of Germanic glass and metalwork on some western sites (E. Campbell 2007) makes such an explanation hard to credit. Finally, there is the appearance of pottery imported from the eastern Mediterranean. The date of the impor-tation of this material is largely reliant on its association with Phocaean or African Red Slipped Ware (ARSW and PRSW). The forms present would suggest that this importation did not start until *c*.450/475 at the earliest (E. Campbell 2007, 14–18 and 26). The combination of these factors would argue that the latest 'Roman' activity ended during the middle third of the fifth century.

Fig. 5.3 A fifth- or sixth-century building at Mothecombe under excavation. Sites of this date are rare and structural remains are even less common (© Sam Turner).

The imported pottery is thinly scattered through Cornwall and the lands bordering the Bristol Channel, and it is also present in Wales and Ireland (E. Campbell 2007). The bulk of the material has been recovered from Tintagel, which would appear to have been the major importation site for these pottery vessels and other cargo (Barrowman, Batey and Morris 2007). In Cornwall and Devon the pottery can also be found on inland sites, such as Trethurgy (Cornwall) (Quinnell 2004) and at a number of coastal sites like Bantham (Devon) (Griffith 1986; Griffith and Reed 1998; Reed, Bidwell and Allan 2011) and Mothecombe (Devon) (Fox 1961; Turner and Gerrard 2004) (Figure 5.3). In Somerset and Wales the pottery seems concentrated on hilltop and hillfort sites like Cadbury Congresbury (Rahtz et al. 1993), Cadbury Castle (Alcock 1995) and Dinas Powys (Alcock 1963). However, there are far more sites where fifth- and sixth-century occupation are suspected than proven (e.g. Burrow 1981). To what extent this distribution is an artefact of archaeological exploration remains debatable. There are some unenclosed lowland sites, like Longbury Bank (Campbell and Lane 1993), Mothecombe (Turner and Roskams 2005) and possibly Carhampton (Somerset) (Webster 2000, 80), that suggest the situation is more complex. Nevertheless, the association of the imported pottery with hilltop settlements is a pattern that has proved stubbornly persistent for more than half a century.

The reoccupation of hillforts superficially represents a significant break with preceding settlement traditions. In the late Roman period hillforts were occasionally used as the sites of Romano-Celtic temples and a number contain evidence of late Roman settlement (Burrow 1981). However, it is

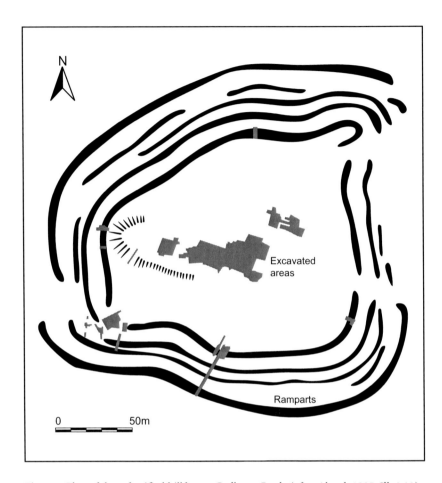

Fig. 5.4 Plan of the refortified hillfort at Cadbury Castle (after Alcock 1995, Ill. 1.11).

extremely rare for that settlement activity to be of high status. Late Roman villas within hillfort ramparts are almost unheard of and the oft-quoted example from Ham Hill (Somerset) is an exception that proves the rule (Beattie and Pythian-Adams 1913; Sharples et al. 2012, 39). When these sites began to be reoccupied remains uncertain. At Cadbury Congresbury there was a phase of activity that appeared to be associated with Romano-British material culture and pre-dated the importation of the Mediterranean pottery (Rahtz et al. 1993, 214–216). The situation at Cadbury Castle is less clear-cut (Figure 5.4). Romano-British building materials, pottery and a coin of Honorius from the rampart indicate a date no earlier than the beginning of the fifth century. However, imported pottery sherds from the rampart may demonstrate that this material was being used on site prior to the refortification. Finally, Crickley Hill has two phases of 'early post-Roman activity' neither of which were associated with imported pottery (Jarrett 1999). They take their *terminus post quem* from some late Roman pottery and a zoomorphic belt buckle of Hawkes and Dunning's (1961) Type IV (Jarrett 2011). This suggests that some overlap should be entertained between the latest 'Roman' and earliest 'medieval' activity.

The discussion in Chapter 3 of hillfort reoccupation and its economic significance has highlighted the main reasons for considering these sites to be those of the late fifth- and sixth-century western elite. However, what prompted the elite to choose these locations? The traditional interpretation would be to see the reoccupation of these sites as primarily defensive in nature. There seems no reason to doubt that defence may well have been a factor. However, these ancient defended sites must have been significant landscape features (Tilley 1994) and it would be foolish to suppose that hillforts in the fifth century were not 'special places' imbued with history, stories and legends (Williams 1998). What that mythology may have been remains impossible to reconstruct. We might suppose that they may have been remembered as pre-Roman power centres, or as the centres of resistance to Rome, or even, as the presence of late Roman temples within the ramparts of some sites might suggest, as religious sites associated with supernatural beings. The reoccupation of the hillforts may have been intended to appropriate some of the symbolic meaning of these places.

One other factor that needs to be considered is that a hilltop site represents the physical separation of its inhabitants from the surrounding hinterland. Cadbury Castle provides an illuminating case study. It is a substantial freestanding hill surrounded by three and in some places four Iron Age ramparts (Figure 5.5). The innermost rampart was refurbished in the fifth century and it encloses the hilltop. Interestingly, the summit of the hill stands proud of the inner defences and is visible. Any inhabitants of the hillfort, their buildings, fires and cooking smoke would be visible for many miles. Yet to access that hillfort an ascent up the deep and steep holloways that lead to the two gateways in the inner rampart would have been required. Cadbury Congresbury presents a similar situation (Figure 5.6): a high and long isolated hilltop, ringed with defences and seemingly accessed through a single entrance at its eastern end. Interestingly, the summit was divided into two in the fifth century by a smaller earthwork, which had the effect of creating an enceinte at the hillfort's higher and western end. Similar zoning of activity is also apparent at Crickley Hill (Jarrett 2011, Fig. 2). Physical separation would seem to be a significant requirement of these communities.

If the inhabitants of these hillforts sought separation from society then the separation was an ideological statement, rather than a physical need.

Fig. 5.5 Cadbury Castle. The Iron Age defences (refurbished in the fifth century) are obscured by the trees but note how the summit is visible (© Clare Randall).

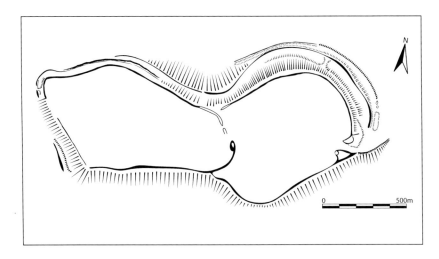

Fig. 5.6 Plan of Cadbury Congresbury (after Rahtz et al. 1993, Fig. 6).

Both Cadbury Castle and Cadbury Congresbury are located on important communications routes. The former site inherited many of the Roman town of Ilchester's geographical advantages (Alcock 1995, 1–5). Major prehistoric and Roman routeways met near the town and, like Cadbury Castle, Ilchester can also be seen as occupying a 'liminal' location between the dry land to the south and the wetter land of the Somerset Levels to the north. Cadbury Congresbury is similarly located between the high and dry land of the Mendips and the flatter coastal plain. The presence of a navigable river giving access to the Bristol Channel is also significant and suggests that the inhabitants of this type of site took care to situate themselves within easy reach of the inter-regional communications networks.

Describing how a hillfort sits in its landscape is a relatively straightforward task. Understanding how the elite functioned within the ramparts is much more problematic. At Cadbury Castle less than 10 per cent of the interior has been excavated but plans of a number of fifth- and sixth-century buildings have been suggested. At the highest point of the hill a large rectangular timber hall, a post-built roundhouse and perhaps another small rectangular structure have been suggested (Alcock 1995, 30–42). The evidence for these structures derives from rock-cut features. However, the length of occupation on the hilltop (which was first used during the Neolithic) means that the summit was riddled with pits, postholes and gullies (Alcock 1995, Ill. 2.2). Determining building plans from this mass of inter-cutting features was far from easy and some of the building plans are more than a little suspect (Figure 5.7). The post-built roundhouse 'L3' seems particularly dubious (Alcock 1995, Ill. 2.20), although the large rectangular timber hall can probably be accepted given its association with sherds of imported pottery (Alcock 1995, Ill. 2.24).

The excavation of Dinas Powys (Alcock 1963, Fig. 6) also revealed a clear 'hall' structure and this also lends credence to the Cadbury example. However, Cadbury Congresbury revealed nothing comparable (Rahtz et al. 1993). Excavation was focussed on the western end of the hilltop, behind a fifth-century enclosure bank that divided the hill in two. The excavated structures include a number of small sub-rectangular buildings and round-houses with eavesdrip gullies (Rahtz et al. 1993, Fig. 168). One had doorway features associated with imported pottery (Rahtz et al. 1993, Fig. 139). Other fifth- and sixth-century roundhouses are known from Crickley Hill (Jarrett 2011). The apparent re-emergence of the roundhouse – an 'Iron Age' architectural form – during the fifth and sixth centuries is often seen as either a return to Iron Age ways of living or sometimes as a conscious rejection of *Romanitas* (Bowles 2007). Neither is a convincing explanation given that

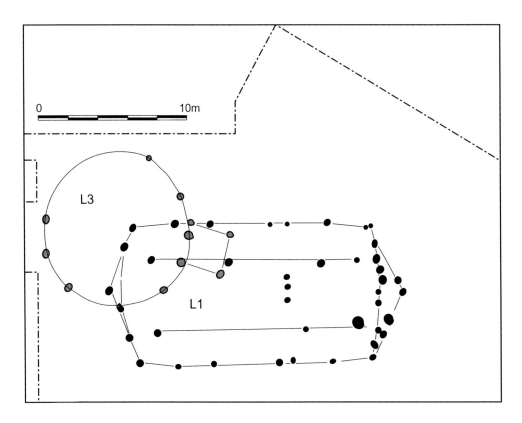

Fig. 5.7 Plan of the post-built structures, including the 'hall' (L1) and 'roundhouse' (L3), on the summit of Cadbury Castle (after Alcock 1995, Ill. 2.20).

roundhouses continued to be built and occupied during the Roman period (Taylor 2007, 31–35). Nevertheless, the appearance of these structures in late fifth- and sixth-century elite contexts is noteworthy.

The relative paucity of material culture from these hillfort sites makes any assessment of how the elite chose to individually display their status problematic. The zoomorphic buckles discussed above may have continued to have been worn if their presence in sixth-century Anglo-Saxon graves (White 1988; Marzinzik 2003) can be taken as indicating their continued circulation in the west. Stratified examples are known from Traprain Law (Hawkes 1974, 389) and Crickley Hill (Jarrett 2011, Fig. 5), and there is also a surface find from Penycorddyn (Clwyd) (Burnham et al. 1993, 271 and Fig. 4). However, they remain strikingly absent from both Cadbury Castle and Cadbury Congresbury.

Other personal adornments that seem to have been in use include penannular brooches. Fowler's (1960) Type G brooch has long been known as a post-Roman form (Dickinson 1982; Campbell and Lane 1993, 32–34) and there are also rarer types, like those from Bath and Calne (Wiltshire) (Youngs 1995), which are also likely to be of fifth- or sixth-century date. Interestingly, production waste for these items has been identified at Dinas Powys (Alcock 1963, 120–121) and Cannington (Rahtz et al. 2000, 352). Glass beads and pierced Roman coins were used as pendants or necklaces and are occasionally recovered from graves and settlement sites.

Some sites have also produced Anglo-Saxon metalwork. Sixth-century button brooches are known from Cadbury Castle (Alcock 1995, 70) and Ham Hill (Leivers et al. 2007, 50–51) and Cadbury Castle also produced a 'sword ring' with Style I decoration (Alcock 1995, 66–70). Anglo-Saxon metalwork, including an equal arm brooch of fifth-century date, has been found close to Hod Hill in Dorset and Anglo-Saxon spearheads were found within the ramparts (Eagles and Mortimer 1993). It is usual to see this material in 'ethnic' terms and the Hod Hill objects have been seen as the property of Germanic mercenaries (Eagles and Mortimer 1993). However, other explanations are both possible and plausible. There seems no reason that this material could not have been incorporated into local systems of display. However, its symbolism may well have been reworked in these western contexts. It need not have carried the same messages that it had in eastern Britain.

The Hod Hill finds are a reminder of the significance of weapons, which are relatively common in fifth- and sixth-century Anglo-Saxon burial contexts (see Chapter 2, 'Violence to the body'). In the west of Britain weapons are almost impossible to find. The excavated cemeteries occasionally produce a burial accompanied by a knife but weapon burials are unheard of. The hillforts have yielded equally poor evidence. Two spearheads of Anglo-Saxon form were found at Hod Hill (Eagles and Mortimer 1993) and Ham Hill produced an Anglo-Saxon shield boss (Burrow 1981, 273), but Cadbury Castle (Alcock 1995), Dinas Powys (Alcock 1963), Cadbury Congresbury (Rahtz et al. 1993) and Tintagel (Barrowman et al. 2007) have produced next to no evidence of weaponry. Nevertheless, they must have existed and the discovery of an axe-hammer in a ritual deposit beneath the fifth- and sixth-century road surface in the south-west gate at Cadbury Castle (Alcock 1995, 75–77) ought to indicate that weapons and tools capable of being used as weapons were symbols of power.

The evidence for toilet implements is somewhat better. Double-sided composite bone or antler combs are known from Dinas Powys (Alcock 1963, 154–159), Poundbury (Sparey-Green 1987, 127), Cadbury Castle (Alcock 1995, 106), Bantham (Griffith 1986; Griffith and Reed 1998) and sites in

Ireland (Dunlevy 1988). Given the apparent growing importance of combs in the later fourth and early fifth century (Cool 2010, 272–274) the use of combs in the later fifth and sixth centuries might suggest a continued interest in particular forms of hair maintenance (Williams 2004; Jackson 2011, 265). Here the presence of a pair of tweezers at Cadbury Congresbury (Rahtz et al. 1993, Fig. 92) that are typologically similar to late Roman and early Anglo-Saxon examples (Eckardt and Crummy 2008, 156–158) may also suggest a continued interest by individuals in their appearance. The importation of olive oil (below), usually seen as a foodstuff, might be better viewed as a component in styling the body. Here Gildas' (*De Excidio* 21.4) allusion to anointing kings may also be significant (Halsall 2007, 313).

In contrast to the relatively small numbers of personal adornments and toilet instruments associated with the reoccupation of hillforts, the evidence for feasting and dining is relatively abundant. The most obvious evidence for this activity is imported glass and pottery vessels. The glassware includes so-called cone beakers of Anglo-Saxon style as well as glass imported from Gaul and the eastern Mediterranean (E. Campbell 2007, 54–73). Most of these vessels were probably used for drinking. Beer and mead would have been available locally, but there are also the imported ceramics to consider. The pottery assemblages from the eastern Mediterranean include red-slipped tablewares and amphorae (E. Campbell 2007, 14–26). The latter vessels are likely to have carried wine and olive oil. This might suggest that the conspicuous consumption of imported luxury foodstuffs formed an important part of elite display.

The imported material is significant and has received considerable academic attention (E. Campbell 2007). However, this should not obscure the fact that this 'trade' with the Eastern Empire is likely to have brought more than glass, pottery, wine and oil into the British Isles (E. Campbell 2007, 75–82). Other perishable commodities like silks and spices may have been far more significant, as might 'diplomatic gifts' of gold and other items (Harris 2003). Here the apparent spike in gold coin finds from the reign of Justin I and Justinian may be significant (Figure 5.8) (Bland and Loriet 2010, Table 32). Further caution needs to be exercised with this material. All too often it is somewhat casually seen as evidence of contact with the Eastern Empire. However, in an insular context we might suppose that it represents contact with Tintagel before hypothesising contact with Byzantine merchants. It is also worth remembering that Roman amphorae often had complex secondary and tertiary uses (van der Werff 2003). There seems no reason to suspect that this was not the case in the fifth and sixth centuries. Therefore,

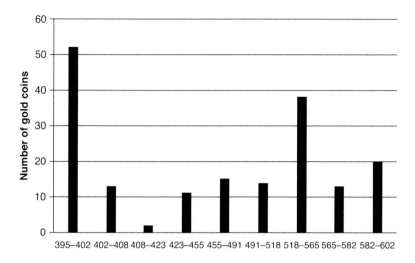

Fig. 5.8 The number of gold coins (single finds from 395 to 602). Note the peak during the reigns of Justin I and Justinian (518–565) (data from Bland and Loriet 2010, Table 32).

the discovery of the amphorae sherds at sites like Carhampton (Webster 2000, 80), Longbury Bank (Campbell and Lane 1993), Trethurgy (Quinnell 2004) or Glastonbury Tor (Rahtz 1971) may not necessarily indicate the consumption of the original contents. This is especially true of the latter site, as imported Mediterranean amphorae sherds have now been recognised in the archives of the antiquarian excavations at Glastonbury Abbey (Allan, Dawson and Kent in press). Evidence for the consumption of the primary contents must come from the discovery of the round discs used to seal the vessels, some of which were identified at Cadbury Castle (Alcock 1995, Ill. 6.3), or from the scientific analysis of the vessels for residues of their contents (Barrowman et al. 2007, 247–256).

The final arena in which elite display may be studied is that of funerary commemoration. In the west of Britain the dominant fourth-century burial rite of east–west orientated inhumations appears to have continued well into the sixth century and beyond (Petts 2004). Cannington (Rahtz et al. 2000) is one of the best examples of this type of cemetery and may be associated with a reoccupied hillfort (Rahtz 1969), like the cemetery at Henley Wood (Somerset) (Watts and Leach 1996), but a number of other examples are known, including Llandough (Glamorgan) (Holbrook and Alan 2005), Filton (Cullen et al. 2006), Caerwent (Campbell 1993) and Bradley Hill (Gerrard 2011a). In contrast to the late Roman urban cemeteries like Poundbury (Farwell and Molleson 1993) the east–west rite seems completely dominant with north–south orientated burials and 'aberrant' grave rituals like decapitation being exceedingly rare. Occasionally a burial will be accompanied by an iron knife or a glass bead but other than this gravegoods are almost unheard of (Rahtz 1977). At some sites particular graves were emphasised by stone linings or surrounded by small ditched enclosures (Murphy 1992; Rahtz et al. 2000, 104–105). This may indicate that even within a social context in which burials were largely undifferentiated, some individuals were singled out for special treatment.

The notion that some individuals were specially commemorated in death receives significant support from the extensive corpus of so-called 'Class I inscribed stones' (Nash-Williams 1950). The distribution of these monuments is focussed on Wales (Edwards 2007; Redknap and Lewis 2007) with outliers in the south-west (Okasha 1993) and as far north as Edinburgh (Alcock 1992, 125–127). They commemorate named individuals, who sometimes use Roman titles, such as *protectoris* and *magistratus*, and occasionally include Christian symbols. This substantial epigraphic record for the post-Roman west has been the subject of considerable study, but their chronology and connections to contemporary continental epigraphy remain the subject of considerable debate (Nash-Williams 1950; Knight 1992, 2010; Handley 2001). However, a number of authors have noted how these monuments are concentrated in the highland zone (Woolf 2003, 370; Halsall 2007, 364). They suggest that this form of commemoration may be derived from either a continuation or reinvention of the epigraphic habit that was so strongly associated with the Roman army in Britain (Handley 2001, 179–180; Halsall 2007, 364).

The supposed relationship of these inscribed stones with the preceding Roman military tradition of epigraphic commemoration would appear to offer evidence of a continuity of practice. However, the story is far more complex. As Petts (2002, 197) has observed, the stones are concentrated in Wales, where there was relatively little Roman period epigraphy. Furthermore, the decline of the epigraphic habit in the fourth century means that derivation from a Roman practice is unlikely. A better view of these inscriptions is that they may represent a new form of display, hybridised from a number of contemporary practices. Here the form of these monoliths, similar superficially at least (Petts 2002) to prehistoric standing stones and Roman milestones (Radford 1971, 8), is noteworthy. The inscriptions are thought to show stylistic and compositional links with contemporary Gallic epigraphy (Knight 2010) and the use of Roman titles and Christian symbols might further reinforce the 'Roman' connotations of these monuments. Thus this type of commemoration may have been used to invoke memories of Roman power, while referencing earlier prehistoric symbolism and contemporary Gallic practices.

The two-phase division of the early post-Roman period into an early phase from 350/370–430/470 and a later phase from 430/470–550/600 allows the development of elite display in western Britain to be charted. In the early phase the elites continued to reference some of the elements of fourth-century display. Villas and urban centres remained important places even if their occupation and function had fundamentally changed. Some forms of late Roman material culture continued in use and these included dress accessories and items used for styling the body. Belt fittings continued to be significant, suggesting that the possible 'martial' connotations of these objects continued to be important. During the later phase many of these elements were lost as greater emphasis was placed on activities like the reoc-cupation of hillforts, which were arguably perceived as being ancestral or mythical locations. Some of the communities inhabiting these locations had links to the eastern Mediterranean that perhaps allowed them to emphasise their position through the consumption of imported exotica. The funerary tradition was rooted in the past, retaining the predominantly unaccom-panied burial tradition of the late Roman period. However, individuals were occasionally commemorated with new forms of display, such as the inscribed stones, that drew on old Roman titles of power.

The distinction between the early and late phase visible in the archaeo-logical material also appears to be broadly visible in the surviving textual accounts of the period. The work of Patrick and Constantius seems to demonstrate that the early fifth-century world was significantly different to the sixth-century world of Gildas. Indeed, the *De Excidio* portrays this very development.

In the second part of this chapter Britain south and east of a line drawn between Berwick-upon-Tweed (Northumberland) and Poole Harbour is examined. The groups inhabiting this area pursued a trajectory that con-tained both similarities and differences to that pursued in the west.

Elite display in the east of Britain during the fifth and sixth centuries

The east of Britain is often characterised as being either 'Anglo-Saxon' or 'Germanic' in the fifth and sixth centuries. The use of these cultural labels to define the region is problematic because ancient identity is written into the vocabulary of the period. 'Anglo-Saxon' is an anachronistic (but commonly used) term to describe the culture of the two supposedly dominant Germanic ethnic groups in Britain. Both Angles and Saxons are known from Classical sources (Springer 2003). However, they were terms applied by literate Roman outsiders to distant communities situated far beyond the empire's frontiers. What the significance of these names was in northern Germany is debatable. By extension it is uncertain whether the earliest Germanic communities in Britain had any clear sense of belonging to these 'tribal' identities. One of the few contemporary witnesses, Gildas (another literate outsider), refers only to Saxons but cared little for the ethnography of barbarians. By the seventh century when the *Tribal Hidage* was written (Dumville 1989), eastern Britain was composed of a number of kingdoms. Some of these were large but others, such as the Suth Gyrwa, were tiny (Yorke 1990, 9–10). Furthermore, the study of charters and toponyms suggests the existence of earlier units, such as the Hæstingas (Welch 1989, 78), which were even smaller in size. The antiquity and significance of these groups and 'identities' remain extremely difficult to resolve but should serve as a reminder of the potential complexity of the fifth and sixth centuries (Scull 1993; Hills 2011, 4).

The more neutral term 'Germanic' is sometimes preferred. However, this label is just as problematic (Goffart 2006). It seems extremely doubtful that anyone in the fifth century referred to themselves as 'Germanic' (although see Bede *Hist. Eccl.* V.9), a term used by Classical authors as a blanket description for the barbarians living east of the Rhine (Kulikowski 2002, Fn. 2; Liebeschuetz 2007, 352–353). It is also, like Celtic (James 1999), a linguistic label and we have very little idea as to what the dominant language was in eastern Britain during the fifth and sixth centuries. It may have been a series of West Germanic dialects (Hines 1990; Green 1998) or it may have been a combination of languages that included the Celtic, Latin and Germanic tongues (Coates 2007; Schrijver 2007; Tristram 2007). Of course, by deconstructing such labels the very grammar and analytical language of the period is dismantled and to invent a new term for the east of Britain would also be a ridiculous affectation. Instead, the label 'Germanic' is used here to describe a series of cultural phenomena that clearly have their origins, at least in part, in northern Germany. The use of this term does not necessarily imply anything about the genetic makeup, or linguistic abilities, or ethnic identity of the individuals and communities to which it is applied.

The significance of 'labels' leads inexorably on to one of the most divisive issues in early medieval archaeology: the scale and nature of the population movement in the fifth century. It seemed to scholars during the nineteenth and much of the twentieth century that various Germanic peoples had invaded the eastern seaboard of the British Isles, driving the indigenous inhabitants west to the Celtic fringe (Collingwood and Myres 1936). Led by the narrative of the 'English Settlement' described by Bede (*Hist. Eccl.* I.15), scholars were at first concerned with which groups of objects could be associated with the Angles, Saxons and Jutes (e.g. Leeds 1912, 1945; Evison 1965) (Figure 5.9). Differences in material culture, such as button (Figure 5.10) and saucer brooches (Figure 5.11) (Avent and Evison 1982; Dickinson 1993; Suzuki 2006) and great square-headed brooches (Hines 1997), were found to broadly reflect the division between the so-called 'Saxon' and 'Anglian' regions of Britain but Kent – the site of supposed 'Jutish' settlement (Richardson 2011) – was different again.

By the end of the twentieth century the invasion/migration hypothesis had been subjected to a sustained critique. That critique questioned whether texts written hundreds of years after the events they purported to describe could be accepted as relevant (e.g. Sims-Williams 1983) and also questioned whether the hitherto unquestioned correlation between material culture and ethnicity was valid (Halsall 1992; Higham 1992, 178–188). This culminated in a model that ran counter to the traditional view of invasion and migration. The Anglo-Saxon 'settlement' of Britain was now seen as an elite takeover by a small number of individuals filling the power vacuum left by the retreat of Roman power (Higham 1992). The new 'Anglo-Saxon' ideology was adopted by the indigenous inhabitants of the former Roman diocese who, within a few generations, spoke and dressed as if, and believed that, they had originated on the far side of the North Sea.

As might be expected this argument was replicated in other arenas (e.g. Halsall 2007; Heather 2005 and 2009) and has led to considerable and sometimes acrimonious academic debate about the nature of ancient migrations and how best to study them (for judicious and recent reviews see Hills 2009 and 2011). That this debate is still very much alive is demonstrated by recent publications (Brookes 2007, 184; Higham 2007; Härke 2011). For the purposes of this volume much of this debate can be side-stepped. That groups of people moved, from what is now northern Germany (Hills 1999) and southern Scandinavia (Hines 1984), into the British Isles during the fifth century cannot be doubted. The artefactual, artistic and linguistic evidence for such a movement of people seems impossible to counter (e.g. Hines 1990; Hills 1999). Nor can it be doubted that those groups had a significant impact in the regions in which they settled. However, even a large migrant population, numbering in the low hundreds of thousands spread over a hundred or so years, will have still been a minority at a 'national' scale.

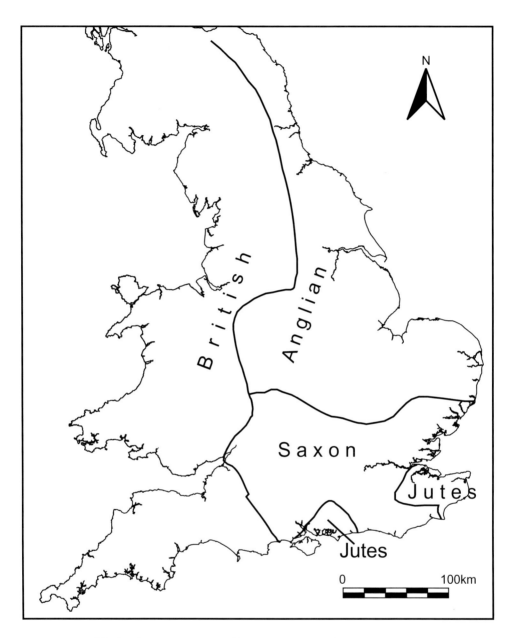

Fig. 5.9 Map of the 'Anglian, Saxon and Jutish' areas of England (after Leeds 1913, Fig. 4).

That said, a thousand people arriving every year in Kent or Essex for twenty or thirty years will quickly have had an enormous impact locally out of all proportion to their percentage of the 'national' population (Brugmann 2011).

Fig. 5.10 Two Anglo-Saxon button brooches (© Trustees of the British Museum).

Fig. 5.11 An Anglo-Saxon saucer brooch (© Trustees of the British Museum).

Migration also plays an important (some might say critical) role in understanding how the material culture of the period was classified. On the continent coin-dated graves from around 400 provided a horizon of dateable objects. As Roman coins became rarer the next apparently fixed point was the migration to Britain, which was dated to *c.*450 (Lucy 2000, 17). Finds of metalwork and pottery that occurred in Britain were thus constrained by the historical dating to occurring no earlier than *c.*450. Objects that only occurred on the continent pre-dated 450 and objects that occurred in Britain and northern Germany post-dated the middle of the fifth century with typological developments of those objects later still (Arnold 1997, 16–17; Brugmann 2011, 40–41).

The difficulties inherent in such an approach seem obvious. Objects may be many years old when deposited; the movement of people from northern Germany to Britain is likely to have been a complex and difficult process that occurred over many years; and finally, typological developments may occur or be adopted in different places at different times (Hills 1979, 326). What this means is that the study of the fifth century is more malleable than one might at first suppose. The 'gap' between Roman Britain ending in *c.*400 and Anglo-Saxon England beginning in *c.*450 has already been shown to be elastic from the Roman perspective and it seems likely to be equally flexible on the Anglo-Saxon side. This has been recently demonstrated by the analysis of the important cremation cemetery at Spong Hill (Hills 1977; Hills and Lucy in press). Such cemeteries have long been seen as 'early' (i.e. mid to late fifth century) (e.g. Williams 2002, 345) but at Spong Hill stratigraphic, stylistic and statistical analysis has demonstrated that two phases of cremation burials (of which there are more than 2,000) pre-date the phase of inhumations (of which there are fewer than a hundred) that can be dated to the late fifth to early sixth century (I am grateful to Drs Catherine Hills and Sam Lucy for discussing this with me prior to publication) (Figure 5.12). Radiocarbon dating of other cemeteries also suggests that Germanic burial traditions start in the first half of the fifth century (Carver, Hills and Scheschkewitz 2009; Hills and O'Connell 2009, 1,104). This suggests that many of the cremations could pre-date the traditional date of 450 for the arrival of the 'Anglo-Saxons'.

This discussion of Spong Hill highlights one of the major differences between the study of the fifth and sixth centuries and the fourth century in the east of Britain (Esmonde-Cleary 1993; Arnold 1997). In contrast to the late Roman period, where settlement sites are commonplace, the most typical and visible fifth- and sixth-century sites are usually cemeteries (Lucy 2000). Their prominence is a product of a funerary tradition that

Fig. 5.12 An Anglo-Saxon cremation urn. The date of these vessels can only be established using relative means. However, the 'fixed' points in the typological development of such vessels are often derived from the historical narrative (© Trustees of the British Museum).

often ensured inhumations and cremations were accompanied by material culture. Pottery urns, iron weapons and copper-alloy brooches are all archaeologically recoverable finds and this visibility contrasts with the often modest assemblages of material culture that are recovered from settlement sites. Thus many archaeologists of the early Anglo-Saxon period have made funerary ritual (e.g. Härke 1992; Stoodley 1997; Penn and Brugmann 2007) and typological analysis (e.g. Hines 1997; Suzuki 2000; Inker 2006) their analytical focus. Settlement sites are less visible and more rarely excavated although recent work is beginning to alter this pattern (e.g. Lucy et al. 2009).

The methodological issues surrounding site identification and the chronology of material culture are significant and go some way to explain the differences in structure and evidence presented in this and the preceding chapter. However, it should also be recognised that these differences in

Fig. 5.13 A great square-headed brooch (© Trustees of the British Museum).

datasets underline the very significant differences in the way society was ordered between the fourth and the fifth and sixth centuries.

New forms of display: settlements in the fifth- and sixth-century east

Like the Roman period the fifth and sixth centuries in the east of Britain suffer from being homogenised by scholarly analysis. This leads to an 'early Anglo-Saxon England' characterised by individuals buried with weapons, great square-headed brooches (Figure 5.13) and bead necklaces who lived in *Grubenhäuser* and timber halls. One reason for this homogenisation is the role that the fifth century plays in the meta-narratives of British and European history: the century is either the *end* of the Classical world, or the *beginning* of the early Middle Ages. This teleology, in which the period is either an afterword to the fate of Roman Britain (e.g. Esmonde-Cleary

1989), or an introduction to the story of the development of Anglo-Saxon England (Hodges 1989), denies the societies of the time independence. They are always studied and judged in relation to something else. Yet much of the stereotypical 'package' that typifies early 'Anglo-Saxon' England is representative of the very late fifth and sixth centuries rather than the fifth century proper (e.g. Scull 1993, 70–71). Opposed caricatures of 'late Roman' and 'early Anglo-Saxon' do little to elucidate the process of transformation that altered life in lowland Britain between 300 and 600.

The final part of this chapter attempts to define an 'early', primarily fifth-century, phase and distinguish it from a 'later', mainly sixth-century, phase. With the early phase the chronological boundaries are set at *c*.400 and *c*.470. The traditional date of the start of the early Anglo-Saxon period *c*.450 is rejected here as a product of a historical tradition that was trying to explain a process as an event: the so-called *adventus Saxonum* (Howe 1989, 54–57). There is also some archaeological evidence that can be best placed before *c*.450. The end point of *c*.470 is derived from the insular adoption of 'Salin's Style I' – a decorative technique used on metalwork that emerges in southern Scandinavia and becomes commonplace in eastern Britain during the sixth century (Hasselhoff 1974; Hines 1990, 25; Rau 2010). As has been attempted for fourth-century Britain and the west of Britain in the fifth and sixth centuries the intention is to discuss the role of architecture, funerary rites and material culture in elite display.

A relatively large number of 'Germanic' settlement sites are known but few of these have been subjected to extensive or comprehensive archaeological investigation (Ulmschneider 2011). Of excavated examples only two sites, Mucking (Hamerow 1993) and West Heslerton (Powlesland 1998), are of a date and dug on a scale that allow meaningful interpretations to be made about their development, function and spatial arrangement. Unfortunately, West Heslerton has not been fully published (Powlesland *pers. comm.*) and this means that a detailed discussion can only be advanced for Mucking.

The site at Mucking was excavated ahead of aggregate extraction between 1965 and 1978 and covered some 18 ha (Hamerow 1993; Hirst and Clark 2009) (Figure 5.14). Located on a high gravel terrace above the Thames the open area excavations revealed a complex multi-phase landscape that included 203 *Grubenhäuser*, 53 post-built structures, 468 cremation burials and approximately 400 inhumations in two cemeteries. The chronology of the site stretched from perhaps the early fifth century until the seventh century.

The settlement was established in a relict late Roman landscape that had been largely abandoned in the mid to later third century. Hamerow

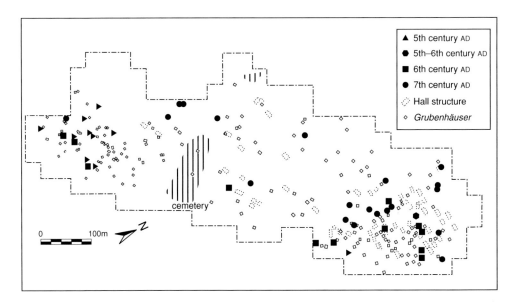

Fig. 5.14 Plan of the early Anglo-Saxon site at Mucking showing how the settlement shifted over time. Note the absence of post-built 'halls' in the southern part of the site (after Hamerow 1993, Fig. 3).

(1993, Fig. 50) proposed that the fifth-century settlement began towards the southern end of the site and moved northwards during the sixth and seventh centuries – a phenomenon suggested for other 'Anglo-Saxon' sites and also identified on the continent (Hamerow 1991, 6–7). This interpretation has not been fully accepted and a bi-focal settlement with a northern and southern core has also been suggested (Tipper 2004, 40). However, fifth-century material remains concentrated in the southern part of the site (Dr Sam Lucy *pers. comm.*).

Architecturally the settlement was dominated by *Grubenhäuser* (Figure 5.15). These are sometimes referred to as 'sunken featured buildings' (Rahtz 1976) and were created by digging a large pit and erecting a timber roof over it. Some of these structures may have utilised suspended timber floors, in others the bottom of the pit may have served as a floor surface. The interpretation of these buildings represents certain challenges because they are often backfilled with large quantities of material culture and other 'rubbish'. It has been tempting to see these deposits as 'occupation debris' derived from the building's use. However, most of the material found in the back fill of a *Grubenhaus* is divorced from its primary context and may not be related functionally to the structure in which it was deposited (Tipper 2004). *Grubenhäuser* are an architectural form that is unknown in Roman

Fig. 5.15 This recent excavation at Needham Market shows a prehistoric enclosure under excavation. During the Anglo-Saxon period a *Grubenhaus* was placed in the centre of the enclosure, which is visible as a large pit overlain by the foundations of a nineteenth-century building (© Pre-Construct Archaeology Ltd).

Britain (although some sunken structures are known: Tipper 2004, 7–9). However, they do occur in North German contexts (Tipper 2004, 4–7) and excavations at Loxstedt in Lower Saxony (Zimmerman 1992, 156–157) have produced almost a hundred such structures.

The timber structures at Mucking were outnumbered almost four to one by the *Grubenhäuser*. They were mostly rectangular and varied from *c.*12 m by 6 m to *c.*9 m by 4 m (Hamerow 1993, Fig. 54–55). It has long been recognised (Addyman 1972) that such post-built timber buildings differ in form and layout from the large three-aisled timber longhouses with byres known from continental sites like Feddersen Wierde in northern Germany (e.g. Zimmerman 1999). At Mucking it is noticeable that the post-built structures are concentrated in the central and northern parts of the site (Hamerow 1993, Fig. 195). The supposedly early phase of fifth-century activity in the southern part of the site lacks these structures (Dixon 1993). It has been argued that this is a consequence of poor excavation techniques in this area (Hamerow 1993, 86). However, this has been countered by the recognition that features were excavated and recorded in this area (Clark 1993, Plans 1, 3 and 4) and that some traces of post-built structures from other periods have been identified (Barford 1995, 108; Tipper 2004, 36–37; Lucy et al. in press).

Grubenhäuser have often been interpreted as ancillary or workshop structures (Tipper 2004, 163–170). If this were the case then one interpretation of the fifth-century phase at Mucking would be that it was characterised by low-status structures. This lack of architectural pretension might in turn imply that the fifth-century community was essentially egalitarian (Leeds 1936, 20–21; Jones 1974, 34; West 1985, 168; Arnold 1997, 176–188). Of course, such an interpretation of the evidence is drawn from a historiographical tradition that sees the Germanic migrations during the fifth century as the movement of a free peasant *völk* (e.g. Hodgkin 1935, 202–203). Alternatively, the supposedly higher-status timber structures could remain unexcavated beyond the limits of the site or based on sill-beam construction that left no visible archaeological traces.

A spatial division between post-built structures and *Grubenhäuser* is visible at West Heslerton where in the northern part of the site the two types of architectural tradition were separated by a stream. This led the excavators to hypothesise functional zoning between dwelling spaces and workshops and other forms of utilitarian structures (Tipper 2004, Fig. C8). Such spatial zoning could exist at Mucking, but if it does then it was not adhered to in subsequent phases when *Grubenhäuser* and post-built structures were constructed in close proximity to one another. Nor was it adhered to at other, less extensively excavated, sites like West Stow (West 1985).

At West Stow a smaller-scale excavation of a site of broadly contemporary date suggested to the excavator that rectangular timber structures were foci for groups of *Grubenhäuser* (Figure 5.16). The timber buildings were described as 'halls' but were relatively modest structures comparable in size to those at Mucking (West 1985, 10–14). Each 'hall' was supposedly associated with a number of *Grubenhäuser* and the settlement was argued to drift from west to east over time (West 1985, Fig. 301). Such an interpretation is attractive and plausible. However, examination of the published plans indicates that both of the putative early 'halls' (Halls 4 and 6) were identified from among a large number of cut features (West 1985, Figs. 6 and 7). The presence of early halls is perhaps not as certain as the published phase plan suggests (West 1985, 11–12).

The proximity of post-built buildings with *Grubenhäuser* also occurs at other sites including Bloodmoor Hill (Suffolk) (Lucy et al. 2009) and Kilverstone (Norfolk) (Garrow et al. 2006). However, at Cowdery's Down

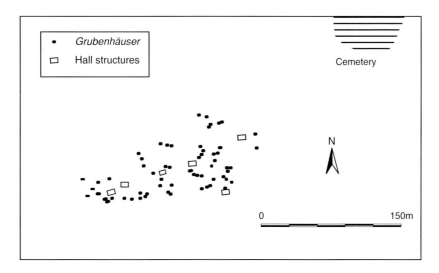

Fig. 5.16 Plan of the early Anglo-Saxon site at West Stow (after Arnold 1997, Fig. 3.8).

(Hampshire) only a single *Grubenhaus* was identified (Millett and James 1983, Fig. 56). This reflects the broad distribution of *Grubenhäuser*, which were restricted to parts of eastern England and far less common in other areas (Arnold 1997, 51–52). It may also be significant that the dating evidence from this site suggests occupation in the sixth and seventh centuries and thus falls in the later phase from *c.*470–550/600 under discussion here.

Cowdery's Down was a large area excavation undertaken ahead of housing development between 1978 and 1981 (Millett and James 1983) (Figure 5.17). The site was shallow with clear features and this, when combined with the large excavated area, allowed the excavators to reconstruct building plans with great confidence. However, there were few stratigraphic relationships and very little material culture to provide chronological information and the date of occupation was established by radiocarbon dating burnt structural timbers. The early medieval phase (the excavators' Phase 4) was subdivided into three sub-phases. The first of these comprised three post-built structures set within or associated within two square, fenced enclosures. In the succeeding sub-phase the building in the northern enclosures was replaced with a larger post-built structure on a different alignment. Additional structures were also located in the southern enclosure.

These post-built buildings varied in size with Building B4 measuring some 14 m × 6.5 m (Figure 5.18). They appear to have had opposed doorways set in the middle of the long walls and there is some evidence for the internal division of space. Building A1 is particularly interesting as it was

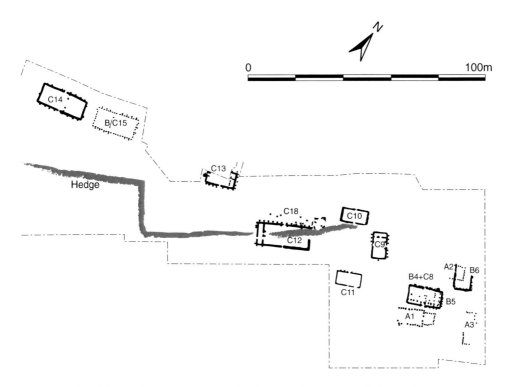

Fig. 5.17 Plan of the Anglo-Saxon site at Cowdery's Down showing several phases of timber 'halls' (after Millett and James 1983, Fig. 31).

some 14 m × 6 m long but also included an annexe at the eastern end that extended its length by another 5 m. In Phase 4C the number of buildings increased from five in the preceding phase to nine rectangular structures and the lone *Grubenhaus* with some evidence for fenced enclosures. Instead of being post-built, construction techniques now favoured a combination of wall trench and post construction. Evidence for internal divisions was more obvious and the size of structures also increased. The dimensions of Building C14 (Millett and James 1983, Fig. 51) were some 20 m × 8 m.

The morphology of the halls and the construction methods suggested that the architecture at these sites represented an 'early medieval building tradition'. A search for the antecedents of this tradition suggested that it represented a development and fusion of indigenous and 'Germanic' construction methods (Dixon 1982; Dixon 1993; James, Marshall and Millett 1984). Attempts have been made to counter this interpretation by suggesting that the structures represent the adaptation of the 'Germanic' longhouse to changed economic and environmental conditions (Zimmerman 1992). The truth probably lies somewhere between these two positions. Either way, the

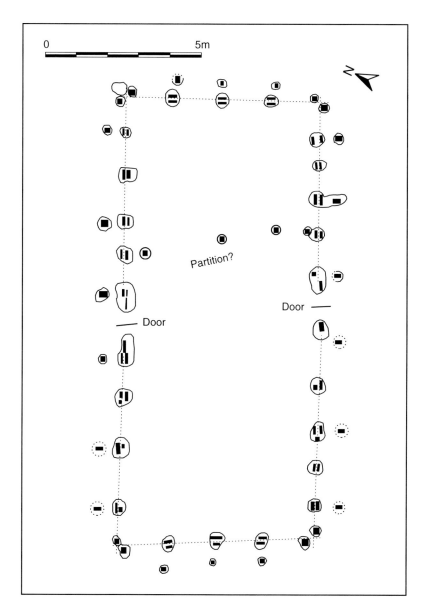

Fig. 5.18 Plan of 'hall' B4 at Cowdery's Down. These large post-built timber buildings required significant quantities of wood for their construction (after Millett and James 1983, Fig. 37).

adoption of this building form over much of lowland Britain is suggestive and may indicate that in the late fifth and sixth centuries these buildings were the preferred form of dwelling, and at sites like Bloodmoor Hill this architectural tradition continued into the seventh century (Lucy et al. 2009).

Compared with a stone-built and elaborately decorated villa these timber buildings might appear as 'simple' structures. However, such an approach denies the complexity of the structures (Millett and James 1983, Figs. 63–71) and ignores the fact that the relatively simple groundplans may disguise complex social structure. Furthermore, the quantities of timber used to construct these buildings were not insignificant, with one estimate suggesting that eighteen fully grown oak trees were required to build one of the larger structures (Arnold 1997, 63). There is no reason to doubt the abilities of fourth- to sixth-century populations to manage woodland (Grocock 2010). However, such mature trees must have been at a premium and their profligate use is indicative of the significant exploitation of woodland resources that could not be easily or quickly replaced. Finally, it should be noted that by the seventh century such timber halls in their most grandiose form were suitable as the residences of kings and princes (Hope Taylor 1977).

This review of the use of architecture at Mucking, Cowdery's Down, West Heslerton and West Stow can be interpreted in various ways. At Mucking the early phase seems to be associated with *Grubenhäuser* and may lack post-built structures. If this phenomenon is real then it suggests that architectural pretension was not an important part of 'Germanic' life in fifth-century Britain. In many respects this is confirmed by the lack of substantial ditched enclosures and other forms of aggrandisement that are often interpreted as highlighting the 'specialness' of specific structures. The next section discusses the funerary evidence from Mucking, which can be interpreted as indicative of significant social stratification. Thus any suggestion that this was an egalitarian community needs to be set aside. How then can the lack of post-built structures be explained?

One potential resolution to the preference for *Grubenhäuser* at Mucking may lie in the history of the site and its location. The gravel terrace, although exploited in the second and third centuries, appears to have been abandoned for most of the fourth century (Lucy et al. in press). This suggests that the 'Germanic' community that settled at Mucking during the early fifth century were fitting into a pre-existing settlement pattern (Lucy 2002, 153). It may also be counter-intuitive to suggest that the 'elite' inhabitants of Mucking in the fifth century needed to signal their status to their followers. It may have been more pressing to advertise status and position within indigenous arenas of power (Brookes 2007, 97–98). As the fifth century progressed and the elite's position stabilised, a drift away from a seaward-facing site might be anticipated. Locations inland, which were suitable for controlling land and resources, may have been more important. Alternatively the supposed division in status between post-built 'hall' and *Grubenhäuser* may reflect nothing more than modern prejudice (Tipper 2004, 183–185).

The sixth- and seventh-century sites at Cowdery's Down and Blood-moor Hill in many respects continue the traditions that occur at Mucking. Both sites have *Grubenhäuser* and include post-built timber structures that might be termed halls. There are the beginnings of signs of division and embellishments with fenced yards, annexes and internal divisions of space possibly indicating an increased interest in these structures as venues for display. Here it should be remembered that archaeology is a very poor witness to the complexities of timber buildings, which may be elaborately decorated without leaving any recoverable trace (Barker 1993, 264). The economic impact of these structures should also be noted. They required large quantities of timber that had to come from managed woodlands. This alone demonstrates the economic pull of the inhabitants of these buildings.

Debate will undoubtedly continue over the extent to which these post-built halls represent a 'Germanic' adaptation to a new environment or the fusion of Romano-British and Germanic building traditions (West 1985, 112). However, the appearance of these buildings in the later fifth and sixth centuries can be taken as evidence of communities coming to terms with new circumstances. It is an architectural tradition that maintains conti-nuities with the Roman and Germanic past while also underscoring the discontinuities with the same past. People no longer lived in rectangular stone-built farmsteads, modified villas or longhouses but they did live in buildings that referenced the forms and layouts of those earlier structures.

Displaying the dead

In contrast to the relatively mute and sometimes fugitive evidence of the architectural traditions the disposal of the dead in the fifth- and sixth-century east of Britain seems to speak volumes. Cremation and inhumation cemeteries contain many hundreds of individuals often accompanied by a rich assortment of gravegoods (Figure 5.19). Both means of disposing of the body were practised in the period under consideration and occasion-ally in the same cemeteries (Lucy 2000). However, cremation cemeteries have a restricted distribution focussed in the east of Britain (Arnold 1997, Fig. 3.9). These cemeteries also mark a significant break in funerary tradition when compared with fourth-century funerary practices (Chapter 4).

Recent statistical and stratigraphic analysis of the more than 2,000 cre-mation burials from Spong Hill places almost all of them in the fifth century

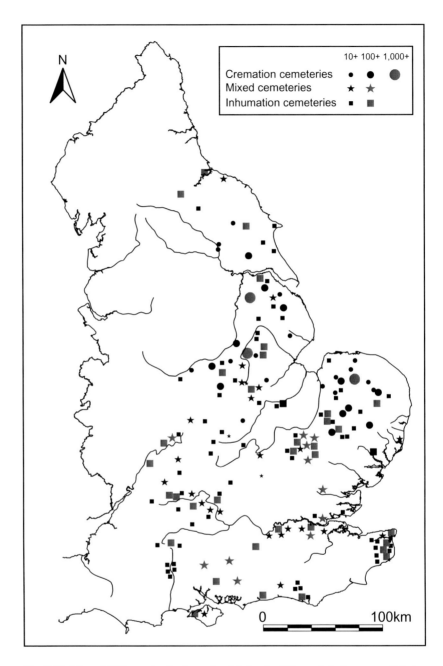

Fig. 5.19 Map of different Anglo-Saxon burial rites in fifth- and sixth-century Britain (after K. Dark 2000, Fig. 14).

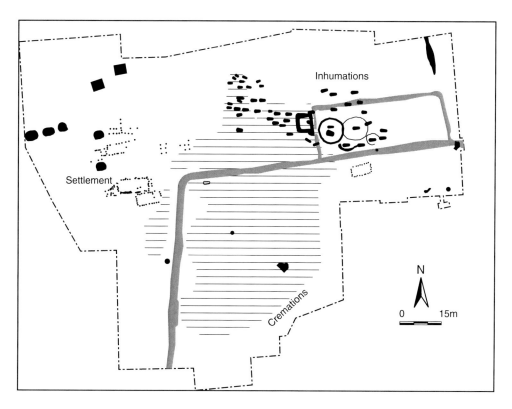

Fig. 5.20 Plan of the early Anglo-Saxon site at Spong Hill showing the large fifth-century cremation cemetery overlying a Roman enclosure. Note the inhumation burials and small settlement (after Rickett 1995, Fig. 60).

(Figure 5.20). Whether this chronology can be extended to other cremation cemeteries remains a matter for discussion. However, it is also noticeable that many cremation cemeteries, such as those at York (Stead 1956), Caistor-by-Norwich (Myres and Green 1973) and Ancaster (Lincolnshire) (Williams 2002, 347–348), were located in close proximity to Roman walled centres. One interpretation of this phenomenon would be to argue that they were founded when these towns still had some lingering significance. Alternatively, the Roman urban centres were focal points in the landscape and controlled Roman roads and other routeways. This may have been a determining factor in choice of location for these burial grounds.

The rite practised at these cemeteries involved cremating the body and putting some of the cremated bones in an urn, occasionally with cremated or uncremated artefacts and faunal remains. The superficial simplicity of this rite and the scale of burial at sites like Spong Hill and Sancton (East Yorkshire) (Myres and Southern 1973) can obscure its importance in signalling the status of the dead. It has already been observed that only a tiny majority of the population of late Roman Britain were buried in a manner that is archaeologically recoverable and the same is surely true of the fifth and sixth centuries (e.g. Devlin 2007, 81). Thus those buried in cremation cemeteries were a sample of the living population chosen for reasons that remain opaque. That said, the very choice of cremation suggests that these individuals were economically privileged.

Corpses are mainly composed of bodily fluids and they do not burn well or easily. Cremating an individual to the state seen in a fifth-century urn would require considerable energy and therefore fuel (McKinley 1994, 84). This requirement is increased by the incorporation of animal carcasses and joints of meat into many (perhaps one in five) funerary pyres (Bond 1998). Clearly, the cremation of animals alongside the cremation of humans suggests that animal sacrifice played a role in the funerary ritual and this further emphasises the economic position of the deceased individuals. Pyre goods are also important and some may have been used to signify status. Relatively common are the types of objects used for styling the body: razors, combs and tweezers (Williams 2004). Some of the combs can appear to be typologically linked to the later Roman examples discussed in Chapter 3 (Hills and Lucy in press) and this group of objects strongly suggests an interest in modifying the appearance of bodily hair. It is, of course, difficult to suggest a direct correlation between funerary ritual and the way the living led their lives, but it might be assumed that these types of activity were an important part of constructing the identities of individuals and kin groups.

Finally, we might observe that the very process of cremation is both a dramatic and visible rite, which contrasts with inhumation burial where the visibility of the mourners is restricted to those in close contact with the actual inhumation and later any funerary marker erected over the site. The process of cremation would generate both smoke and light. Smoke would make the site of the event visible for some distance and the same would be true of the light if the cremation were undertaken at night. Of course, it is possible that individuals were cremated in one location and buried elsewhere but the movement of the dead to a specific point in the landscape only emphasises their importance (Williams 2002). This, and the economic resources that underpin the cremation rite, suggests that those treated in this fashion could be interpreted as an elite demarcated by their position in death.

Furnished inhumation burials also occurred in the fifth century south and east. This is a tradition that may have its origins in the late Roman period. At Lankhills (Winchester, Hampshire) the late

Fig. 5.21 The Quoit Brooch Style belt set from Mucking (© Trustees of the British Museum).

fourth-century cemetery includes a number of individuals buried with a variety of belt fittings, personal adornments and other items (Booth et al. 2010). It remains unique in Britain but two unusual burials from London's eastern cemetery offer a parallel (Barber, Bowsher and Whittaker 1990). The first was that of a man interred with a chip-carved belt set and gilded crossbow brooch; the second that of a woman wearing two so-called *tutulus* brooches and buried with a bone comb. The belt set sits comfortably within the late Roman military tradition of wearing such equipment and the brooches point to contact with the lands beyond the Rhine. Other accompanied inhumations include an individual at Richborough accompanied by a spear, shield boss and pewter bowl (Bushe-Fox 1949, 80) and the famous early fifth-century burials from Dyke Hills (Dorchester-upon-Thames, Oxfordshire) (Kirk and Leeds 1954). These include a man buried with an elaborate belt set and possibly a weapon; a woman buried with an early cruciform brooch and an insular belt set decorated with horses' heads; and another female buried with a collection of Romano-British objects including bracelets and a key as well as two Germanic 'applied' brooches. These burials have recently been joined by another inhumation from Dyke Hills that appears to have been accompanied by a so-called *francisca* type axe (P. Booth *pers. comm.*).

Two fifth-century burials at Mucking continue and extend this tradition. The first contained an important and prestigious belt set in the Quoit Brooch Style and decorated with silver wire and foil inlay (Evison 1968; Hirst and Clark 2009, 662–668) (Figure 5.21). It is clearly linked in form to the wide chip-carved belts like that from London discussed above (Hirst and Clark 2009, 666). The second included a mid fifth-century belt set of Hawkes and Dunning's (1961) Type IIIB in a burial that was also accompanied by similarly dated spear and ferrule and an iron penannular brooch (Hirst and Clark 2009, 568) (Figure 5.22).

Grave 979
Mucking

Fig. 5.22 Reconstruction drawing of a fifth-century individual buried at Mucking (© English Heritage).

Much of the debate surrounding these burials has focussed on whether they might be the last resting places of some of the earliest Germanic settlers in Britain (Böhme 1986). There is, of course, no need to insist that the gravegoods indicate the ethnicity of the deceased (Halsall 1992; Böhme 1997). A more useful approach is to see these burials as the beginnings of a form of display that straddles the late Roman and early medieval worlds. They do not necessarily indicate that the individuals buried with this material were warriors (Härke 1992). However, they can be interpreted as indicating that some parts of society were appropriating the symbols of martial prowess such as belt sets (Marzinzik 2003) and weapons (Halsall 1992). That some of those symbols would have been recognisable in a late Roman context is significant and this point will be returned to in Chapter 7.

The importance of 'martial qualities' may not have been restricted to male display and funerary contexts. The equal arm brooch (Brun 2003) is an uncommon form in Britain that does occur in some cremation cemeteries (Hills et al. 1987, 41) and rarely as stray finds. These brooches are a 'Germanic' type and are usually assumed to have been female personal adornments. They were often decorated in the chip-carved style that was also used to embellish the large belt sets discussed above. How this decorative style came to be reinterpreted beyond the frontiers of the Roman Empire as a one suitable for a female personal adornment is unknown (Brun 2003, 42). However, a recent discussion of this phenomenon suggested that such brooches with their 'martial' decoration may have been imbued with protective and amuletic qualities (Brun 2003, 49).

Other forms of 'early Anglo-Saxon' brooch present a number of difficulties as their chronology is imperfectly understood. Nevertheless, examples of cruciform brooches, disc brooches and saucer brooches probably all circulated during the fifth century (Lucy 2000, 27–40). Often interpreted as ethnic indicators, their presence in eastern Britain might be alternatively seen as a new means of signalling position, status and belonging. The Quoit Brooch Style, of which the Mucking belt set is one example, is also of relevance to this discussion (Inker 2000; Suzuki 2000). Like the equal arm brooches it is a very small category of material and is often found in contexts later than the date of its manufacture (Hines 1990, 24). Typical products are belt fittings and brooches and they have a restricted distribution south of the Thames, in Kent, the Isle of Wight and Hampshire. The origins and development of the style have been the subject of considerable debate, although there seems to be a growing consensus that late Roman provincial art styles and metalworking traditions were an important influence (Suzuki 2000;

Hirst and Clark 2009, 666–668). This is suggestive of a situation in which traditional and new styles were being reworked to carry new significances.

Finally, it is worth noting that alongside the evidence of belt sets, brooches, toilet equipment and faunal remains other items also occur in burials. The presence of fragments of glass beads and drinking vessels (Evison 1982), which are sometimes found partially melted in cremation urns (Hills et al. 1987, 105) and even occur on sites in the west of Britain, is significant. These are likely to have been 'high-status' objects and hint at the role of communal drinking and eating in the maintenance of the status.

The late fifth and early sixth century mark a significant period of transformation in the east of Britain. Between *c.*450 and *c.*470 a new art style arose in southern Scandinavia and northern Germany (Rau 2010, 31–123). Defined as Salin's Style I this new decoration was mainly applied to female dress accessories and, although it ultimately descends from late provincial art, clearly originates beyond the frontiers of what had been the Roman Empire (Hasselhoff 1974; Hines 1990, 25; Rau 2010). The style quickly became an important ornamental grammar and was transmitted to Britain at an unknown date, but certainly before 500 (Prof. J. Hines *pers. comm.*). It was soon used to decorate diverse forms of metalwork that include items which tend to be categorised as stereotypically 'Anglo-Saxon': great square-headed brooches and cast and applied saucer brooches.

At approximately the same time as Style I was being transmitted to eastern Britain, other Scandinavian cultural influences were also beginning to make themselves felt. The most visible of these was the adoption of so-called wrist clasps in the East Anglia, Lincolnshire, around the Humber and East Yorkshire (Hines 1984; Arnold 1997, Fig 7.5). These decorated fasteners were dress accessories principally found in female graves and appear to originate in south-western Norway.

These new influences were accompanied by a transformation in burial rites (Lucy 2000). Cremation burial at Spong Hill appears to have first overlapped with inhumation burial and then been replaced by it as the only rite. In other regions new inhumation cemeteries were founded, as at Great Chesterford in Essex (Evison and Evans 1994, 45). Sixth-century female burials were also often accompanied by significant quantities of gravegoods. In the areas of Britain which Bede (*Hist. Eccl.* I.15) would later describe as being Anglian, the wrist clasps mentioned above were often accompanied by brooches of great square-headed or cruciform type (Hines 1997), and in those areas which Bede would describe as 'Saxon' saucer and button brooches predominated (Suzuki 2006; Dickinson 2010). Of course, this was not a sudden appearance and 'Saxon' style objects occur earlier in the fifth century as well. However, it is the later fifth and sixth centuries that see the crystallisation of female funerary (and perhaps day-to-day) dress into broad regional styles. Other items accompanying female burials include keys, necklaces of beads, and knives.

The study of female dress accessories and personal adornments in these funerary contexts suggests that they were indicative not just of a regional identity but were also used to signal complex messages about social position, status and an individual's lifecycle. Whether these objects define an elite or elites is a debatable point. However, the economic resources and some-times distance that items had travelled before deposition in graves indicate that those accompanied by such items were far from being an economic underclass.

The later fifth and sixth centuries also see the floruit of weapon burials. Swords, such as the seven from Mucking dated to the late fifth, sixth and seventh centuries (Hirst and Clark 2009, 564; Menghin 1983), are always relatively rare, but spears and shields are commonplace. Other forms of weaponry such as axes and seaxes also occur. It has been suggested that weapon burials were one of the most significant means of indicating social position (Härke 1992). In an extension of the pattern emerging at the end of the fourth and during the early fifth centuries, weapons and war-gear had become one of the primary means of creating and indicating male position and status. Nor should the economic value of these items be disregarded. Manufacturing a sword was a highly complex, technical and time-consuming business (Gilmour 2007). Spears and shields involved fewer resources in their manufacture. That said, the deposition of all of these items in the grave on a significant scale clearly indicates a class of individuals who could withstand the loss of such valuable and prestigious items. Here Crawford's (2004) suggestion that the scale of this phenomenon is such that it should be considered as a 'votive horizon' demonstrates the value that was placed on the social messages this war-gear signified.

Horses and equestrian gear, such as bridle bits, also occur, albeit in small numbers, in sixth-century burials (Figure 5.23). The importance of the horse as a means of transportation, an elite status symbol and a weapon of war should not be overlooked. Indeed, there is some evidence that horses included in ritual deposits were selected with some intention to choose visibly impressive animals. Given that horse-gear and animals appear rarer than the uncommon swords it would seem clear that their use was the prerogative and symbol of a small elite minority (Fern 2005, 67).

Finally, it is worth considering the location of these inhumation ceme-teries (Figure 5.24). Many were positioned in close proximity to extant

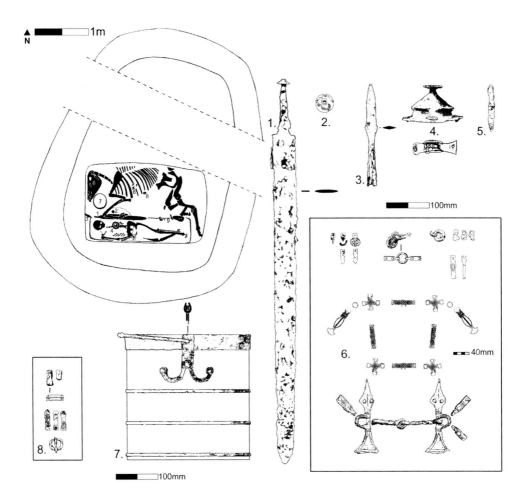

Fig. 5.23 Burial from Lakenheath (Suffolk) accompanied by a horse, weaponry and a bucket: 1) sword, 2) sword-bead, 3) spearhead, 4) shield, 5) knife, 6) bridle, 7) bucket, 8) saddle fittings, 9) sheep remains (Fern 2005) (© Chris Fern, reproduced by kind permission).

prehistoric and Roman sites or natural topographic features (Williams 1998). At Barton Court Farm (Oxfordshire) a number of inhumations were cut through a small Roman 'villa' and a small Anglo-Saxon settlement lay nearby (Miles 1986), and this pattern is repeated at other sites (Williams 1997). The most common prehistoric feature to attract Anglo-Saxon burials were the ubiquitous barrows (burial mounds) that dot considerable swathes of southern England to this day. The significance of this phenomenon arguably lay in claiming important points in the landscape that could be used to reinforce and legitimate claims to the land.

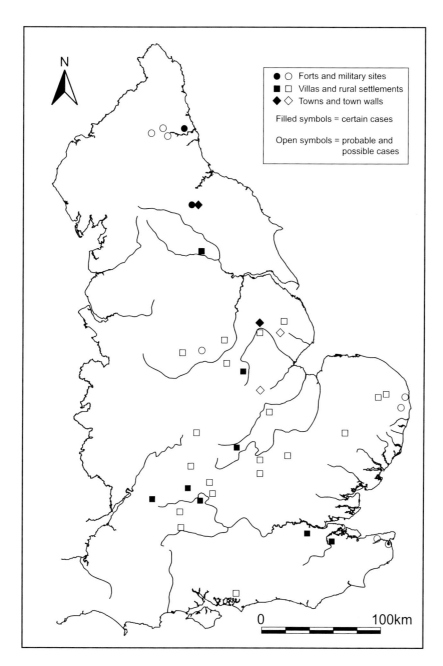

Fig. 5.24 Map of Roman sites reused in the early Anglo-Saxon period as cemetery locations (after Williams 1997, Fig. 7).

A time of transformation

Britain during the immediately post-Roman period, perhaps a time running from the late fourth century until the late fifth century, can be described as living in the shadow of the Roman Empire. In the west of Britain this time saw significant changes in the ways in which 'Roman' places of power were being used and perceived. Villas and monumental urban or military structures continued to be the focus for activity and 'Romano-British' material culture remained important. There are also hints that some 'Roman' activities (such as the consumption of suckling pig) were emphasised in particular social contexts (Gerrard 2007b; Hammon 2011). The continued use of late Roman style belt fittings suggests a maintained interest in forms of material culture and personal adornment that had martial connotations.

At the same time in the east of Britain new forms of material culture, architectural styles and funerary rites were being introduced. This influx of new 'Germanic' cultural influences was accompanied by some population movement across the North Sea, although the scale of this is debatable. The location of sites like Mucking (Hamerow 1993) might suggest that the earliest sites demonstrating Germanic cultural influences were positioned in areas that had previously been peripheral. The architecture of these sites appears to lack pretension but early burials display signs of economic wealth and social stratification (McKinley 1994, 84). This suggests that the settlements may not have been arenas for significant social display in contrast to the cemeteries. The continuing importance of Roman inspired objects, like belt sets, parallels the situation in the west, and the occurrence of occasional weapon burials is indicative of the importance of a martial ideology. Possibly the inhabitants of sites like Mucking in their early phases used items like belt sets as objects of personal adornment and elite status in indigenous contexts.

By the later fifth century many of the 'Roman' focussed activities in the west of Britain seem to have been transformed. Villas and towns were of diminished significance but ancestral locations like hillforts were becoming the focus of elite activity. Contacts with the eastern Mediterranean emphasised, perhaps, a new form of *Romanitas* as the old symbols of martial and civil power were rejected for monumental earthwork defences (Alcock 1995; E. Campbell 2007). New forms of display, such as inscribed stones with Latin and Ogham texts, arguably represent a hybridisation, or reinvention, of Roman epigraphic traditions (Handley 2001, 179–180; Petts 2002) but burial rites generally continued a custom derived from the late Roman tradition of unaccompanied inhumation. Meanwhile in the east the burgeoning Germanic communities were looking across the North Sea for cultural inspiration. Internal distinctions were emphasised in funerary dress, and perhaps daily life and male status were displayed using martial accoutrements.

If we were to summarise the complexities of this process it could be argued that the fifth century saw the rejection of the fourth-century civilian ideology based on *paideia*. Roman civilian and especially martial symbols were important to all communities. Once the Roman state disappeared the opportunity to appropriate a military role presumably appealed to both the indigenous population and 'barbarians'. The adoption of first a martial and then an increasingly Germanic ideology in the east of Britain perhaps forced a transformation in the west. As the 'Anglo-Saxon' east defined itself from the later fifth century by an increasingly territorially defined approach to dress, which signalled a variety of social and economic messages, the population in the west of Britain chose a different path. They eschewed the overt forms of display that were becoming dominant in the Anglo-Saxon regions (Lucy 2000) and instead pursued an elite lifestyle that was advertised by architecture and landscape context that also indicated their martial power.

6 | *Civitates*, kingdoms, estates and regions

Back to the Iron Age?

It is easy to contrast Britain's situation in the year 300 with its position in the year 600. In 300 the province was part of a pan-European and Mediterranean empire. It was part of the Roman economic system, tax-paying, money-using with urban centres and long-distance exchange. Governed by Roman law with a literate Latin-speaking elite and protected by standing armies, Britain was an integral part of the Roman Empire. By 600 the situation was very different. The province of Britannia had been replaced by a series of polyglot kingdoms many of which were smaller than a modern county. Long-distance exchange in bulk commodities had largely ceased and, when such exchange did take place, was on a much reduced scale at the new *wic* (emporia) sites (e.g. Hodges 1982). The early medieval period was a time of small communities and small worlds (Kolb and Snead 1997) in contrast to the earlier globalised Roman world system.

Like many of the debates surrounding the end of the Roman Empire the contrasts drawn between the situation in 300 and 600 offer only one view of the period. The hidden hand of decline, fall and catastrophe steers the interpretation along a predetermined and teleological path where Roman complexity regressively gave way to early medieval simplicity (Ward-Perkins 2005). This view also has the advantage of being undoubtedly true. However, the opposition of high-order *versus* low-order polities camouflages the fact that Roman Britain's coherence was both constructed and imposed. It is the mosaic of differences that characterise the regions of fourth-century Britain that deserve more attention. This shifting, blurred and overlapping pattern of social practice provides a stark contrast to the stereotypical 'Roman Britain'. It also offers another lens through which the transformation of Roman Britain into early medieval successor polities may be studied.

Under Domitian Roman arms in Britain were carried far north of the Forth–Clyde line (Hanson 1987) and during the early third century Severus was to repeat this feat (Birley 1999, 170–188). Yet the practical realities of terrain, logistics and indigenous opposition forced the Roman state to acknowledge that the total conquest of Britain was undesirable and unsustainable. From the late first century onwards there was a recognition that the lands north of Hadrian's Wall and west of the Irish Sea were to remain free of Roman rule, if not Roman influence (Mattingly 2007). Even within the area incorporated into the empire the incoherence of 'Britain' as a practical concept was recognised. First the province was subdivided during the early third century into Britannia Inferior and Superior (Graham 1966) and this was followed by the late Roman creation of the Diocese of the Britains, which comprised four or five provinces (*Not. Dig. Occ.* XXIII).

The archaeological study of 'Roman Britain' has long recognised that different parts of Britain had diverse experiences of the 'Roman period' (Figure 6.1). For the north of England and southern Scotland, Wales and the far south-west the Roman period could be seen as little more than an 'interlude' (for which see Fraser 2009, 116–117) and this different experience of the Roman period has often been explained as due to a lack of 'Romanisation'. The topography of these regions (all of which fall within the highland zone), the nature of Roman state control, the presence of the army as well as resistance to Rome have all been cited as explanations for this phenomenon (Haverfield 1912, 10; Frere 1967, 5; Millett 1990, 100; Mattingly 2007, 402–427).

The remaining areas, often described as the lowland or civilian zone, have sometimes been portrayed as a homogeneous fusion of Roman and indigenous civilisation (e.g. Leeds 1913, 13). Recently such views have been the subject of vigorous theoretical critiques, which suggest that any interaction between communities was likely to lead to a complex and diverse set of cultural responses (Webster 2001; Pitts 2008; Mattingly 2011). There have also been attempts to argue that the Roman Conquest was little more than a veneer laid over an indigenous society (Reece 1988b; Russell and Laycock 2010). At its most extreme this approach suggests that Iron Age tribal groupings were ethnic units whose antipathies were controlled and fossilised by the overarching imperial state.

The Iron Age may seem a long way from the fifth century. However, if the social and political structure of earlier 'tribal units' survived, then the transformation of Britain from a high-order polity to a series of small-scale polities could be recast as the re-emergence of a pre-existing order. This approach has dual benefits that play into two significantly different interpretations of Roman Britain's end. First, it can be seen as evidence of long-term continuities that run through the structure of society. No matter how great the transformations and changes were, a significant substratum of British society continued unchanged (Dark 1994) underpinned by a sense of antiquity (Carver 2009, 334; 2012). The alternative view uses the notion

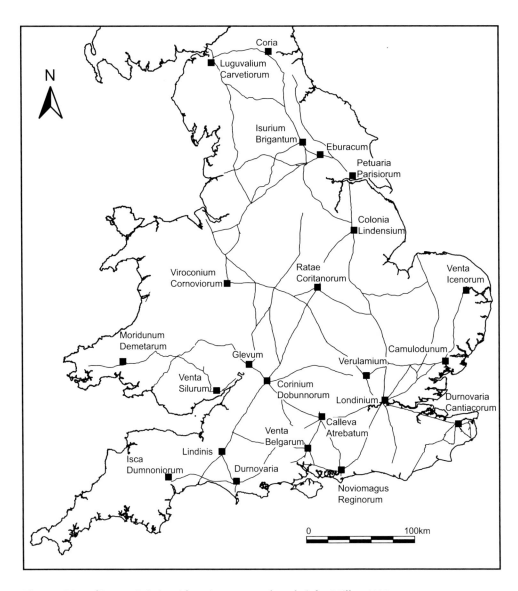

Fig. 6.1 Map of Roman Britain with major towns and roads (after Millett 1990, Fig. 17).

of Iron Age ethnic antipathies to explain the catastrophe of Roman Britain's end and the later dominance of the Anglo-Saxons (Laycock 2008). The veracity of such approaches depends to a large extent on their evidential basis and this lies in the Iron Age.

Caesar's (Caes., *B. Gall.*) account of his conquest of Gaul depicts an Iron Age situation in which a large number of tribal groups, ruled by kings and narrow oligarchies, were overcome militarily. These groupings

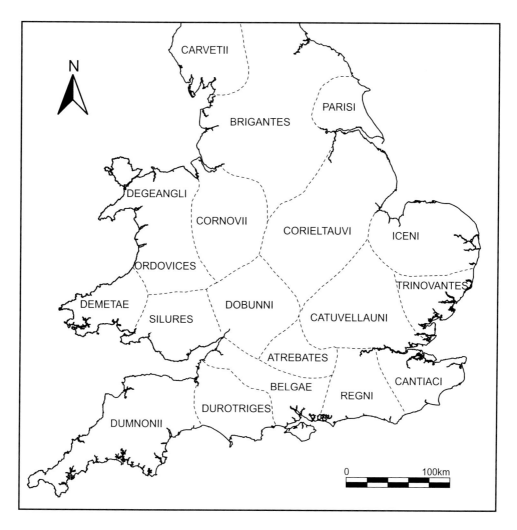

Fig. 6.2 The tribes/*civitates* of Roman Britain (after Millett 1990, Fig. 16).

shared, in Caesar's view, some attributes such as religion, language and, when confronted by an external threat (like the Germani), 'Gallic identity'. However, they also competed with one another and inter-tribal relationships were extremely fluid. Once Gaul had been conquered these tribal groups were used as the basis of the Roman administration. They became *civitates*, each headed by an urban settlement bearing the tribal name (Woolf 1998, 115). Britain's experience appears to have been structured along similar lines, and maps of Britain's Iron Age tribes and Romano-British *civitates* grace most standard textbooks (e.g. Millett 1990, Fig. 16; Mattingly 2007, Figs 3. and 10) (Figure 6.2). Roman documentary sources, such as Ptolemy's

Geography, the *Antonine Itinerary* and the *Ravenna Cosmography* (Rivet and Smith 1979), as well as epigraphy (e.g. *RIB* 1,673), superficially support this interpretation.

Difficulties emerge when a more critical approach is taken. The term 'tribe' is far from neutral and comes with significant modern and colonial-era baggage (Mattingly 2007, 59). It is in common usage as a means of Othering (Said 2003), whereby complexities in troubled parts of the modern world are discussed and dismissed from a western viewpoint as the result of largely irrational and anachronistic 'tribal' or 'ethnic' tensions. Yet many of these modern tensions are the direct product of colonial experiences where European powers sought to categorise, control and exploit indigenous communities. This is a reminder that the Roman view of 'tribes' was far from neutral. They too were seeking to exploit and control and were just as capable of imposing simplifying worldviews on fluid and complex realities.

During the period of Rome's expansion various Mediterranean social units were taken under control (e.g. James 2011a). Mainly these social units were of some complexity and included city states and established kingdoms. However, in north-western Europe such complexities were largely lacking. Roman understanding of indigenous groups, whether so-called tribes or temporary alliances treated as tribal units, was structured by the Mediter-ranean model of cities and territories. In areas such as northern Britain, which appear to have lacked much of the organisation and complexity that characterised polities in the south of Britain during the Late Iron Age (Cun-liffe 2005), Rome manufactured such groups either deliberately or through happenstance. The Belgae of southern Britain may have been a Roman invention (Rivet and Smith 1979, 267) and the Brigantes (whose name means the 'high' or 'mighty ones') may have simply been a Roman label of convenience for a complex patchwork of small hill-dwelling groups (Rivet and Smith 1979, 279).

The archaeological material from the Late Iron Age also has a part to play in this argument. The location of Iron Age polities is usually fixed by the later position of the Romano-British *civitas* capital. However, the territory is defined by the distribution of material culture, in particular coins and types of pottery. Iron Age coinage occasionally bears tribal names and the distribution of stylistically related types can be used to define the territories of individual tribes (Cunliffe 2005). Pottery styles, some of which have antecedents stretching back into the Middle Iron Age, can also be mapped into zones that are more or less contiguous with the distributions of the 'tribal' coinages. Acceptance of the correlation of these types of material culture as equating to a 'tribe' suggests acquiescence to a Childean

(1929) view of material culture and identity. Yet considerable work over the last thirty years has demonstrated that such an approach is problematic. Material culture was and remains an active part of human social relations, used to define and negotiate elements of individual identity (Jones 1997). Suggesting that the Iron Age was inhabited by tribes that underwent no significant changes during either the Late Iron Age or the Roman period and were to re-emerge in some fashion in the fifth or sixth century stretches credulity. Such arguments become even more strained when their details are examined. The supposed transformation of the Iron Age Dobunni into the Middle Saxon Hwicce provides an illuminating case study.

The lower Severn Valley is the focus for a distribution of Iron Age coins and pottery attributed to the Dobunnic polity (Cunliffe 2005, 189–190 and Fig. 8.10). In the Roman period Cirencester – Corinium Dobunnorum – was the *civitas* capital and an important urban centre associated with a particular style of mosaics known as the 'Corinian School' (Millett 1990, Fig. 72). An argument has been advanced that this *civitas* became the post-Roman kingdom of the Hwicce (Figure 6.3). This is based on an entry in *The Anglo-Saxon Chronicle* for the year 577 recording the fall of Bath, Gloucester and Cirencester to the West Saxon kings Cuthwine and Ceawlin and the boundaries of the medieval See of Worcester, which is thought to approximate to the kingdom of the Hwicce (Hooke 1985; Gelling 1992, 80).

Clearly, the basis of the argument is a comparison of apples and oranges. There is no Romano-British pottery with a purely 'Dobunnic' distribution and the inhabitants of Cirencester were happy to acquire their pots from Dorset, Oxfordshire and elsewhere in the later Roman period (e.g. McWhirr 1986, 158–189). Furthermore, there is a suggestion that Dobunnic ceramics in the Late Iron Age may indicate two different groupings separated by the Bristol Avon (Cunliffe 2005, 189). The medieval evidence is equally problematic. It has long been recognised that *The Anglo-Saxon Chronicle* entry for 577 may be a later invention, created to justify later West Saxon claims to the territory of the Hwicce (which had been under the Mercian sphere of influence in the Middle Saxon period) (Sims-Williams 1983, 33). Nor has it been demonstrated that the later boundaries of the See of Worcester were coterminous with the earlier Anglo-Saxon polity.

The case of the Dobunni/Hwicce demonstrates many of the difficulties inherent in any attempt to identify long-term political continuities through the distribution of material culture. Nevertheless, this type of argument has been developed even further and it has been suggested that the early medieval geography of Britain respects the preceding Roman provincial boundaries within the diocese (White 2007). Under this argument the areas

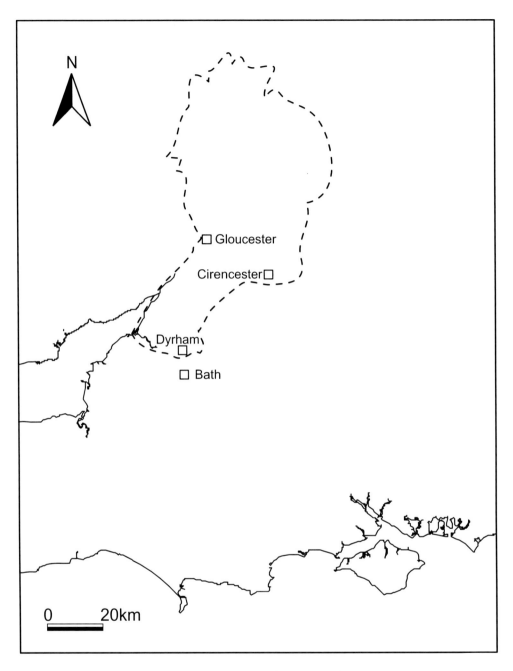

Fig. 6.3 A map of the Dobunni/Hwicce. The outline of the diocese of Worcester is indicated as well as four locations linked to *The Anglo-Saxon Chronicle*'s entry for 577 (after Dark 1994, Fig. 25).

that remained free of Germanic cultural influence the longest (Wales and the west of Britain) are seen as coterminous with Britannia Prima and the areas of Anglian and Saxon influence correspond with other late Roman provincial boundaries (White 2007). Interesting as this hypothesis is, it is ultimately speculative because there is not a single extant document that defines the boundaries between the four (or five) provinces.

The notion that Iron Age polities became Romano-British *civitates*, or provinces, and emerged as early medieval kingdoms is an interesting hypothesis and the occurrence of names such as the Gododdin (derived from the Roman period Votadini) (Jarman 1988) and the Dumnonii of the south-western peninsula (Pearce 2004, 22–23) in the early Middle Ages suggests that earlier 'tribal' names continued in use among groups on Roman Britain's peripheries (Dark 1994). However, this is slim evidence on which to suggest institutional or political continuity. This is not to say that regions in the Roman period failed to maintain a distinct character influenced by their inhabitants' past as well as new factors and stimuli. What it does deny is the ahistorical notion of political and social units surviving, come what may, unchanged in their outlooks and agendas for nearly a thousand years. A more sophisticated approach to regionalism abandons these imposed notions of supposed 'tribal group' and illusory polities as unhelpful. In their place we can examine how material culture and the environment were used and shaped to produce contrasting worldviews across and within regions.

Regions and regionality: living differently in the fourth century

In Chapter 3 attention was focussed on the majority of the Romano-British population – the 90 per cent or so who lived in the countryside (Figure 6.4). The lives of these rural dwellers were dominated by the landscape they inhabited, the agricultural cycle and their relationships with their crops and herds. Elements of this cycle are embodied in a mid fourth-century calendar produced in Rome (Salzman 1990). They arguably shared this close relationship with the agricultural cycle with medieval peasants (Hill 1998; Karkov 2010), and the prehistoric communities of the Neolithic and Bronze Age (Williams 2003). Those relationships were influenced by a myriad of factors: some physical, like relief, rainfall, drainage and soil fertility; and others cultural, like economic systems, elite control, religious beliefs, diet and dialect or language. It is impossible to assess all of these factors for late Roman Britain. Much of the evidence simply does not exist. Yet the

Fig. 6.4 An aerial photograph of modern field systems in Devon.
This patchwork of small fields provides an impression of the nature
of the late Roman agricultural landscape (© Sam Turner).

enormous increase in archaeological research over the past thirty years does
allow some of these issues to be investigated.

One of the most common archaeological features encountered in a rural
situation is the field boundary. These can survive as upstanding earthworks,
or as infilled ditches visible on aerial photographs, geophysical surveys or
in an excavation. Many of these field systems and their attendant settlement
enclosures have been excavated recently since the advent of developer-
funded archaeology in the mid 1990s. The excavations themselves can cover
significant swathes of landscape. Housing developments may cover tens of
acres, linear developments like road or pipelines may run for hundreds
of kilometres and these interventions have allowed the morphology and
chronology of how the landscape was organised to be understood at a
previously unheard of level of detail.

A recent survey attempted to draw much of this information together into an *Atlas of Roman Rural Settlement in England* (Taylor 2007). This demonstrated that field systems across Britain were far from uniform. In the north and west the landscape was largely open (Taylor 2007, 55–61) (Figure 6.5). This outfield was sometimes divided by long boundaries and characterised by small enclosed settlements with a patchwork of infields (Taylor 2007, Figs. 5.1 and 5.2). This is probably indicative of communities practising mixed agriculture, but with an emphasis on livestock rearing. The open outfield can be interpreted as grazing land held in common and the smaller enclosures typical of the infield as arable plots, worked either individually or with their neighbours. However, it should be noted that the morphology of settlements in these regions differed in small but significant ways.

Further south and east the landscape was far more intensively divided (Taylor 2007, 65–71). Patchworks of fields and larger and hierarchical set-tlement foci were linked by tracks, droveways and roads over long distances. These landscapes were varied in subtle ways between regions, and field sys-tems characteristic of the East Midlands, East Anglia, the Thames Valley and the Southern Downs can be postulated. Clearly, it seems reasonable to sug-gest that these were landscapes dominated by intensive arable agriculture.

This conclusion could have been reached by the same kind of environ-mental determinism that produced the dichotomy between the 'highland' and 'lowland' zones (Haverfield 1912, 10) (Figure 6.6). The topography, rainfall and soils in the north and far south-west of England and Wales have, until the advent of modern industrial agriculture, all emphasised live-stock within a mixed farming economy and a dispersed settlement pattern. The difference is not unexpected. However, this data can be incorporated into a broader analysis of the worldview of the Romano-British inhabitants of this region.

The lived experience of communities dwelling in Cumbria, Northumber-land, Wales or parts of Cornwall will have been dominated by their relative isolation (Figure 6.7). Compared to southern communities the settlements were smaller, and presumably contained fewer inhabitants. Those who dwelt in farmsteads like those excavated near Penrith in Cumbria (Higham and Jones 1983), Huckhoe and Pegswood in Northumberland (Jobey 1959; Proctor 2009), Cefn Cwmwd and Melin y Plas in Anglesey (Cuttler, David-son and Hughes 2012) or Bryn Eryr and Bush Farm in Gwynedd (Longley, Johnstone and Evans 1998, 185–246), as well as Trethurgy in Cornwall (Quinnell 2004) will undoubtedly have come together with their neigh-bours to trade, celebrate festivals and arguably pay their taxes to Rome.

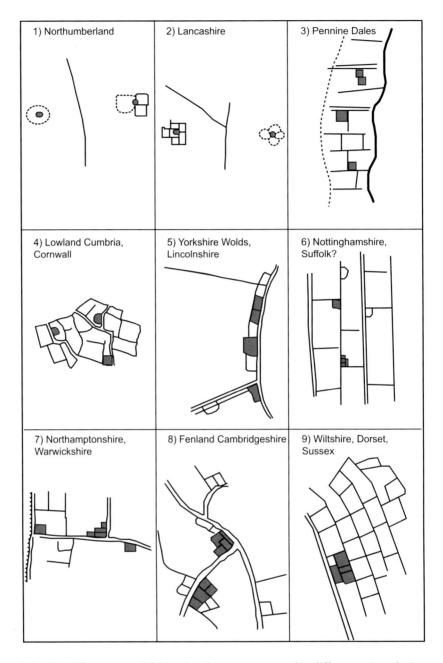

Fig. 6.5 Different types of field and enclosure systems used in different regions during the Roman period (after Taylor 2007, Fig. 5.2).

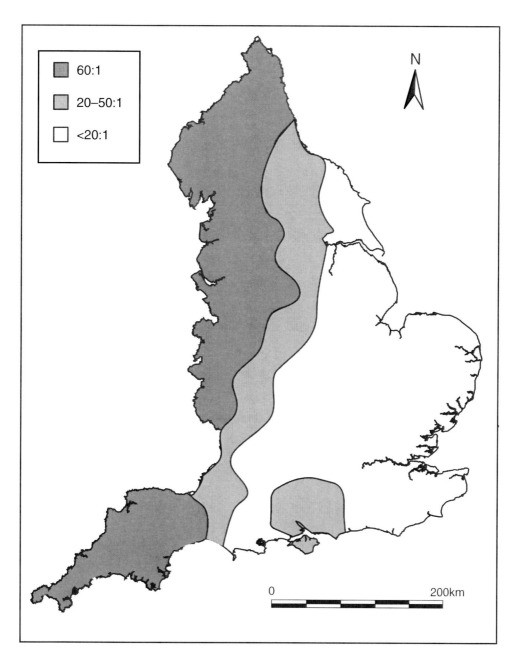

Fig. 6.6 Map showing the ratio of enclosed settlements to linear field systems in England (after Taylor 2007, Fig. 4.6).

Fig. 6.7 Reconstruction of the settlement at Pegswood. This is an early Roman site but
it is typical of many upland settlements (© Pre-Construct Archaeology Ltd).

However, their day-to-day lives, the routine of working in a mixed economy
with an emphasis on livestock rearing, will have provided a shared sense
of values and experiences. This sense of community will have been further
reinforced by cultural factors. The presence of the frontier will have been
one of these (James 2001). The significant role that the Roman army played
in controlling movement, or the opportunities it offered as an alternative
'career', should not be underestimated. Equally, on the far side of the frontiers were groups with whom the inhabitants of northern England will have
shared much, but who also represented a threat and perhaps also an alternative way of life. In Wales the impact of the army will have been less intense
but still important given garrisons at sites like Segontium.

There is a growing body of archaeological evidence that supports the
suggestion that life in the north and far west of Roman Britain was significantly different to that lived elsewhere (Mattingly 2007). The use of 'Roman'
material culture was severely restricted. In Wales (excluding the southern
coastal plain), Cumbria and Northumberland relatively few sites produce
significant finds assemblages. The excavators of two rural sites in Gwynedd
commented that they had yielded above average quantities of Romano-
British pottery, but the totals still amounted to little more than a dozen
vessels per generation (Longley et al. 1998, 244). Even the distribution of
Roman coinage echoes this pattern, with coin loss being far more common
in southern and eastern England than in the north and west (Walton 2011).
To some extent this is a product of preservational circumstances, but it is
also a reflection of a different way of life in these areas.

The paucity of material culture does not extend to the Roman military sites in the north and their attendant civilian settlements (e.g. Collins and Allason-Jones 2010). The occupation of the latter class of site falls largely before our period of interest, with many so-called *vici* being abandoned by the fourth century (Sommer 1984b). However, the finds assemblages from these sites reinforce the differences between the north and the south. Brooches from such sites tend to be of the 'plate' form, while southern sites produce 'bow' brooches (Snape 1993). The wearing of brooches was a primarily early Roman phenomenon (Mackreth 2011) but this broad division in material culture and the existence of forms such as the 'dragonesque brooch', which is clearly a northern type (Mackreth 2011, 188), suggest differences in the use of material culture across regions. In the late Roman period this north–south divide is visible in the relative absence of Hawkes and Dunning (1961) style belt fittings from the north (see Chapter 2). Late Roman ceramics reveal a slightly different story. In the third and early fourth centuries pottery was being sourced from kilns as far south as Dorset (Gillam 1976). However, by the late fourth century pottery supply across the northern regions was dominated by vessels manufactured in kilns located in East Yorkshire (Bidwell and Croom 2010).

Archaeobotanical evidence from the same region indicates that a variety of arable crops were raised and these included wheat, barley, rye and oats, with barley the most significant crop (van der Veen 1992). A similar pattern is discernible in Wales and this contrasts to the situation in the south where wheat was more commonly grown. It has been suggested that this distinction reflects a division between those preferring to eat barley bannocks and those favouring loaves of bread (Cool 2006, 77–79). Cool (2006, 77) argues for a 'Roman' preference for wheat consumption, with barley characterised in some sources as little more than animal fodder, and culinary prejudice may have been a significant component in the creation of regional identities.

This evidence demonstrates that at a broad level life in the north or far west and the south of Britain was not homogeneous. Lived experience for a community in Cumbria reflected the realities of an upland environment, the close proximity of the Roman army, a dispersed settlement pattern and an agricultural economy which emphasised animals, alongside significant arable production. Socio-cultural factors, such as a preference for wearing particular brooch designs or consuming barley as a staple, may have been further signifiers of the distinctiveness of these regions. Such patterns, discernible in dumps of carbonised grain or in collections of metalwork, are all that survive of what must have surely been a rich tapestry of regional identities and networks. Local dialects may have been important indicators of regional affiliation (Weber 1976, 67–94), but the absence of written Celtic means that this is a matter for speculation (Tomlin 1987). Religious affiliations and rituals are another aspect for which, outside of the military cultural milieu of the forts (e.g. Allason-Jones and McKay 1985), next to nothing is known. These possibilities and more, for which archaeology is an intractable witness, suggest that the pattern of regionalism may be even more complex than the broad strokes of the picture outlined here indicate.

The situation in the south of Britain – the so-called lowland zone – was probably just as complicated as that in the north. There has been a tendency among scholars to homogenise this phenomenon and this approach has been driven by an intellectual paradigm that has, until recently, been concerned primarily with establishing how 'Roman' a particular site was. Thus villas, with their stone walls, tiled roofs, mosaics, hypocausts and bath blocks, were perceived as statements of *Romanitas*, rather than indicating the structure of society (for an honourable exception to this generalisation see Smith 1997). This thinking was applied to many other site types and artefact assemblages. The emphasis was on measuring how Roman a site was rather than the context in which the material culture was used. Recently this paradigm has begun to shift and the differences in lived experience in Britain during the Roman period are beginning to be explored.

The distribution and use of fourth-century pottery

Much of the research has been concentrated on studying the spatial distributions of material culture and then attempting to link them back to supposed Iron Age patterns. This has been attempted with mosaic styles as well as ceramic distributions and is convincing to a greater or lesser extent. It has been argued here that such approaches are simplistic and are based on largely ahistorical assumptions about societies within particular regions. This is not to say that some are more or less convincing. The significant and rapid fall off in the distribution of Dorset BB1 a few miles east of the kiln sites is clearly a significant phenomenon that would seem to echo preceding boundaries between cultural zones (Allen and Fulford 1996, Fig. 8). Similarly, on the Isle of Wight 'Vectis Ware' (Tomalin 1987), an Iron Age pottery tradition, continued until the third century, when the inhabitants of the island went over to using BB1 and New Forest grey wares (Lyne 2011). Interestingly, the Isle of Wight also emerges as a distinct 'zone' in Walton's (2011, 209–260) recent discussion of coin loss in Roman Britain. It would be easy to interpret these patterns as demonstrating the continued existence of earlier cultural boundaries into the Roman period. Such an analysis may be true but it has also been suggested that in the late Roman period pottery producers consciously chose to be located close to boundaries of *civitates* (and by extension earlier Iron Age polities) in order to take advantage of the marketing opportunities such liminal positions offered (Millett 1990, 167–169). If the interpretations of these contrasting phenomena are correct then it would suggest that different types of pottery carried different social messages.

In Somerset and Dorset, BB1 would be an indicator of local regional identity that differentiated the 'Durotrigian' inhabitants from those to the west in Devon (Dumnonia) and to the east (the 'Belgae'). However, to the north-east ('Dobunnic' territory) BB1 was accepted and used quite happily, as it was to varying degrees in places further afield like South Wales, London and Kent (Pollard 1988; Tyers 1996). Oxfordshire Ware, produced on the boundary of a number of *civitates*, achieved a significant distribution over much of southern England during the fourth century (Young 1977). This suggests that it was socially acceptable to the majority of communities who encountered it. However, in the Midlands the ware is rare even though there were few producers manufacturing competing forms (Tyers 1996, Fig. 221).

The late Roman grog-tempered industries of southern Britain are also of interest (Figure 6.8). Produced during the fourth century in Kent, Hampshire and the Isle of Wight (Pollard 1988, Fig. 53; Lyne 1994), these vessels have often been derided as crude and argued to represent the degenerate state of late Roman pottery production (Faulkner 2000, 148). The localised distribution of these wares indicates that their use was restricted (Tyers 1996, Fig. 240). Yet in many of the same regions other types of Romano-British pottery, such as BB1 or Alice Holt/Farnham Ware, were being used. These grog-tempered wares may well represent a simpler mode of production than that used to produce the major wares like BB1 (Peacock 1982). If so, then the use of this pottery might reflect a society structured in a different way. Here it may be noted that the distribution of grog-tempered pottery in the fourth century (Tyers 1996, Fig. 240; Dr M. Lyne *pers. comm.*) can be broadly correlated with the later distribution of Quoit Brooch Style objects (Suzuki 2000, Figs. 78 and 79) (Figure 6.9). It would be foolish to push this correlation too far but the suggestion of a 'cultural zone', however such an ambiguous term may be defined, that can be perceived in the fourth century and also in the fifth century is an interesting one.

A final late Roman pottery fabric – so-called 'Pevensey Ware' – presents another facet of ceramic distribution in fourth-century Britain. Pevensey

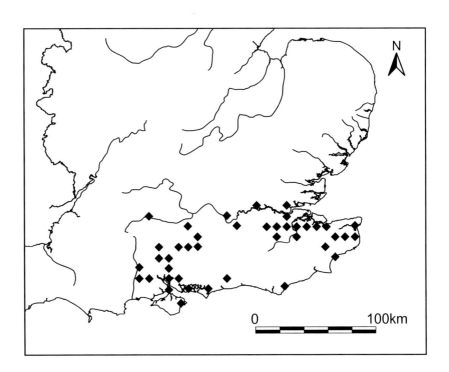

Fig. 6.8 The distribution of late Roman grog-tempered ware in south-eastern Britain (after Tyers 1996, Fig. 240).

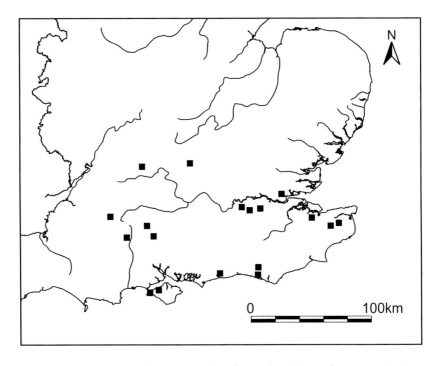

Fig. 6.9 The distribution of Quoit Brooch Style metalwork in south-eastern Britain (after Suzuki 2000, Fig. 78).

Ware is a minor red-slipped tableware fabric manufactured and used, as the name suggests, in a restricted corner of Sussex focussed on the shore fort at Pevensey (Fulford 1973; Lyne 1994, 365). Stylistically the vessel forms manufactured in this fabric are very closely linked to those produced in Oxfordshire (Young 1977) and it has been suggested that the kilns were established by a migrant potter (Bird and Young 1981). That such a small-scale producer could flourish, albeit in a small area, during the late fourth century stands as a warning: late Roman ceramic distributions should not be characterised simply as a series of interlocking and competing pan-regional producers. There were small-scale distributions even of 'fine wares' and perhaps 'small worlds' to accompany these restricted distributions.

These observations about the nature of late Roman pottery use in southern Britain need to be tempered with the recognition that different types of pottery will have fulfilled different social roles. For instance, grog-tempered coarse wares from Kent are not comparable with red-slipped tablewares from Oxfordshire. The likelihood of uneven and periodic supply (Going 1992) may also be noted and could explain the co-existence of small local producers alongside larger supra-regional industries (Figure 6.10). The resulting conclusion must be that the ceramic evidence, when studied as the distribution of the products of particular kilns, is equivocal evidence of regionality. In some circumstances the use (or rejection) of particular forms of ceramic material culture may have been a significant component in the creation and maintenance of local identities. However, this should be assessed alongside equally compelling evidence for such material culture being accepted in a wide variety of contexts. From this it might be suggested that the role of pottery as a signifier of regional affiliation was both blurred and complex. For an inhabitant of the southern Midlands not using red-slipped tableware from Oxfordshire may have been a deliberate choice carrying important messages about their worldview. In contrast, the use of Oxfordshire Ware in Kent or Somerset may have not have been seen in these terms.

The analysis of the distributions of Romano-British pottery and other types of material culture demonstrates that there are nested regional patterns of some complexity. Unfortunately this conclusion can be questioned by observing that such distributions do not necessarily underline regional differences or local identities. The distributions might, for instance, be the result of differing workshops fulfilling demand in geographically restricted markets. However, a more detailed examination of a number of ceramic case studies from Roman Britain conclusively reveals regional differences in social practice.

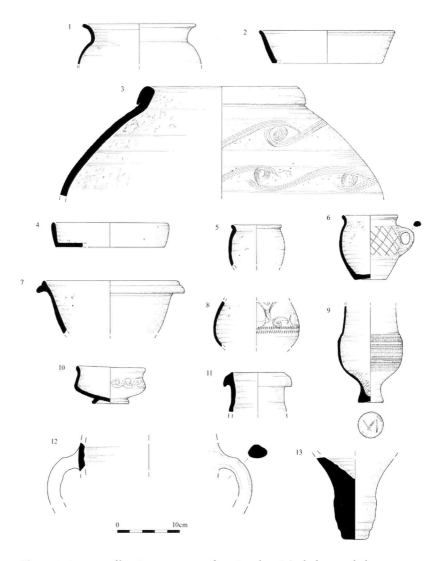

Fig. 6.10 A group of late Roman pottery from London. It includes vessels from a range of sources: 1–3) Alice Holt/Farnham Ware jars and a dish, 4–5) Dorset Black Burnished Ware dish and beaker, 6–7) unsourced beaker and bowl, 8–9) fineware bottle and beaker from the Nene Valley, 10) Red Slipped fineware bowl from Oxfordshire and 11–13) fragments of rare North African amphora (© Pre-Construct Archaeology Ltd).

The first of these case studies concerns large pottery storage jars (Figure 6.10 No. 3), which were manufactured at a number of centres across southern England. In the south-west of Britain they were produced in a variety of fabrics and they also formed an important element within the repertoire of late Roman pottery producers in the New Forest (Fulford 1975),

Oxfordshire (Young 1977), Harrold (Bedfordshire) (Brown 1994) and the Alice Holt/Farnham region (Lyne and Jefferies 1979). Other centres of production have been postulated at Norton Fitzwarren (Somerset) (Holbrook and Bidwell 1991, 177), as well as in northern Somerset and Gloucestershire (Wedlake 1958, Fig. 49.645–648; Wedlake 1982, 250; Leach and Evans 2001, Fig. 35.J14) and the Milton Keynes/Towcester region (Booth and Green 1989). Of these production centres the vessels made in the Alice Holt/Farnham region were perhaps distributed most widely and they occur in London, Essex and Kent (Lyne and Jefferies 1979, Fig. 41). Large vessels such as these storage jars may have been manufactured as packaging for some otherwise invisible commodity, although the use of lead rivets to repair examples in Essex (Wickenden 1988, Fig. 54.22) suggests that they were also valued as vessels in their own right.

In Dorset large storage jars are notably absent (e.g. Seager Smith and Davies 1993). Of course, this was the heartland of the BB1 producers and ceramic assemblages in the region are dominated by black burnished vessels manufactured on the fringes of Poole Harbour (Allen and Fulford 1996). It is true that these kilns occasionally produced oversize versions of smaller jars but large storage jars only appear in the latter half of the fourth century in a variant fabric (Gerrard 2010). This absence is reinforced when the use of large storage jars in Somerset and Hampshire was relatively commonplace. Interestingly, in the north of Britain storage jars were always rare (Holbrook and Bidwell 1991, 175) and industries located at Crambeck and elsewhere in East Yorkshire did not produce this vessel form (Gillam 1970; Corder 1989; Bidwell and Croom 2010).

The decision by some groups in late Roman Britain to not use storage jars appears to be a case of localised social practice that did not require a particular vessel form. The following examples deal with a related phenomenon: the localised use of unique vessel forms.

The Romano-British pottery industry located in the Nene Valley is well studied and comparatively well understood (Howe, Perrin and Mackreth 1980; Perrin 1999). Established in the late second century the kilns produced a variety of coarsewares and finewares, the latter of which included decorated beakers, bowls, flagons and mortaria that travelled in some quantity. Among this repertoire is a unique vessel form known as the 'Castor box' (Figure 6.11). This vessel is often accompanied by a lid and was only copied for a short time by kilns located near Colchester. The Castor box achieved a wide (if thin) distribution. Examples are known from across southern England with one even occurring at Ilchester in Somerset, where it was misidentified as a New Forest beaker (Leach 1982, Fig. 70.165). The origins

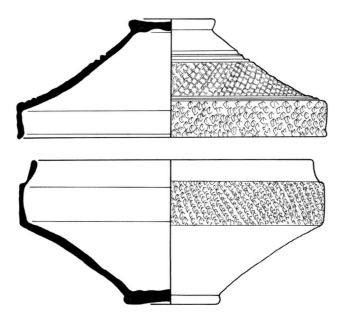

Fig. 6.11 A Nene Valley Ware 'Castor box' (after Howe et al. 1980, Fig. 7.89).

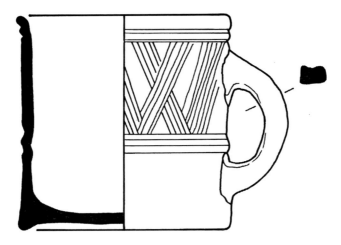

Fig. 6.12 A Severn Valley Ware tankard (after Timby 1990, Fig. 4.45).

of the Castor box and its function are unknown, although it has been suggested that it may have served in a fashion analogous to a tureen (Perrin 1999, 100).

The other vessel of relevance was the so-called Severn Valley Ware 'tankard' (Figure 6.12). As the name suggests this was a handled mug-like vessel. It was originally produced in small quantities by the BB1 potters of south-east Dorset (Holbrook and Bidwell 1991, 124) and went on to be copied by potters in the Lower Severn Valley (Webster 1976; Timby 1990) and parts of the Midlands (Booth 1986, 31). This vessel is distinctive: it surely functioned as a drinking vessel and is sometimes found as far north as the frontier zone (Gillam 1970, Fig. 20, No. 180).

The use of both the Castor box and the Severn Valley Ware tankard highlights the differences in social practices between regions. The communities located close to the kilns that produced these vessels clearly felt that these unusual pots were needed. The failure to copy these vessels elsewhere suggests that other groups did not require them. Of course, both of these unusual vessel types were also distributed over reasonably long distances in very small quantities. This pattern might indicate the movement of people who found these objects necessary in areas where they were unavailable. Alternatively, these 'boxes' and 'tankards' may have travelled alongside other more typical suites of vessels (such as bowls and jars) and been used by distant consumers in ways not envisaged at the site of production (Webster 2001).

The role of material culture in defining the regional distinctiveness of late Roman Britain should not be underestimated. The examples drawn from the study of ceramics can be elaborated further with reference to other classes of artefacts. The distribution of late fourth- and fifth-century belt buckles has been alluded to in an earlier chapter (Chapter 2), but metal hairpins (Cool 1990), nail cleaners (Crummy and Eckardt 2003) and even coins (Walton 2011) are distributed in ways that might be interpreted as regionally significant. However, rather than labour this point through the continued study of material culture it seems more appropriate to discuss this topic using other forms of evidence such as architecture.

Fourth-century architectural styles

The traditional division of Roman Britain between a northern/upland region dominated by military installations and 'indigenous' architectural traditions and a southern/lowland region characterised by villas and rectilinear buildings is one which generally holds true (Figure 6.13). However, as is the case with all generalisations this observation belies a far more complex situation.

The dominant domestic architectural style in the north and west of Britain was the roundhouse. Within England roundhouses occurred in smaller numbers but apparently more frequently in parts of the Midlands, particularly around Worcestershire and in Derbyshire, Leicestershire and Nottinghamshire. They were much rarer in south-eastern counties

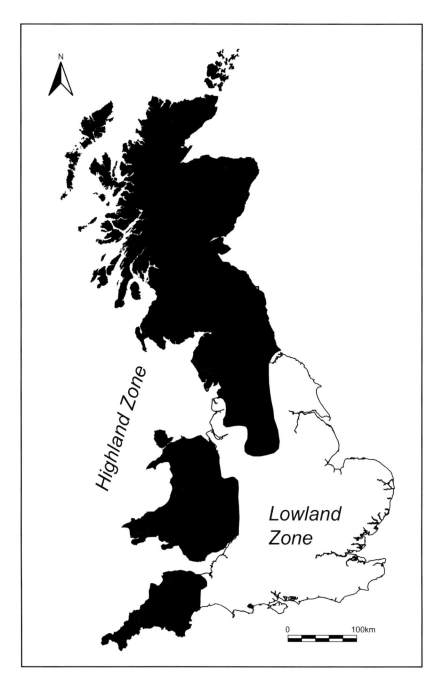

Fig. 6.13 The Highland and Lowland Zones of Britain (after Hill 1981, Fig. 7).

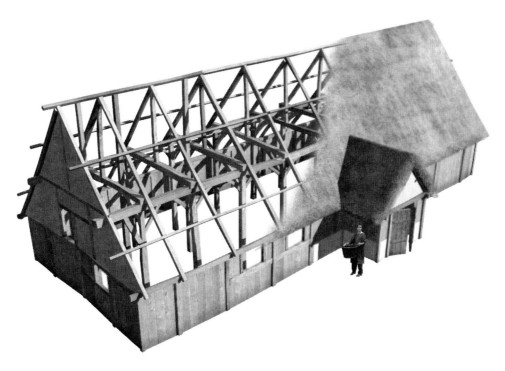

Fig. 6.14 Reconstruction drawing of the large aisled building at Shiptonthorpe (drawn by Mark Faulkner and reproduced by the kind permission of Martin Millett and the Shiptonthorpe Project).

including Kent, Essex, Hertfordshire, Surrey and Kent (Taylor 2007, 31 and Fig. 4.7).

The so-called 'villa', an architectural form that exists in a bewildering variety (Smith 1997), is often seen as the 'Roman' architectural counterpart to the 'native' roundhouse. Yet it has long been recognised that villas are not evenly spread across the lowlands of Roman Britain. Concentrations exist in the West Country and these structures can be identified occurring in a broad swathe from the Exe to The Wash (Taylor 2007, Fig. 4.9). Elsewhere villa type buildings are distributed more thinly. They are largely absent from the Weald and are rare around London and in parts of Norfolk and Suffolk.

The distributions of other forms of buildings are harder to plot because there is little consistent vocabulary to describe them. Rectilinear buildings are commonplace and largely echo the distribution of villa structures. However, this unsatisfactory category includes so-called aisled buildings (Figure 6.14). These large structures are rectangular in plan and divided lengthways into aisles by rows of columns or pillars (Perring 2002, 53–55). First occurring during the early Roman period, they are a significant rural architectural form that occurs closely linked to some villa buildings and also as stand-alone structures. They have variously been interpreted as barns or as housing for estate workers. However, some are elaborately constructed and decorated and contain evidence such as groups of hearths and other features that suggest the use of space within them was tightly structured. It has been argued that this phenomenon replicates the structuring of space within earlier Iron Age buildings, but Taylor (2001, 52) has demonstrated that the architecturally embellished late Roman examples seem to represent a hybrid architectural form, incorporating traditional indigenous patterns of life as well as referencing Classicising mores. The distribution of aisled buildings has not been fully mapped but they are particularly common in the East Midlands, where they may have been the dominant architectural form (Taylor 2007, 33).

Funerary practices provide another example of regional variation in architectural tradition. Mausolea are a rare monument type frequently associated with late Roman urban cemeteries. A number of examples have been investigated in London (Barber and Bowsher 2000), at Dorchester (Farwell and Molleson 1993) and more recently next to the Roman fort at Binchester (Co. Durham) (Birbeck in press). However, in south-eastern England and particularly in Kent these funerary monuments occasionally existed in relative isolation – as at Gillingham (G. Seddon *pers. comm.*) and Stone-by-Faversham (Taylor and Yonge 1981) – or juxtaposed with villa buildings. Examples of the latter phenomenon exist at Bancroft (Buckinghamshire) (Zeepvat 1994), Lullingstone (Meates 1979) and Keston (Kent) (Philp et al. 1999). This form of commemorating the dead does not occur in other areas where villa buildings are common and suggests that this type of funerary architecture was another manifestation of regionality. The particular concentration of this type of funerary display in Kent has been linked to cultural connections with areas such as Gallia Belgica (Millett 2007, 159). This is a useful reminder that some of Britain's late Roman regions may have looked towards northern Gaul.

Roundhouses, 'villas', aisled buildings and mausolea were not distributed evenly and as such they were architectural statements that highlighted the distinctiveness of particular regions. The contrast between an area (like the Cotswolds) where villas were a dominant architectural form and a region (like the East Midlands) where aisled buildings were more common would have been obvious. It is likely that these regional differences in architectural traditions were further highlighted by construction techniques. The architecture of the medieval and early modern periods is characterised by the use of regionally specific materials (Morriss 2001) and a similar situation is likely to have existed in the Roman period.

Material culture and architectural traditions appear to present a picture of widespread regional differences. These differences in dress, architecture and consumption present a complex spatial picture that cannot be simply overlaid on supposed pre-existing and latent Iron Age tribal structures. The pattern that emerges from this admittedly selective examination of the evidence is of nested and overlapping spatial distributions. The presence of broad distinctions (such as north *versus* south, or highland *versus* lowland) cannot be denied. However, elsewhere it seems clear that aspects of material culture were not viewed consistently. The use of a particular piece of material culture may have been important in the construction of regional difference, but in other regions such items may have played no part in constructing worldviews.

The patterns that can be charted through the distribution of material culture and architectural traditions offer a vision of 'small worlds' (Kolb and Snead 1997) where economics and social practice appear to have been restricted and regionally distinct. It may be inappropriate to frame these distinctions solely in terms of identities but the idea of communities at varying geographical scales provides an interesting model of fourth-century Britain at odds with the top-down vision of provinces and *civitates*-cum-tribes.

Ilchester and its hinterland: an elite 'small world'

In Chapter 4 elite groupings in late Roman Britain were introduced along with the manner in which they demonstrated their *paideia* and ideological commitment to *Romanitas*. Developing the concept advanced above – that the landscape was fractured into different communities defined in a variety of ways – allows a speculative reconstruction and analysis of the micro-regional relationships of a series of 'elite' sites in fourth-century Somerset to be undertaken. Traditional interpretations have tended to view the late Roman landscape in a flat cartographic fashion with each site being categorised and plotted (Tilley 1994; Taylor 2007) with simple hierarchies used to order the data. In this discussion we can use the *estate* as a unit of analysis. Estates have featured prominently in early medieval landscape studies (e.g. Jones 1961) but discussion in the Roman period has been thwarted by the lack of contemporary documentary evidence. Here the estate is used as a means of conceptualising socio-economic relationships between sites.

The Roman town of Lindinis (Ilchester) in Somerset (Leach 1982, 1994) was a relatively small urban centre that was arguably promoted to the status of a *civitas* capital during the late empire (Stevens 1952). It stood at a nodal point on the local communications routes. The Fosse Way, the long-distance route that ran from Lincoln to Exeter, skirts the marshes of the Somerset Levels and crosses the Yeo at Ilchester and another route running from Dorchester (Dorset), which used the dryland of the Polden Hills to cross the Somerset Levels, ran on to the port of Combwich at the mouth of the Parrett on the Somerset Coast (Rippon 2008). The town has long been recognised as a focus for some of the densest villa settlement in Britain (Figure 6.15) and it is one group of such structures located to the south and west of the town that concerns us here.

Within an area crudely defined as everything bounded by the River Yeo to the north and east, the modern county boundary to the south and the Fosse Way to the west, there are at least eight buildings that have been excavated to various degrees, have evidence for contemporaneous activity and can be termed villas. These include the structures at Seavington St Mary (Graham and Mills 1995), Dinnington (Adcock and Wood 2005; Prof. A. King *pers. comm.*), Lopen (Brunning 2001) in the south-west; Lufton (Hayward 1952 and 1972), Westlands (Radford 1928) and Bedmore Barn (Ham Hill) (Beattie and Pythian-Adams 1913; Sharples et al. 2012, 39) in the centre and east (Haverfield 1906, 330); and West Coker (Moore 1862) on the southern edge. In addition to these sites there are also a number of possible villas known from stray finds. These have been excluded and, given that Lopen and Dinnington were both discovered since 2000, a number of other sites probably remain to be identified. The significance of this distribution lies in the simple fact that not one of these sites is located more than eight miles away from Ilchester or its furthest neighbour (i.e. less than three hours walk). Indeed, with some of the buildings, such as those at East and West Coker or Seavington St Mary and Dinnington, the structures are located in such close proximity that walking between them, let alone riding, would be a matter of tens of minutes.

If it is accepted that these buildings were the dwelling places of members of the local elite then it seems clear that some of these elite individuals and family groups lived in close proximity to one another. It is inconceivable that they did not know one another and their relationships will have been structured through some of the mechanisms discussed in Chapter 4. Super-ficially these individuals may have been equals and peers, and they may, for instance, all have been members of the local *ordo* (town council). However, there would also be complex webs of power within these groups. Some

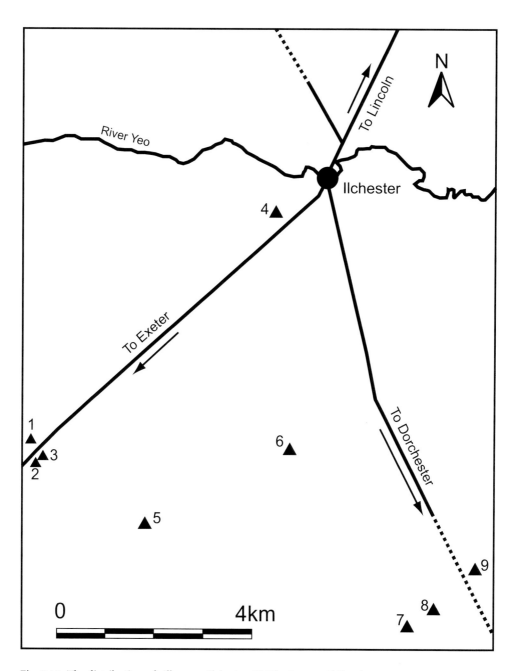

Fig. 6.15 The distribution of villas near Ilchester: 1) Dinnington, 2) Seavington St Mary, 3) Lopen, 4) Ilchester Mead, 5) Bedmore Barn, 6) Lufton, 7) West Coker, 8) East Coker, 9) Westlands (drawn by Mark Roughley).

may have been linked by marriage to one another, others obligated through patronage or debt, and some neighbours may also have been vehemently opposed to one another. If these connections of kin, obligation and coercion were mapped geographically then they would reveal a shifting kaleidoscope of relationships that may have covered large parts of the landscape.

The late fourth-century writings of Ausonius of Bordeaux provide a glimpse of the sorts of social relations that might concentrate land and wealth in a single individual's hands (Hopkins 1961). He owned at least four estates and possibly as many as seven and these he seems to have gained through inheritance and marriage. The much discussed *herediolum* (little heritage) was one of these estates and covered more than 1,000 *iugera* or approximately 238 ha (Sivan 1993, 66–69). If, for the sake of argument, the four estates totalled 1,000 ha and we imagine four individuals, allied to one another by blood and marriage, controlling territory on this scale, then those individuals would between them control a significant portion of a modern county or an early medieval kingdom. Of course, not all of these estates will have been coterminous and Ausonius' testimony exists in isolation and therefore may be atypical or not applicable to the Romano-British situation. King (1990, 104), for instance, suggests 100 ha as the average estate size based on site densities in Gaul and Germany. Nevertheless, it is illustrative of the scale at which some late antique landowners operated.

Late Roman inequality

The agricultural estates that may have accompanied the villa buildings around Ilchester remain poorly understood but other nearby lower-status sites, such as those at Yeovilton (Lovell 2006) (Figure 6.16), Bradley Hill (Leech 1981) and Sigwells (Tabor and Johnson 2000), should indicate a relatively densely settled landscape. Understanding the social and tenurial structure of this and other parts of late Roman Britain is fraught with difficulty. Traditionally those interested in social structure sought inspiration from late antique documentary sources. The argument developed considered the impact of an increasingly hierarchical social structure and the oppression of the lower social orders (Jones 1964, 1049–1053). It suggested that, from the reign of Diocletian, the peasantry, who were heavily taxed by the rapacious late Roman state, were driven into the arms of powerful landowners and would eventually become tied tenants, servile in outlook and almost indistinguishable from slaves (e.g. Percival 1967; Sarris 2004, 308–309). Historical sources, especially *The Theodosian Code* (*Cod. Theod.*)

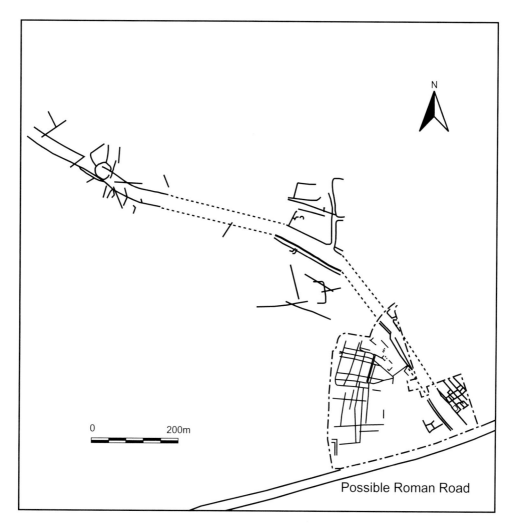

Fig. 6.16 Plan of the late Roman low-status settlement at Yeovilton. The buildings here were small and unpretentious rectangular structures set among ditched enclosures and trackways (after Lovell 2006, Fig. 20).

and Justinian's *Digest*, were thought to name this class *coloni*. This interpretation was a significant argument on two different levels. First, it tied into a Marxist meta-narrative that sought to explain social change through class conflict and also attempted to identify the origins of feudalism (Thompson 1952; Wickham 2005). Secondly, this view of the late Roman situation allowed a small Germanic warrior class the opportunity of an 'elite takeover' against an emasculated sub-Roman aristocracy, cut off from their 'Roman' ideology (Higham 1992, 233). During the course of this elite takeover the bulk of the population were argued to be so downtrodden that they neither knew, nor cared, how their overlords described themselves.

This historical formulation of late Roman social structure rests on unstable foundations. That *coloni* existed in Britain seems assured by an entry in *The Theodosian Code* (*Cod. Theod.* XI.7.2), addressed to the *vicarius* of Britain in 319 (Stevens 1947). However, the nature and position of the *coloni* discussed in the documentary sources is far from clear-cut (e.g. Mirkovíc 1997; Grey 2007). By the sixth century *coloni* were almost synonymous with slaves (Sirks 2008, 122). Yet the coherence of the colonate as an institution and its development has been a subject that has generated considerable historical debate that has produced little modern consensus (Wickham 2005, 521–527; Grey 2007). Some argue that the *coloni* were little more than a means of ensuring the efficient raising of tax revenues (Wickham 2005, 525). Others prefer a position closer to the traditional narrative espoused by Jones (1958, 1964, 794–802), while arguing for greater variety in the economic and social relationships that governed how elite and non-elite groups interacted in late antiquity (Banaji 2001, 2009).

Interpretations derived from late antique documentary sources are occasionally joined by models of so-called 'Celtic' social structures (Stevens 1966; Jones 1996, 105). These attempts serve as an interesting reminder of the possibility of local custom and social structure in Roman Britain. However, they are too often based on ahistorical formulations of 'Celtic Society' (James 1999) and back-projection from later medieval sources.

The absence of meaningful documentary evidence, like that from late antique Egypt (Banaji 2001), regarding the lower orders of late Roman society in Britain means that any attempt to assess their position must rely on archaeological evidence. This is not an attempt to deny the existence of *coloni*, peasants, slaves and other classes. Instead, it is an attempt to examine their position in society free of the intellectual baggage that accompanies such labels.

Within any given region fourth-century archaeological sites and assemblages of artefacts and ecofacts have been and continue to be identified and excavated in significant numbers. This data is a far from objective sample. The vagaries of development and archaeological research agendas are combined with factors – such as geology, stone walls, ditched enclosures and durable pottery – that either aid or hinder site identification. Nevertheless, the dataset represents a significant cross-section through the settlement hierarchy. Often this data is interpreted blandly as evidence of differing 'status' but what it really represents are the complex relations that social groups within a single region had with one another.

These issues are, as we have seen already, arguably most acute when studying settlement morphology. At the top of the settlement hierarchy were the bewildering variety of 'villa' buildings and other forms of elaborate structures (like aisled buildings), beneath which were the other forms of settlement often described simply as 'farmsteads' or as 'villages'. The latter term has uncomfortable and anachronistic overtones derived from later medieval nucleated rural settlements. However, there is emerging evidence from the analysis of settlement morphology that the later Roman period saw a rise in the number of nucleated rural settlements and a related decline in the number of farmsteads (Taylor 2007, 111–113). These agglomerations of settlement have rarely been the subject of extensive excavations. Three of the most famous of these types of settlement have been excavated in the West Country at Catsgore (Somerset) (Leech 1982) (Figure 6.17), Gatcombe (North Somerset) (Branigan 1977) and Kingscote (Gloucestershire) (Timby 1998), and other examples can be cited or are suspected elsewhere (e.g. Lawrence and Smith 2009). They are formed from a significant number of rectilinear stone buildings that otherwise show few signs of architectural embellishments. Gatcombe has the unusual distinction of being surrounded by a 3m-thick stone wall and has been interpreted variously as a villa and a small town (Branigan 1977). However, if the unique wall circuit is ignored the site conforms to the general pattern.

The standing of these communities within their local settlement hierarchy remains opaque. They may have been linked through tenurial obligations to local villa-owning families but this is difficult to prove. Catsgore is located in close proximity to a number of villas (Leech 1982, 176) and contains one building with tessellated pavements (Ellis 1984), which could conceivably have belonged to a 'bailiff', 'headman' or village elder. There are also apsidal buildings and shrines at some of these sites that may have functioned as communal meeting places (Leech 1982, Figs. 12 and 13; Lawrence and Smith 2009, 98–99).

A more profitable line of enquiry is to consider how life was characterised within these settlements. The buildings were often densely packed within small plots demarcated by ditched boundaries. These boundaries were often zealously maintained and, by the end of the Roman period, were replaced by walls at some sites (Leech 1982, Figs. 12–14; Lawrence and Smith 2009, 114). Given the time scales involved – the late Roman period lasted for 150 years (seven generations) and some of these sites were founded in the second century – this maintenance of property boundaries could suggest that property was in some way inalienable, otherwise the consolidation of holdings might have occasionally occurred. The replacement of ditched

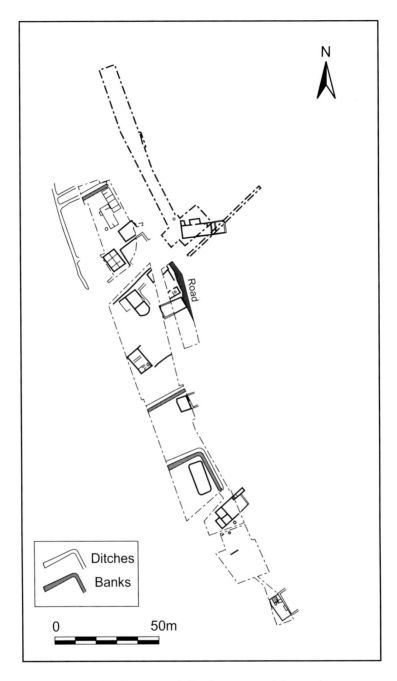

Fig. 6.17 Plan of the late Roman 'village' at Catsgore (after Leech 1982, Fig. 5).

boundaries with walls may also be significant. Ditches require periodic maintenance, and walls, once built, provide a less labour-intensive and more formidable barrier. They also have the benefit of not only defining and securing property but also enhancing the levels of privacy within an individual plot. This should be set against the general observation that complex locking mechanisms are more common in urban centres (Manning 1985, 88). If security was a primary concern then the absence of complex locks might be significant. Perhaps community cohesion was greater in a rural context, or rural dwellings were more secure because they were rarely left unattended.

The notion of community cohesion can be related to another aspect of material culture. In a simple but incisive paper Evans (2001, 33–34) demonstrated that the ratio of literate graffiti to sherds could be used to classify sites. Military installations, towns and villas had the highest ratios of graffiti and rural centres the lowest. This was interpreted as an index of the site's incorporation into the literate Roman world. However, Catsgore – one of Evans' (2001, Fig. 12) rural sites – also produced styli suggestive of a literate population not visible in graffiti on portable objects from the site (Leach 1982, Fig. 84.29–34). As many of the graffiti encountered on artefacts are names and other ownership marks it seems equally likely that such marks were primarily used in situations where conflict over the ownership of property might arise. Therefore the absence of graffiti in rural situations might be reflective of the implicit trust that these communities and their inhabitants had in one another.

Another archaeologically recoverable characteristic of life at these sites concerns the consumption of foodstuffs. Significant assemblages of animal bones from a large number of sites have demonstrated that rural settlements consumed more mutton than beef or pigs, which were characteristic of villas, towns and forts (King 1988; Cool 2006, 111–118). It would be useful to know whether particular cuts of meat were consumed at different site types. Unfortunately this type of detail is difficult to recover because it is rarely possible to identify primary 'kitchen' waste (Dobney 2001). This dietary distinction is echoed in the ceramic assemblages. Rural settlements tend to be characterised by jar- and bowl/dish-dominated assemblages and have lower levels of so-called finewares than villas and urban centres (Evans 2001, Fig. 10). Taken together this evidence could plausibly be seen as suggesting that the most common dish in late Roman Britain was mutton stew and a heel of bread. As the isotopic evidence from burials confirms that the upper echelons of society consumed a far more varied diet (Richards et al. 1998; Cummings and Hedges 2010, 419) this dietary division may have been a significant indicator of difference in status between groups within a region.

The isotopic evidence for dietary differences serves as a reminder of the important osteological work that has been undertaken on ancient human remains. The large sample of excavated burials of all periods from Britain has allowed some long-term trends in the health of the population to be identified (Roberts and Cox 2003). The Roman period saw a number of changes, some of which – such as an increase in dental caries – can be attributed to a richer diet for some elements within society. Others, which include an increase in the numbers of individuals with DISH (a condition whose cause is unknown, but which may be linked to diet and environment), as well as increases in arthritis and infectious diseases, suggest that life was hard for many.

In contrast, the early medieval period saw a decrease in the prevalence of many of these illnesses and complaints. This observation should be viewed next to considerable evidence for an increase in height between the Roman and early medieval periods. Roberts and Cox (2003, 389–390) have published figures suggesting that men were some 3 cm taller than the Roman mean during the early medieval period and the women were 2 cm taller and this is confirmed by regional studies (e.g. Klingle 2012). This has sometimes been seen as indicative of migration and population replacement (Härke 1990, 40). However, current thinking would emphasise stature as an indicator of increased access to nutrients. Interestingly, the increase in mean height is seen not only in Britain but also across Western Europe (Köpke and Baten 2005). If the association between height and better diet, calorific intake and living conditions is correct then it suggests that for many the early Middle Ages were more comfortable than the Roman period had been.

The picture of rural life outside of elite contexts (such as villa buildings) can only be sketched in broad outlines, and considerable variation across sites and regions is to be expected. However, the themes highlighted here serve to demonstrate that life at the lower end of the settlement hierarchy was far from simple. Many communities lived in close proximity to their neighbours within nucleated settlements and, at some sites, architecture and finds allow us to hypothesise the existence of village elders, councils and headmen or women. Materially many of these fourth-century communities were well endowed with possessions. Pottery, copper-alloy jewellery and other objects were relatively common and certainly far more common than they would be for the next half a millennium or more. Nevertheless, against this relative material 'wealth' it is worth noting that the inhabitants of sites like Catsgore or Gatcombe ate a diet that, in comparison with their local elite, was relatively restricted. This observation can be combined with the evidence for an increased prevalence of disease and medical conditions in the Roman period and the apparent early medieval increase in stature. The price of a 'Roman' lifestyle for the lower orders was harder work, less food and a greater risk of illness. This, when set alongside the clear evidence for elite settlement and intensive economic exploitation during the later Roman period, is suggestive of deeply rooted inequalities within late Roman society (James 2011a, 254). This conclusion cannot be directly related to late antique historical evidence which, as has been discussed, does not exist in sufficient detail or quantity for late Roman Britain. However, the similarities in trajectory of argument are notable.

Small worlds and new horizons

At the beginning of this chapter a contrast was drawn between a vision of Britain as an integrated part of the Roman Empire and the disparate and polyglot communities that inhabited the island during the early Middle Ages. It has long been recognised that Roman Britain was never a unified whole. Divisions between upland and lowland or military and civilian have coloured the interpretation of the period since the very beginnings of its study. Yet the search for ancient social and political units that survive from prehistory into the early medieval period has been something of a dead end. Hamstrung by a lack of the most basic evidence, these discussions have made inappropriate comparisons and condemned the inhabitants of Late Iron Age, Roman and 'Dark Age' Britain to an ahistorical procession from tribe to kingdom *via* the *civitas* (Dark 1994; Laycock 2008).

The rejection of these approaches and their replacement with a less simplistic and therefore less clear-cut vision of regionality offers new interpretative avenues. The physical remains of the past suggest a more complex story where some Roman period distributions echo patterns established in prehistory, other socio-economic phenomena reflect large-scale topographical or environmental divisions and further patterning presents less explicable differences. Alongside these contrasts other factors such as religion, dialect and diet may also have played a role in constructing these regional worldviews. Together the confusion and complexity of this vision presents a late Roman world that was integrated into the rest of the Roman Empire but was also fractured into small worlds and communities.

The fourth-century elites (discussed above and in Chapter 4) had feet in both camps. Their adoption of *paideia* and a Roman provincial lifestyle saw them integrated into a pan-European and Mediterranean network. Yet the foundations of their power and position rested on the agricultural and rural economy of small worlds. It is a pretty contradiction that the 'globalising' nature of the Roman Empire led to the emergence of introspective and small-scale communities. To maintain its structures the state needed resources and the elites were charged with gathering the revenues and taxes necessary to furnish the state with its requirements. This in turn allowed elite groups to create, maintain and strengthen their position over the rural economy and productive classes. Elite control, exercised through patronage and land ownership (estates), offered another set of 'small worlds' that co-existed with other possibilities explored above. For the agricultural producers the fourth century was a time of burdens, hard work, shrinking horizons and declining influence.

Events in Gaul during the early fifth century led to Britain being severed from the Roman Empire. This brought with it the collapse of the state structures needed to maintain Britain's existence in the Roman Empire. With the disappearance or jettisoning of these state structures Romano-British communities became even more reliant on their small worlds. These were not necessarily *civitates*, but may have included estates, economic zones or areas united by cultural preference or prejudice. It was in this complex and fluid situation that the changes of the fifth century unfolded. Germanic migration, changes in elite display and the new world of the late fifth and sixth centuries were all written on this mosaic of difference and had to cope with the 'small worlds' left as the Roman tide retreated. The fifth century was not a return to the Iron Age but a time to refocus on the local basis of economic power and control.

7 | The ruin of Roman Britain

As the fifth century opened Britain still held its Roman character. Changes and transformations were evident, particularly in urban contexts and villas, but the diocese still retained its late Roman shape. By the close of the fifth century this pattern had largely been swept away. Towns and villas were abandoned, the rural economy transformed and the provinces of the old Diocese of the Britains divided among squabbling and competing warbands. In the west of Britain potentates looked to the Roman past and the eastern Mediterranean, as well as a reinvented indigenous 'Iron Age' warrior culture. The east of Britain was now focussed on the North Sea with Germanic influence the dominant cultural vocabulary.

This transformation has at various times been explained as a consequence of both external and internal dynamics. Violent barbarians, internal crisis and economic collapse as the Roman imperial system disintegrated have all played their part at one time or another. In earlier chapters it has been argued that the barbarian threat to late Roman Britain has been over-stated – a consequence of the meta-narrative of decline and fall, taking fourth-century historical sources out of context and misunderstanding what has recently been described as the 'politics of fear' in Roman political and military ideology (Drinkwater 2007, 12). Internal economic collapse, wrought by the disappearance of the imperial tax–pay cycle, has also been examined in some detail. Significant economic changes did occur but these damaged the visible parts of the economy most catastrophically. The biggest slice of Romano-British 'GDP' – the largely invisible agricultural economy – remained resilient and may even have prospered once the burdens of the Roman Empire had been lifted. This allowed diversification and a move to a less efficient pastoral economy, which manifested itself in the way landscapes were managed and perhaps increased calorific intake.

The flaws in these explanatory models suggest that the changes which manifested themselves during the course of the fifth century need to be understood in different terms. In the second half of this volume considerable attention was focussed on issues related to social complexity and elite display. It was argued that elites during the fourth, fifth and sixth centuries used material culture to display their adherence to specific ideologies and reinforce their social position and power. It was further suggested that analysis has been distracted by the over-arching superstructure of the Roman world. Exploitation of the rural economy actually rested on the control of relatively small blocks of land. These estates were connected in some cases by ownership, tenurial obligations and kinship. Together the adherence to these and other forms of social practice, as well as economic linkages, defined so-called 'small worlds'. In this the late Roman period may not have been much different to the early medieval world.

This chapter develops and extends the arguments advanced in the preceding chapters. It presents a model of change for lowland Britain during the period *c.*350–550. This model is intended as a means of exploring and explaining the very real and significant differences between 300 and 600. It is intended to highlight a number of social and political trajectories that may have been followed during the fifth century. It attempts to introduce complexity into our analyses, rather than seeking a one-size-fits-all explanation for the changes of the fifth century. However, the complexity can never be complex enough to portray the reality of the period and lived human experience. Therefore the model is in the final analysis a gross simplification of a period of profound change.

Fourth-century stability

Fourth-century Britain can be divided into four zones. North of Hadrian's Wall were lands and communities where Rome's writ never, or only intermittently, ran. South of the *limes*, in what is today northern England, was a region where the influence of the army and military communities was strong (Collins 2012). In the far west of Wales and Cornwall were communities seemingly little changed from the Iron Age, where Rome's influence was feebly felt and restricted to specific times and locations. Meanwhile England south and east of the Fosse Way exhibited a culture that was part of a late antique mainstream and perhaps spoke a primarily Romance language, in contrast to the Celtic dialects spoken in the far west. The broad outlines of these cultural zones had been fixed in the second century and, with some alteration, remained more or less stable until the end of the Roman period.

In the lowland zone the structure of society was primarily civilian. Elite display was focussed on villas and the outward signs that demonstrated an individual's social position and adoption of the late antique social norms of *paideia*. This civilian ideology, the details of which were explored in

Chapter 4 above, was a response to two stimuli. First, the Roman state exercised a monopoly over violence. Military glory was the preserve of the emperor and the ideological role of the soldiers was the protection of the state. To usurp either of these prerogatives would doom the user to oblivion as a rebel, bandit or *Bagauda*. Secondly, even in the fourth century Britain remained a 'frontier province', with a significant military garrison. This military community of soldiers represented an alternative structure of power and patronage. For those in the civilian south of Britain there was also a need to define themselves in opposition to the boorish and uncouth soldiers and officers of the north. The southern communities needed to adhere to *paideia* and the civilian power structures or risk having their interests conflated on the imperial stage with those of the military communities.

The adherence to a civilian ideology brought with it a number of advantages. The Roman state theoretically offered tools of control, like the legal system, and protection in the form of a standing garrison. The state demanded tax to fund these 'services' but even taxation offered the lowland elite a means of increasing their power and position. Together this symbiotic relationship had worked reasonably well for 200 years or more depending on the location.

The civilian ideology also provided a means of establishing social distance within the lowlands. For the elites *paideia* and the gradations of status offered by the Roman state demonstrated the elites' unique entitlement to power and position. The social boundaries between elite groups and the lower order created a social structure in which the layers of stratification presented the local landlord as the parochial equivalent of the semi-divine emperor. The difference between the *honestiores* and the *humiliores* was signalled so comprehensively that there could be no doubt that the elite's position was predestined.

For the lower orders, bound into webs of patronage with the local elite, position and status were largely fixed. In exchange for economic control the landowner and local elite achieved a significant level of exploitation that benefited them personally and the Roman state. Arguably this control became enshrined in legalistic terms used to denote status such as *coloni*. For the lower orders the relationship was not, and should not, be seen as completely negative. The elites offered protection from the Roman state and its unruly agents: soldiers and tax collectors. The landlord also provided a means of resolving local disputes and was a potential source of aid in times of crisis (like famine).

The relationships between the elites in lowland Britain and the agricultural producers were the foundations of the elites' power. It was agriculture that provided the surpluses and wealth that were used to maintain their economic position and social status. In such a situation, where the demands of one group had to be supplied by another for benefits that may not always have been either readily visible or valuable, it is likely that friction and conflict would arise.

Rebellious and recalcitrant peasants and tenants or troublesome elite neighbours would find themselves confronted by two main methods of control wielded by elite landowners. It was through local custom and Roman law that control of the land and the means of production were secured (Van Dam 1985, 14). Disputes could then be ensnared in the complexities of the late Roman law courts, where social position, favour and money spoke louder than the technicalities of a case (Harries 1999; Kelly 2004). The legally inferior position of tenants and peasants further underlined the bias in favour of the elite landowner. Those same landowners could also coerce their neighbours and the lower social orders with relative impunity, as they were protected by their close links to the apparatus of the late Roman state (Salvian, *De Gub. Dei* IV.3).

At first sight coercion appears at odds with the Roman state's monopoly of violence and the civilian ideology of the elite with their cultured and non-military attributes (Sivonen 2006, 100–104 and 115–117). However, the state's monopoly of violence was always flexible. In a time when the dispossessed and the desperate could turn to 'banditry', wild animals (such as wolves) still roamed the countryside and political enemies could seek to take direct action, it was impossible to deny provincials some recourse to violence. Similarly, the ideology of *paideia* may have denied the elite the opportunity to publicly revel in violence and military or paramilitary trappings and insisted that a *dominus* keep his distance from such activities. Yet it did not deny the elites the opportunity to sub-contract violence to trusted clients, freedmen and knives-for-hire who could serve a dual function as bodyguards and enforcers.

The individuals who became these bodyguards and enforcers were unlikely to have solely functioned in this capacity. These trusted clients are likely to have fulfilled other roles as 'community leaders' or 'headmen' in settlements like Catsgore or Higham Ferrers or functioned as personal servants, or grooms. Occasional weapon finds from villa sites will have served not only as hunting equipment but also as the sharp edge of the landlord's will (Brodribb, Hands and Walker 1971, Fig. 51.107; Neal 1996, Fig. 40.93; Light and Ellis 2009, Fig. 35.47) along with more commonplace tools – the woodsman's axe or butcher's cleaver – that could also have served dual functions.

Evidence for the existence of these retinues is not unequivocal. Of course, the imperial *comitatus* (Sivonen 2006, 29) offered a model for such groups in keeping with the villa owner's perception of himself as emperor of his own 'small world'. The oft-quoted Ecdicius and his eighteen men (Whittaker 1993, 296; Halsall 2003, 124) may hint at the scale of such retinues (although these eighteen may have been the notables among a larger group of armed retainers: Whittaker 1998, 295–296), which may, by the end of the fourth century, have been so widespread that they were labelled *bucellarii*. The term, loosely translated as biscuit or bread eaters (Jones 1964, 657, 665–667; Whittaker 1998, 294), and the use of armed retainers are encountered in the late antique east (e.g. *Cod. Just.* IX, xii, 10). The term seems to have come into being in the west during the fourth century (Diesner 1972; Whittaker 1998, 294) and Olympiodorus suggests the term was first coined during the reign of Honorius (Olympiodorus frags 7.4 and 12; Blockley 1983, 159 and 171).

The shadowy existence of the retinue in fourth-century Britain provides the other side of the overtly civilian ideology displayed by elite landowners in the lowlands. Reliance on the Roman state with its law courts and soldiers was all very well, but faced with wolves, bandits or the need to protect or coerce one's clients, having trusted men close to home was a necessity. These retinues provide the key to understanding the ideological transformation that swept across Britain in the fifth century.

The winds of change: the fifth century

In 406 Britain saw a succession of three short-lived usurpations. Of the first two usurpers – Marcus and Gratian – we know relatively little (Stevens 1957; Thompson 1977, 304; Kulikowski 2000b, 332), although Orosius (Oros. 7.40) described Marcus as a *municeps* (i.e. a civilian). The third usurper was more successful and is known to history as Constantine III. Taking troops from Britain he crossed the Channel and established a short-lived regime that was briefly recognised by Honorius' court in Ravenna (Drinkwater 1998). To all intents and purposes it would seem that Constantine III was a conservative usurper, cast from the same mould as Magnus Maximus and Constantine I (Kulikowski 2000b, 333), and driven by the centripetal forces of imperial power to lay claim to the Western Empire.

The disintegration of Constantine III's regime, following a series of military reverses in 409, was followed by the famous 'British revolt' in 410. Zosimus, writing in the Greek east during the early sixth century, but drawing on Olympiodorus' largely lost fifth-century history (Blockley 1981, 28; Rohrbacher 2002, 75), tells us that:

The barbarians above the Rhine, assaulting everything at their pleasure, reduced the inhabitants of Britain and some of the Celtic peoples to defecting from Roman rule and living their own lives disassociated from Roman law. The Britons, therefore, taking up arms and fighting on their own behalf, freed the *poleis* [towns] from the barbarians who were pressing upon them: and the whole of Armorica and other provinces of Gaul, imitating the Britons, freed themselves in the same way, expelling the Roman officials and establishing a sovereign constitution on their own authority. (Zos. 6.5.3)

This passage has been the subject of considerable and often contradic-tory debate (Thompson 1977, 312; Esmonde-Cleary 1989, 137; Higham 1992, 72–72; Jones 1996, 248–249; Faulkner 2000, 174–180). One possible and plausible interpretation would be to suggest that the Romano-British elite, confronted with a barbarian menace and Constantine III's waning star, decided to take matters into their own hands. Constantine, struggling against the forces of the legitimate administration in southern Gaul and Spain, had shown himself incapable of fulfilling the promise of success indicated by his auspicious name. With the consequences of the failure of both Magnentius' revolt in 353 and, perhaps more importantly, Magnus Maximus' revolt only a generation earlier still fresh (Stevens 1957, 334), it probably appeared wise to remove the usurper's administration.

With hindsight the consequences of this action have been seen as marking the 'end' of Roman Britain. However, at the time the situation must have seemed very different. Constantine III surely left some garrisons, many of whom had deep local roots by this time, along the northern frontier and these troops (Collins 2012), as well as the Romano-British elite, surely expected the legitimate regime of Honorius to restore control of the diocese sooner or later. This expectation may also have existed in Ravenna at the imperial court. We know that the *Notitia Dignitatum*'s western portion was updated into the first quarter of the fifth century and retained information on Britain. It has also been convincingly argued that the appearance of Britain in fifth-century continental sources reflects the proximity of Roman power in Gaul to Britain (Wood 1987). Events such as St Germanus' visit could be seen as preludes to planned, but never undertaken, reoccupa-tions of Britain, and Gildas' account of Britons writing to Aëtius for aid in 446 also implies that some groups in Britain still sought the return of Roman authority.

   The failure of the Western Empire to reassert control marks a fundamental turning point in the trajectory of social and political development in Britain. There was, of course, no conscious decision, just an increasing realisation that the situation in Gaul made Britain's reincorporation into the empire a task whose risk outweighed any potential benefits. For lowland Britain the disappearance of Roman power was a catalyst that propelled social, political and economic changes along trajectories they had been moving towards for much of the late Roman period.

   The collapse of Roman power in Britain during the early fifth century brought with it two significant changes. The first of these concerned legitimation. It was the Roman state that made the garrison commander at a fort like Birdoswald on Hadrian's Wall an army officer and not a warlord; it was the Roman state that made taking a percentage of the grain harvest tax collection rather than thievery; and it was the Roman state that confirmed a landowner's ownership of the land. The second change concerned the economy. It was no longer necessary to produce the kinds of surpluses that had been previously required. Who in the south of Britain was going to send grain to the Rhineland, or Hadrian's Wall, if there was no legitimate state to compel them to do so? These two changes cascaded through society in southern Britain and in the following discussion their impact is speculatively charted.

   The disappearance of Roman power left the villa-dwelling elite of southern Britain in a precarious position. In the fourth century their position had been assured by the Roman state and its structures. However, as the fifth century unfolded life became more complex. The lower social orders, resentful of the control exercised by the elites, may have seized the opportunity to overthrow long-established tenurial customs and avoid obligations to their patrons and landlords. Some may even have sought new outlets for their ambitions. Here parallels with fifth-century Gaul, where peasants ran away from their landlords and estates to join passing warbands or barbarian groups (e.g. Sid. *Epistola* III.9; Samson 1992, 226), are indicative of the type of situation confronting fifth-century elites. Without control over agricultural labour the elites' economic system and position would begin to look vulnerable.

   Peer-to-peer interaction within the landowning classes will also have presented new challenges. In the fourth century disputes over land ownership, inheritance and grazing rights may have been resolved in law courts. Such law courts may have continued to exist but their decisions will have lacked legitimacy (see Jones 2001 for an alternative interpretation) and there was no external force capable of (however ineffectively) ensuring that decisions were abided by. In this changed environment any grievances between landowners could have gone to court, but the unlucky party now had the previously denied opportunity to settle matters more favourably at the point of a sword (Jones 2001).

There were also the potential predations of armed groups to consider. These might include barbarian warbands, groups of the disaffected that conform to some interpretations of the *Bagaudae* and the remnants of the garrisons left by Constantine III. Here the lowland distribution of certain forms of 'Pictish' material culture in Roman Britain indicates that the north could visit the south and *vice versa* (Hunter 2010, Fig. 11.5). Last but by no means least was the possibility of a reconquest by the Western Empire. Aëtius' use of Alans to chastise the Armoricans (Halsall 2007, 249) suggests that those who appealed to him in 446 may have looked to a positive answer to their letter with some trepidation (Drinkwater 1992, 217).

Faced with these possibilities the villa-owning elite can be divided for the purposes of this study into two groups that might be labelled 'traditional' and 'reactionary'. Under the 'traditional' model the elites would attempt to maintain the status quo. Adherence to *paideia* and an outwardly civilian ideology, gradations of social status and the importance of social difference and distinction would be important. Attempts might also be made to maintain the traditional structures of power, such as law courts (Woolf 2003).

Choosing to maintain the fourth-century 'civilian' lifestyle (Mathisen 1993, 39–47, 50–57), perhaps in the hope that the status quo would be restored by a 'reconquest' of Britain by forces loyal to the western imperial court, was probably a route that offered oblivion in one form or another. Peasants and clients were no longer bound to heed their customary obligations and the very difference that defined the landowning class marked them as vulnerable. Rebellious peasants, bandits, warbands and disputes with other members of the landowning class could all have destroyed this way of life and the collapse in elements of the economic system will also have contributed to this conclusion.

In contrast to the attempts to maintain the status quo the 'reactionary' model offers a different trajectory. It might be assumed that those interested in maintaining the traditional way of life sought to bolster their position by recruiting armed groups of men. These would serve to defend the elite and to enforce the landowning classes' will on those who would oppose it. There are two different but interlinked ways in which this attempt to cope with the fifth century would have been made effective.

The earliest account of the interactions between the indigenous communities of fifth-century Britain and the Germanic barbarians is Gildas' *De Excidio* (23–24). In this account the *superbus tyrannus* invited the Saxons into Britain to fight against the Picts and provided them with supplies in return for their military service. The extent to which this testimony can be relied upon is debatable but the theme is not implausible. Germanic barbarians taking such service would simply be following in the footsteps of their forefathers (Halsall 2007, 102–103 and 158), who had sought fame, fortune and a career within the Roman army and administration. The three keels of later tradition that shipped Hengist and Horsa (Bede, *Hist. Eccl.* I.15; *ASC(A)*, sa449) are undoubtedly legendary, as are the protagonists of this origin myth, but the scale need not be (Carr 2007). Three ships with around thirty men each could amount to the core of a warband.

To a member of the Romano-British elite, faced with having to militarise in the fifth century, recruiting Germanic barbarians probably seemed like a sensible plan. Such individuals had served with distinction in the Western Empire's armies and offered significant benefits to the recruiter. A hundred armed men, used to working and fighting together and cemented by their shared experiences crossing the North Sea, were likely to offer advantages over the bodyguards, retainers, servants and rustics that were the alternative options.

Perhaps most importantly groups of Germanic warriors may not have been perceived as barbarians. One fourth-century epitaph from Aquincum (Budapest) states: 'I am a Frankish citizen but a Roman soldier in arms' (*CIL* 3.3567) and this neatly illustrates the blurring that might have occurred between the military and barbarian identity (James 2011a, 268–270). In Britain the provision of some individuals with 'military' style dress accessories such as the Quoit Brooch Style belt plate from Mucking (Hirst and Clark 2009) and Hawkes and Dunning type (1961) belt fittings may indicate that these armed men were perceived not as barbarians but as Roman soldiers. The presence of one of the latter types of buckle at Westerwanna (Böhme 1986, 520) suggests that some who travelled from Germany to Britain returned. However, an example from Iruña (Spain) suggests alternative narratives (Fernandez 1999, 55–56). From a fifth-century perspective recruiting these groups of warriors probably looked less like inviting the wolf over the threshold than following time-honoured tradition.

The late Roman landlord hiring these 'barbarians' to serve in his retinue presumably considered their martial skills important. However, it must soon have become clear that the power of such an individual was largely reliant on the loyalty of the Germanic warriors that made up the nucleus of his retinue (Mathisen 1993, 31–32). This may have led to Germanic warriors betraying their would-be employers and lords and this model is, of course, enshrined in early medieval myth (Nennius *HB* 36–37). Alternatively, the elite and the Germanic adventurers may have moved closer together. The late Roman aristocrat, recognising his vulnerability, may have attempted to ensure the position of his family by drawing the Germans and Romano-Britons tighter together. Inter-marriage would have been one way of achieving this aim and the marriage of Gallia Placidia to Ataulf is an example of such a political alliance at an imperial level (Harlow 2004) and the presence of 'British' names in some Anglo-Saxon regnal lists may indicate that political marriages were commonplace (Yorke 1995, 49–50). Alternatively, given the increasing irrelevancy of the late Roman civilian ideology, individuals may have made themselves or their children follow the dress, custom and language of the incomers. Sidonius' (*Epistola* 5.5) Burgundian-speaking Gallo-Roman friend Syagrius hints at such a process (Adams 2003, 277).

This process of 'takeover' and acculturation is difficult to identify archaeologically. However, the reuse of villa sites and ancient earthworks for 'Anglo-Saxon' cemeteries suggests the appropriation of the significance of these places. Such burials are therefore likely to indicate claims on the land and ancestral geography of a region. This process rooted fifth- and sixth-century communities in the past and confirmed their 'ownership' and legitimacy in a particular region. A villa that had functioned in the fourth century as an arena of elite power now performed a similar function for the elite in death.

The alternative 'reactionary' approach sees a more radical adaptation to the changed circumstances of the fifth century. The elites, recognising that their privileged position separated from their retainers and clients by the architecture of their dwellings and the richness of their dress and adornments was no longer secure, sought to proactively transform their social position. In a time when the loyalty of armed retainers counted for more than subtle divisions of status that needed to be signalled under the late Roman system, discarding those divisions of status was an obvious move. The decline in elite display, discussed in Chapters 4 and 5, was thus not a product of an economic collapse. Instead, it was the result of a conscious decision to superficially reduce the social hierarchy in order to preserve some measure of elite power. The villa owner had to change from aping the court of a semi-divine emperor, distant from his subjects, all powerful and surrounded by ritual and ceremony, to being the first among the equals that made up the retinue he could use to coerce his neighbours, clients and enemies.

It is thus unsurprising that the new forms of display that emerged at the end of the fourth century and during the early fifth century seem to be solidly focussed on the trappings of military power. The proliferation of zoomorphic buckles suggests that across much of lowland Britain the wearing of belts had become a 'fashion' of importance. As these belts surely reference the military belt sets worn by late Roman soldiers and state officials (Leahy 2007b; Speidel 2006) it would seem that in civilian areas 'para-military' dress had become acceptable in a way that had previously been unheard of. This phenomenon can also be discerned elsewhere in the Western Empire (e.g. Périn and Kazanski 2011, 327). Later the use of Roman titles, such as *protectoris*, on inscribed stones (Edwards 2007) might suggest that some trappings of this 'Roman military identity' continued to be used into the sixth century. Arguably the elite had turned to the methods of martial display used by the Roman state to emphasise the position of their retinues and warbands.

These changes in social dynamics can also be seen on the ground. The changing function of villa buildings at the end of the fourth century and during the early fifth century is indicative of significant changes in the social use of space. Many buildings and rooms that had previously been used for elite dining, bathing or receiving clients were converted to other uses. These often included the subdivision of rooms with partition walls suggesting that more people were dwelling in these buildings (Ellis 1988; Petts 1997). This could be interpreted as the opening up of these previously restricted and private spaces to a greater number of users – arguably the owner's retinue and their dependants.

The relocation of noisome activities such as metalworking (Figure 7.1) and grain drying into formerly elite residences is also significant. During the Roman period metalworking was an important economic activity carried out both at a very small scale and also on an almost industrial scale at some locations (Sim 1998). In the early fifth century, as long-distance exchange decreased in both volume and intensity, access to metalworkers and their products may well have been considered vital. The goods they produced were necessary to equip and maintain not only the retinue but also the tools and equipment needed for everyday life. As the fifth century progressed the individual metalworkers would have become an integral part of a retinue and it is no surprise to discover metalworking closely connected to elite sites during the early medieval period (Alcock 2003).

Grain-driers are the other form of structure of relevance to this argument. Created by suspending a floor over a flue these kiln-like structures are often associated with assemblages of burnt cereal grains. Analysis of these

Fig. 7.1 A late Roman hearth at the Butleigh villa (© Absolute Archaeology).

carbonised archaeobotanical assemblages indicates that in many cases grain-driers were used to parch grain, either to aid in its preservation or to stimulate germination as part of the malting process for brewing (van der Veen 1989). A recent study of their distribution reveals that they are typical of the lowland 'villa' zone and have been interpreted as indicating the specialised processing of a significant arable surplus (Taylor 2007, 115 and Fig. 7.3).

   If grain-driers are indicative of the production and processing of a substantial grain surplus then they allow us to investigate the spatial distribution of these activities and, by extension, economic relationships. Here it is noticeable that during the fourth century many of these grain-driers appear as relatively isolated features situated on the peripheries of relatively low-status settlements. Three good examples are: Roundstone Lane, Angmering (Sussex), Popley, near Basingstoke (Hampshire), and Fordington Bottom (Dorset). At the first site a grain-drier was located among fields and trackways and associated with several ovens but there were few traces of any associated buildings (Griffin 2003). Popley had a grain-drier located within a field system but seemingly divorced from significant settlement activity (Wright, Powell and Barclay 2009, 31–35). At Fordington Bottom a revetment protected a terraced area at the base of the valley, which was occupied by a grain-drier and a large tank (Smith et al. 1997, 216–217). Low-status domestic buildings were excavated some distance to the north of these features. Finally, it is important to note that many other such sites could be added to this list (Taylor 2007, Fig. 7.3).

The comparative isolation of these grain-driers may in part be a consequence of their function. Keeping a source of fire at a distance from easily combustible dwellings and agricultural buildings would appear to be common sense. However, at a number of sites grain-driers are located within structures: at Worth Matravers (Dorset) a rectangular building, interpreted as a barn, contained a grain-drier in an extension at one end (Graham, Hinton and Peacock 2002, 24); two buildings in the nucleated settlement at Catsgore contained grain-driers (Leech 1982, Fig. 58), as did an aisled building at Monk Sherborne (Hampshire) (Teague 2005).

The separation of grain-driers from villa buildings is an important phenomenon. The dispersal of these crop-processing structures across the landscape suggests that during much of the late Roman period there was no need to closely supervise their positioning and, by extension, the agricultural surpluses being processed at these sites. The relocation of grain-driers within buildings previously associated with elite functions – as at Chedworth (George 1999), Butleigh (Somerset) (Absolute Archaeology 2012) (Figure 7.2), Brading and Rock (Isle of Wight) (Lyne 2011), North Wraxall (Wiltshire) (Wessex Archaeology 2009) and other sites – is suggestive. It may indicate that the landlord could no longer trust his tenants to process their crops for him and instead needed to ensure that this was done under the close supervision of his household and retinue.

The provision of grain-driers within villa buildings may therefore indicate a weakening of the obligations that ensured the smooth rendering of agricultural surpluses to the elite. Equally important is the change in social dynamics that the presence of these structures indicates. No longer were these noisome activities distanced from elite dwelling places and it may also be assumed that the workers needed to process the crops were also relocated to ensure that the processing happened.

As a final aside it is worth considering the end product of these grain-driers. The crops may have been dried as a means of preserving the grain for longer in storage. However, there is a considerable body of evidence that suggests these structures were used primarily for malting (Reynolds and Langley 1979). The conversion of grain into ale and beer represents a significant economic choice that may have been partially guided by a desire to turn grains into a commodity that kept for longer (Pearson 1997, 12). Attention should also be paid to the importance of drinking

Fig. 7.2   A late Roman grain-drier at the Butleigh villa (© Absolute Archaeology).

alcohol as a component in conspicuous consumption during the early Middle Ages (Alcock 1995, 119–120; *Beowulf*, *Y Gododdin*). Given this, it is
worth speculating whether one of the drivers behind the relocation of
grain-driers was the need to ensure a supply of beer for feasting, now that
many villa buildings were apparently taking on an increasingly communal
outlook.

   By drawing these threads together it is possible to argue that some villas,
built as private dwellings displaying the power and status of their inhabitants, changed their role during the late fourth century and early fifth
century. No longer were they the private and reserved space of an elite class
separated physically from their clients and tenants. Instead, they functioned
as nodal points in the landscape storing and processing foodstuffs that
fed the specialists that formed the lord's retinue. Some of these specialists
we might term *bucellarii* (Diesner 1972), fighting men who were loyal to
the lord and fought to preserve and extend his power. Others were skilled
metalworkers, like blacksmiths, and it is likely that the villa buildings now
sheltered the families and servants of these individuals. From these locations
the remnants of the Romano-British elite exercised control from what was
a traditional seat of power.

The blocks of territories controlled during the early fifth century are beyond reconstruction, but patterning in the distribution and use of material culture during the late fourth century suggests that there were geographically extensive territories sharing similar worldviews and also micro-regions or 'small worlds'. We have also seen how the links of patronage, blood and marriage could have brought large 'estates' together into loose federations with allied interests, which are likely to have been wide and varied. It can be suggested that attempting to control the arguably recalcitrant peasantry was one ambition, but acquiring and defending territory against neighbouring communities and 'barbarians' are also likely to have been important factors (Woolf 2003, 345).

The scale at which this sort of activity took place is difficult to reconstruct. Ambrosius Aurelianus is the only fifth-century potentate who can definitely be associated with Britain and Gildas' account of him (*De Excidio* 25.3) is short on the sort of details modern historians are interested in. Nevertheless, Gallic analogies are illuminating. Ecdicius and his eighteen men have been mentioned above. The figure sounds small and opinion is divided over whether this was the total number of his warband or just the 'notables' commanding groups of lower-status fighters (Whittaker 1998; Halsall 2003, 122). The raising of a militia by Honorius' relatives in Spain during Constantine III's usurpation is instructive and suggests some landlords could muster significant forces (Arce 2003, 136). Similarly, Syagrius in the late fifth century attempted to oppose the Franks and other barbarian groups (MacGeorge 2002, 113).

These examples are significant but one of the most interesting fifth-century warlords was a Briton/Breton named Riothamus (e.g. MacGeorge 2002, 72–74; Halsall 2007, 276–277). He was active in the Loire against the Goths during the 470s and Sidonius (*Epistola* III.9) remonstrated with him by letter in an attempt to stop the peasants of one of Sidonius' clients joining Riothamus' warband. Jordanes (Jord. *Get.* XLV), writing in the sixth century, gives the figure of 12,000 men for this group of fighters, but such figures should be treated with scepticism. Nevertheless, it is clear that Riothamus was able to bring a force of men across the sea in an attempt to intervene in Gaul on behalf of the Western emperor Anthemius. This shows that sizeable forces could be raised and organised in Britain or Brittany. Arguments over the exact origin of the force are irrelevant: if a warband could be raised on this scale in Brittany then it is inconceivable that similar forces could not have been raised in Britain. The career of Riothamus can thus be seen as either the last flickering of the centripetal forces that drew Constantine III and Magnus Maximus across the English

Channel, or as indicative of sub-Roman Britain's (or Brittany's) elevation to the status of 'barbarian other', intervening militarily in the hope of gaining high office and reward from the emperor (Wickham 2005, 169).

The transformation of late Roman aristocrats into fifth-century warlords over the course of two or three generations was thus a response to the collapse in the relevancy of the late antique ideology of a civilian cultured elite. The other avenue of power – military strength – offered an alternative direction, one which had been suppressed or disguised during the Roman period (Sivonen 2006, 117). The future was to be based on the sword, personal obligations and local power.

Two other groups of 'actors' should be considered in this model of fifth-century change. Introduced above as 'Germanic barbarians' and the 'lower orders, or the peasantry', these groups also played an important role in the transformations that were occurring between the late fourth and late fifth century.

The 'Germanic barbarians' have primarily functioned in this model as military specialists: groups of male warriors recruited into the retinues or warbands of the indigenous elite. The martial ideology and abilities of these groups then either allowed them to usurp the indigenous power structures, or encouraged indigenous potentates to adopt the new martial lifestyle and its attendant customs and cultural traits. This is one route, but alternatives should also be considered.

Much of the historiography of the so-called 'English Settlements' has been coloured by a search for the founding fathers (and mothers) of the modern English. There has thus been a temptation to cast the earliest Germanic groups in Britain as conquering heroes in a reworking of early medieval origin myths. Even under the 'elite takeover' model a tiny number of 'Anglo-Saxons' ultimately succeed in dominating lowland Britain with their language, culture and, in some versions, their genes (Härke 2011). The implications of this model are as disturbing as the concept of a mass Germanic folk migration driving the hapless Britons into the mountain fastnesses of the west.

It is unlikely that the arrival of groups of Germanic warriors in Britain in the years after 400 was a straightforward process leading to cultural dominance. Archaeological and historical analysis has almost entirely been focussed on Germanic groups that were 'successful'. Yet it seems equally plausible that groups of Germanic warriors could become British as easily as Britons adopted Germanic cultural traits. Here the occurrence of 'Anglo-Saxon' material culture along the Gallic seaboard is instructive (Soulat 2009). If North Germanic (i.e. not 'Frankish') cultural influence can be found in Normandy then its absence west of Hampshire in Britain requires explanation. The odd 'Anglo-Saxon' artefact from West Country sites, such as the equal armed brooch from near Hod Hill (Dorset) (Eagles and Mortimer 1993), may have reached the region through a variety of mechanisms. However, the recruitment of Germanic (and Irish) warriors may have occurred in the west of Britain with very different results to those that occurred along the eastern coast. A two-way process where Germanic cultural influence was more or less successful in different regions should be entertained. There was no predestination involved.

The social structure of the earliest 'Germanic' groups in Britain should also be considered. The notion of coherent groups migrating to Britain is probably a fallacy (Yorke 2003, 386–388). One of the great ironies of the debate over Bede's (*Hist. Eccl.* I.15) 'Angles, Saxons and Jutes' is that he also supplies a much more extensive list of 'barbarians' that settled in Britain (*Hist. Eccl.* V.9). This longer list is probably no more reliable than the trinity of tribes but it serves to give a flavour of what was probably a very mixed situation in which identities were poorly defined. For Germanic migrants who were not the sword-wielding elite the experience of moving to Britain may have been very different.

Much has been made of the disappearance of the Roman tax–pay system and the likely impact that this had on the nature of agricultural production. Changes in the way the landscape was managed suggest a shift to less intensive forms of agricultural production. This, combined with the indigenous landowning elite's potential difficulties in maintaining their control over the land, may have led to less pressure on land. The appearance of the fifth-century settlement at Mucking on land that had fallen from intensive Romano-British occupation perhaps a hundred years before may imply that settlement was either guided towards, or tolerated in, areas that indigenous communities saw as marginal. Groups of low-status migrants (who by definition would be difficult to identify archaeologically) may have been viewed by the indigenous fifth-century elite with more pity than fear. Indeed, such settlements may have been allowed because they potentially offered that elite a new group of clients to exploit.

For the lower orders of indigenous society the fifth century presented a number of stark choices and opportunities. They could stand by their patrons and landlords, who demanded their loyalty and a portion of their surplus. Or the agricultural producers could recognise that the world had changed and seize the moment to free themselves of burdens that were no longer relevant without fear of imperial retribution. This path may have offered destruction as patrons sought to re-impose control over their clients.

Freedom from the elite and its burdens may also have had unforeseen consequences. The patron's retinue, or nascent warband, may have been both an instrument of oppression and also a means of protection, preserving peasant communities from other predatory groups.

The fifth century also offered the indigenous peasantry the means to alter their position. Individuals could use the confusion of the time to usurp power, or to flee traditional bonds. Here the new 'Germanic' groups were a destabilising factor. The lower social orders could flee to the 'barbarians' in search of new identities and patrons that would either protect them, or offer hitherto unheard of opportunities for advancement. The hybridisation visible in timber architecture (James et al. 1984) suggests that indigenous communities could find new lives in the emerging Germanic world. Indeed, such groups may have provided the earliest migrant communities with the local knowledge and skills to flourish in what was a foreign land.

This discussion has attempted to sketch a model of the decisions that fifth-century society in Britain could have taken. The three groups (the indigenous elite, the 'Germanic migrants' and the indigenous peasantry) were confronted with different choices and responses to what was a fluid and changing situation. This model is, of course, a gross simplification of reality but it serves to demonstrate how the late Roman forms of elite display, focussed on an overtly civilian ideology of *paideia*, were abandoned in favour of more martial elements in the fifth century. Power, which had been guaranteed by the Roman state, now devolved to local landowners and their personal ability to enforce their will and control. The incoming Germanic groups offered a martial ideology that at first may have been to all intents and purposes indistinguishable from that espoused by Roman military communities. For the peasantry the fifth century offered a means to break free of traditional bonds and obligations. The fact that traditional power structures did buckle in the years after 400 allowed the peasantry the potential for advancement either through the appropriation of the elite's power, or the adoption of novel Germanic alternatives. By the last quarter of the fifth century this period of flux was beginning to resolve itself and different trajectories were emerging from the chaos.

The sixth century and the emergence of a new order

It is clear from the preceding discussion that during the early to mid fifth century identities and ethnicities were in a state of flux. This situation in which 'Romano-British', 'Roman military', 'barbarian' and other forms of identity co-existed in a mutable, blurred and malleable fashion is suggestive of a time of crisis in how populations conceptualised their position in the world. In contrast to this unstable position the late fifth and sixth centuries present a world in which identities were beginning to crystallise and solidify in southern Britain.

In the east of Britain the fluid fifth century gave way to a sixth century in which the structures of elite display were relatively clear-cut. Furnished inhumation became the dominant burial rite, even replacing cremation in those areas where it had been popular (Lucy 2000). For males the major components of funerary display were items of war-gear: weaponry, shields, belt buckles and the like (Härke 1990). For women complex suites of jewellery and personal adornments accompanied many individuals into the grave. Analysis of female grave assemblages appears to demonstrate combinations of objects that were most appropriate to specific age groups. Thus these objects indicate a tightly defined female identity and lifecycle (Stoodley 1997, 2000). There are also significant regional differences in female jewellery. Great square-headed, developed cruciform and annular brooches and so-called 'wrist clasps' appear typical of those areas that Bede was to later describe as 'Anglian' (Figure 7.3) and saucer and button brooches occur in 'Saxon' areas. Bede's so-called Jutish areas (especially Kent) follow a different trajectory that hybridises southern Scandinavian and Frankish material culture to produce another distinctive package (Brooks 1989; Brookes 2007).

The creation and adoption of these packages of objects seem to indicate the development of relatively proscribed identities in which men aspired to, or claimed, martial (whether real or fictive) roles and women conformed to an equally regulated series of identities. Some of these identities, which are apparently signalled in material culture, correlate more or less with cultural zones which Bede was later to define in ethnic terms. It is logical to conclude from this that one of the functions of brooch types in the eastern portion of sixth-century Britain was to indicate the discreteness of individual communities and groups. At around the same time we also see the apparent aggrandisement of settlements like Cowdery's Down. Together these phenomena would seem to indicate an emerging stability in display and identity.

At more or less the same time as these changes were happening in eastern Britain significant cultural transformations were occurring in the west and the two processes were probably inter-related. The use of zoomorphic belt fittings, which had been common in the decades either side of *c.*400, seems to have declined and these items are only rarely encountered at refortified

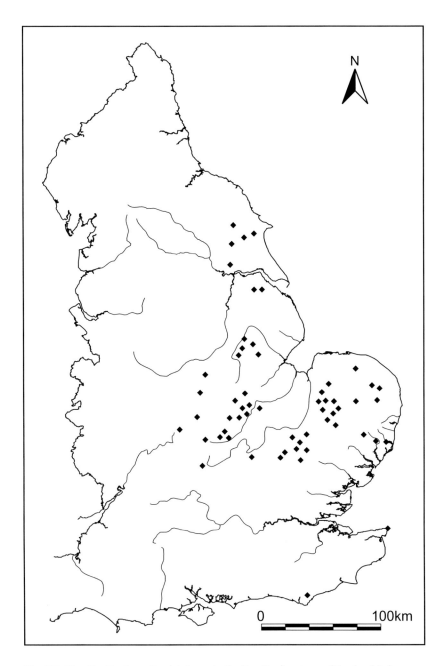

Fig. 7.3 The distribution of wrist clasps in the 'Anglian' regions of England (after Arnold 1997, Fig. 7.5).

hillforts. Given that this form of elite display had arguably originated in late Roman military dress its disappearance demonstrates that perceptions of what was appropriate had changed. It is surely no coincidence that belt buckles and martial dress were a significant component in Anglo-Saxon society and thus a conscious decision may have been made by western societies to reject a form of personal adornment that was becoming associated with populations in the east. Similarly, the decline in other forms of personal adornment may be related to the apparent profligacy with which such items were worn in the east.

The refortification of hillforts and the rejection of particular items of material culture and modes of social display may be linked with other changes. It has long been noted that the late fifth or early sixth century saw a shift in western naming practices (Woolf 2003, 367). Latin and Roman names fell out of favour and British or Celtic names came into use. This could be seen as a rejection of *Romanitas*. However, it is clear that the Roman past remained an important ideological touchstone for the communities of western Britain. The use of Latin titles on memorial stones (Redknap and Lewis 2007), contacts (however tenuous) with the eastern Roman Empire and the important part played by Magnus Maximus (Davies 2007, 222–233) in the genealogies of western polities and myth all point to this conclusion.

It is tempting to see the developments in both east and west as part of a process of ethnogenesis. After a period of fifth-century fluidity successful ethnicities emerged and propagated themselves in the sixth century. In the west the ethnicity could be seen as 'Brythonic' and in the east as Anglian, Saxon or Jutish/Kentish.

For Wenskus (1961), whose work has been encountered earlier in this volume, ancient 'tribes' were not sealed and racially pure groups. Instead, he suggested that fragmented peoples coalesced under the inspiration and leadership of particularly prominent and successful noble families. These groups maintained collective traditions and memories – the so-called *Traditionskern* – over long periods of time. Individuals joining the group had to subscribe to these traditions and through this mechanism a people or ethnic identity was born. Wenskus' ideas have long been applied and developed in the field of early medieval studies (Wolfram 1988 and 1997; Pohl 1998a and 1998b; Geary 2002; Liebeschuetz 2007; Heather 2009) and the notion of a tradition-bearing Germanic aristocracy bringing a fresh ideology and identity to a rudderless indigenous population is a familiar one (Higham 1992). Nevertheless, ethnogenesis and the *Traditionskern* model present certain difficulties.

Ethnogenesis was developed as a reaction to earlier Nazi era scholarship that had emphasised the supposed racial purity of ancient communities. *Stammesbildung und Verfassung* broke with this tradition of scholarship by emphasising the malleability of ancient identity. However, it has been observed that this model perpetuates visions of ancient Germanic structure based on the warband and aristocratic leadership that had appealed to Nazi historians (Callender Murray 2002; Halsall 2007, 15). The *Traditionskern* model also allows historians to project 'Germanic' identities back into the distant and prehistoric past. Here the recent use of Classical antiquity and the migration period as an origin myth for the modern German nation state is an important undercurrent. Of course, rejecting an idea because the intellectual framework that produced it appears unpalatable is poor scholarship. Such intellectual prejudice runs the risk of throwing the baby out with the bathwater. However, these are not the only methods for deconstructing the idea of a 'core of tradition'.

The mechanisms through which a group's core identity can be transmitted over time are unclear (Goffart 2002). Considerable emphasis is placed on religious beliefs, oral histories and group memories. However, the evidence for each of these phenomena is derived from later textual sources. These include such dubious materials as genealogies and mythology. Rules of thumb and hypotheses about social and political development are also utilised in unconvincing ways (e.g. Callender Murray 2002; Goffart 2002). Even Heather's (2005, 94–96; 2009, 65–67) suggestion that this kernel of tradition was maintained by a significant (in this case 'Gothic') social stratum composed of freemen is problematic. As Halsall (2007, 472–473) observes there is no compelling evidence for the existence of such a group, and it is uncomfortably close to the discarded concept of *Königsfreie* or 'King's freemen' for whom there is little evidence (Staab 1980).

This debate has a direct relevance for our understanding of the sixth-century situation in Britain. Were there nuclei of 'Anglian, Saxon and Jutish' groups that were transferred from northern Germany to Britain in the fifth century? Did these nuclei achieve success in the confusion of the fifth century and thus attract and assimilate others, both Germanic and indigenous?

The answers to these questions depend on the extent to which the three groups can be shown to have existed in the centuries prior to the sixth century (Springer 2003). Here traditional narratives draw attention to the occurrence of Anglii and Eudoses in Tacitus' first-century *Germania*. Ptolemy's second-century *Geography* also names these groups and is sometimes argued to also contain the first occurrence of the term 'Saxons'. However, it is likely that this is a later confusion arising from the misspelling of a group Tacitus knew as the Aviones and the first indisputable use of the name 'Saxon' occurs in the middle of the fourth century (Springer 2003, 14–15).

'Saxons' probably means something akin to 'knife-wielders' (Wolfram 1997, 42) and the seemingly generic nature of the name has encouraged scholars to talk of a 'Saxon confederacy'. Parallels can be drawn with the Franks (e.g. Goetz 2003) and Alamanni (e.g. Drinkwater 2007) as well as other barbarian groups. The Franks may mean 'the free or fierce men' (Wolfram 1997, 47) and the Alamanni seems to mean 'all the men' (Wolfram 1997, 40). The latter may have had a dual meaning. To the Alamanni it may have been a positive label – All-Men – with martial connotations. However, to groups external to the Alamanni it may have been used pejoratively (i.e.'the mixed group or mongrels') (Drinkwater 2007, 67). For both the Franks and the Alamanni there is some evidence for sub-groups, clans or septs (Halsall 2007, 134) but the sources are silent about the more distant Saxons. It has been assumed that they too must have been a confederacy of tribes during the fourth century. This interpretation sees the term Saxon as a label used in northern Germany as an identity in which smaller-scale identities such as Angle, Jute, Frisian and others were subsumed.

This is interesting because there seems to be no meaningful trace (Heather 1996, 96) of either the Anglii or the Eudoses between Tacitus in the first century and their reappearance in various sixth-century and later sources. Of course, these 'reappearing tribes' require explanation and the simplest suggestion has been to assume that their identities only re-emerged once the dominance of the over-arching group was broken (Heather 1996). Such an explanation would indicate that identities were firmly fixed in the period under question. However, given that four centuries separate Tacitus' Anglii from the sixth-century Angles of Procopius, this stretches credulity.

It should also be clearly noted that the presence of archaeological 'cultures' in northern Germany does not prove the existence of the Angles, Saxons or Jutes before their first literary appearances (e.g. Todd 1987, 64–65). The communities that produced these packages of material culture were prehistoric and labelling them with these terms is both anachronistic and unhelpful.

Late Roman military commanders and writers probably had at best a limited – and more commonly no – interest in the precise composition of the barbarian groups they were dealing with. During the fourth century there may well have been a Roman desire to discriminate between those barbarian groups along the Lower Rhine and those that they confronted on the North Sea littoral. The former were the 'Franks' and the latter became the 'Saxons', a term which is likely to have meant little more than 'boat-borne barbarian' and may be analogous to the later use of the term 'Viking'. Of course, the name may have been adopted and used by barbarian groups but it undermines the idea that there was a Saxon 'core of tradition' to be transmitted to Britain. Equally the silence in the sources about Angles and Jutes until the sixth and seventh centuries should make us extremely wary about hypothesising the existence of these identities in the fourth century, camouflaged by a so-called Saxon confederacy.

The movement of groups of Germanic individuals to Britain probably involved a multiplicity of identities. Bede, for all of his Angles, Saxons and Jutes (*Hist. Eccl.* I.15), had some concept of this (*Hist. Eccl.* V.9). The long-term and complex process of 'migration' and subsequent adjustment to British conditions, which probably included the incorporation of signifi-cant numbers of 'Romano-Britons' into the 'Germanic lifestyle', may well have proved so traumatic that any large-scale group identities and ethnic-ities were left in a state of incoherence. The later origin myths about the 'English' support this view of the situation. There were no meaningful sto-ries or legends about the position before the migration across the North Sea (Howe 1989). There were no *Traditionskerne* for aristocratic warrior bands to perpetuate or, if there had been, they were lost (Goffart 2002) and reinvented by the time Bede was writing. For these new myths the migration was the defining point for the origins of the Germanic kingdoms in Britain (e.g. Howe 1989).

During the mid to late fifth century the key social unit in eastern Britain was probably not a 'tribe' but extended kin groups, communities defined by localised geographical areas and those tied to the elite through 'lordship': obligation, service and patronage (Yorke 1995, 39–45; Semple 2008). The existence of these groups can only be seen obliquely through the funerary record and placenames, such as those which record the existence of the Hæstingas (Welch 1989, 78). During the later fifth century these small-scale communities and their elites begin to coalesce. Broad cultural distinctions, including dress, funerary ritual and perhaps dialect, become the focus for a higher level of identity. This led to the emergence of cultural zones, which modern authors, labouring under Bede's model, describe as discrete ethnic units and label as 'Anglian', 'Saxon' and 'Jutish'. Whether or not the small communities considered themselves as belonging to these ethnicities is a moot point. However, the existence of these cultural norms was a means of unifying disparate groups and providing social cohesion. It allowed small-scale social units to see themselves as part of a larger whole and this was useful

Table 7.1 *The* Tribal Hidage

Name	Area (Hides)	Name	Area (Hides)
Myrcna Landes	30,000	Hwinca	7,000
Wocensætna	7,000	Cilternsætna	4,000
Westerna	7,000	Hendrica	3,500
Pecsætna	1,200	Unecung(a)ga	1,200
Elmedsætna	600	Arosætna	600
Lindesfarona mit Hæthfeldlande	7,000	Færpinga	300
Suth Gyrwa	600	Bilmiga	600
North Gyrwa	600	Widerigga	600
East Wixna	300	East Willa	600
West Wixna	600	West Willa	600
Spalda	600	East Engle	30,000
Wigesta	900	East Sexena	7,000
Herefinna	1,200	Cantwarena	15,000
Sweordora	300	Suth Sexena	7,000
Gifla	300	West Sexena	100,000
Hicca	300		
Wihtgara	600		
Noxgaga	5,000		
Ohtgaga	2,000		
Total	66,100	Total	242,700 (correct total 244,100)

Source: The figure for West Sexena is likely to be a later interpolation (after Yorke 1990, 10).

because it provided a framework in which groups could define themselves as 'us' in opposition to 'them'. In this case 'them' may have been the Britons, whom Gildas records as being militarily resurgent in the late fifth century, or other 'Germanic' groups.

As the sixth century progressed these small-scale groups were crystallising into bigger polities. The composition of the *Tribal Hidage* in the seventh century (Dumville 1989) marks the beginning of the end of this process. The thirty-five recorded kingdoms include the emergent super-powers of Middle Saxon England: Mercia, Kent, the East Angles and the West Saxons (Table 7.1 and Figure 7.4). The absence of Northumbria can probably be explained by the suggestion that the document was Northumbrian in origin (Dumville 1989). However, alongside these kingdoms are a host of smaller communities, and almost half of the list records groups of 600 hides or less.

Fig. 7.4 Map of Britain in the seventh century with named kingdoms/groups derived from the *Tribal Hidage* (after Yorke 1990, Maps 1 and 2).

Some of these tiny polities are obscure but Bede (*Hist. Eccl.* IV.19) indicates that others had their own rulers.

It seems reasonable to suggest that the small territories of a few hundred hides with their kinglets reflect the situation during the sixth century (Yorke 1990, 11–13). Here it is noticeable that all of the kingdoms with 'Saxon' or 'Angle' in their names were large units measured in the thousands of hides. This suggests that these were 'new' names coined to unite the diverse groups that were being forged into kingdoms during the sixth century. As part of this process, invented tradition and mythmaking were used to link the groups ethnically through the shared history of the migration of coherent peoples to Britain in the fifth century. The origin myth provided kin groups and later kingdoms with a shared ancestry of heroic forefathers, gods and a history of victorious conflict with the Britons.

The culmination of this process was the unification of large social units, such as the South Folk and North Folk into the East Angles (Yorke 1990, 61), or the Gewisse's possible change to a West Saxon identity once the 'Jutish province' in Hampshire had been conquered (Yorke 1995, 34). The taking of these super-identities following territorial aggrandisement is less clear in other cases. The East Saxons seem to have controlled much of what would later in the eighth century be termed 'Middlesex', as well as parts of Hertfordshire and Surrey in the seventh century (Yorke 1990, 46–47). This abortive dominance or 'overlordship' may have prompted the promulgation of an East Saxon identity. In contrast, Bernicia and Deira adopted a purely geographical name: Northumbria (Yorke 1990, 74). However, Bede (*Hist. Eccl.* I.15) was certain that both the Northumbrians and Mercians were Angles.

Why the inhabitants of eastern Britain chose the names 'Saxons, Angles and Jutes' is beyond reconstruction. However, 'Saxon' was probably chosen because the name had a sound Classical pedigree and it was in British usage. The existence of the 'Continental Saxons' may also have been a significant factor. The terms 'Angle' and 'Jute' may have been chosen simply because they were geographical names in northern Germany. The fact that continental Angeln was known to be thinly populated (Bede *Hist. Eccl.* I. 15) might have encouraged its designation as the mythical point of origin for the 'Angles'.

The process of ethnogenesis for the 'Anglo-Saxons' took place in Britain during the late fifth and early sixth centuries. The first step was the development of origin myths that rationalised similarities between disparate kin groups and defined the position of small-scale communities in the wider world. As those communities coalesced into small kingdoms the 'tribal

ethnicity' provided a means to portray territorial expansion as the unification of an ancient and shared ethnic group. By the time early medieval
authors began to record these myths these fictive identities were fixed and
even formed the names of kingdoms. However, this process did not occur
in a vacuum. During much of the fifth and sixth centuries the greater part
of the Roman diocese was free of Germanic cultural influence. Even in the
seventh century significant areas were following an indigenous trajectory of
development (White 2007). These groups and communities were arguably
undergoing their own process of ethnogenesis in the late fifth century.

In the west this process is likely to have followed two intertwined paths. In
some regions an identity that looked to the Iron Age for inspiration appears
to have developed. Ancient power centres such as hillforts were refortified
(Alcock 1995) and 'Celtic' names appear on inscribed stones (e.g. Okasha
1993, 329–331; Redknap and Lewis 2007). This suggests that the distant past
was used as a focus for the newly emerging 'British' identities. Interestingly,
it is during the late fifth or early sixth centuries that later Welsh royal lineages
seem to shift from Latin names to 'Celtic' names (Woolf 2003, 369–370).
However, the Roman past also played a key role. Some inscribed stones use
Roman titles like *protectoris* or *magistratus* and Magnus Maximus features
prominently in Welsh myth (Davies 2007, 222–233). This suggests that the
trappings of Roman power were still relevant in the new post-Roman world.

The origins of these identities are opaque. However, unlike the Germanic
groups in the east, communities in the west could potentially draw inspiration from the 'un-Romanised' upland zone (Bowles 2007). Those regions
clearly maintained a very different social structure to the lowlands in the
Roman period and this may have been one model for post-Roman societies.
Connections with the Eastern Roman Empire could also have reinforced lingering notions of real or imagined *Romanitas* (Fulford 1989; Harris 2003).
Here the role of the remnants of the literate elite, perhaps largely confined
to ecclesiastics like Gildas, should not be underestimated. They provided
one means that might have perpetuated knowledge of the distant past both
'Iron Age' and 'Roman'.

The most striking element of sixth-century western society is the way
in which it differed from societies in the east. Yet the societies that left
traces of themselves in both the east and west were not so different in terms
of organisation and economy. The ostentatious martial funerary displays
and funerary deposition of female personal adornments in the east mark
(Stoodley 1997) a very different tradition to that seen in the west. The
unfurnished burials perpetuate a late antique tradition (Petts 2004) and it is
hard to escape the conclusion that once the use of weaponry and jewellery

became signifiers of identity in the east the west chose to follow a completely different path. The Roman symbols of martial identity (like belt plates) and female status (jewellery) had become Germanic ones. The communities in the west had defined themselves in opposition to this new 'Anglo-Saxon' identity by rejecting the overt use of these forms of material culture in funerary display.

It is possible that religion formed a major element in this late fifth- and sixth-century ethnic dividing line. The extent to which fourth-century Britain was Christianised is often overestimated (Petts 2003) but there is ample evidence for paganism in the fourth-century lowlands (e.g. Henig 1995; King 2005). This paganism is unlikely to have been exclusive and there may have been significant similarities in practice with Germanic paganism, about which almost nothing is known in fifth- and sixth-century Britain (Morris 1989, 57–61; Blair 2005, 52; Semple 2007). However, by the time of Gildas (*De Excidio*) the Britons were supposedly guilty of almost every sin imaginable except paganism, which seems to have been part of the distant past. Perhaps one of the key transformations in the fifth century was a shift in religious belief as those communities in the west, who saw themselves as indigenous and 'Roman', adopted Christianity in opposition to the Germanic 'pagans' in the east. Such a change may also have influenced attitudes in the west to material culture and the ostentatious display of material wealth.

By the middle of the sixth century the west and east of Britain were defined as 'British' and 'Anglo-Saxon'. Language, religion and the use of material culture described two societies defined in opposition to one another. Yet it would be wrong to think in terms of a 'Dark Age iron curtain'. The societies, based on small kingdoms and warbands, were not that dissimilar and the ideological differences between them were not sufficient to stop them cooperating with one another when needed. The rejection of the Roman civilian ideology of *paideia* and the adoption of a militarised identity in the fifth century had led to this sixth-century situation. It led to small-scale personalised power and fragmentation of Roman Britain's superficial unity.

8 | Final thoughts

The recent publication of a major site in the City of London reported the discovery of a semi-articulated and headless human corpse in a roadside ditch (Hill and Rowsome 2011, 386 and Fig. 331). This discovery was dated to around the end of the fourth century and linked to the supposedly hasty abandonment of nearby buildings (Hill and Rowsome 2011, 447). Some forty years ago a late Roman building was excavated in Bath. Dug into its floors was an oven and in the oven the excavators discovered the head of a young woman (Cunliffe 1969, 159).

Both of these phenomena have been interpreted by archaeologists, themselves separated by four decades of research and intellectual development, in historical terms. The headless corpse in the ditch and the skull in the oven are argued to be the victims of insecurity at the end of the Roman Empire. Recourse to Gildas' (*De Excidio* 24.4) narrative of cataclysm and the framework of 'Decline and Fall' has produced a teleological approach to interpretation. The interpretation has in turn become self-referencing and tautological. The end of the Roman Empire was a violent catastrophe; the collapse of a complex society. History and archaeology are blended together in such a way as to make this a seamless narrative.

Tautologies and teleology undermine alternative narratives, forcing discourse down predetermined paths without ever assessing the impact of multi-vocal interpretations on the evidential basis which underpins the narrative framework. The examples of interpretation from London and Bath discussed above highlight this issue and on closer examination demonstrate in microcosm some of the wider difficulties that confront those of us working on the vexing transition from Roman Britain to early medieval Britain.

The London discovery presents a number of interpretative issues that are worthy of fuller consideration. The implication is that the headless semi-articulated skeleton is the hastily buried victim of violence at the very end of the Roman period. To substantiate this interpretation it would need to be demonstrated that the individual met a traumatic end, through the osteological analysis of the skeleton. If the link between the historical framework and the archaeological material is severed then different interpretations can emerge.

Rather than see the human remains as the victim of barbarians it may be more fruitful to place the discovery in a broader context. Research in prehistory and more recent studies looking at the Roman period have demonstrated that societies engaged in all kinds of practices with human remains. So-called 'corpse manipulation' where body parts, or odd bones were kept, curated and then deposited in unusual places is a phenomenon with a long history (Beasley 2006, 41–45) that is beginning to receive archaeological attention (Crerar 2013). In late antiquity the cult of saints and relics throws this interest in pieces of dead people into a new, Christian light. Of course, the burial also marks a clear break with tradition because intramural burial was not a regular feature of Romano-British funerary practice. Together these elements might be united to suggest that there were significant changes occurring at the end of the fourth century in London but that these were more complex than the arrival of barbarian invaders.

The suggestion that the buildings were abandoned in a hurry can also be disputed. The evidence for this phenomenon was the supposedly large number of bulky items and personal adornments left in some of the structures. However, the decision to discard large items such as furniture does not necessarily indicate haste. Again the archaeological evidence is being forced to conform to a predetermined narrative.

The skull in the oven at Bath also repays closer examination. It was discovered during the small-scale excavation of a complex urban site. The skull lacked a jaw or vertebrae and thus does not look like the severed head of a victim of barbarian raiders and it has been suggested that the skull was displaced from an overlying late Saxon cemetery. Here a sequence of actions that seem to indicate the decline and fall of Roman Britain – late Roman townhouse; 'squatter's' oven and head of the last occupant – may indicate a very different tale that serves as a reminder of the methodological challenges that confront archaeologists.

Understanding the processes that led to the 'end' of the Roman Empire in Britain, a small and peripheral region, is not just a case of reading the outlines of a historical narrative on to the physical remains of the past. In Chapter 2 it was shown that the historical narratives are malleable and this serves as a strong indicator that interpretations of the period should also be flexible and able to countenance alternative perspectives. The recent trend for totalising pan-European narratives constricts debate by trying to shoehorn the experiences and trajectories of diverse and geographically distant regions within a single framework. The dynamics of the Western Empire were such that different stimuli had different impacts depending on their location. This volume has attempted to demonstrate this point by its detailed analysis of the minutiae of some aspects of late Roman Britain's material culture.

The 'end' of Roman Britain was a process of adjustment. Beginning in the third century material culture shows the shortening of the networks that maintained the province. The control of violence by the Roman state and its symbiotic relationship with the provincial elites provided those elites with legitimated power and control over local economic systems. However, as part of the bargain the elites had to eschew the trappings of military power, which were the emperor's preserve. At the dawn of the fifth century the indigenous elites adopted some elements of martial display, perhaps in response to weakening state influence. The failure of the Western Empire to recover Britain in the aftermath of Constantine III's revolt proved to be a catalyst that allowed latent social tensions to be explored as the fifth-century scramble for power unfolded.

It was military power that allowed elites to control and protect their clients and the format for this power was personalised as the retinue. From this point it was a small step to the creation of petty kingdoms and war-bands. For Germanic migrants the fifth century offered employment and opportunities for bands of warriors. The appearance of these groups at first probably conformed to Romano-British society's expectations of 'soldiers' but over time they, and other less martial groups of settlers, began to offer an alternative to the Romano-British socio-economic system. By the sixth century 'ethnic' identities had emerged which rationalised Britain into a situation of 'them' and 'us' based on a shared and fictive origin myth of conflict, conquest and migration.

The end of Roman Britain was thus not a consequence of economic collapse or barbarian invasion/migration. Instead it was the result of a complex scrabble to maintain, reinforce and acquire position and economic control. The tools to achieve these ends were the sword and the spear. These could be wielded as edged steel but also served as symbols and statements that demonstrated who was in control and why. The early medieval future was based, not on the supposed legitimation of status that came from a state, but on personalised power based on localised relationships and social structures. These had always existed in the Roman world but could flourish in the early Middle Ages free of any ideology (except religion) that sought to constrain them and their excesses.

Appendix A

Table A1 *Roman cemeteries with and without evidence of weapon trauma*

Site name	Number of skeletons	Number of skeletons with weapon trauma	Reference
Eyewell Fm, Chilmark	7	0	Fitzpatrick and Crockett 1998
Lankhills OA	335	0	Booth et al. 2010
Ilchester	7	0	Leach 1994
Gloucester	32	0	Heighway 1981
E. London Cemetery	545	0	Barber and Bowsher 2000
Chesterton	57	0	Casa Hatton and Wall 2005
Butt Rd, Colchester	669	0	Crummy, Crummy and Crossan 1993
Clarence St, Leicester	92	1	Gardner 2005
Poundbury	1,431	1	Farwell and Molleson 1993
Cirencester	407	8	McWhirr et al. 1982
Spitalfields	36	0	Sudds in press
Old Ford	6	0	Gary Brown *pers.comm.*
Stanton Harcourt	34	0	McGavin 1980
Queenford Fm, Dorch.-upon-Thames	275	1	Harman et al. 1978; Chambers 1987
Newarke St, Leicester	30	0	Cooper 1996
Lant St, Southwark	83	0	Sayer, Sudds and Ridgeway in press
Southwark Bridge Road	18	0	Sayer et al. in press
Alcester N.	17	0	Booth and Evans 2001
Alcester S.	31	0	Mahoney 1994
Wanborough	19	0	Anderson, Wacher and Fitzpatrick 2001
Bancroft	8	0	Williams and Zeepvat 1994
Lynch Fm, Peterborough	50	0	Jones 1975
Great Welden, Northamptonshire	2	0	Smith, Hird and Dix 1989
Kemble	11	0	King, Barker and Timby 1996

(*cont.*)

Table A1 (*cont.*)

Site name	Number of skeletons	Number of skeletons with weapon trauma	Reference
Yeovilton	13	0	Lovell 2006
Ilchester Gt Yard	5	0	Broomhead 1999
Barrow Hills, Radley	62	0	Chambers and McAdam 2007
Bow, Old Ford	2	0	Schwab 1993
Trinity St	44	0	Killock 2007
165 Gt Dover St, London	25	0	Mackinder 2000
Cambridgeshire Sites	265	5	Klingle 2012
Alington Ave, Dorset	91	0	Davies et al. 2002
Maiden Castle Rd, Dorset	22	0	Smith et al. 1997
Fordington Bottom, Dorset	4	0	Smith et al. 1997
Castle Fm, Somerset	2	0	C. Randall *pers. comm.*
Little Keep, Dorchester	29	2	Egging-Dinwiddy 2007
Kempston, Bedford	88	0	Boylston et al. 2000
Higham Ferrers, Northamptonshire	38	0	Lawrence and Smith 2009
Godmanchester	62	0	Jones 2003
Dartford	23	0	Wessex Archaeology 2006

Table A2 *Western British burials of the fifth and sixth century with and without weapon trauma*

Site name	Number of skeletons	Number of skeletons with weapon trauma	Reference
Henley Wood	70	0	Watts and Leach 1996
Cannington	542	0	Rahtz et al. 2000
Shepton Mallet	45	0	Leach and Evans 2001
Ulwell	57	0	Cox 1988
Filton	51	0	Cullen et al. 2006
Exeter	5	0	Bidwell 1979
Tolpuddle	48	0	Hearne and Birbeck 1999
Bradley Hill	21	0	Leech 1981; Gerrard 2011b
Portbury	15	2	Aston 2011

Table A3 *Anglo-Saxon burials with and without weapon trauma*

Site name	Number of skeletons	Number of skeletons with weapon trauma	Reference
Norton, Cleveland	109	1	Sherlock and Welch 1992
Great Chesterford	171	1	Evison and Evans 1994
Apple Down	175	0	Down and Welch 1990
Quarrington	15	2	Dickinson 2004
Buckland, Dover	243	2	Anderson 1996
Alton	49	1	Evison 1988
Castledyke South	199	0	Drinkall and Foreman 1998
Berinsfield	114	0	Boyle et al. 1995
Didcot	17	0	Boyle et al. 1995
Empingham II	150	0	Timby 1996
Buckland, Dover	164	0	Evison 1987
Butler's Field, Lechlade	219	3	Boyle et al. 1998
Eccles, Kent	200	7	Shaw 1995 and Wenham 1989
Stafford Rd, Brighton	3	1	Gardiner 1988
Goblin Works, Leatherhead	33	0	Poulton 1989
Park Lane, Croydon	21	0	McKinley 2003
Tadworth, near Banstead	36	0	Harp and Hines 2003
Market Lavington	42	0	Williams and Newman 2006
Broughton Lodge	121	0	Kinsley 1994
Worthy Park	99	2	Chadwick Hawkes and Grainger 2003
Beckford, Hereford and Worcester	106	1	Evison and Hill 1996
Blacknall Field	102	3	Annable and Eagles 2010
Mill Hill, Deal	76	0	Parfitt and Brugmann 1997
Harwell, Oxford	7	1	Brown 1967
Shavard's Fm, Meonstoke	21	0	Stoodley and Stedman 2001
Dinton, Buckinghamshire	20	0	Hunn, Lawson and Farley 1994
Dunstable, Bedfordshire	8	1	Matthews and Chadwick Hawkes 1985
Gallows Hill, Swaffham Prior	4	0	Malin 2005
Bishop's Cleeve	20	0	Holbrook 2000
Kemble	5	0	King et al. 1996
Barrow Hills, Radley	2	0	Chambers and McAdam 2007
Gunthorpe, Peterborough	36	0	Patrick, French and Osborne 2007

(cont.)

Table A3 (*cont.*)

Site name	Number of skeletons	Number of skeletons with weapon trauma	Reference
Portway, Andover	69	0	Cook and Dacre 1985
Ports Down, Portsmouth	17	1	Corney 1967
'Cambridgeshire'	345	13	Klingle 2012
Hicknoll Slait, Somerset	2	0	C. Randall *pers. comm.*

Appendix B

Table B1 *Early Roman groups quantified by Estimated Vessel Equivalents (%)*

Site Name	Flagons	Jars	Beakers	Bowls	Dishes	Cups	Mortaria	Amphorae	Others	Reference
London 1A	16.5	43	4.25	8.75	8.75	9.75	3	4.5	1.5	Davies, Richardson and Tomber 1993
London 1B	17	40	7	13.9	6.7	7.4	1.3	0.7	6	Davies et al. 1993
London 2	18.4	31.4	12.4	14.7	7.05	5.1	2	2.25	6.7	Davies et al. 1993
London 3	13.5	30.5	11.5	17.2	7.4	0.6	2.7	1.4	15.2	Davies et al. 1993
London 4	17.5	27.4	5.5	14.4	6.8	1.9	2	7	17.5	Davies et al. 1993
London 5	17.7	28.4	6.7	26.5	4.5	2.5	2	2	9.7	Davies et al. 1993
Drapers' Gardens P3	18.45	24.39	4.72	14.25	11.97	8.66	5.84	6.39	5.33	Author
Drapers' Gardens P4	17.90	19.88	5.93	20.16	8.06	7.89	3.15	9.52	7.52	Author
Drapers' Gardens P5	18.94	22.60	4.52	23.02	9.05	7.61	4.49	3.43	6.33	Author
9 Blake St, York P1	28	25	0	11	16	0	5	0	17	Monaghan 1993, Table 106
9 Blake St, York P2	26	46	4	11	4	0	2	0	6	Monaghan 1993, Table 106
9 Blake St, York P3	12	46	5	17	5	0	5	0	8	Monaghan 1993, Table 106
9 Blake St, York P4a	15	35	6	19	15	0	2	0	7	Monaghan 1993, Table 106
Tabard Sq., Southwark KG2	15.65	25.26	7.85	24.50	10.04	6.10	2.24	2.51	5.84	Author
Totals	252.54	444.83	85.37	235.38	120.32	57.51	42.72	39.7	119.62	1,397.99

Table B2 *Late Roman groups quantified by Estimated Vessel Equivalents (%)*

Site name	Flagons	Jars	Beakers	Bowls	Dishes	Cups	Mortaria	Amphorae	Others	Reference
Lincoln *	3.5	45.8	9.4	18.5	14.1	0	0.6	0	8.1	Darling 1977, 22
Silchester 1044	0	76	0	10	14	0	0	0	0	Fulford et al. 2006, Table 25
Silchester 1300	11	62.5	3	6	8.5	2	0	2	3.5	Fulford et al. 2006
Silchester 2554	15	47	0	14	19	2.5	0	0	2.5	Fulford et al. 2006
Segontium P10 *	0.5	46.5	0	23.2	9	5.7	10.9	0	4.3	Casey et al. 1993, Table 17.4
Segontium P10a *	1.2	48.1	0	24.2	16.4	3.9	5.4	0.3	0.6	Casey et al. 1993, Table 17.4
Segontium P11 *	0.8	56.6	0	26.4	7	0.8	8.5	0	0	Casey et al. 1993, Table 17.4
Boxfield Fm, Herts P5.2	1	54	2	35	6	0	0	1	1	Going and Hunn 1999, Fig. 35
Higham Ferrers P5	3	47.2	10	16.1	18.6	1.3	2.6	0	1.2	Lawrence and Smith 2009, Table 5.4
Cirencester Beeches DE/DF	11.36	44.81	1.84	20.4	15.43	0.19	5.36	0	0.61	McWhirr 1986, Table 28
Cirencester CQ and CX/CY PIII	8.15	41.6	3.39	21.88	10.65	0.47	10.53	0.81	2.52	McWhirr 1986, Table 28
9 Blake St, York P4c	4	38	7	14	29	0	3	0	5	Monaghan 1993, Table 106
9 Blake St, York P5	7	38	11	7	32	0	3	0	2	Monaghan 1993, Table 106
FCC95	1.6	32.17	4.43	33.25	10.12	0.33	7.47	6.25	4.39	Brigham, with Nielsen and Bluer
Old Ford, pit	13.87	49.45	1.05	16.65	9.99	4.83	3.66	0	0.5	Author
Old Ford, layer	0	49.03	2.86	26.4	17.26	0	4.46	0	0	Author
Drapers' Gardens P7	15.98	27.31	7.64	22.35	10.88	4.2	5.91	2.3	3.42	Author
Drapers' Gardens P8	15.74	23.5	7.43	24.44	13.09	2.82	9.53	0.72	2.73	Author
Shadwell, well	0	24.3	0	51.9	12.8	0	11	0	0	Author

(cont.)

Table B2 (*cont.*)

Site name	Flagons	Jars	Beakers	Bowls	Dishes	Cups	Mortaria	Amphorae	Others	Reference
Shadwell, layer	2.2	31.4	6	37.4	13.7	0	9.3	0	0	Author
Tabard Sq., Southwark KG9	0	41.87	5.48	17.67	15.69	7.84	3.69	1.51	6.24	Author
Tarrant Hinton	9.62	55.82	17.9	7.53	7.34	0	0.85	0	0.94	Lyne 1994, 140A
Heybridge, well	0	69.14	11.4	14.05	2.31	0	3.1	0	0	Lyne 1994, 88A
Chalk	20.91	34.23	7.14	15.68	9.49	0	11.5	0	1.05	Lyne 1994, 84A
Orpington	11.63	38.95	7.47	27.64	4.91	0	4.59	0	4.8	Lyne 1994, 83A
Neatham, well	9.67	56.67	9.77	12.57	4.84	0	0.68	0	5.8	Lyne 1994, 60A
Dickets Mead	16.48	37.07	6.74	28.37	8.78	0	0.11	0	2.44	Lyne 1994, 51A
Limbury	4.82	38.16	7.33	29.37	13.03	0	6.22	0	1.07	Lyne 1994, 33
Findon	6.95	61.1	7.37	11.88	9.72	0	0.13	0	2.85	Lyne 1994, 157
Brentford	10.32	58.41	11.11	11.39	7.16	0	0.62	0	0.99	Lyne 1994, 36A
Downton, villa	5.75	57.38	9.51	14.45	5.12	0	1.29	0	6.51	Lyne 1994, 1
Staines	12.24	42.58	20.59	14.58	4.95	0	1.75	0	3.32	Lyne 1994, 34
Alton Priors	3.1	66.4	1.6	15.5	7.3	0	1	0	5.1	Lyne 1994, 54
Hall Place	1.56	66.26	4.67	12.33	14.41	0	0.52	0	0.26	Lyne 1994, 74
Winchester	1.3	42.87	22.21	21	6.91	0	2.51	0	3.2	Lyne 1994, 7C
Winchester	2.75	40.19	15.93	20.05	9.03	0	3.73	0	8.32	Lyne 1994, 7B
Stockton	9.7	37.44	15.01	33.22	1.18	0	2.19	0	1.26	Lyne 1994, 98
Dummer	5.87	55.11	12.09	16.14	9.62	0	0.47	0	0.7	Lyne 1994, 61
Bradwell	19.65	44.2	1.38	17.58	11	0	5.11	0	1.08	Lyne 1994, 75
Portchester	0	45.02	13.56	29.41	8.85	0	3.16	0	0	Lyne 1994, 6A
Winchester	0.63	39.27	41.88	10.1	8.12	0	0	0	0	Lyne 1994, 7D
Brockley Hill	5.89	58.5	2.99	24.21	3.36	0	4.49	0	0.56	Lyne 1994, 94
Chilgrove	10.3	58.4	4.88	12.26	6.5	0	2.51	0	5.15	Lyne 1994, 92

Rock, villa	5.58	64.57	2.7	4.68	22.48	0	0	0	0	Lyne 1994, 91
Park St	7.56	33.11	7.71	33.11	13.53	0	0	0	4.99	Lyne 1994, 50A
Chichester Tower St	5.52	39.91	4.73	35.17	10.09	0	4.57	0	0	Lyne 1994, 15F
Bush Lane	0.49	30.41	7.42	34.21	17.17	0	7.51	0	2.77	Lyne 1994, 73D
Braishfield	0	55.83	10.31	16.85	15.26	0	0.59	0	1.17	Lyne 1994, 57
West Blanchington	2.47	60.47	3.91	22.39	5.61	0	3.91	0	1.24	Lyne 1994, 24C
Chilgrove	7.24	58.49	2.9	18.36	4.87	0	1.03	0	7.1	Lyne 1994, 20B
Wiggonholt	0	59.69	2.36	20.74	13.44	0	0	0	3.77	Lyne 1994, 67B
Owslebury	24.12	35.53	8.04	20.66	10.53	0	1.13	0	0	Lyne 1994, 10B
Witchampton, villa	14.72	37.16	2.94	24.21	20.24	0	0.74	0	0	Lyne 1994, 151
Cheniers Latimer	0	43.53	3.27	33.47	15.72	0	2.93	0	1.09	Lyne 1994, 49
Cobham Chatley	0	68.64	1.36	16.89	10.58	0	0.49	0	2.04	Lyne 1994, 96
Portchester	7.52	47.03	8.32	23.39	12.31	0	1.31	0	0.12	Lyne 1994, 6B
Brentford	8.25	68.59	1.74	10.77	9.85	0	0	0	0.82	Lyne 1994, 36B
Cox Green	3.41	61.57	8.11	8.11	11.34	0	4.33	0	3.13	Lyne 1994, 28B
Datchworth	2.87	65.63	0.84	23.28	6.19	0	0.94	0	0.25	Lyne 1994, 138B
Bokerley Dyke	2.52	48	26.56	7.36	14.65	0	0	0	0.91	Lyne 1994, 110
Orsett Cock	1.3	64.05	8.03	13.67	11.79	0	0	0	1.17	Lyne 1994, 173b
Datchworth	9.64	50.33	1.33	25.8	6.32	0	6.25	0	0.33	Lyne 1994, 138b
Wye	3.56	65.71	2.91	13.09	8.65	0	2.67	0	3.42	Lyne 1994, 127
Ickham	0	53.28	1.84	23.93	13.02	0	7.34	0	0.59	Lyne 1994, 126
Ware Lock	3.45	54.26	8.6	18.26	12.55	0	1.35	0	1.53	Lyne 1994, 109A
Bishopstone	8.28	62.11	0.26	21.51	5.04	0	2.1	0	0.7	Lyne 1994, 105

(cont.)

Table B2 (*cont.*)

Site name	Flagons	Jars	Beakers	Bowls	Dishes	Cups	Mortaria	Amphorae	Others	Reference
Mildenhall	1.93	42.24	7.49	34.29	6.64	0	7.41	0	0	Lyne 1994, 100
Radwinter	2.76	64.25	16.56	5.59	9.8	0	0	0	1.04	Lyne 1994, 76
Dickets Mead	4.51	61.43	1.02	18.5	12.56	0	1.3	0	0.69	Lyne 1994, 51B
Chichester, E. Gate	4.67	56.87	3.75	24.49	8.72	0	1.5	0	0	Lyne 1994, 15E
Winchester	10.23	42.34	20.1	17.34	6.68	0	3.31	0	0	Lyne 1994, 7H
Portchester	13.79	47.62	4.41	20.19	10.56	0	3.43	0	0	Lyne 1994, 6C
Truleigh Hill	0.6	71.36	2.37	18.18	6.18	0	0.08	0	1.23	Lyne 1994, 153
Verulamium	0	77.92	4.75	11.18	6.14	0	0	0	0	Lyne 1994, 47J
Netherwylde	1.51	61.85	2.75	16.16	9.69	0	7.4	0	0.65	Lyne 1994, 95B
Chalk	4.46	53.65	5.06	20.57	8.41	0	4.66	0	3.19	Lyne 1994, 84C
Fulham Palace	0.64	50.27	5.38	25.36	17.52	0	0.46	0	0.36	Lyne 1994, 71D
Baldock, well	7.87	56.38	0.43	22.84	8.19	0	4.29	0	0	Lyne 1994, 48C
Pevensey	2.07	57.81	1.24	29.67	7.54	0	0.69	0	0.97	Lyne 1994, 26D
Chilgrove	8.16	62.57	5.36	16.45	6.32	0	0.42	0	0.72	Lyne 1994, 20C
Burgess Hill	0	75.53	2.21	17.02	0	0	1.1	0	4.14	Sawyer 1999, Table 2
Billingsgate	1.94	48.63	9.31	28.06	8.69	0	1.38	0	2	Lyne 1994, 73H
Neatham	6.93	59.46	5.52	16.72	10.2	0	0	0	1.17	Lyne 1994, 60C
Dorchester-upon-Thames	9.24	55.55	12.94	9.77	7.22	0	4.58	0	0.7	Lyne 1994, 29D
Ware Lock	5.46	49.06	0.47	33.85	9.13	0	0.47	0	1.56	Lyne 1994, 109C
Ware Lock	0	22.49	0	8.19	2.67	0	0.86	0	65.79	Lyne 1994, 109B
TOTAL	490.31	4,373.49	572.36	1,730.38	901.23	36.88	253.97	14.89	225.36	8,598.87

Source: Sites marked * are quantified by rim counts; references to Lyne 1994 are to groups quantified in his Appendix 3.

Ancient Sources

Amm. Marc. *Ammianus Marcellinus Vols I–III.* Translated by J. Rolfe (1958 and 1972). London.

ASC. *The Anglo-Saxon Chronicle.* Translated and edited by M. Swanton (1996). London.

Ausonius of Bordeaux, *Ausonius Volume I.* Translated by H. Evelyn White (2002). London.

Bede, *Hist. Eccl. The Ecclesiastical History of the English Church and People.* Translated by J. McClure and R. Collins (1994). Oxford.

Beowulf. *Beowulf: A new translation.* Translated by S. Heaney (1999). London.

Caes. *B. Gall. Caesar, De Bello Gallico. Caesar: The Gallic War.* Translated by H. Edwards (1979). London.

CIL. *Corpus Inscriptionum Latinarum* (1862–). Berlin.

Cod. Just. Codex Justinianus. Annotated Code of Justinian. Translated by F. Blume, edited by T. Kearley (2012) https://uwacadweb.uwyo.edu/blume&justinian/default1.asp (accessed 20/9/2012).

Cod. Theod. The Theodosian Code and Novels and the Sirmondian Constitutions. Translated by C. Pharr (1952). Princeton.

Constantius, *Life of St Germanus* in 'Constantius of Lyon: The Life of St Germanus of Auxerre', edited and translated by T. Noble and T. Head in *Soldiers of Christ: Saints' Lives from Late Antiquity and the Early Middle Ages* (1994). Philadelphia: 75–106.

Digest. The Digest of Justinian. Latin text edited by Theodore Mommsen with the aid of Paul Krueger. Translated by A. Watson (1985). Philadelphia.

Firm. Mat. *Err. prof. rel.* Firmicus Maternus, *De errore profanarum religionum.* Translated by Clarence A. Forbes as *The Error of the Pagan Religions* (1970). New York.

Gallic Chronicle of 452. 'The Gallic Chronicle of 452: A new critical edition with brief introduction', by R. Burgess in R. Mathisen and D. Shanzer (eds.) *Society and Culture in Late Antique Gaul* (2001). Aldershot: 52–84.

Gildas, *De Excidio. Gildas: The Ruin of Britain and Other Works.* Edited and translated by M. Winterbottom (1978). Arthurian Period Sources 7. Chichester.

Jerome, *Epistles. Select Letters of St Jerome.* Translated by F. A. Wright (1933). London.

Jord. *Get.* Jordanes, *Getica. The Origins and Deeds of the Goths by Jordanes.* Translated by C. Mierow (1908). Princeton.

Joshua the Stylite, *Chronicon. The Chronicle of Pseudo-Joshua the Stylite.* Translated with notes by F. Trombley and J. Watt (2000). Liverpool.

Lib. *Or.* Libanius, *Oration* 59 in S. Lieu and D. Montserrat, *From Constantine to Julian: Pagan and Byzantine Views. A Source History* (1996). London.

Nennius *HB. Nennius: British History and the Welsh Annals.* Edited and translated by J. Morris (1980). Arthurian Period Sources 9. London.

Not. Dig. Occ. Notitia Dignitatum: Accedunt Notitia Urbis Constantinopolitanae Et Laterculi Provincarium. Edited by O. Seeck (1876). Berlin.

Olympiodorus, 'Olympiodorus', *The Fragmentary Classicizing Historians of the Later Roman Empire.* Translated by R. Blockley (1983). Liverpool: 152–211.

Oros. *Orosius. Seven Books of History against the Pagans.* Translated with an introduction and notes by A. T. Fear (2010). Liverpool.

Patrick, *Confessio* and *Epistola. St Patrick: His Writings and Muirchu's Life.* Edited and translated by A. Hood (1978). Arthurian Period Sources 9. Chichester.

Patrick, *Letter to Coroticus. St Patrick: His Writings and Muirchu's Life.* Edited and translated by A. Hood (1978). Arthurian Period Sources 9. Chichester.

PLRE. The Prosopography of the Later Roman Empire. A. Jones, J. Martindale and J. Morris (1971). Cambridge.

RIB. The Roman Inscriptions of Britain Vols. I–III. R. Collingwood, R. Wright and R. Tomlin (1995–2009). Oxford.

Salvian, *De Gub. Dei. De Gubernatione Dei. The Writings of Salvian the Presbyter.* Translated by J. O'Sullivan (1947). Washington.

Sid. Apoll. *Epistola* and *Carmina. Sidonius: Poems and Letters.* Translated by W. Anderson (1965). London.

Tac. *Hist.* Tacitus, *Histories Book I.* Edited by C. Damon (2003). Cambridge.

Y Gododdin. Aneirin: Y Gododdin. Translated by A. Jarman (1998). Llandysul.

Zos. *Zosimus: A New History.* A translation and commentary by Ronald T. Ridley (1982). Sydney.

Bibliography

Abdy, R. (2006) 'After Patching: imported and recycled coinage in fifth- and sixth-century Britain', in *Coinage and History in the North Sea World 500–1250: Essays in Honour of Marion Archibald*, B. Cook and G. Williams (eds.). Leiden: 75–98.

Absolute Archaeology (2012) *Butleigh Roman Villa Investigations 2005–2011*. Unpublished Absolute Archaeology Report. http://butleigh.org/images/2010% 20excavation.pdf (accessed 15/3/2012).

Adams, J. (2003) *Bilingualism and the Latin Language*. Cambridge.

Adcock, J. and Wood, E. (2005) *Geophysical Survey Report: Dinnington, Somerset*. Unpublished GSB Prospection Report No. 2,005/33.

Addyman, P. (1972) 'The Anglo-Saxon house: a review', *Anglo-Saxon England* 1: 273–307.

Africa, T. (1971) 'Urban violence in imperial Rome', *Journal of Interdisciplinary History* 2(1): 3–21.

Alcock, L. (1963) *Dinas Powys: An Iron Age, Dark Age and Early Medieval Settlement in Glamorgan*. Cardiff.

Alcock, L. (1971) *Arthur's Britain*. London.

Alcock, L. (1972) *By South Cadbury, is that Camelot?* London.

Alcock, L. (1982) 'Cadbury-Camelot, a fifteen year perspective', *PBA* 68: 355–388.

Alcock, L. (1992) 'Burials and cemeteries in Scotland', in *The Early Church in Wales and the West*, N. Edwards and A. Lane (eds.). Oxford: 125–129.

Alcock, L. (1995) *Cadbury Castle, Somerset: The Early Medieval Archaeology*. Cardiff.

Alcock, L. (2003) *Kings and Warriors, Craftsmen and Priests in Northern Britain AD 550–850*. Edinburgh.

Allan, J., Dawson, D. and Kent, O. (in press) 'The post-Roman pottery', in *Excavations at Glastonbury Abbey 1907–1979*, R. Gilchrist and C. Allum (eds.). London.

Allason-Jones, L. (1989) *Ear-rings in Roman Britain*. Oxford.

Allason-Jones, L. (1996) *Roman Jet in the Yorkshire Museum*. York.

Allason-Jones, L. and McKay, B. (1985) *Coventina's Well: A Shrine on Hadrian's Wall*. Oxford.

Allen, M. and Fulford, M. (1996) 'The distribution of south-east Dorset Black Burnished category 1 pottery in South-West Britain', *Britannia* 27: 223–281.

Almond, P. (2006) 'Beware the New Goths are coming', *The Sunday Times*, 11/6/2006.

Anderson, T. (1996) 'Cranial weapon injuries from Anglo-Saxon Dover', *International Journal of Osteoarchaeology* 6: 10–14.

Anderson, A., Wacher, J. and Fitzpatrick, A. (2001) *The Romano-British 'Small Town' at Wanborough, Wilts.* London.

Annable, K. and Eagles, B. (2010) *The Anglo-Saxon Cemetery at Blacknall Field, Pewsey, Wiltshire.* Salisbury.

Arce, J. (2003) 'The fifth century in Hispania', in *Regna and Gentes: The Relationship between Late Antique and Early Medieval Peoples and Kingdoms in the Transformation of the Roman World,* H. Goetz, J. Jarnut and W. Pohl (eds.). Leiden: 135–159.

Arnold, C. (1984) *Roman Britain to Saxon England.* London.

Arnold, C. (1997) *The Archaeology of the Early Anglo-Saxon Kingdoms.* London.

Aston, M. (2011) 'New radiocarbon dates for early medieval Somerset', *Proceedings of the Somerset Archaeological and Natural History Society* 154: 185–189.

Atkinson, D. (1932) 'Caister-by-Norwich', *JRS* 21: 232–233.

Avent, R. and Evison, V. (1982) 'Anglo-Saxon button brooches', *Archaeologia* 107: 77–124.

Baatz, D. (1983) 'Town walls and defensive weapons', in *Roman Urban Defences in the West,* J. Maloney and B. Hobley (eds.). London: 136–140.

Babcock, W. (1916) 'The races of Britain', *The Scientific Monthly* 2(2): 149–169.

Bachrach, B. (2000) 'Imperial walled cities in the West: an examination of their early medieval *nachleben*', in *City Walls: The Urban Enceinte in Global Perspective,* J. Tracy (ed.). Cambridge: 192–218.

Baillie, M. (2010) 'Volcanoes, ice cores and tree rings: one story or two?', *Antiquity* 84: 202–215.

Baker, S. (2002) 'Prehistoric and Romano-British landscapes at Little Wittenham and Long Wittenham, Oxfordshire', *Oxoniensia* 67: 1–28.

Banaji, J. (2001) *Agrarian Change in Late Antiquity: Gold, Labour and Aristocratic Dominance.* Oxford.

Banaji, J. (2009) 'Aristocracies, peasantries and framing the early Middle Ages', *Journal of Agrarian Change* 9(1): 59–91.

Bang, P. (2007a) 'Trade and Empire – In search of organizing concepts for the Roman economy', *P&P* 195: 3–54.

Bang, P. (2007b) *The Roman Bazaar: A Comparative Study of Trade and Markets in a Tributary Empire.* Cambridge.

Barber, B. and Bowsher, D. (2000) *The Eastern Cemetery of Roman London: Excavations 1983–1990.* London.

Barber, B., Bowsher, D. and Whittaker, K. (1990) 'Recent excavations of a cemetery of Londinium', *Britannia* 21: 1–12.

Barford, P. (1995) 'Reinterpreting Mucking: countering the Black Legend', *Anglo-Saxon Studies in Archaeology and History* 8: 103–109.

Barker, P. (1993) *Techniques of Archaeological Excavation.* London.

Barker, P., White, R., Pretty, K., Bird, H. and Corbishley, M. (1997) *The Baths-Basilica Wroxeter: Excavations 1966–90.* London.

Barnes, T. (1998) *Ammianus Marcellinus and the Representation of Historical Reality.* London and Ithaca NY.

Barrett, J. (1997) 'Romanization: a critical comment', in *Dialogues in Roman Imperialism*, D. Mattingly (ed.), *Journal of Roman Archaeology* Supplementary Series. Portsmouth, Rhode Island: 51–64.

Barrett, J., Freeman, P. and Woodward, A. (2000) *Cadbury Castle, Somerset: The Later Prehistoric and Early Historic Archaeology.* London.

Barrowman, R., Batey, C. and Morris, C. (2007) *Excavations at Tintagel Castle, Cornwall, 1990–1999.* London.

Bartholomew, P. (1982) 'Fifth-century facts', *Britannia* 13: 261–270.

Bartholomew, P. (1984) 'Fourth-century Saxons', *Britannia* 15: 169–185.

Bassett, S. (1989) *The Origins of Anglo-Saxon Kingdoms.* Leicester.

Bayley, J. and Butcher, S. (2004) *Roman Brooches in Britain: A Technological and Typological Study Based on the Richborough Collection.* London.

Beagrie, N. (1989) 'The Romano-British pewter industry', *Britannia* 20: 169–191.

Beasley, M. (2006) 'Roman boundaries, roads and ritual: excavations at the Old Sorting Office, Swan Street, Southwark', *Transactions of the London and Middlesex Archaeological Society* 57: 23–68.

Beattie, I. and Pythian-Adams, W. (1913) 'A Romano-British house near Bedmore Barn, Ham Hill, Somerset', *JRS* 3(1): 127–133.

Biddle, M. and Kjølbye-Biddle, B. (2001) 'The origins of St Albans Abbey: Romano-British cemetery and Anglo-Saxon monastery', in *Alban and St Albans: Roman and Medieval Architecture, Art and Archaeology*, M. Henig and P. Lindley (eds.). London: 45–77.

Bidwell, P. (1979) *The Legionary Bath-house and Basilica and Forum at Exeter.* Exeter.

Bidwell, P. (2006) 'Constantius and Constantine at York', in *Constantine the Great: York's Roman Emperor*, E. Hartley, J. Hawkes, M. Henig and F. Mee (eds.). York: 31–40.

Bidwell, P. and Croom, A. (2010) 'The supply and use of pottery on Hadrian's Wall in the 4th century AD', in *Finds from the Frontier*, R. Collins and L. Allason-Jones (eds.). London: 20–36.

Bidwell, P. and Speak, S. (1994) *Excavations at South Shields Roman Fort Volume 1.* Newcastle.

Bindler, R., Renberg, I., Rydberg, J. and Andrén, T. (2009) 'Widespread waterborne pollution in central Swedish lakes and the Baltic Sea from pre-industrial mining and metallurgy', *Environmental Pollution* 157(7): 2132–2141.

Birbeck, V. (in press) 'A Time Team evaluation at Binchester Roman fort, County Durham', *Durham Archaeological Journal.*

Birbeck, V. and Schuster, J. (2009) *Living and Working in Roman and Later London: Excavations at 60–63 Fenchurch Street.* Salisbury.

Bird, J. and Young, C. (1981) 'Migrant potters – the Oxford connection', in *Roman Pottery Research in Britain and North-West Europe*, A. Anderson and

A. Anderson (eds.). Oxford British Archaeological Reports International Series 123(ii). Oxford: 295–312.

Birley, A. (1999) *Septimius Severus: The African Emperor*. London.

Birley, A. (2005) *The Roman Government of Britain*. Oxford.

Birley, E. (1961) *Research on Hadrian's Wall*. Kendal.

Bishop, B. (2000) 'A keyhole through the gateway: a watching brief at Aldgate', *London Archaeologist* 9(7): 179–184.

Blair, J. (2005) *The Church in Anglo-Saxon Society*. Oxford.

Bland, R. and Loriet, X. (2010) *Roman and Early Byzantine Gold Coins found in Britain and Ireland with an Appendix of New Finds from Gaul*. London.

Blockley, R. (1980) 'The date of the "barbarian conspiracy" ', *Britannia* 11: 223–225.

Blockley, R. (1981) *The Fragmentary Classicizing Historians of the Later Roman Empire: Eunapius, Olympiodorus, Priscus and Malchus*. Liverpool.

Blockley, R. (1982) 'Constantius II and his generals', *Studies in Latin Literature and History* 2: 467–486.

Blockley, R. (1983) *The Fragmentary Classicizing Historians of the Later Roman Empire: Volume II*. Liverpool.

Böhme, H. (1974) *Germanische Grabfunde des 4. bis 5. Jahrhunderts*. Munich.

Böhme, H. (1986) 'Das Ende der Römerherrschaft in Britannien und die Angelsächsich Besiedlung Englands im 5. Jahrhundert', *JRGZ* 33: 469–574.

Böhme, H. (1997) 'Söldner und Siedler im spätantiken Nordgallien', *Die Franken* 1: 91–101.

Bond, J. (1998) 'Burnt offerings: animal bones in Anglo-Saxon cremations', *World Archaeology* 28(1): 76–88.

Bonfield, L. (1989) 'The nature of customary law in the manor courts of medieval England', *CSSH* 31(3): 514–534.

Boon, G. (1987) *The Legionary Fortress of Caerleon – Isca*. Cardiff.

Booth, P. M. (1986) 'Roman pottery in Warwickshire, production and demand', *Journal of Roman Pottery Studies* 1: 22–41.

Booth, P. and Evans, J. (2001) *Roman Alcester: Northern Extra-mural Areas*. London.

Booth, P. and Green, S. (1989) 'The nature and distribution of certain pink grog-tempered vessels', *Journal of Roman Pottery Studies* 2: 77–84.

Booth, P., Simmonds, A., Boyle, A., Clough, S., Cool, H. and Poore, D. (2010) *The Late Roman Cemetery at Lankhills, Winchester: Excavations 2000–2005*. Oxford.

Bosworth, J. (1838) *A Dictionary of the Anglo-Saxon Language*. London.

Bowersock, G. (1996) 'The vanishing paradigm of the fall of Rome', *Bulletin of the American Academy of Arts and Sciences* 49(8): 29–43.

Bowes, K. (2010) *Houses and Society in the Later Roman Empire*. London.

Bowles, C. (2007) *Rebuilding the Britons: The Post-Colonial Archaeology of Culture and Identity in the Late Antique Bristol Channel Region*. Oxford.

Bowman, A. (1993) *Life and Letters on the Roman Frontier: Vindolanda and its People*. London.

Boyle, A., Dodd, A., Miles, D. and Mudd, A. (1995) *Two Oxfordshire Anglo-Saxon Cemeteries: Berinsfield and Didcot*, Thames Valley Landscapes Monograph 8. Oxford.

Boyle, A., Jennings, D., Miles, D. and Palmer, S. (1998) *The Anglo-Saxon Cemetery at Butler's Field, Lechlade, Gloucestershire: Volume 1 Prehistoric and Roman Activity and Anglo-Saxon Grave Catalogue*. Oxford.

Boylston, A. (2000) 'Evidence for weapon-related trauma in British archaeological samples', in *Human Osteology in Archaeology and Forensic Science*, M. Cox and S. Mays (eds.). London: 357–380.

Boylston, A., Knüsel, C., Roberts, C. and Dawson, M. (2000) 'Investigation of a Romano-British rural ritual in Bedford, England', *Journal of Archaeological Science* 27: 241–254.

Bradley, R. (2006) 'Bridging two cultures: commercial archaeology and the study of prehistoric Britain', *The Antiquaries Journal* 86, 1–13.

Bradley, T. and Butler, J. (2008) *From Temples to Thames Street – 2000 Years of Riverside Development*. London.

Branigan, K. (1977) *Gatcombe: The Excavation and Study of a Romano-British Villa Estate*. Oxford.

Branigan, K. and Miles, D. (1988) *The Economies of Romano-British Villas*. Sheffield.

Breeze, A. (2010) 'Gildas and the schools of Cirencester', *AntJ* 90: 131–138.

Breeze, D. (1982) *The Northern Frontiers of Roman Britain*. London.

Brenan, J. (1991) *Hanging Bowls and their Context*. Oxford.

Brewer, R. (1993) '*Venta Silurum*: a *civitas* capital', in *Roman Towns: The Wheeler Inheritance*, S. Greep (ed.). London: 56–65.

Brickstock, R. (2000) 'Coin supply in the north in the late Roman period', in *The Late Roman Transition in the North*, T. Wilmott and P. Wilson (eds.). Oxford: 33–37.

Brigham, T. (1990a) 'The late Roman waterfront in London', *Britannia* 21: 99–183.

Brigham, T. (1990b) 'A reassessment of the second basilica in London AD 100–400', *Britannia* 21: 53–97.

Brigham, T. with Nielsen, R. and Bluer, R. (2006) *Roman and Later Development East of the Forum and Cornhill: Excavations at Lloyd's Register, 71 Fenchurch Street, City of London*. London.

Broadberry, S. Campbell, B. and van Leuwen, B. (2010) *English Medieval Population: Reconciling Time Series and Cross Sectional Evidence*. Unpublished University of Warwick Working Paper.

Brodribb, A., Hands, A. and Walker, D. (1971) *Excavations at Shakenoak II*. Oxford.

Brooke, J. (1920) 'The excavation of a late Roman well at Cunetio (Mildenhall)', *Wiltshire Archaeology and Natural History Magazine* 41: 151–152.

Brookes, S. (2007) *Economies and Social Change in Anglo-Saxon Kent AD 400–900*. Oxford.

Brooks, N. (1989) 'The creation and early structure of the kingdom of Kent', in *The Origins of Anglo-Saxon Kingdoms*, S. Bassett (ed.). Leicester: 55–74.

Broomhead, R. (1999) 'Ilchester: Great Yard excavations 1995', *Proceedings of the Somerset Archaeological and Natural History Society* 142: 139–191.

Brown, A. (1994) 'A Romano-British shell-gritted pottery and its manufacturing site', *Bedfordshire Archaeology* 21: 19–107.

Brown, G., Bishop, B., Douglas, A., Leary, J. Ridgeway, V. and Taylor-Wilson, R. (in press) *Excavations at Old Ford, London*. London.

Brown, D. (1967) 'The Anglo-Saxon cemetery at Harlow', *Oxoniensia* 32: 72–74.

Brown, D. (1973) 'A Roman pewter hoard from Appleford, Berks.', *Oxoniensia* 38: 184–206.

Brown, P. D. (1971) 'The church at Richborough', *Britannia* 2: 225–231.

Brown, P. R. (1971) *The World of Late Antiquity*. London.

Brown, P. R. (1992) *Power and Persuasion in Late Antiquity: Towards a Christian Empire*. Madison.

Bruce-Mitford, R. (1975) *The Sutton Hoo Ship Burial Volume 1*. London.

Bruce-Mitford, R. and Raven, S. (2005) *The Corpus of Late Celtic Hanging-Bowls*. Oxford.

Brugmann, B. (2011) 'Migration and endogenous change', in *The Oxford Handbook of Anglo-Saxon Archaeology*, H. Hamerow, D. Hinton and S. Crawford (eds.). Oxford: 30–45.

Brun, D. (2003) *Germanic Equal Arm Brooches of the Migration Period: A Study of Style, Chronology and Distribution, including a Full Catalogue of Finds and Contexts*. Oxford.

Brunn, C. (2003) 'The Antonine plague: Rome and Ostia', *JRA* 16: 426–434.

Brunning, R. (2001) 'Lopen, Bridge Farm', *Somerset Archaeology and Natural History* 145: 142–143.

Brunt, P. (1975) 'Did Imperial Rome disarm her subjects?', *Phoenix* 29(3): 260–270.

Buckland, P., Hartley, K. and Vigby, V. (2001) 'The Roman pottery kilns at Rossington Bridge excavations 1956–1961', *Journal of Roman Pottery Studies* 9: 1–96.

Bull, R. and Davis, S. (2006) *Becoming Roman: Excavation of a Late Iron Age to Romano-British Landscape at Monkston Park, Milton Keynes*. London.

Büntgen, U., Tegel, W., Nicolussi, K., McCormick, M., Frank, D., Trouet, V., Kaplan, J., Herzig, F., Heussner, K., Wanner, H., Lüterbacher, J. and Esper, J. (2011) '2,500 years of climate variability and human susceptibility', *Science* 331(6,017): 578–582.

Burnett, A. (1984) 'Clipped siliquae and the end of Roman Britain', *Britannia* 15: 163–168.

Burnham, B. and Wacher, J. (1990) *The 'Small Towns' of Roman Britain*. London.

Burnham, B., Keppie, L., Esmonde-Cleary, A. and Hassall, M. (1993) 'Roman Britain in 1992', *Britannia* 24: 267–322.

Burrow, I. (1981) *Hillfort and Hilltop Settlement in Somerset in the First to Eighth Centuries AD*. Oxford.

Burrow, I. (1982) 'Hillforts and hilltops 1000 BC–1000 AD', in *The Archaeology of Somerset*, M. Aston and I. Burrows (eds.). Taunton: 83–98.

Bushe-Fox, J. (1926) *First Report on the Excavation of the Roman Fort at Richborough, Kent.* London.

Bushe-Fox, J. (1949) *Fourth Report on the Excavation of the Roman Fort at Richborough, Kent.* London.

Butler, J. (2001) 'The city defences at Aldersgate', *Transactions of the London and Middlesex Archaeological Society* 52: 41–112.

Butler, J. (2006) *Reclaiming the Marsh: Archaeological Investigations at Moor House, City of London.* London.

Callender Murray, A. (2002) 'Reinhard Wenskus on "Ethnogenesis", ethnicity and the origin of the Franks', in *On Barbarian Identity: Critical Approaches to Ethnicity in the Early Middle Ages*, A. Gillett (ed.). Turnhout: 85–122.

Camden, W. (1586) *Britannia siue Florentissimorum regnorum, Angli, Scoti, Hiberni, et insularum adiacentium ex intima antiquitate chorographica descriptio.* London.

Cameron, A. (1993) *The Later Roman Empire.* London.

Campbell, B. (2007) *Three Centuries of English Crop Yield 1211–1491.* www.cropyields.ac.uk (accessed 6/2/2011).

Campbell, E. (1993) 'Excavations at Caerwent vicarage orchard garden, 1973: an extra-mural post-Roman cemetery', *Archaeologia Cambrensis* 142: 74–98.

Campbell, E. (2007)*Continental and Mediterranean Imports to Atlantic Britain and Ireland AD 400–800.* London.

Campbell, E. and Lane, A. (1993) 'Excavations at Longbury Bank, Dyfed and early medieval settlement in South Wales', *Medieval Archaeology* 37: 15–77.

Campbell, E. and MacDonald, P. (1993) 'Excavations at Caerwent Vicarage Garden 1973: an extra mural post-Roman cemetery', *Archaeologia Cambrensis* 142: 74–98.

Carr, L. (2007) 'Sonia Chadwick Hawkes and the "three ships" ', in *Collectanea Antiqua: Essays in Memory of Sonia Chadwick Hawkes*, M. Henig and J. Smith (eds.). Oxford: 49–52.

Carver, M. (1994) 'Environment and commodity in early Anglo-Saxon society', in *Environment and Economy in Anglo-Saxon England*, J. Rackham (ed.). London: 1–6.

Carver, M. (2009) 'Early Scottish monasteries and prehistory: a preliminary dialogue', *The Scottish Historical Review* 88(2): 332–351.

Carver, M. (2012) 'Intellectual communities in early Northumbria', in *Early Medieval Northumbria. Kingdoms and Communities, AD 400–1100*, D. Petts and S. Turner (eds.). Turnhout: 185–206.

Carver, M., Hills, C. and Scheschkewitz, J. (2009) *Wasperton: A Roman, British and Anglo-Saxon Community in Central England.* Woodbridge.

Casa Hatton, R. and Wall, W. (2005) 'A late Roman cemetery at Durobrivae, Chesterton', *Proceedings of the Cambridge Antiquarian Society* 95: 5–24.

Casey, P. (1974) 'A coin of Valentinian III from Wroxeter', *Britannia* 5: 383–386.

Casey, P. (1983) 'Imperial campaigns and 4th century defences in Britain', in *Roman Urban Defences in the West*, J. Maloney and B. Hobley (eds.). London: 121–124.

Casey, P. (1994) *Roman Coinage in Britain*. Aylesbury.

Casey, P., Davies, J. and Evans, J. (1993) *Excavations at Segontium (Caernarfon) Roman Fort: 1975–1979*. London.

Casson, L. (1974) *Travel in the Ancient World*. London.

Chadwick Hawkes, S. and Grainger, G. (2003) *The Anglo-Saxon Cemetery at Worthy Park, Kingsworthy, near Winchester, Hampshire*. Oxford.

Chambers, R. (1987) 'The late and sub-Roman cemetery at Queenford farm, Dorchester upon Thames, Oxon', *Oxoniensia* 52: 35–69.

Chambers, R. and McAdam, E. (2007) *Excavations at Barrow Hills, Radley, Oxfordshire*. Oxford.

Chase, A. and Chase, D. (1992) 'Mesoamerican elites: assumptions, definitions and models', in *Mesoamerican Elites: An Archaeological Assessment*, A. Chase and D. Chase (eds.). Norman OK.

Childe, V. (1929) *The Danube in Prehistory*. Oxford.

Christie, N. (2000) 'Towns, land and power: German-Roman survivals and interaction in fifth and sixth-century Pannonia', in *Towns and their Territories between Late Antiquity and the Early Middle Ages*, G. Broglio, N. Gunther and N. Christie (eds.). Leiden: 275–297.

Christie, N. (2011) *The Fall of the Western Roman Empire: An Archaeological and Historical Perspective*. London.

Clark, A. (1993) *Excavations at Mucking. Volume 1: The Site Atlas*. London.

Clark, C. and Haswell, M. (1970) *The Economics of Subsistence Agriculture*. London.

Clark, E. (1984) *The Life of Melania the Younger. Introduction, translation and commentary*. Lampeter.

Clarke, D. (1978) *Analytical Archaeology*. Cambridge.

Clarke, G., Rigby, V. and Shepherd, J. (1982) 'The Roman villa at Woodchester', *Britannia* 13: 197–228.

Coates, R. (2007) 'Invisible Britons: the view from linguistics', in *Britons in Anglo-Saxon England*, N. Higham (ed.). Woodbridge: 172–191.

Collingwood, R. (1930) *The Archaeology of Roman Britain*. London.

Collingwood, R. and Myres, J. (1936) *Roman Britain and the English Settlements*. Oxford.

Collins, R. (2007) 'Decline, collapse or transformation? Hadrian's Wall in the 4th to 5th centuries AD'. Unpublished PhD thesis, Department of Archaeology, University of York.

Collins, R. (2008) 'The latest Roman coin from Hadrian's Wall: a small fifth-century purse group', *Britannia* 39: 256–261.

Collins, R. (2009) 'Hadrian's Wall and the collapse of Roman frontiers', in *Limes XX*, A. Morillo. N. Hanel and E. Martín (eds.). Madrid: 181–197.

Collins, R. (2010) 'Brooch use in the 4th- to 5th-century frontier', in *Finds from the Frontier: Material Culture in the 4th–5th Centuries*, R. Collins and L. Allason-Jones (eds.). London: 64–77.

Collins, R. (2012) *Hadrian's Wall and the End of Empire: The Roman Frontier in the 4th–5th Centuries*. New York.

Collins, R. and Allason-Jones, L. (2010) *Finds from the Frontier: Material Culture in the 4th to 5th Centuries AD*. London.

Cook, A. and Dacre, M. (1985) *Excavations at Portway, Andover*. Oxford.

Cooke, N. (2003) 'Excavation of Roman features and deposits on the outskirts of Cunetio, Marlborough in 1997', *Wiltshire Archaeological and Natural History Magazine* 96: 26–32.

Cool, H. (1990) 'Roman metal hairpins from southern Britain', *AJ* 147: 148–182.

Cool, H. (2000a) 'The parts left over: material culture into the fifth century', in *The Late Roman Transition in the North*, T. Wilmott and P. Wilson (eds.). Oxford: 47–65.

Cool, H. (2000b) 'Hairstyles and lifestyles', *Lucerna: Roman Finds Group Newsletter* 19: 3–6.

Cool, H. (2006) *Eating and Drinking in Roman Britain*. Cambridge.

Cool, H. (2010) 'Objects of glass, shale, bone and metal (except nails)', in *The Late Roman Cemetery at Lankhills, Winchester: Excavations 2000–2005*, P. Booth, A. Simmonds, A. Boyle, S. Clough, H. Cool and D. Poore (eds.). Oxford: 266–309.

Cool, H. (2011) 'Funerary contexts', in *Artefacts in Roman Britain: Their Purpose and Use*, L. Allason-Jones (ed.). Cambridge: 293–313.

Cool, H. and Mason, D. (2008) *Roman Piercebridge: Excavations by D. W. Harding and Peter Scott 1969–1981*. Durham.

Cooper, L. (1996) 'A Roman cemetery in Newarke St, Leicester', *Transactions of the Leicester Archaeological and Historical Society* 70: 1–90.

Corcoran, S. (2000) *The Empire of the Tetrarchs: Imperial Pronouncements and Government 284–324*. Oxford.

Corder, P. (1956) 'The reorganisation of the defences of Romano-British towns in the fourth century', *AJ* 112: 20–42.

Corder, P. (1989) 'The Roman pottery at Crambeck, Castle Howard', in *Crambeck Roman Pottery Industry*, P. Wilson (ed.). York: 3–40.

Corney, A. (1967) 'A prehistoric and Anglo-Saxon burial ground, Ports Down, Portsmouth', *Proceedings of the Hampshire Field Club* 24: 20–41.

Corney, M. (1997) 'The origins and development of the small town of Cunetio, Mildenhall, Wiltshire', *Britannia* 28: 337–350.

Corney, M. (2002) *The Roman Villa at Bradford on Avon: The Investigations of 2002*. Bradford on Avon.

Corney, M. (2003) *The Roman Villa at Bradford on Avon: The Investigations of 2003*. Bradford on Avon.

Cosh, S. (2001) 'Seasonal-dining rooms in Romano-British houses', *Britannia* 32: 219–242.

Costen, M. (2011) *Anglo-Saxon Somerset*. Oxford.

Cotterill, J. (1993) 'Saxon raiding and the role of the late Roman coastal forts of Britain', *Britannia* 24: 227–239.

Coulston, J. (2010) 'Military equipment of the "long" 4th century on Hadrian's Wall', in *Finds from the Frontier: Material Culture in the 4th–5th Centuries*, R. Collins and L. Allason-Jones (eds.). London: 50–63.

Cox, P. (1988) 'A seventh century inhumation cemetery at Shepherd's Farm, Ulwell, near Swanage, Dorset', *Proceedings of the Dorset Natural History and Archaeological Society* 110: 37–47.

Crabtree, P. (2010) 'Agricultural innovation and socio-economic change in early medieval Europe: evidence from Britain and France', *World Archaeology* 42(1): 122–136.

Crawford, S. (2004) 'Votive deposition, religion and the Anglo-Saxon furnished burial rite', *World Archaeology* 36(1): 87–102.

Crerar, B. (2013) 'Conceptualising deviancy: a regional approach to decapitated inhumation in late Roman Britain'. PhD thesis, Department of Classics, Cambridge University.

Croom, A. (2000) *Roman Clothing and Fashion*. Stroud.

Croom, A. (2007) *Roman Furniture*. Stroud.

Crummy, N. (1983) *The Roman Small Finds from Excavations in Colchester*. Colchester.

Crummy, N. (2006) 'The small finds', in *Life and Labour in Late Roman Silchester: Excavations in Insula IX since 1997*, M. Fulford, A. Clarke and H. Eckard (eds.). London: 120–132.

Crummy, N. and Eckardt, H. (2003) 'Regional identities and technologies of the self: nail cleaners in Roman Britain', *AJ* 160: 44–69.

Crummy, N., Crummy, P. and Crossan, C. (1993) *Excavations of Roman and Later Cemeteries, Churches and Monastic Sites in Colchester 1971–99*. Colchester.

Cullen, K., Holbrook, N., Watts, N. Caffell, A. and Holst, M. (2006) *A Post-Roman Cemetery at Hewlett Packard, Filton, South Gloucestershire: Excavations in 2005*. Unpublished Cotswold Archaeology Report.

Cummings, C. and Hedges, R. (2010) 'Carbon and nitrogen stable isotope analysis', in *The Late Roman Cemetery at Lankhills, Winchester: Excavations 2000–2005*, P. Booth, A. Simmonds, A. Boyle, S. Clough, H. Cool and D. Poore (eds.). Oxford: 411–421.

Cunha, E. and Silva, A. (1997) 'War lesions from the famous Portuguese medieval battle of Aljubarrota', *International Journal of Osteoarchaeology* 7: 595–599.

Cunliffe, B. (1968) *Richborough: Fifth Report on the Excavations of the Roman Fort at Richborough, Kent*. London.

Cunliffe, B. (1969) *Roman Bath*. London.

Cunliffe, B. (2005) *Iron Age Communities in Britain*. London.

Cunliffe, B. and Davenport, P. (1985) *Excavations at the Temple of Sulis Minerva Bath Volume 1: The Site*. Oxford.

Curle, A. (1923) *The Treasure of Traprain*. Edinburgh.

Cuttler, R., Davidson, A. and Hughes, G. (2012) *A Corridor Through Time: The Archaeology of the A55 Anglesey Road Scheme*. Oxford.

Dark, K. (1992) 'A sub-Roman re-defence of Hadrian's Wall?', *Britannia* 23: 111–120.

Dark, K. (1993) 'St Patrick's *villula* and the fifth-century occupation of Romano-British villas', in *St. Patrick AD 493–1993*, D. Dumville (ed.). Woodbridge: 19–24.

Dark, K. (1994) *Civitas to Kingdom: British Political Continuity 300–800*. Leicester.

Dark, K. (2000) *Britain and the End of the Roman Empire*. Stroud.

Dark, K. (2005) *Archaeology and the Origins of Insular Monasticism*. Cambridge.

Dark, K. and Dark, P. (1997) *The Landscape of Roman Britain*. Stroud.

Dark, P. (1996) 'Palaeoecological evidence for landscape continuity and change in Britain AD 400–800', in *External Contacts and the Economy of Late and Post-Roman Britain*, K. Dark (ed.). Boydell: 23–51.

Dark, P. (2000) *The Environment of Britain in the First Millennium AD*. London.

Darling, M. (1977) *A Group of Late Roman Pottery from Lincoln*, Lincoln Archaeological Trust Monograph Series 16. Lincoln.

Darling, M. (1987) 'The Caister-by-Norwich massacre reconsidered', *Britannia* 18: 263–272.

Darling, M. and Gurney, D. (1993) *Caister-On-Sea: Excavations by Charles Green 1951–1955*. Dereham.

Das, V., Kleinman, A., Ramphele, M. and Reynolds, P. (2000) *Violence and Subjectivity*. Berkeley.

Davey, J. (2005) *The Roman to Medieval Transition in the Environs of South Cadbury, Somerset*. Oxford.

Davies, B., Richardson, B. and Tomber, B. (1993) *A Dated Corpus of Early Roman Pottery from the City of London*, The Archaeology of London 5. London.

Davies, J. (1991) 'Roman military deployment in Wales and the Marches from Pius to Theodosius I', in *Roman Frontier Studies 1989: Proceedings of the 15th International Congress of Roman Frontier Studies*, V. Maxfield and M. Dobson (eds.). Exeter: 52–57.

Davies, S. (2007) *The Mabinogion*. Oxford.

Davies, S., Bellamy, P., Heaton, M. and Woodward, P. (2002) *Excavations at Alington Avenue, Fordington, Dorset, 1984–1987*. Dorchester.

Deetz, J. (1991) 'Introduction: archaeological evidence of sixteenth and seventeenth century colonial encounters', in *Historical Archaeology in Global Perspective*, L. Falk (ed.). Washington, DC: 1–9.

Delogu, P. (1998) 'Reading Pirenne again', in *The Sixth Century: Production, Distribution and Demand*, R. Hodges and W. Bowden (eds.). Cologne: 15–42.

Demandt, A. (1972) 'Die Feldzüge des Älteren Theodosius', *Hermes* 100: 81–113.

Devlin, Z. (2007) *Remembering the Dead in Anglo-Saxon England: Memory Theory in Archaeology and History*. Oxford.

Diamond, J. (2005) *Collapse: How Societies Choose to Fail or Survive.* London.

Dickinson, T. (1982) 'Fowler's Type G penannular brooch reconsidered', *Medieval Archaeology* 26: 41–68.

Dickinson, T. (1993) 'Early Saxon saucer brooches: a preliminary overview', *Anglo-Saxon Studies in Archaeology and History* 6: 11–44.

Dickinson, T. (2004) 'An Early Anglo-Saxon cemetery at Quarrington, near Sleaford, Lincolnshire: a report on the excavations 2000–2001', *Lincolnshire Archaeology and History* 39: 29–45.

Dickinson, T. (2010) 'The changing face of saucer-brooch distribution, 1912–1977–1997–2007', in *A Decade of Discovery: Proceedings of the Portable Antiquities Scheme's Conference 2007*, S. Worrell, G. Egan, K. Leahy, J. Naylor and M. Lewis (eds.). Oxford: 181–191.

Diesner, H.-J. (1972) 'Das Bucellarietum von Stilicho und Sarus bis auf Aetius (454–455)', *Klio* 54: 321–350.

Dixon, P. (1982) 'How Saxon is the Saxon house?', in *Structural Reconstruction: Approaches to the Interpretation of Excavated Remains of Buildings*, P. Drury (ed.). Oxford: 275–286.

Dixon, P. H. (1993) 'The Anglo-Saxon settlement at Mucking: an interpretation', *Anglo-Saxon Studies in Archaeology and History* 6: 125–147.

Dobney, K. (2001) 'A place at the table: the role of vertebrate zooarchaeology within a Roman research agenda for Britain', in *Britons and Romans: Advancing an Archaeological Agenda*, S. James and M. Millett (eds.). London: 36–45.

Dodds, B. (2004) 'Estimating arable output using Durham Priory tithe receipts, 1341–1450', *Economic History Review* (Second Series) 57: 245–285.

Donaldson, H. (1990) 'A reinterpretation of RIB 1912 from Hadrian's Wall', *Britannia* 21: 207–214.

Douglas, A., Gerrard, J. and Sudds, B. (2011) *A Roman Settlement and Bath House at Shadwell: Excavations at Tobacco Dock and Babe Ruth's Restaurant, The Highway, London.* London.

Down, A. and Welch, M. (1990) *Apple Down and The Mardens. Chichester, Volume VII.* Chichester.

Drake, H. (2006) 'Gauging violence in Late Antiquity', in *Violence in Late Antiquity: Perceptions and Practices*, H. Drake (ed.). Aldershot: 1–11.

Drinkall, G. and Foreman, M. (1998) *The Anglo-Saxon Cemetery at Castledyke South, Barton-on-Humber.* Sheffield.

Drinkwater, J. (1983) 'The "pagan underground", Constantius II's "secret service", and the survival and usurpation of Julian the Apostate', *Studies in Latin Literature and Roman History* 3: 348–387.

Drinkwater, J. (1992) 'The bacaudae of fifth-century Gaul', in *Fifth-Century Gaul: A Crisis of Identity?*, J. Drinkwater and H. Elton (eds.). Cambridge: 208–217.

Drinkwater, J. (1998) 'The usurpers Constantine III (407–411) and Jovinus 411–413', *Britannia* 29: 269–298.

Drinkwater, J. (1999) 'Ammianus, Valentinian and the Rhine Germans', in *The Late Roman World and its Historian: Interpreting Ammianus Marcellinus*, J. Drijvers and D. Hunt (eds.). London: 127–137.

Drinkwater, J. (2007) *The Alamanni and Rome 213–496: Caracalla to Clovis*. Oxford.

Dumville, D. (1977) 'Sub-Roman Britain: history and legend', *History* 62: 173–192.

Dumville D. (1989) 'The Tribal Hidage: an introduction to its texts and history', in *The Origins of Anglo-Saxon Kingdoms*, S. Bassett (ed.). Leicester: 225–230.

Dumville, D. (1993) *St. Patrick AD 493–1993*, Woodbridge.

Dunbabin, K. (2003) *The Roman Banquet: Images of Conviviality*. Cambridge.

Dunlevy, M. (1988) 'A classification of early Irish combs', *Proceedings of the Royal Irish Academy* 88C: 341–422.

Dunwoodie, L. (2004) *Pre-Boudican and Later Activity on the Site of the Forum: Excavations at 168 Fenchurch Street, City of London*. London.

Eagles, B. and Mortimer, C. (1993) 'Early Anglo-Saxon artefacts from Hod Hill, Dorset', *AJ* 73: 132–140.

Eckardt, H. (2002) *Illuminating Roman Britain*. Montagnac.

Eckardt, H. and Crummy, N. (2006) ' "Roman" or "native" bodies in Britain: the evidence of late Roman nail-cleaner strap-ends', *Oxford Journal of Archaeology* 25(1): 83–103.

Eckardt, H. and Crummy, N. (2008) *Styling the Body in Late Iron Age and Roman Britain*. Montagnac.

Edwards, N. (2007) *A Corpus of Early Medieval Inscribed Stones and Stone Sculpture in Wales: Volume II*. Cardiff.

Edwards, R. (2001) 'Mid- to late-Holocene sea level change in Poole Harbour, southern England', *Journal of Quaternary Science* 16(3): 221–235.

Eggers, H. (1951) *Der Römische Import im Freien Germanien*. Hamburg.

Egging-Dinwiddy, K. (2007) *A Late Roman Cemetery at Dorchester, Dorset*. Salisbury.

Ellis, P. (1984) *Catsgore 1979; Further Excavation of the Romano-British Village*. Bristol.

Ellis, S. (1988) 'The end of the Roman house', *AJA* 92(4): 565–576.

Ellis, S. (1991) 'Power, architecture and decor: how the late Roman aristocrat appeared to his guests', in *Roman Art in the Private Sphere*, E. Gazda (ed.). Ann Arbor: 117–134.

Ellis, S. (1995) 'Classical reception rooms in Romano-British houses', *Britannia* 26: 163–178.

Ellis, S. (1997) 'Late Antique dining: architecture, furnishings and behaviour', in *Domestic Space in the Roman World: Pompeii and Beyond*, R. Laurence and A. Wallace-Hadrill (eds.). Portsmouth, Rhode Island: 41–52.

Elton, H. (1996) *Warfare in Roman Europe, 350–425*. Oxford.

Engleheart, G. (1898) 'On some buildings of the Romano-British period discovered at Clanville, near Andover, and on a deposit of pewter vessels of the same period found at Appleshaw, Hants.', *Archaeologia* 56: 1–20.

Esmonde-Cleary, S. (1989) *The Ending of Roman Britain*. London.

Esmonde-Cleary, S. (1993) 'Approaches to the differences between late Romano-British and early Anglo-Saxon archaeology', *Anglo-Saxon Studies in Archaeology and History* 6: 57–63.

Esmonde-Cleary, S. (2001) 'The Roman to medieval transition', in *Britons and Romans: Advancing an Archaeological Agenda*, S. James and M. Millett (eds.). London: 90–97.

Esmonde-Cleary, S. (2003) 'Civil defences in the west under the High Empire', in *The Archaeology of Roman Towns: Studies in Honour of J. S. Wacher*, P. Wilson (ed.). Oxford: 72–85.

Esmonde-Cleary, S. (2007) 'Fortificación en la Britannia Romana: ¿defensa militar o monumento cívico?', in *Murallas de Ciudades en el Occidente del Impero Romano: Lucus Augusti como Paradigma, Diputación*, A. Rodríguez Colmenero and I. Rodá de Llanza (eds.). Lugo: 155–165.

Esmonde-Cleary, S. (in press) *The Roman West AD 200–500*. Cambridge.

Evans, J. (1981) 'Wheat production and its social consequences in the Roman world', *CQ* 31(2): 428–442.

Evans, J. (1990) 'From the end of Roman Britain to the "Celtic West"', *OJA* 9(1): 91–103.

Evans, J. (2001) 'Material approaches to the identification of different Romano-British site types', in *Britons and Romans: Advancing an Archaeological Agenda*, S. James and M. Millett (eds.). London: 26–35.

Evans, P. (2003) 'Excavations in Cardiff Castle 2003', *Archaeology in Wales* 44: 43–60.

Evison, V. (1965) *The Fifth-Century Invasions South of the Thames*. London.

Evison, V. (1968) 'Quoit Brooch Style buckles', *AJ* 48: 231–249.

Evison, V. (1982) 'Anglo-Saxon glass claw beakers', *Archaeologia* 107: 77–124.

Evison, V. (1987) *Dover: Buckland Anglo-Saxon Cemetery*. London.

Evison, V. (1988) *An Anglo-Saxon Cemetery at Alton, Hampshire*. Stroud.

Evison, V. and Evans, J. (1994) *An Anglo-Saxon Cemetery at Great Chesterford, Essex*. London.

Evison, V. and Hill, P. (1996) *Two Anglo-Saxon Cemeteries at Beckford, Hereford and Worcester*. London.

Fagerlie, J. (1967) *Late Roman and Byzantine Solidi found in Sweden and Denmark*. New York.

Farley, M., Henig, M. and Taylor, J. (1988) 'A hoard of late Roman bronze bowls and mounts from the Misbourne Valley, near Amersham, Buckinghamshire', *Britannia* 19: 357–366.

Farwell, D. and Molleson, T. (1993) *Poundbury Volume 2: The Cemeteries*. Dorchester.

Faulkner, N. (2000) *The Decline and Fall of Roman Britain*. Stroud.

Faulkner, N. (2004) 'The case for the Dark Ages', in *Debating Late Antiquity in Britain AD 300–700*, R. Collins and J. Gerrard (eds.). Oxford: 5–12.

Ferguson, N. (2011) *Civilization: The West and the Rest*. London.

Fern, C. (2005) 'The archaeological evidence for equestrianism in Early Anglo-Saxon England AD 450–700', in *Just Skin and Bones: New Perspectives on Human–Animal Interactions in the Historical Past*, A. Pluskowski (ed.). Oxford: 43–71.

Fernandez, J. (1999) 'Late Roman belts in Hispania', *JRMES* 10: 55–62.

Fernández-Ochoa, C. and Morillo, A. (2005) 'Walls in the urban landscape of late Roman Spain: defense and imperial strategy', in *Hispania in Late Antiquity: Current Perspectives*, K. Bowes and M. Kulikowski (eds.). Leiden, 299–340.

Ferrill, A. (1986) *The Fall of the Roman Empire: The Military Explanation*. London.

Finley, M. (1985) *The Ancient Economy*. London.

Fiorato, V., Boylston, A. and Knusel, C. (2007) *Blood Red Roses: The Archaeology of a Mass Grave from the Battle of Towton 1461*. Oxford.

Fitzpatrick, A. and Crockett, A. (1998) 'A Romano-British settlement and inhumation cemetery at Eyewell Farm, Chilmark', *Wiltshire Archaeology and Natural History Magazine* 91: 11–33.

Fleming, R. (2012) 'Recycling in Britain after the fall of Rome's metal economy', *Past and Present* 217(1): 3–45.

Fowler, E. (1960) 'The origins of the penannular brooch reconsidered', *Proceedings of the Prehistoric Society* 26: 14–77.

Fowler, P. (2001) 'Wansdyke in the Woods: an unfinished Roman military earthwork for a non-event', in *Roman Wiltshire and After: Papers in Honour of Ken Annable*, P. Ellis (ed.). Devizes: 179–198.

Fowler, P. (2002) *Farming in the First Millennium AD*. Cambridge.

Fox, A. (1961) 'Holbeton: Mothecombe', *Reports and Transactions of the Devonshire Association for the Advancement of Science, Literature and Art*, 93: 79–80.

Fraser, J. (2009) *The New Edinburgh History of Scotland Volume I: From Caledonia to Pictland*. Edinburgh.

Freeman, E. (1867) *The History of the Norman Conquest of England: Its Causes and Results*. Oxford.

Freeman, P. (1993) 'Romanization and material culture', *Journal of Roman Archaeology* 6: 438–445.

Freeman, P. (1995) 'The archaeology of Roman material in Ireland', *Proceedings of the Harvard Celtic Colloquium* 15: 69–74.

Freeman, P. (2007) *The Best Training Ground for Archaeologists: Francis Haverfield and the Invention of Romano-British Archaeology*. Oxford.

Frere, S. (1967) *Britannia: A History of Roman Britain*. London.

Frere, S. (1972) *Verulamium Excavations*. London.

Frere, S. (1984) 'British urban defences in earthwork', *Britannia* 15: 63–74.

Fulford, M. (1973) 'A fourth-century colour-coated fabric and its types in south-east England', *Sussex Archaeological Collections* 111: 41–44.

Fulford, M. (1975) *New Forest Roman Pottery*. Oxford.

Fulford, M. (1979) 'Pottery production and trade at the end of Roman Britain: the case against continuity', in *The End of Roman Britain*, P. Casey (ed.). Oxford: 120–132.

Fulford, M. (1984) *Silchester Defences 1974–1980*. London.

Fulford, M. (1989) 'Byzantium and Britain: a Mediterranean perspective on post-Roman imports into Western Britain and Ireland', *Medieval Archaeology* 33: 1–6.

Fulford, M. (2002) 'Wroxeter, legionary fortress baths and the "Great Rebuilding" of 450–550', *JRA* 15(2): 639–645.

Fulford, M. (2006) 'Corvées and civitates', in *Romanitas: Essays on Roman Archaeology in Honour of Shepherd Frere on the Occasion of his Ninetieth Birthday*, R. Wilson (ed.). Oxford: 65–71.

Fulford, M. and Hodder, I. (1975) 'A regression analysis of some late Romano-British pottery: a case study', *Oxoniensia* 39: 26–33.

Fulford, M. and Rippon, S. (2011) *Pevensey Castle, Sussex: Excavations in the Roman Fort and Medieval Keep, 1993–1995*. Salisbury.

Fulford, M. and Timby, J. (2000) *Late Iron Age and Roman Silchester: Excavations on the Site of the Forum Basilica, 1977, 1980–86*. London.

Fulford, M. and Tyers, I. (1995) 'The date of Pevensey and the defence of an *Imperium Britanniarum*', *Antiquity* 69: 1009–1014.

Fulford, M., Clarke, A. and Eckardt, H. (2006) *Life and Labour in Late Roman Silchester: Excavations in Insula IX since 1997*. London.

Fulford, M., Handley, M. and Clarke, A. (2000) 'An early date for Ogham: the Silchester Ogham stone rehabilitated', *Medieval Archaeology* 44: 1–23.

Fulford, M., Burnett, A., Henig, M. and Johns, C. (1989) 'A hoard of late Roman rings and silver coins from Silchester, Hampshire', *Britannia* 20: 219–228.

Funari, P. (1996) *Dressel 20 Inscriptions from Britain and the Consumption of Spanish Olive Oil*. Oxford.

Fyfe, F. and Rippon, S. (2004) 'A landscape in transition? Palaeoenvironmental evidence for the "end" of the Romano-British period in southwest England', in *Debating Late Antiquity in Britain AD 300–700*, R. Collins and J. Gerrard (eds.). Oxford: 33–42.

Gaddis, M. (2005) *There is No Crime for Those Who Have Christ: Religious Violence in the Christian Roman Empire*. Berkeley.

Gaffney, J. and Gater, J. (2002) *Geophysical Survey: Dinnington, Somerset*. Unpublished GSB Prospection Report No. 2002/47.

Garbsch, J. (1967) 'Die Burgi von Meckatz und Untersaal und die valentinianische Grenzbefestigung zwischen Basel und Passau', *Bayerische Vorgeschichtsblätter* 32: 51–82.

Gardiner, M. (1988) 'Early Anglo-Saxon burials from Stafford Road, Brighton, East Sussex', *Sussex Archaeological Collections* 126: 53–76.

Gardner, A. (2007) *An Archaeology of Identity: Soldiers and Society in Late Roman Britain*. California.

Gardner, R. (2005) 'A Roman cemetery in Clarence Street, Leicester', *Transactions of the Leicestershire Archaeological and Historical Society* 79: 27–90.

Garnsey, P. (1970) *Social Status and Legal Privilege in the Roman Empire*. Oxford.

Garrow, D., Lucy, S. and Gibson, D. (2006) *Excavations at Kilverston, Norfolk: An Episodic Landscape History*. Dereham.

Geake, H. (1999) 'When were hanging bowls deposited in Anglo-Saxon graves?', *Medieval Archaeology* 43: 1–18.

Geary, P. (2002) *The Myth of Nations: The Medieval Origins of Europe*. Princeton.

Gelling, M. (1992) *The West Midlands in the Early Middle Ages*. Leicester.

Gentili, G. (1999) *La Villa romana di Piazza Armerina Palazzo Erculio*. Osimo.

George, K. (2009) *Gildas's 'De Excidio Britonum' and the Early British Church*. Woodbridge.

George, M. (1999) 'Chedworth Roman villa', *National Trust Annual Archaeological Review 1998–1999*, 42.

Germany, M. (2003) *Excavations at Great Holts Farm, Boreham, Essex 1992–1994*. Dereham.

Gerrard, J. (2004) 'How late is late? Pottery and the fifth century in south west Britain', in *Debating Late Antiquity in Britain AD 300–700*, R. Collins and J. Gerrard (eds.). Oxford: 65–76.

Gerrard, J. (2005) 'Bradley, Hill Somerset, and the end of Roman Britain: a study in continuity?', *Proceedings of the Somerset Archaeological and Natural History Society* 148: 1–10.

Gerrard, J. (2007a) 'The temple of Sulis Minerva at Bath and the end of Roman Britain', *AJ* 87: 148–164.

Gerrard, J. (2007b) 'Rethinking the "small pig horizon" at York Minster', *OJA* 26(3): 303–307.

Gerrard, J. (2008) 'Feeding the army from Dorset: pottery, salt and the Roman state', in *Feeding the Roman Army: The Archaeology of Production and Supply in NW Europe*, S. Stallibrass and R. Thomas (eds.). Oxford: 116–127.

Gerrard, J. (2009) 'The Drapers' Gardens hoard: a preliminary account', *Britannia* 40: 163–183.

Gerrard, J. (2010) 'Finding the fifth century: a late fourth- and early fifth-century pottery fabric from south-east Dorset', *Britannia* 41: 293–412.

Gerrard, J. (2011a) 'New radiocarbon dates from the cemetery at Bradley Hill, Somerton', *Proceedings of the Somerset Archaeological and Natural History Society* 154: 189–192.

Gerrard, J. (2011b) 'Wells and belief systems at the end of the Roman Britain: a case study from London', in *The Archaeology of Late Antique Paganism*, L. Lavan (ed.). Leiden: 551–572.

Gerrard, J. (2012) 'New light on the end of Roman London', *AJ* 168: 181–194.

Gibbon, E. (1993) *The Decline and Fall of the Roman Empire*. London.

Gillam, J. (1970) *Types of Roman Coarse Pottery Vessels in Northern Britain*. Newcastle-upon-Tyne.

Gillam, J. (1976) 'Coarse fumed ware in northern Britain and beyond', *Glasgow Archaeological Journal* 4: 57–80.

Gilmour, B. (2007) 'Swords, seaxes and Saxons: pattern welding and edged weapon technology from late Roman Britain to early Anglo-Saxon England', in *Collectanea Antiqua: Essays in Memory of Sonia Chadwick Hawkes*, M. Henig and T. Smith (eds.). Oxford: 91–110.

Goetz, H.-W. (2003) '*Gens*, kings and kingdoms: the Franks', in *Regna and Gentes: The Relationship between Late Antique and Early Medieval Peoples and Kingdoms in the Transformation of the Roman World*, H.-W. Goetz, J. Jarnut and W. Pohl (eds.). Leiden: 307–344.

Goffart, W. (1980) *Barbarians and Romans: Techniques of Accommodation*. Princeton NJ.

Goffart, W. (2002) 'Does the distant past impinge on the Invasion Age Germans?', in *On Barbarian Identity: Critical Approaches to Ethnicity in the Early Middle Ages*, A. Gillett (ed.). Brepols: 21–38.

Goffart, W. (2006) *Barbarian Tides: The Migration Age and the Later Roman Empire*. Philadelphia.

Going, C. (1992) 'Economic long waves in the Roman period? A reconnaissance of the Romano-British ceramic evidence', *OJA* 11(1): 93–117.

Going, C. and Hunn, J. (1999) *Excavations at Boxfield Farm, Chells, Stevenage, Hertfordshire*. Hertford.

Goodburn, R. and Bartholomew, P. (eds.) (1976) *Aspects of the Notitia Dignitatum: Papers Presented to a Conference in Oxford December 13 to 15, 1974*. Oxford.

Graham, A. (1966) 'The division of Britain', *JRS* 56: 92–107.

Graham, A. and Mills, J. (1995) 'A Romano-British building at Crimbleford Knap, Seavington St Mary', *Somerset Archaeology and Natural History* 139: 119–134.

Graham, A., Hinton, D. and Peacock, D. (2002) 'The excavation of an Iron Age and Romano-British settlement in Quarry Field, south of Compact Farm, Worth Matravers, Dorset', in *Purbeck Papers*, D. Hinton (ed.). Oxford: 1–83.

Green, D. (1998) *Language and History in the Early Germanic World*. Cambridge.

Greenberg, J. (2003) 'Plagued by doubt: reconsidering the impact of a mortality crisis in the 2nd century AD', *JRA* 16: 413–425.

Greene, K. (2005) 'The economy of Roman Britain: representation and historiography', in *TRAC 2004: Proceedings of the Fourteenth Annual Theoretical Roman Archaeology Conference*, J. Bruhn, B. Croxford and D. Grigoropoulos (eds.). Oxford: 1–15.

Gregory, T. (1977) 'A hoard of late Roman metalwork from Weeting, Norfolk', *Norfolk Archaeology* 36: 265–272.

Grey, C. (2007) 'Contextualizing the colonate: the *Origo* of the Late Roman Empire', *JRS* 97: 155–175.

Griffin, N. (2003) *Archaeological Excavations at Roundstone Lane, Angmering, West Sussex*. Unpublished Archaeology South East Report No. 1,333.

Griffith, F. (1986) 'Salvage observations at the Dark Age site at Bantham Ham, Thurlston, in 1982', *Proceedings of the Devon Archaeological Society* 44: 39–58.

Griffith, F. and Reed, S. (1998) 'Rescue recording at Bantham Ham, south Devon in 1977', *Proceedings of the Devon Archaeological Society* 56: 109–132.

Grocock, C. (2010) 'Barriers to knowledge: coppicing and landscape usage in the Anglo-Saxon economy', in *The Landscape Archaeology of Anglo-Saxon England*, N. Higham and M. Ryan (eds.). Woodbridge: 23–38.

Grünewald, T. (2004) *Bandits in the Roman Empire: Myth and Reality* (J. Drinkwater trans.). London.

Grunwald, L. (1998) 'Grabfunde des Neuwieder Beckens von der Völkerwanderungszeit bis zum frühen Mittelalter', *Internationale Archäologie* 44, 1–219.

GSB (2009) *Cunetio, Wiltshire SAM 224765.* Unpublished Geophysical Surveys of Bradford Report No. 2,009/41.

Guest, P. (1993) 'Hoards from the end of Roman Britain', *Coin Hoards from Roman Britain* 10: 411–423.

Guest, P. (2002) 'Manning the defences', in *Artefacts and Archaeology: Aspects of the Celtic and Roman World*, M. Aldhouse-Green and P. Webster (eds.). Cardiff: 76–89.

Guest, P. (2005) *The Late Roman Gold and Silver Coins from the Hoxne Hoard.* London.

Guest, P. (2008) 'Roman gold and the Hun Kings: The use and hoarding of solidi in the late fourth and fifth centuries', in *Roman Coins Outside the Empire: Ways and Phases, Contexts and Functions*, A. Bursche, R. Ciolek and R. Wolters (eds.). Warsaw: 295–307.

Guest, P. (2013) '*Siliquae* from the Traprain Law treasure: silver and society in later fourth- and fifth-century Britain', in *Late Roman Silver and the End of Empire: The Traprain Treasure in Context*, F. Hunter and K. Painter (eds.). Edinburgh: 93–106.

Guggisberg, M. and Kaufmann-Heinimann, A. (2003) *Der spätrömische Silberschatz von Kaiseraugst, die neuen Funde: Silber im Spannungsfeld von Geschichte, Politik und Gesellschaft der Spätantike.* Augst.

Guido, M. (1978) *The Glass Beads of the Prehistoric and Roman Periods in Britain and Ireland.* London.

Guiraud, H. (1989) 'Bagues et anneaux a l'époque romaine en Gaule', *Gallia* 46: 173–211.

Hales, S. (2003) *The Roman House and Social Identity.* Cambridge.

Halsall, G. (1992) 'The origins of the Reihengräberzivilisation: forty years on', in *Fifth-Century Gaul: A Crisis of Identity?*, J. Drinkwater and H. Elton (eds.). Cambridge: 196–207.

Halsall, G. (1997) 'Archaeology and historiography', in *Companion to Historiography*, M. Bentley (ed.). London: 788–810.

Halsall, G. (2003) *Warfare and Society in the Barbarian West 450–900.* London.

Halsall, G. (2007) *Barbarian Migrations and the Roman West 376–568.* Cambridge.

Hamerow, H. (1991) 'Settlement mobility and the "Middle Saxon Shift": rural settlements and settlement patterns in Anglo-Saxon England', *Anglo-Saxon England* 20: 1–17.

Hamerow, H. (1993) *Excavations at Mucking. Volume 2: The Anglo-Saxon Settlement.* London.

Hamerow, H. (2002) *Early Medieval Settlements: The Archaeology of Rural Communities in Northwest Europe 400–900.* Oxford.

Hamerow, H. (2004) 'The archaeology of early Anglo-Saxon settlements: past, present and future' in *Landscapes of Change: Rural Evolutions in Late Antiquity and the Early Middle Ages,* N. Christie (ed.). Aldershot: 301–316.

Hamerow, H. (2011) 'Anglo-Saxon timber buildings and their social context', in *The Oxford Handbook of Anglo-Saxon Archaeology,* H. Hamerow, D. Hinton and S. Crawford (eds.). Oxford: 128–155.

Hammon, A. (2011) 'Understanding the Romano-British–early medieval transition: a zooarchaeological perspective from Wroxeter', *Britannia* 42: 275–305.

Handley, M. (2001) 'The origins of Christian commemoration in Late Antique Britain', *Early Medieval Europe* 10(2): 177–199.

Hanson, W. (1987) *Agricola and the Conquest of the North.* London.

Harbison, P. (2004) 'The Helgö crozier-head', in *Excavations at Helgö XVI: Exotic and Sacral Finds from Helgö,* B. Gyllensvärd, P. Harbison, M. Axboe, J. Lamm, T. Zachrisson and S. Reisborg (eds.). Stockholm: 29–34.

Härke, H. (1990) ' "Warrior Graves?" The background of the Anglo-Saxon weapon burial rite', *P&P* 126: 22–43.

Härke, H. (1992) *Angelsächsische waffengräber des 5. bis 7. Jahrhunderts.* Cologne.

Härke, H. (2011) 'Anglo-Saxon immigration and ethnogenesis', *Medieval Archaeology* 55: 1–28.

Härke, H. and Dickinson, T. (1992) 'Early Anglo-Saxon shields', *Archaeologia* 110: 1–94.

Harlow, M. (2004) 'Gallia Placidia: conduit of culture?', in *Women's Influence on Classical Civilization,* F. McHardy and E. Marshall (eds.). London: 138–150.

Harman, M., Lambrick, G., Miles, D. and Rowley, T. (1978) 'Roman burials around Dorchester upon Thames', *Oxoniensia* 43: 1–16.

Harp, P. and Hines, J. (2003) 'An Anglo-Saxon cemetery at Headley Drive, Tadworth, near Banstead', *Surrey Archaeological Collections* 90: 117–145.

Harries, J. (1999) *Law and Empire in Late Antiquity.* Cambridge.

Harries, J. (2007) *Law and Crime in the Roman World.* Cambridge.

Harris, J. (2003) *Byzantium, Britain and the West: The Archaeology of Cultural Identity AD 400–650.* Stroud.

Hassall, M. (1978) 'Britain and the Rhine provinces: epigraphic evidence for Roman trade', in *Roman Shipping and Trade: Britain and the Rhine Provinces,* J. Taylor and H. Cleere (eds.). London: 41–48.

Hassall, M. (2004) 'The defence of Britain in the 4th century', in *L'armée romaine de Dioclétien à Valentinien Ier: Actes du Congrès Lyon (12–14 Septembre 2002)*, Y. Bohec and C. Wolff (eds.). Lyons: 179–189.

Hasselhoff, G. (1974) 'Salin's Style I', *Medieval Archaeology* 18: 1–15.

Hattatt, R. (2000) *A Visual Catalogue of Richard Hattatt's Ancient Brooches*. Oxford.

Hauken, A. (2005) *The Westland Cauldrons in Norway*. Stavanger.

Haverfield, F. (1904) 'The last days of Silchester', *EHR* 19(76): 625–631.

Haverfield, F. (1906) 'Romano-British Somerset', in *Victoria County History of Somerset* I: 207–371.

Haverfield, F. (1912) *The Romanization of Roman Britain*. Oxford.

Haverfield, F. and MacDonald, G. (1924) *The Roman Occupation of Britain*. Oxford.

Hawkes, S. (1974) 'Some recent finds of late Roman buckles', *Britannia* 5: 386–393.

Hawkes, S. and Dunning, G. (1961) 'Soldiers and settlers in Britain: fourth to fifth century', *Mediaeval Archaeology* 5: 1–70.

Haynes, I. and Johnson, P. (1996) (eds.) *Architecture in Roman Britain*. London.

Hayward, L. (1952) 'The Roman villa at Lufton, near Yeovil', *Proceedings of the Somerset Archaeological and Natural History Society* 97: 91–112.

Hayward, L. (1972) 'The Roman villa at Lufton, near Yeovil', *Proceedings of the Somerset Archaeological and Natural History Society* 116: 59–77.

Hearne, C. and Birbeck, V. (1999) *A35 Tolpuddle to Puddletown Bypass DBFO, Dorset, 1996–8*. Salisbury.

Heather, P. (1996) *The Goths*. Oxford.

Heather, P. (2005) *The Fall of the Roman Empire: A New History*. London.

Heather, P. (2009) *Empires and Barbarians: Migration, Development and the Birth of Europe*. London.

Hedeager, L. (1992) *Iron Age Societies*. London.

Heighway, C. (1981) 'Romano-British cemeteries in the Gloucester district', *Transactions of the Bristol and Gloucester Archaeological Society* 98: 57–72.

Hemp, W. (1918) 'A Roman gold brooch from Carnarvon', *Proceedings of the Society of Antiquaries of London* 30: 184–187.

Henig, M. (1978) *A Corpus of Roman Engraved Gemstones from British Sites*. Oxford.

Henig, M. (1995) *Religion in Roman Britain*. London.

Herschend, F. (1979) 'Två studier i öländska guldfynd. I. Det myntade guldet', *Tor* 18: 33–194.

Higham, N. (1992) *Rome, Britain and the Anglo-Saxons*. London.

Higham, N. (1994) 'Literary evidence for towns, villas and hillforts in fifth-century Britain', *Britannia* 25: 229–232.

Higham, N. (2007) 'Britons in Anglo-Saxon England: an introduction', in *Britons in Anglo-Saxon England*, N. Higham (ed.). Woodbridge: 1–15.

Higham, N. and Jones, G. (1983) 'The excavation of two Romano-British farm sites in North Cumbria', *Britannia* 14: 45–72.

Hill, D. (1981) *An Atlas of Anglo-Saxon England*. Toronto.

Hill, D. (1998) 'Eleventh century labours of the month in prose and pictures', *Landscape History* 20: 30–39.

Hill, J. and Rowsome, P. (2011) *Roman London and the Walbrook Stream Crossing: Excavations at 1 Poultry and Vicinity, City of London*. London.

Hillner, J. (2007) 'Review: D. Slootjes *The Governor and his Subjects in Late Antiquity*', *JRS* 97: 379–381.

Hills, C. (1977) *The Anglo-Saxon Cemetery at Spong Hill, North Elmham. Part I*. Gressenhall.

Hills, C. (1979) 'The archaeology of Anglo-Saxon England in the pagan period: A review', *ASE* 8: 297–330.

Hills, C. (1999) 'Did the people of Spong Hill come from Schleswig-Holstein?', *Studien zur Sachsenforschung* 11: 145–155.

Hills, C. (2003) *The Origins of the English*. London.

Hills, C. (2009) 'Anglo-Saxon DNA?', in *Mortuary Practices and Social Identities in the Middle Ages*, D. Sayer and H. Williams (eds.). Exeter: 123–140.

Hills, C. (2011) 'Overview: Anglo-Saxon identity', in *The Oxford Handbook of Anglo-Saxon Archaeology*, H. Hamerow, D. Hinton and S. Crawford (eds.). Oxford: 3–12.

Hills, C. and Lucy, S. (in press) *Spong Hill Part IX: Chronology and Synthesis*. Cambridge.

Hills, C. and O'Connell, T. (2009) 'New light on the Anglo-Saxon succession: two cemeteries and their dates', *Antiquity* 83: 1096–1108.

Hills, C., Penn, K. and Rickett, R. (1984) *The Anglo-Saxon Cemetery at Spong Hill, North Elmham, Part III: Catalogue of Inhumations*. Dereham.

Hills, C., Penn, K. and Rickett, R. (1987) *The Anglo-Saxon Cemetery at Spong Hill, North Elmham. Part IV: Catalogue of Cremations*. Norwich.

Hinchcliffe, J. and Sparey Green, C. (1985) *Excavations at Brancaster 1974 and 1977*. Dereham.

Hines, J. (1984) *The Scandinavian Character of Anglian England in the Pre-Viking Period*. Oxford.

Hines, J. (1990) 'Philology, archaeology and the adventus Saxonum vel Anglorum', in *Britain AD 400–600: Language and History*, A. Bammesberger and A. Wollman (eds.). Heidelberg: 17–36.

Hines, J. (1997) *A New Corpus of Anglo-Saxon Great Square Headed Brooches*. London.

Hingley, R. (2000) *Roman Officers and English Gentlemen*. London.

Hinman, M. (2003) *A Late Iron Age Farmstead and Romano-British Site at Haddon, Peterborough*. Oxford.

Hirst, S. and Clark, D. (2009) *Excavations at Mucking. Volume 3: The Anglo-Saxon Cemeteries Part II, Analysis and Discussion*. London.

Hirt, A. (2010) *Imperial Mines and Quarries in the Roman World*. Oxford.

Hobbs, R. (2006) *Late Roman Precious Metal Deposits c. AD 200–700: Changes over Time and Space*. Oxford.

Hobley, B. (1983) 'Roman urban defences: a review of research in Britain', in *Roman Urban Defences in the West*, J. Maloney and B. Hobley (eds.). London: 77–84.

Hobsbawm, E. and Ranger, T. (1983) *The Invention of Tradition*. Cambridge.

Hodder, I. (1974) 'Some marketing models for Romano-British coarse pottery', *Britannia* 5: 340–359.

Hodder, I. and Hutso, S. (2003) *Reading the Past: Current Approaches to Interpretation in Archaeology*. Cambridge.

Hodges, R. (1982) *Dark Age Economics: The Origins of Towns and Trade AD 600–1000*. London.

Hodges, R. (1989) *The Anglo-Saxon Achievement*. London.

Hodgkin, R. (1935) *A History of the Anglo-Saxons: Volume I*. Oxford.

Hodgson, N. (1991) 'The *Notitia Dignitatum* and the late Roman garrison of Britain', in *Roman Frontier Studies 1989: Proceedings of the 15th International Congress of Roman Frontier Studies*, V. Maxfield and M. Dobson (eds.). Exeter: 52–57.

Hodgson, N. (1996) 'A late Roman courtyard house at South Shields and its parallels', in *Architecture in Roman Britain*, P. Johnson and I. Haynes (eds.). London: 135–151.

Hodgson, N. (2008) 'After the Wall-Periods: What is our historical framework for Hadrian's Wall in the twenty-first century?', in *Understanding Hadrian's Wall*, P. Bidwell (ed.). South Shields: 11–24.

Hoeper, M. (1999) 'Kochkessel – Opfergrabe – Urne – Grabbeigabe – Altmetall: Zur Funktien und Typologie der Westlandkessel auf dem Kontinent', in *Archäologie als Sozialgeschichte: Studien zu Siedlung Wirtschaft und Gesellschaft im frühgeschichtlichen Mitteleuropa*, S. Brather, C. Bücker and M. Hoeper (eds.). Rahden: 235–249.

Holbrook, N. (1998) *Cirencester: The Roman Town Defences, Public Buildings and Shops*. Cirencester.

Holbrook, N. (2000) 'The Anglo-Saxon cemetery at Lower Farm, Bishop's Cleeve: excavations directed by Kenneth Brown 1969', *Transactions of the Bristol and Gloucester Archaeological Society* 118: 61–92.

Holbrook, N. (2004) 'Turkdean Roman Villa, Gloucestershire: archaeological investigations 1997–1998', *Britannia* 35: 39–76.

Holbrook, N. and Bidwell, P. (1991) *Roman Finds from Exeter*. Exeter.

Holbrook, N. and Alan, T. (2005) 'An early-medieval monastic cemetery at Llandough Glamorgan: excavations in 1994', *Medieval Archaeology* 49: 1–92.

Honoré, T. (2004) 'Roman Law AD 200–400: from Cosmopolis to Reichsstaat', in *Approaching Late Antiquity: Transformation from Early to Late Empire*, S. Swain and M. Edwards (eds.). Oxford: 109–132.

Hooke, D. (1985) *The Anglo-Saxon Landscape*. Manchester.

Hope Taylor, B. (1977) *Yeavering: An Anglo-British Centre of Early Northumbria*. London.

Hopkins, K. (1980) 'Taxes and trade in the Roman Empire', *JRS* 70: 101–125.

Hopkins, K. (1995/6) 'Rome, taxes, rents and trade', *Kodai* 6/7: 41–75.

Hopkins, M. (1961) 'Social mobility in the later Roman Empire: the evidence of Ausonius'. *CQ* 11(2): 239–249.

Horsnaes, H. (2002) 'New gold hoards from Bornholm with new types of Valentinian III *solidi*', *RN* 158: 131–138.

Howe, E. and Lakin, D. (2004) *Roman and Medieval Cripplegate, City of London.* London.

Howe, M., Perrin, J. and Mackreth, D. (1980) *Roman Pottery from the Nene Valley: A Guide.* Peterborough.

Howe, N. (1989) *Migration and Mythmaking in Anglo-Saxon England.* London.

Howell, R. (2000) 'The demolition of the Roman tetrapylon in Caerleon: an erasure of memory?', *OJA* 19(4): 387–395.

Hume, I. (1964) 'Handmaiden to history', *North Carolina Historical Review* 41(2): 215–225.

Humfrers, C. (2006) 'Poverty and Roman law', in *Poverty in the Roman World*, M. Atkins and R. Osborn (eds.). Cambridge: 183–203.

Hunn, J., Lawson, J. and Farley, M. (1994) 'The Anglo-Saxon cemetery at Dinton, Buckinghamshire', *Anglo-Saxon Studies in Archaeology and History* 7: 85–148.

Hunter, F. (2007) *Beyond the Edge of Empire: Caledonians, Picts and Romans.* Rosemarkie.

Hunter, F. (2010) 'Beyond the frontier: interpreting late Roman Iron Age indigenous and imported material culture', in *Finds from the Frontier*, R. Collins and L. Allason-Jones (eds.). London: 96–109.

Ingelmark, B. (1939) 'The skeletons', in *Armour from the Battle of Visby, 1361 Volume 2*, B. Thordman, O. Norlund, and B. Ingelmark (eds.). Stockholm: 149–209.

Inker, P. (2000) 'Technology as active material culture: the Quoit Brooch Style', *Medieval Archaeology* 44: 25–42.

Inker, P. (2006) *The Anglo-Saxon Relief Style.* Oxford.

Insoll, T. (ed.) (2007) *The Archaeology of Identities.* London.

Isings, C. (1957) *Roman Glass from Dated Finds.* Groningen.

Jackson, R. (2011) 'Medicine and hygiene', in *Artefacts in Roman Britain: Their Purpose and Use*, L. Allason-Jones (ed.). Cambridge: 243–268.

James, S. (1984) 'Britain and the late Roman army', in *Military and Civilian in Roman Britain*, T. Blagg and A. King (eds.). Oxford: 161–186.

James, S. (1999) *The Atlantic Celts: Ancient People or Modern Invention?* London.

James, S. (2001) 'Soldiers and civilians: identity and interaction in Roman Britain', in *Britons and Romans: Advancing an Archaeological Agenda*, S. James and M. Millett (eds.). London: 77–89.

James, S. (2011a) *Rome and the Sword.* London.

James, S. (2011b) 'Stratagems, combat and "chemical warfare" in the siege mines of Dura-Europos', *AJA* 115(1): 69–101.

James, S., Marshall, A. and Millett, M. (1984) 'An early medieval building tradition', *AJ* 141: 182–215.

Janes, D. (1996) 'The golden clasp of the late Roman state', *Early Medieval Europe* 5(2): 127–153.

Jarman, A. (1988) *Aneirin: Y Gododdin*. Llandysul.

Jarrett, K. (1999) 'The late/post-Roman settlement at Crickley Hill, Gloucestershire'. Unpublished MA dissertation, University of Nottingham.

Jarrett, K. (2011) *An Interim Report on Roman and Early Medieval Activity at Crickley Hill, Gloucestershire.* Unpublished manuscript kindly provided by the author.

Jobey, G. (1959) 'Excavations at the native settlement at Huckhoe, Northumberland, 1955–7', *Archaeologia Aeliana 4th Series* 37: 217–278.

Johns, C. (1996a) *The Jewellery of Roman Britain: Celtic and Classical Traditions.* London.

Johns, C. (1996b) 'The classification and interpretation of Romano-British treasures', *Britannia* 27: 1–16.

Johns, C. (2007) 'The last chance', in *Roman Finds: Context and Theory*, R. Hingley and S. Willis (eds.). Oxford: 29–34.

Johns, C. (2010) *The Hoxne Late Roman Treasure: Gold Jewellery and Silver Plate.* London.

Johns, C. and Potter, T. (1983) *The Thetford Treasure: Roman Jewellery and Silver.* London.

Johnson, P. (1993) 'Town mosaics and urban officinae', in *Roman Towns: The Wheeler Inheritance*, S. Greep (ed.). London: 147–165.

Johnson, S. (1976) *The Roman Forts of the Saxon Shore.* London.

Johnson, S. (1983a) *Late Roman Fortifications.* London.

Johnson, S. (1983b) 'Late Roman urban defences in Europe', in *Roman Urban Defences in the West*, J. Maloney and B. Hobley (eds.). London: 68–76.

Jones, A. (1958) 'The Roman colonate', *P&P* 13: 1–13.

Jones, A. (1964) *The Later Roman Empire 284–602: A Social, Economic and Administrative Survey.* Baltimore.

Jones, A. (2003) *Settlement, Burial and Industry in Roman Godmanchester.* Oxford.

Jones, F. (1961) 'Early territorial organisation in England and Wales', *Geografiskar Annaler* 43: 174–181.

Jones, G. and Shotter, D. (1988) *Roman Lancaster: Rescue Archaeology in an Historic City 1970–75.* Manchester.

Jones, M. (1974) 'The Mucking excavations 1974', *Journal of the Thurrock Local History Society* 18: 32–41.

Jones, M. (1994) 'St Paul in the Bail, Lincoln. Britain in Europe?', in '*Churches Built in Ancient Times': Recent Studies in Early Christian Archaeology*, K. Painter (ed.). London: 325–348.

Jones, M. (1996) *The End of Roman Britain.* Ithaca and London.

Jones, M. (2001) 'The legacy of Roman law in post-Roman Britain', in *Law, Society and Authority in Late Antiquity*, R. Mathisen (ed.). Oxford: 52–67.

Jones, M. and Gilmour, T. (1980) 'Lincoln, Principia and Forum: A Preliminary Report', *Britannia* 11: 61–72.

Jones, R. (1975) 'The Romano-British farmstead and its cemetery at Lynch Farm, near Peterborough', *Northamptonshire Archaeology* 10: 94–137.

Jones, S. (1997) *The Archaeology of Identity*. London.

Kampen, N. (2009) *Family Fictions in Roman Art*. Cambridge.

Kandler, M. and Vetters, H. (1986) *Der römische Limes in Österreich. Ein Führer*. Vienna.

Kanz, F. and Grossschmidt, K. (2006) 'Head injuries of Roman gladiators', *Forensic Science International* 160: 207–216.

Karkov, C. (2010) 'Calendar illustration in Anglo-Saxon England: realities and fictions of the Anglo-Saxon landscape', in *The Landscape Archaeology of Anglo-Saxon England*, N. Higham and N. Ryan (eds.). Woodbridge: 157–168.

Keen, L. (1988) 'Medieval salt working in Dorset', *Proceedings of the Dorset Archaeological and Natural History Society* 109: 25–28.

Kehoe, D. (2007) *Law and the Rural Economy in the Roman Empire*. Michigan.

Keller, E. (1971) *Die spätrömischen Grabfunde in Südbayern*. Munich.

Kelly, C. (2004) *Ruling the Later Roman Empire*. Harvard.

Kelly, G. (2008) *Ammianus Marcellinus: The Allusive Historian*. Cambridge.

Kennett, D. (1971) 'Late Roman bronze vessel hoards in Britain', *JRGZ* 16: 123–148.

Kent, J. and Painter, K. (1977) *Wealth of the Roman World: Gold and Silver AD 300–700*. London.

Killock, D. (2007) *An Assessment of an Archaeological Excavation at 28–30 Trinity St, London Borough of Southwark*. Unpublished PCA report, London.

King, A. (1981) 'The decline of samian manufacture in the North West Provinces: problems of chronology and interpretation', in *The Roman West in the Third Century*, A. King and M. Henig (eds.). Oxford: 187–218.

King, A. (1988) 'Villas and animal bones', in *The Economies of Romano-British Villas*, K. Branigan and D. Miles (eds.). Sheffield: 51–59.

King, A. (1990) *Roman Gaul and Germany*. Los Angeles.

King, A. (1991) 'The Roman defences of Bitterne', in *Roman Frontier Studies 1989: Proceedings of the 15th International Congress of Roman Frontier Studies*, V. Maxfield and M. Dobson (eds.). Exeter: 108–110.

King, A. (2005) 'Animal remains from Roman temples in Britain', *Britannia* 36: 329–370.

King, R., Barker, A. and Timby, J. (1996) 'Excavations at West Alne, Kemble: an Iron Age, Roman and Saxon burial site and a medieval building', *Transactions of the Bristol and Gloucester Archaeological Society* 114: 15–54.

Kinsley, A. (1994) *Broughton Lodge: Excavations on the Romano-British Settlement and Anglo-Saxon Cemetery at Broughton Lodge, Willoughby-on-the-Wolds, Nottinghamshire 1964–8*. Nottingham.

Kirby, D. and Williams, J. (1976) 'Review of *The Age of Arthur*'. *Studia Celtica* 10–11: 454–486.

Kirk, J. and Leeds, E. (1954) 'Three early Saxon graves from Dorchester, Oxon.', *Oxoniensia* 17–18: 63–76.

Klingle, D. (2012). *The Use of Skeletal and Mortuary Evidence to Understand the Transition from Roman to Anglo-Saxon England in Cambridgeshire and Bedfordshire.* British Archaeological Report British Series 569. Oxford.

Knight, J. (1992) 'The early Christian Latin inscriptions of Britain and Gaul: chronology and context', in *The Early Church in Wales and the West*, N. Edwards and A. Lane (eds.). Oxford: 45–50.

Knight, J. (2007) *The End of Antiquity.* Stroud.

Knight, J. (2010) 'An inscription from Bavai and the fifth-century Christian epigraphy of Britain', *Britannia* 41: 283–292.

Kolb, M. and Snead, J. (1997) 'It's a small world after all: comparative analyses of community organization in archaeology', *American Antiquity* 62(4): 609–628.

Köpke, N. and Baten, J. (2005) 'The biological standard of living in Europe during the last two millennia', *European Review of Economic History* 9(1): 61–95.

Kossinna, G. (1928) *Ursprung und Verbreitung der Germanen in der vor- und frühgeschichtlicher Zeit.* Berlin.

Kulikowski, M. (2002) 'Nation versus army a necessary contrast?', in *On Barbarian Identity: Critical Approaches to Ethnicity in the Early Middle Ages*, A. Gillett (ed.). Brepols: 69–84.

Kulikowski, M. (2000a) 'The "Notitia Dignitatum" as a historical source', *Historia* 49(3): 358–377.

Kulikowski, M. (2000b) 'Barbarians in Gaul, usurpers in Britain', *Britannia* 31: 325–345.

Kulikowski, M. (2004) *Late Roman Spain and its Cities.* Baltimore.

Künzl, E. (1993) *Die Alamannenbeute aus dem Rhein bei Neupotz Plünderungsgut aus dem römischen Gallien.* Mainz.

Lander, J. (1984) *Roman Stone Fortifications: Variation and Change from the First Century to the Fourth.* Oxford.

Lapidge, M. (1984) '"Gildas" education and the Latin culture of sub-Roman Britain', in *Gildas: New Approaches*, M. Lapidge and D. Dumville (eds.). Woodbridge: 27–50.

Lapidge, M. and Dumville, D. (eds.) (1984) *Gildas: New Approaches.* Woodbridge.

Larsen, B., Vinther, B., Briffa, K., Melvin, T., Clausen, H., Jones, P., Siggaard-Andersen, M., Hammer, C., Eronen, M., Grudd, H., Gunnarson, B., Hantemirov, R., Naurzbaev, M. and Nicolussi, K. (2008) 'New ice core evidence for a volcanic cause of the AD 536 dust veil event', *Geophysical Research Letters* 35, L04708.

Lavan, L. (2001) 'The *praetoria* of civil governors in Late Antiquity', in *Recent Research in Late Antique Urbanism*, L. Lavan (ed.). Portsmouth, Rhode Island: 39–56.

Lawrence, S. and Smith, A. (2009) *Between Villa and Town: Excavations of a Roman Roadside Settlement and Shrine at Higham Ferrers, Northamptonshire.* Oxford.

Laycock, S. (2008) *Britannia the Failed State: Tribal Conflicts and the End of Roman Britain.* Stroud.

Leach, P. (1982) *Ilchester Excavations Volume I.* Bristol.

Leach, P. (1994) *Ilchester Volume 2: Archaeology, Excavations and Fieldwork to 1984.* Sheffield.

Leach, P. and Evans, J. (2001) *Fosse Lane, Shepton Mallet, 1990: The Excavation of a Romano-British Roadside Settlement and Cemetery.* London.

Leader-Newby, R. (2004) *Silver and Society in Late Antiquity.* London.

Leahy, K. (2007a) 'Interrupting the Pots': The Excavation of Cleatham Anglo-Saxon Cemetery. London.

Leahy, K. (2007b) 'Soldiers and settlers in Britain, fourth to fifth century – revisited', in *Collectanea Antiqua: Essays in Memory of Sonia Chadwick Hawkes*, M. Henig and T. Smith (eds.). Oxford: 133–144.

Leary, R. (1994) *Excavations at the Romano-British Settlement at Pasture Lodge Farm, Long Bennington, Lincolnshire, 1975–77 by H. M. Wheeler.* Lincoln.

Lee, R. (2009) *The Production, Use and Disposal of Romano-British Pewter Tableware.* Oxford.

Leech, R. (1981) 'The excavation of a Romano-British farmstead and cemetery on Bradley Hill, Somerset', *Britannia* 12: 177–252.

Leech, R. (1982) *Excavations at Catsgore 1970–73: A Romano-British Village.* Bristol.

Leeds, E. (1912) 'The distribution of the Anglo-Saxon saucer brooch in relation to the Battle of Bedford (AD 571)', *Archaeologia* 63: 159–202.

Leeds, E. (1913) *The Archaeology of the Anglo-Saxon Settlements.* Oxford.

Leeds, E. (1936) *Early Anglo-Saxon Art and Archaeology.* Oxford.

Leeds, E. (1945) 'The distribution of Angles and Saxons archaeologically considered', *Archaeologia* 91: 1–106.

Leivers, M., Chisham, C., Knight, S. and Stevens, C. (2007) 'Excavations at Ham Hill Quarry, Hamdon Hill, Montacute, 2002', *Proceedings of the Somerset Archaeological and Natural History Society* 150: 39–62.

Lennard, R. (1933) 'The character of the Anglo-Saxon Conquests: a disputed point', *History* 18(71): 204–215.

Lenski, N. (2002) *Failure of Empire: Valens and the Roman State in the Fourth Century AD.* Berkeley.

Lewis, J. (2008) 'Identifying sword marks on bone: criteria for distinguishing between cut marks made by different classes of weapons', *Journal of Archaeological Science* 35: 2001–2008.

Lewit, T. (2003) ' "Vanishing villas": What happened to elite rural habitation in the west in the 5th–6th century?', *JRA* 16: 260–274.

Liebeschuetz, W. (2006) 'Violence in barbarian successor kingdoms', in *Violence in Late Antiquity: Perceptions and Practices*, H. Drake (ed.). Aldershot: 37–46.

Liebeschuetz, W. (2007) 'The debate about the ethnogenesis of Germanic tribes', in *From Rome to Constantinople: Studies in Honour of Averil Cameron*, H. Amirav and B. Romeny (eds.). Leuven: 341–356.

Lieu, S. and Montserrat, D. (1996) *From Constantine to Julian: Pagan and Byzantine Views. A Source History.* London.

Light, T. and Ellis, P. (2009) *Bucknowle: A Romano-British Villa and its Antecedents*. Dorchester.

Ling, R. (1991) *Roman Painting*. Cambridge.

Longley, D., Johnstone, N. and Evans, J. (1998) 'Excavations at two farms of the Romano-British period at Bryn Eryr and Bush Farm, Gwynedd', *Britannia* 29: 185–246.

Loseby, S. (2000) 'Power and towns in late Roman Britain and early Anglo-Saxon England', in *Sedes regiae (ann. 400–800)*, G. Ripoll and J. Gurt (eds.). Barcelona: 319–370.

Lovell, J. (2006) 'Excavation of a Romano-British farmstead at RNAS Yeovilton', *Proceedings of the Somerset Archaeological and Natural History Society* 149: 7–70.

Lucy, S. (2000) *The Anglo-Saxon Way of Death*. Stroud.

Lucy, S. (2002) 'From pots to people: two hundred years of Anglo-Saxon archaeology', in *'Lastworda Betst': Essays in Memory of Christine E. Fell with Her Unpublished Writings*, C. Hough and K. Lowe (eds.). Donington: 144–169.

Lucy, S., Tipper, J. and Dickens, A. (2009) *The Anglo-Saxon Settlement and Cemetery at Bloodmoor Hill, Carlton Colville, Suffolk*. Norwich.

Lucy, S., Evans, C., Jefferies, R., Appleby, G. and Going, C. (in press) *The Romano-British Settlement and Cemeteries at Mucking: Excavations by Margaret and Tom Jones 1965–1978*. Cambridge.

Lyne, M. (1994) 'Late Roman handmade wares in south-east Britain'. Unpublished PhD thesis, University of Reading.

Lyne, M. (1999) 'The end of the Saxon Shore fort system in Britain: new evidence from Richborough, Pevensey and Portchester', in *Proceedings of the XVIIth International Congress of Roman Frontier Studies*, N. Gudea (ed.). Zalau: 283–292.

Lyne, M. (2011) *Roman Wight*. http://thehumanjourney.net/pdf_store/sthames/iow%20Roman.pdf (accessed 11/4/2013).

Lyne, M. and Jefferies, R. (1979) *The Alice Holt Farnham Roman Pottery Industry*. London.

Lyon, J. (2007) *Within these Walls: Roman and Medieval Defences North of Newgate at the Merrill Lynch Financial Centre, City of London*. London.

Lysons, S. (1797) *An Account of the Roman Antiquities Discovered at Woodchester in the County of Gloucestershire*. London.

MacDougall, H. (1982) *Racial Myth in English History: Trojans, Teutons and Anglo-Saxons*. London.

MacGeorge, P. (2002) *Late Roman Warlords*. Oxford.

MacGregor, A. (1976) 'Finds from a Roman sewer system and an adjacent building in Church Street', *The Archaeology of York* 17(1): 1–30.

Mackensen, M. (1994) 'Das Kastell Caelius Mons (Kellmünz an der Iller) – eine tetrarchische Festungsbaumaßnahme in der Provinz Raetien', *Arheolski Vestnik* 45: 145–163.

Mackensen, M. (1995) *Das spätrömische Grenzkastell Caelius Mons – Kellmünz.* Stuttgart.

Mackensen, M. (1999) 'Late Roman fortifications and building programmes in the province of Raetia: the evidence of recent excavations and some new reflections', in *Roman Germany: Studies in Cultural Interaction*, J. Creighton and R. Wilson (eds.). Portsmouth, Rhode Island: 199–244.

Mackinder, A. (2000) *A Romano-British Cemetery on Watling St: Excavations at 165 Great Dover Street, Southwark, London.* London.

Mackreth, D. (2011) *Brooches in Late Iron Age and Roman Britain.* Oxford.

MacMullen, R. (1963) *Soldier and Civilian in the Late Empire.* Cambridge MA.

MacMullen, R. (1982) 'The epigraphic habit in the Roman Empire', *AJPh* 103(3): 233–246.

Macphail, R., Galinie, H. and Verhaeghe, F. (2002) 'A future for dark earth?', *Antiquity* 77: 349–358.

Maddicott, J. (1997) 'Plague in seventh century England', *P&P* 156: 7–24.

Maddicott, J. (2005) 'London and Droitwich *c.*650–750: trade, industry and the rise of Mercia', *ASE* 34: 7–58.

Magilton, J. (2003) 'The defences of Roman Chichester', in *The Archaeology of Roman Towns: Studies in Honour of J. S. Wacher*, P. Wilson (ed.). Oxford: 156–167.

Mahoney, C. (1994) *Roman Alcester: Southern Extramural Areas 1964–1966.* London: 144–145.

Maier, I. (2012) *The Compilation of Notitia Dignitatum.* http://members.ozemail. com.au/~igmaier/notitia.htm (accessed 24/5/2012).

Malin, T. (2005) 'A Romano-British temple complex and Anglo-Saxon burials at Gallows Hill, Swaffham Prior', *Proceedings of the Cambridge Antiquarian Society* 95: 91–114.

Maloney, J. (1979) 'Excavations at Dukes Place: the Roman defences', *London Archaeologist* 3(11): 292–297.

Maloney, J. (1983) 'Recent work on London's urban defences', in *Roman Urban Defences in the West*, J. Maloney and B. Hobley (eds.). London: 96–117.

Malosse, P. (1999) 'Qu'est donc allé faire Constant 1er en Bretagne pendant l'hiver 343?', *Historia* 48(4): 465–476.

Manning, W. (1983) 'The cauldron chains of Iron Age and Roman Britain', in *Rome and her Northern Provinces*, B. Hartley and J. Wacher (eds.). Stroud: 132–154.

Manning, W. (1985) *Catalogue of the Romano-British Iron Tools, Fittings and Weapons in the British Museum.* London.

Manning, W. (2003) 'The defences of Caerwent', in *The Archaeology of Roman Towns: Studies in Honour of J. S. Wacher*, P. Wilson (ed.). Oxford: 168–183.

Marsden, P. (1980) *Roman London.* London.

Marsden, P. (1987) *The Roman Forum Site in London: Discoveries Before 1985.* London.

Marsden, P. (1994) *Ships of the Port of London. First to Eleventh Centuries.* London.

Marsden, P. and West, B. (1995) 'Population change in Roman London', *Britannia* 23: 133–140.

Marshall, A. and Marshall, G. (1991) 'A survey and analysis of the buildings of early and middle Anglo-Saxon England', *Medieval Archaeology* 35: 29–43.

Martin, M. (1997) 'Wealth and treasure in the west 400–700', in *The Transformation of the Roman World*, L. Webster and M. Brown (eds.). London: 48–66.

Marzinzik, S. (2003) *Early Anglo-Saxon Belt Buckles (Late 5th to Early 8th Centuries AD): Their Classification and Context.* Oxford.

Mathisen, R. (1993) *Roman Aristocrats in Barbarian Gaul: Strategies for Survival in an Age of Transition.* Austin.

Mathisen, R. (2001) 'Imperial honorifics and senatorial status in Late Roman legal documents', in *Law, Society and Authority in Late Antiquity*, R. Mathisen (ed.). Oxford: 179–207.

Matthews, C. and Chadwick Hawkes, S. (1985) 'Early Anglo-Saxon settlements and burial on Puddlehill, near Dunstable, Bedfordshire', *Anglo-Saxon Studies in Archaeology and History* 4: 59–116.

Matthews, J. (1975) *Western Aristocracies and the Imperial Court AD 364–425.* Oxford.

Matthews, J. (1989) *The Roman Empire of Ammianus.* London.

Mattingly, D. (2007) *An Imperial Possession: Britain in the Roman Empire.* London.

Mattingly, D. (2011) *Imperialism, Power and Identity: Experiencing the Roman Empire.* Princeton.

Mattingly, H., Pearce, J. and Kendrick, T. (1937) 'The Coleraine Hoard', *Antiquity* 11(41): 39–45.

Maurin, L. (1992) 'Remparts et cités dans les trois provinces du Sud-Ouest de la Gaule au Bas-Empire (dernier quart du IIIe siècle–début du Ve siècle)', in *Villes et agglomerations urbaines antiques du Sud-Ouest de la Gaule. Histoire et Archéologie.* Paris: 365–389.

Mayerson, P. (1984) 'Roman wheat production: an addendum', *CQ* 34(1): 243–245.

McCarthy, M. and Brooks, C. (1988) *Medieval Pottery in Britain AD 900–1600.* Leicester.

McCormick, M. (1986) *Eternal Victory: Triumphal Rulership in Late Antiquity, Byzantium and the Early Medieval West.* Cambridge.

McCormick, M. (2002) *Origins of the European Economy: Communications and Commerce AD 300–900.* Cambridge.

McGavin, N. (1980) 'A Roman cemetery and trackway at Stanton Harcourt', *Oxoniensia* 45: 112–123.

McGill, S. (2010) *From the Tetrarchs to the Theodosians: Later Roman History and Culture.* Cambridge.

McKinley, J. (1994) *The Anglo-Saxon Cemetery at Spong Hill, North Elmham Part VIII: The Cremations.* Norwich.

McKinley, J. (2003) 'The early Saxon cemetery at Park Lane, Croydon', *Surrey Archaeological Collections* 90: 1–116.

McPeake, J. (1978) 'The end of the affair', in *New Evidence for Roman Chester*, T. Strickland and P. Davey (eds.). Liverpool: 41–45.

McWhirr, A. (1986) *Houses in Roman Cirencester*. Cirencester.

McWhirr, A., Viner, L. and Wells, C. (1982) *Romano-British Cemeteries at Cirencester*. Cirencester.

Meates, G. (1987) *The Lullingstone Roman Villa Volume II: The Wall Paintings and Finds*. Maidstone.

Menghin, W. (1983) *Das Schwert im Frühen Mittelalter*. Stuttgart.

Merrifield, R. (1983) *London: City of the Romans*. London.

Miles, D. (1986) *Archaeology at Barton Court Farm, Abingdon, Oxfordshire*. London.

Miles, D., Smith, A. and Perpetua-Jones, G. (2007) *Iron Age and Roman Settlement in the Upper Thames Valley: Excavations at Claydon Pike and Other Sites within the Cotswold Water Park*. Oxford.

Miller, M. (1975) 'Stilicho's Pictish war', *Britannia* 6: 141–145.

Miller, L., Schofield, J. and Rhodes, M. (1986) *The Roman Quay at St Magnus House, London: Excavations at New Fresh Wharf, Lower Thames Street, London, 1974–78*. London.

Millett, M. (1987) 'The question of continuity: Rivenhall revisited', *AJ* 144: 434–438.

Millett, M. (1990) *The Romanization of Britain: An Essay in Archaeological Interpretation*. Cambridge.

Millett, M. (1994) 'Treasure: interpreting Roman hoards', in *Proceedings of the 4th Theoretical Roman Archaeology Conference*, S. Cottam, D. Dungworth, S. Scott and J. Taylor (eds.). Oxford: 99–106.

Millett, M. (2007) 'Roman Kent', in *The Archaeology of Kent to AD 800*, J. Williams (ed.). Woodbridge: 135–186.

Millett, M. and James, S. (1983) 'Excavations at Cowdery's Down, Basingstoke, Hants. 1978–1981', *AJ* 140: 151–279.

Millett, M. and Wilmott, T. (2003) 'Rethinking Richborough', in *The Archaeology of Roman Towns: Studies in Honour of J. S. Wacher*, P. Wilson (ed.). Oxford: 243–261.

Millett, M., Allason-Jones, L. and Barclay, C. (2006) *Shiptonthorpe, East Yorkshire: Archaeological Studies of a Roadside Romano-British Settlement*. Leeds.

Milne, G. (1996) 'A palace disproved: reassessing the provincial governor's presence in 1st-century London', in *Interpreting Roman London*, D. Bird, M. Hassall and H. Sheldon (eds.). Oxford: 49–55.

Mirkovíc, M. (1997) 'The later Roman colonate and freedom', *Transactions of the American Philosophical Society New Series* 87(2): 1–144.

Mitchell, P., Nagar, R. and Ellenblum, R. (2006) 'Weapon injuries in the 12th century crusader garrison of Vadum Iacob castle, Galilee', *International Journal of Osteoarchaeology* 16: 145–155.

Monaghan, J. (1993) 'Roman pottery from the fortress: 9 Blake St', *Archaeology of York* 16(7): 667–824.

Moore, J. (1862) 'Roman villa at West Coker, Somersetshire', *JBAA* 18: 392–395.

Moorhead, S. (1997) 'A reappraisal of the Roman coins found in J. W. Brooke's excavation of a late Roman well at Cunetio, Mildenhall 1912', *Wiltshire Archaeological and Natural History Magazine* 90: 42–54.

Moorhead, S. (2006) 'Roman bronze coinage in sub-Roman and early Anglo-Saxon England', in *Coinage and History in the North Sea World 500–1250: Essays in Honour of Marion Archibald*, B. Cook and G. Williams (eds.). Leiden: 99–109.

Moorhead, S., Booth, A. and Bland, R. (2010) *The Frome Hoard*. London.

Moreland, J. (2000) 'Ethnicity, power and the English', in *Social Identity in Early Medieval Britain*, W. Frazer and O. Tyrell (eds.). Leicester: 23–52.

Moreland, J. (2001) *Archaeology and Text*. London.

Moreland, J. (2006) 'Archaeology and texts: subservience or enlightenment?', *Annual Review of Archaeology* 35: 135–151.

Morris, J. (1973) *The Age of Arthur*. London.

Morris, R. (1989) *Churches in the Landscape*. London.

Morriss, R. (2001) *The Archaeology of Buildings*. Stroud.

Mratschek, S. (2007) 'Et ne quid coturni terribilis fabulae relinquerent intemptatum . . . (Amm. Marc. 28.6.29): Die Göttin der Derechtigkeit und der comes Romanus', in *Ammianus after Julian: The Reign of Valentinian and Valens in Books 26–31 of the Res Gestae*, J. den Boeft, J. Drijvers, D. Den Hengst and H. Teitler (eds.). Leiden: 245–270.

Muhlberger, S. (1992) 'Looking back from the mid century: the Gallic Chronicler of 452 and the crisis of Honorius' reign', in *Fifth-Century Gaul: A Crisis of Identity?*, J. Drinkwater and H. Elton (eds.). Cambridge: 28–37.

Murphy, C. (2007) *Are We Rome? The Fall of an Empire and the Fate of America*. New York.

Murphy, K. (1992) 'Plas Gogerddan, Dyfed: A multiperiod burial and ritual site', *AJ* 149: 1–39.

Myres, J. (1969) *Anglo-Saxon Pottery and the Settlement of England*. Oxford.

Myres, J. (1986) *The English Settlements*. London.

Myres, J. and Green, B. (1973) *The Anglo-Saxon Cemeteries of Caistor-by-Norwich and Marshall, Norfolk*. London.

Myres, J. and Southern, W. (1973) *The Anglo-Saxon Cremation Cemetery at Sancton*. Hull.

Näf, B. (1995) *Senatorisches Standesbewusstsein in Spätrömischer Zeit*. Freiburg.

Nash-Williams, V. (1950) *The Early Christian Monuments of Wales*. Cardiff.

National Trust (2010) *Chedworth Roman Villa* [data-set]. York, Archaeology Data Service (doi:10.5284/1000107).

Neal, D. (1996) *Excavations on the Roman Villa at Beadlam, Yorkshire*. York.

Neal, D. and Cosh, S. (2006) *The Roman Mosaics of Britain Volume II: South-West Britain*. London.

Neal, D. and Cosh, S. (2009) *The Roman Mosaics of Britain Volume III: SE Britain (Parts 1 and 2)*. London.

Nicassie, M. (1998) *Twilight of Empire: The Roman Army from the Reign of Diocletian to the Battle of Adrianople.* Amsterdam.

Nuber, H. and Reddé, M. (2002) 'Das Römische Oedenburg/Le site romain d'Oedenburg (Biesheim/Kunheim, Haut Rhin France)', *Germania* 80: 169–242.

Okasha, E. (1993) *Corpus of Early Christian Inscribed Stones of South-West Britain.* Leicester.

Oosthuizen, S. (1998) 'Prehistoric fields into medieval furlongs? Evidence from Caxton, south Cambridgeshire', *Proceedings of the Cambridge Antiquarian Society* 86: 145–152.

Oosthuizen, S. (2011a) 'Anglo-Saxon fields', in *Handbook of Anglo-Saxon Archaeology*, D. Hinton, S. Hamerow and S. Chapman (eds.). Oxford: 377–401.

Oosthuizen, S. (2011b) 'Archaeology, common rights and the origins of Anglo-Saxon identity', *Early Medieval Europe* 19(2): 153–181.

Orton, C., Tyers, P. and Vince, A. (1993) *Pottery in Archaeology.* Cambridge.

Ottaway, P. (1993) *Roman York.* London.

Ottaway, P. (1997) 'Recent excavations of the late Roman signal station at Filey, North Yorkshire', in *Proceedings of the Sixteenth International Congress of Roman Frontier Studies*, W. Groeman-van Waateringe, B. van Beek, W. Willems and S. Wynia (eds.). Oxford: 135–141.

Ottaway, P. (2000) 'Excavations on the site of the Roman signal station at Carr Naze, Filey, 1993–94', *AJ* 157: 79–199.

Ottaway, P. (2011) *The Products of the Blacksmith in Mid-Late Anglo-Saxon England Part 3.* www.pjoarchaeology.co.uk/docs/17/anglosaxon-ironwork-part-3.pdf (accessed 27/2/2011).

Pace, B. (1955) *I Mosaici di Piazza Armerina.* Sicily.

Parfitt, K. and Brugmann, B. (1997) *The Anglo-Saxon Cemetery on Mill Hill, Deal, Kent.* London.

Parnell, G. (1985) 'The Roman and medieval defences and the later development of the inmost ward, Tower of London: excavations 1955–77', *Transactions of the London and Middlesex Archaeological Society* 36: 1–79.

Patrick, P., French, C. and Osborne, C. (2007) 'Rescue excavation of an Early Saxon cemetery at Gunthorpe, Peterborough', *Anglo-Saxon Studies in Archaeology and History* 14: 204–237.

Pattison J. (2008) 'Is it necessary to assume an apartheid-like social structure in early Anglo-Saxon England?', *Proceedings of the Royal Society* B275: 2423–2429.

Paul, C. (2010) 'As a fish swims in the sea: relationships between factors contributing to support for terrorists or insurgent groups', *Studies in Conflict and Terrorism* 33(6): 488–510.

PCA (2009) *Secrets of the Gardens: Archaeologists Unearth the Lives of Roman Londoners at Drapers' Gardens.* London.

Peacock, D. (1982) *Pottery in the Roman World.* London.

Peacock, D. and Williams, D. (1986) *Amphorae and the Roman Economy.* London.

Peal, C. (1967) 'Romano-British pewter plates and dishes', *Proceedings of the Cambridge Antiquarian Society* 60: 19–37.

Pearce, S. (1999) 'The dispersed dead: preliminary observations on burial and settlement space in rural Roman Britain', in *TRAC98: Proceedings of the Eighth Annual Theoretical Roman Archaeology Conference*, P. Baker, C. Forcey, S. Jundi and R. Witcher (eds.). Oxford: 151–162.

Pearce, S. (2004) *South-Western Britain in the Early Middle Ages*. Leicester.

Pearson, A. (2002) *The Roman Shore Forts – Coastal Defence of Southern Britain*. Stroud.

Pearson, A. (2005) 'Barbarian piracy and the Saxon Shore: a reappraisal', *OJA* 24(1): 73–88.

Pearson, A. (2006) 'Piracy in late Roman Britain: a perspective from the Viking Age', *Britannia* 37: 337–353.

Pearson, K. (1997) 'Nutrition and the early medieval diet', *Speculum* 72(1): 1–32.

Penn, K. and Brugmann, B. (2007) *Aspects of Anglo-Saxon Inhumation Burial: Morningthorpe, Spong Hill, Burgh Apton and Westgarth Gardens*. Norwich.

Percival, J. (1967) 'Seigneurial aspects of late Roman estate management', *EHR* 84: 449–473.

Percival, J. (1992) 'The fifth-century villa: new life or death postponed?', in *Fifth-Century Gaul: A Crisis of Identity?*, J. Drinkwater and H. Elton (eds.). Cambridge: 156–164.

Périn, P. and Kazanski, M. (2011) 'Identity and ethnicity during the era of migrations and barbarian kingdoms in the light of archaeology in Gaul', in *Romans, Barbarians and the Transformation of the Roman World*, R. Mathisen and D. Shanzer (eds.). Farnham: 299–330.

Perrin, J. (1999) 'Roman pottery from excavations at and near to the Roman small town of *Durobrivae*, Water Newton, Cambridgeshire, 1956–58', *Journal of Roman Pottery Studies* 8: 1–139.

Perring, D. (2002) *The Roman House in Britain*. London.

Petts, D. (1997) 'Elite settlements in the Roman and Sub-Roman period', in *Proceedings of the Sixth Theoretical Roman Archaeology Conference: Sheffield 1996*, K. Meadows, C. Lemke and J. Heron (eds.). Oxford: 101–112.

Petts, D. (2002) 'The reuse of prehistoric standing stones in western Britain? A critical consideration of an aspect of early medieval monument reuse', *OJA* 21(2): 195–209.

Petts, D. (2003) *Christianity in Roman Britain*. Stroud.

Petts, D. (2004) 'Burial in western Britain AD 400–800: Late Antique or Early Medieval?', in *Debating Late Antiquity in Britain AD 300–700*, R. Collins and J. Gerrard (eds.). Oxford: 77–88.

Pharr, C. (trans.) (1952) *The Theodosian Code and Novels and the Sirmondian Constitutions: A Translation with Commentary, Glossary and Bibliography*. Princeton NJ.

Phillips, D. and Heywood, B. (1995) *Excavations at York Minster Volume 1: From Roman Fortress to Norman Cathedral.* London.

Philp, B. (2005) *The Excavation of the Roman Fort at Reculver, Kent.* Dover.

Philp, B., Parfitt, K., Wilson, J,. and Williams, W. (1999) *The Roman Villa Site at Keston: Second Report.* Dover.

Philpott, R. (1991) *Burial Practices in Roman Britain: A Survey of Grave Treatment and Furnishing* AD *43–410.* Oxford.

Pirenne, H. (1939) *Mohammed and Charlemagne.* London.

Pitts, L. and St. Joseph, J. (1985) *Inchtuthil: The Roman Legionary Fortress Excavations 1952–1965.* London.

Pitts, M. (2007) 'The emperor's new clothes? The utility of identity in Roman archaeology', *AJA* 111: 693–713.

Pitts, M. (2008) 'Globalizing the local in Roman Britain: an anthropological approach to social change', *Journal of Anthropological Archaeology* 27: 493–506.

Pocock, J. (1999) *Barbarism and Religion: The Enlightenments of Edward Gibbon, Volume I.* Cambridge.

Pohl, W. (1998a) 'Telling the difference: signs of ethnic identity', in *Strategies of Distinction: The Construction of Ethnic Communities 300–800,* W. Pohl and H. Reimitz (eds.). Leiden: 17–69.

Pohl, W. (1998b) 'Conceptions of ethnicity in early medieval studies', in *Debating the Middle Ages,* L. Little and B. Rosenwein (eds.). Oxford: 15–24.

Pohl, W. (2006) 'Perceptions of barbarian violence', in *Violence in Late Antiquity: Perceptions and Practices,* H. Drake (ed.). Aldershot: 15–26.

Polanyi, K. (1957) 'The economy as instituted process', in *Trade and Markets in the Early Empires,* K. Polanyi, C. Arensberg and H. Pearson (eds.). New York: 243–270.

Pollard, R. (1988) *The Roman Pottery of Kent.* Maidstone.

Portmann, W. (1999) 'Die politische Krise zwischen den Kaisern Constantius II und Constans', *Historia* 48(3): 301–329.

Poulter, A. (2004) 'Cataclysm on the Lower Danube: the destruction of a complex Roman landscape', in *Landscapes of Change: Rural Evolutions in Late Antiquity and the Early Middle Ages,* N. Christie (ed.). Aldershot: 233–254.

Poulter, A. (2009) 'A late Roman fort – but one built for foederati?', in *Limes XX,* A. Morillo, N. Hanel and E. Martín (eds.). Madrid: 223–236.

Poulton, R. (1989) 'Rescue excavations on an early Saxon cemetery site and a later (probably late Saxon) execution site at the former Goblin Works, Ashstead, near Leatherhead', *Surrey Archaeological Collections* 79: 67–98.

Powlesland, D. (1998) 'The West Heslerton assessment', *Internet Archaeology* 5. http://intarch.ac.uk/journal/issue5/westhes_index.html (accessed 5/12/2010).

Proctor, J. (2009) *Pegswood, Morpeth: A Later Iron Age and Romano British Farmstead Settlement.* London.

Putnam, B. (2007) *Roman Dorset.* Stroud.

Quinnell, H. (2004) *Trethurgy. Excavations at Trethurgy Round: Community and Status in Roman and Post-Roman Cornwall.* Plymouth.

Rackham, D. (1995) 'Animal bone from post-Roman contexts', in *Excavations at York Minster Volume 1: From Roman Fortress to Norman Cathedral*, D. Phillips and B. Heywood (eds.). London: 533–573.

Radford, C. (1928) 'The Roman site at Westland', *Proceedings of the Somerset Archaeological and Natural History Society* 74: 122–143.

Radford, C. (1970) 'The later pre-Conquest boroughs and their defences', *Medieval Archaeology* 14: 83–103.

Radford, C. (1971) 'Christian origins in Britain', *Medieval Archaeology* 15: 1–12.

Raepsaet-Charlier, M. and Vanderhoeven, A. (2004) 'Tongres au Bas-Empire romain', in *Capitales éphémères: Des capitals de cités perdent leur statut dans l'antiquité tardive*, A. Ferdière (ed.). Tours: 51–73.

Rahtz, P. (1951) 'The Roman temple at Pagans Hill, Chew Stoke, Somerset', *Proceedings of the Somerset Archaeological and Natural History Society* 96: 112–142.

Rahtz, P. (1969) 'Cannington Hillfort 1963', *Proceedings of the Somerset Archaeological and Natural History Society* 113: 56–68.

Rahtz, P. (1971) 'Excavations on Glastonbury Tor, Somerset', *AJ* 127: 1–81.

Rahtz, P. (1976) 'Buildings and rural settlement', in *The Archaeology of Anglo-Saxon England*, D. Wilson (ed.). London: 49–98.

Rahtz, P. (1977) 'Late Roman cemeteries and beyond', in *Burial in the Roman World*, R. Reece (ed.). London: 53–64.

Rahtz, P., Hayfield, C. and Bateman, J. (1986) *Two Roman Villas at Wharram Le Street.* York.

Rahtz, P., Hirst, S. and Wright, S. (2000) *Cannington Cemetery.* London.

Rahtz, P., Woodward, A., Burrow, I., Everton, A., Watts, L., Leach, P., Hirst, S., Fowler, P. and Gardner, K. (1993) *Cadbury Congresbury 1968–73: A Late/Post-Roman Hilltop Settlement in Somerset.* Oxford.

Randall, C. (2010) 'South Cadbury, Castle Farm', *Somerset Archaeology and Natural History* 153: 213.

Rankov, B. (2002) 'Now you see it, now you don't. The British fleet in Vegetius IV.37', in *Limes XVIII*, P. Freeman, J. Bennett, Z. Fiema and B. Hoffman (eds.). Oxford: 921–924.

Rau, A. (2010) *Nydam Mose 1–2: Die Personengebundenen Gegenstände.* Aarhus.

RCHM (1962) *Eburacum: Roman York.* London.

Redknap, M. and Lewis, J. (2007) *A Corpus of Early Medieval Inscribed Stones and Stone Sculpture in Wales: Volume I.* Cardiff.

Reece, R. (1980) 'Town and country: the end of Roman Britain', *World Archaeology* 12: 77–92.

Reece, R. (1984) 'Mints, markets and the military', in *Military and Civilian in Roman Britain*, T. Blagg and A. King (eds.). Oxford: 143–160.

Reece, R. (1988a) 'Hoards and hoarding', *World Archaeology* 20(2): 261–269.

Reece, R. (1988b) *My Roman Britain.* Cirencester.

Reece, R. (1992) 'The end of the city in Roman Britain', in *The City in Late Antiquity*, J. Rich (ed.). London: 136–144.

Reece, R. (1994) '353, 367 or 357? Splitting the difference or taking a new approach?', *Britannia* 25: 236–238.

Reece, R. (1997) 'Writing Roman Britain: past indicative, future perfect?', *Britannia* 28: 473–478.

Reece, R. (2008) 'Satellite, parasite or just London?', in *Londinium and Beyond: Essays on Roman London and its Hinterland for Harvey Sheldon*, J. Clark, J. Cotton, J. Hall, R. Sherris and H. Swain (eds.). London: 46–48.

Reed, S., Bidwell, P. and Allan, J. (2011) 'Excavation at Bantham, Devon and post-Roman trade in South-West England', *Medieval Archaeology* 55: 82–138.

Reynolds, A. and Langlands, A. (2006) 'Social identities on the macro scale: a maximum view of Wansdyke', in *People and Space in the Early Middle Ages, 300–1300*, W. Davies, G. Halsall and A. Reynolds (eds.). Turnhout, 13–44.

Reynolds, P. and Langley, J. (1979) 'Romano-British corn-drying oven: an experiment', *AJ* 136: 27–42.

Rice, P. (1987) *Pottery Analysis: A Sourcebook*. Chicago.

Richards, J. (1987) *The Significance of Form and Decoration on Anglo-Saxon Cremation Urns*. Oxford.

Richards, J. (1992) 'Anglo-Saxon symbolism', in *The Age of Sutton Hoo*, M. Carver (ed.). Woodbridge: 131–148.

Richards, M., Hedges, R., Molleson, T. and Vogel, J. (1998) 'Stable isotope analysis reveals variations in human diet at the Poundbury Camp Cemetery Sites', *Journal of Archaeological Science* 25: 1247–1252.

Richards, P. (1980) 'Byzantine bronze vessels in England and Europe'. Unpublished PhD thesis, University of Cambridge.

Richardson, A. (2011) 'The Third Way – thoughts on non-Saxon identity south of the Thames AD 450–600', in *Studies in Anglo-Saxon Antiquities and Archaeology: Papers in Honour of Martin G. Welch*, S. Brookes, S. Harrington and A. Reynolds (eds.). Oxford: 49–54.

Riches, D. (1986) 'The phenomenon of violence', in *The Anthropology of Violence*, D. Riches (ed.). Oxford: 1–27.

Rickett, R. (1995) *Spong Hill Part VII: The Iron Age, Roman and Anglo-Saxon Settlement*. Dereham.

Riddler, I. (1988) 'Late Saxon or late Roman? A comb from Pudding Lane', *London Archaeologist* 5(14): 372–374.

Ripoll, G. and Arce, J. (2000) 'The transformation and end of Roman *villae* in the West (fourth to sixth centuries): problems and perspectives', in *Towns and Their Territories between Late Antiquity and the Early Middle Ages*, G. Brogilo, N. Gauther and N. Christie (eds.). Leiden: 63–114.

Rippon, S. (1991) 'Early planned landscapes in South-East Essex', *Essex Archaeology and History* 22: 46–60.

Rippon, S. (2000) *The Transformation of Coastal Wetlands*. Oxford.

Rippon, S. (2006) *Landscape, Community and Colonisation: The North Somerset Levels During the 1st to 2nd Millennia A D*. London.

Rippon, S. (2008) 'Coastal trade in Roman Britain: the investigation of Crandon Bridge, Somerset, a Romano-British transhipment port beside the Severn Estuary', *Britannia* 39: 35–144.

Rippon, S., Fyfe, R. and Brown, A. (2006) 'Beyond villages and open fields: the origins and development of a historic landscape characterised by dispersed settlement in South-West England', *Medieval Archaeology* 50: 31–70.

Rivet, A. and Smith, C. (1979) *The Place-Names of Roman Britain*. London.

Rivet, L. (1964) *Town and Country in Roman Britain*. London.

Rivet, L. and Smith, C. (1979) *The Place-Names of Roman Britain*. London.

Roberts, C. (2000) 'Trauma in bio-cultural perspective', in *Human Osteology in Archaeology and Forensic Science*, M. Cox and S. Mays (eds.). London: 337–350.

Roberts, C. and Cox, M. (2003) *Health and Disease in Britain: From Prehistory until the Present Day*. Stroud.

Robertson, A. (1970) 'Roman finds from non-Roman sites in Scotland: More Roman "drift" in Caledonia', *Britannia* 1: 198–226.

Robertson, A. (2000) *An Inventory of Romano-British Coin Hoards*. London.

Roblin, M. (1951) 'Cités ou citadelles? Les enceintes romaines du Bas-Empire d'après de Paris', *Revue archéologique de l'Est et de Centre-Est* 53: 301–311.

Roblin, M. (1965) 'Cités ou citadelles? Les enceintes romaines du Bas-Empire d'après de Senlis', *Revue archéologique de l'Est et de Centre-Est* 67: 368–391.

Rogers, A. (2005) 'Metalworking and late Roman power: a study of towns in later Roman Britain', in *TRAC2004: Proceedings of the Fourteenth Theoretical Roman Archaeology Conference, Durham, 2004*, J. Bruhn, B. Croxford and D. Grigoropoulos (eds.). Oxford: 27–38.

Rogers, A. (2011) *Late Roman Towns in Britain*. Cambridge.

Rohrbacher, D. (2002) *The Historians of Late Antiquity*. London.

Roskams, S. (1996) 'Urban transition in early medieval Britain: the case of York', in *Towns in Transition: Urban Evolution in Late Antiquity and the Early Middle Ages*, N. Christie and S. Loseby (eds.). Aldershot: 159–183.

Rostovtzeff, M. (1926) *The Social and Economic History of the Roman Empire*. Oxford.

Russell, J. (1968) 'That earlier plague', *Demography* 5(1): 174–184.

Russell, M. and Laycock, S. (2010) *Unroman Britain*. Stroud.

Said, E. (2003) *Orientalism*. London.

Salway, P. (1981) *Roman Britain*. Oxford.

Salzman, M. (1990) *On Roman Time: The Codex Calendar of 354 and the Rhythms of Urban Life in Antiquity*. Los Angeles.

Samson, R. (1992) 'Slavery, the Roman legacy', in *Fifth-Century Gaul: A Crisis of Identity?*, N. Christie and S. Loseby (eds.). Cambridge: 218–227.

Sánchez León, J. (1996) *Les sources de l'histoire des bagaudes: Traduction et commentaire.* Paris.

Sankey, D. (1998) 'Cathedrals, granaries and urban vitality in Late Roman London', in *Roman London: Recent Archaeological Work*, B. Watson (ed.). Portsmouth, Rhode Island: 78–82.

Sankey, D. and Stephenson, A. (1991) 'Recent work on London's defences', in *Roman Frontier Studies 1989: Proceedings of the 15th International Congress of Roman Frontier Studies*, V. Maxfield and M. Dobson (eds.). Exeter: 117–124.

Sarris, P. (2002) 'The Justinianic plague: origins and effects', *Continuity and Change* 17(2): 169–182.

Sarris, P. (2004) 'The origins of the manorial economy: new insights from late antiquity', *EHR* 119: 279–311.

Sawyer, J. (1999) 'The excavation of a Romano-British site at Burgess Hill, West Sussex', *Sussex Archaeological Collections* 137: 49–58.

Sayer, K., Sudds, B. and Ridgeway, V. (in press) *Roman Burials in Southwark: Excavations at Lant Street and Southwark Bridge Road.* London.

Scheidel, W. and Friesen, S. (2009) 'The size of the economy and the distribution of income in the Roman empire', *JRS* 99: 61–91.

Schindler, C. (2009) *Per Carmina Laudes: Untersuchungen zur spätantiken Verspanegyrik von Claudian bis Coripp.* Berlin and New York.

Schönberger, H. (1969) 'The Roman frontier in Germany: an archaeological survey', *JRS* 59: 144–197.

Schrijver, P. (2007) 'What Britons spoke around 400 AD', in *Britons in Anglo-Saxon England*, N. Higham (ed.). Woodbridge: 165–171.

Schwab, I. (1993) 'A Roman burial group from Bow', *London Archaeologist* 2(2): 27–31.

Schwarz, P. (2004) 'Kaiseraugst et Bâle (Suisse) aux premières temps chrétiens', in *Capitales éphémères: Des capitals de cités perdent leur statut dans l'antiquité tardive*, A. Ferdière (ed.). Tours: 103–126.

Scott, E. (1994) *A Gazetteer of Roman Villas in Britain.* Leicester.

Scott, S. (1997) 'The power of image in the late Roman house', in *Domestic Space in the Roman World: Pompeii and Beyond*, R. Laurence and A. Wallace-Hadrill (eds.). Portsmouth, Rhode Island: 53–67.

Scott, S. (2000) *Art and Society in Fourth-Century Britain: Villa Mosaics in Context.* Oxford.

Scull, C. (1993) 'Archaeology, early Anglo-Saxon society and the origins of the early Anglo-Saxon kingdoms', *Anglo-Saxon Studies in Archaeology and History* 6: 65–82.

Seager Smith, R. and Davies, S. (1993) 'Black Burnished ware and other southern British coarsewares', in *Excavations at Greyhound Yard, Dorchester 1981–4*, P. Woodward, S. Davies and A. Graham (eds.). Dorchester: 229–289.

Seaman, A. (2010) 'The Roman to early medieval transition in South-East Wales'. Unpublished PhD thesis, Department of Archaeology, University of Cardiff.

Semple, S. (2007) 'Defining the OE *hearg*: a preliminary archaeological and topographic examination of *hearg* placenames and their hinterlands', *Early Medieval Europe* 15(4): 364–385.

Semple, S. (2008) 'Polities and princes 400–800: new perspectives on the landscape of the South Saxon kingdom', *OJA* 27(4): 407–429.

Sharples, N. (1991) *Maiden Castle*. London.

Sharples, N., Evans, C., Slater, A., Payne, A., Linford, P. and Linford, N. (2012) 'Ham Hill', *British Archaeology* 123: 34–39.

Shaw, R. (1995) 'The Anglo-Saxon cemetery at Eccles: a preliminary account', *Archaeologia Cantiana* 114: 165–188.

Sherlock, S. and Welch, M. (1992) *An Anglo-Saxon Cemetery at Norton, Cleveland*. London.

Sim, D. (1998) *Beyond the Bloom: Iron Refining and Iron Artefact Production in the Roman World*. Oxford.

Sims-Williams, P. (1983) 'The settlement of England in Bede and the Chronicle', *ASE* 12: 1–41.

Sirks, A. (2001) 'The farmer, the landlord and the law in the fifth century', in *Law, Society and Authority in Late Antiquity*, R. Mathisen (ed.). Oxford: 256–271.

Sirks, A. (2008) 'The colonate in Justinian's reign', *JRS* 98: 120–143.

Sivan, H. (1993) *Ausonius of Bordeaux: Genesis of a Gallic Aristocracy*. London.

Sivonen, P. (2006) *Being a Roman Magistrate: Office Holding and Roman Identity in Late Antique Gaul*. Helsinki.

Slootjes, D. (2006) *The Governor and his Subjects in the Later Roman Empire*. Leiden.

Smith, D., Hird, L. and Dix, B. (1989) 'The Roman villa at Great Welden, Northamptonshire', *Northamptonshire Archaeology* 22: 23–68.

Smith, J. (1997) *Roman Villas: A Study in Social Structure*. London.

Smith, R. (1999) 'Late Antique portraits in a public context: Honorific statuary at Aphrodisias in Caria AD 300–600', *JRS* 89: 155–189.

Smith, R., Healy, F., Allen, M., Morris, E., Barnes, I. and Woodward, P. (1997) *Excavations Along the Route of the Dorchester By-pass, Dorset, 1986–8*. Salisbury.

Snape, M. (1992) 'Sub-Roman brooches from Roman sites on the Northern Frontier', *Archaeologia Aeliana Fifth Series* 20: 158–159.

Snape, M. (1993) *Roman Brooches from North Britain*. Oxford.

Snyder, C. (1998) *An Age of Tyrants: Britain and the Britons AD 400–600*. Stroud.

Sommer, M. (1984a) *Die Gürtel und Gürtelbeschläge des 4. und 5. Jahrhunderts im Römischen Reich*. Bonn.

Sommer, S. (1984b) *The Military Vici in Roman Britain*. Oxford.

Soulat, J. (2009) *Le matériel archéologique de type Saxon et Anglo-Saxon en Gaule Mérovingienne*. Paris.

Southern, P. and Dixon, K. (1996) *The Late Roman Army*. London.

Sparey-Green, C. (1987) *Excavations at Poundbury Volume I: The Settlements.* Dorchester.

Sparey-Green, C. (1996) 'Poundbury, Dorset: settlement and economy in Late and Post Roman Dorchester', in *External Contacts and the Economy of Late and Post Roman Britain*, K. Dark (ed.). Woodbridge: 121–152.

Sparey-Green, C. (2004) 'Living amongst the dead: from Roman cemetery to post-Roman monastic settlement at Poundbury', in *Debating Late Antiquity in Britain AD 300–700*, R. Collins and J. Gerrard (eds.). Oxford: 103–111.

Speake, G. (1989) *A Saxon Bed Burial on Swallowcliffe Down.* London.

Speidel, M. (2006) 'Militia: Zu Sprachgebrauch und Militarisierung in der kaiserzeitlich Verwaltung', *Herrschaftsstrukturen und Herrschaftspraxis*, A. Kolb (ed.). Berlin: 263–269.

Springer, M. (2003) 'Location in time and space', in *The Continental Saxons: An Ethnographic Perspective*, D. Green and F. Siegmund (eds.). Woodbridge: 11–36.

Staab, F. (1980) 'A reconsideration of the ancestry of modern political liberty: the problem of the "King's Freemen" ', *Viator* 11: 51–69.

Starkey, D. (2010) *Crown and Country: A History of England through the Monarchy.* London.

Stead, I. (1956) 'An Anglian cemetery on the Mount, York', *Yorkshire Archaeological Journal* 39: 427–435.

Stenton, F. (1971) *Anglo-Saxon England.* Oxford.

Stevens, C. (1947) 'A possible conflict of Roman laws in Britain', *JRS* 37: 132–134.

Stevens, C. (1952) 'The Roman name of Ilchester', *Proceedings of the Somerset Archaeological and Natural History Society* 96: 188–192.

Stevens, C. (1957) 'Marcus, Gratian and Constantine', *Athenaeum* 35: 316–347.

Stevens, C. (1966) 'The social and economic aspects of rural settlement', in *Rural Settlement in Roman Britain*, C. Thomas (ed.). London: 108–128.

Stoodley, N. (1997) *The Spindle and the Spear: A Critical Enquiry into the Construction and Meaning of Gender in the Early Anglo-Saxon Burial Rite.* Oxford.

Stoodley, N. (2000) 'From the cradle to the grave: age organization and the early Anglo-Saxon burial rite', *World Archaeology* 31(3): 456–472.

Stoodley, N. and Stedman, M. (2001) 'Excavations at Shavard's Farm, Meonstoke: the Anglo-Saxon cemetery', *Proceedings of the Hampshire Field Club* 56: 129–169.

Stout, A. (1994) 'Jewelry as a symbol of status in the Roman Empire', in *The World of Roman Costume*, J. Sebesta and L. Bonfante (eds.). Madison: 77–100.

Stubbs, W. (1926) *The Constitutional History of England.* Oxford.

Sudds, B. (2011) 'Building materials', in *A Roman Settlement and Bath House at Shadwell: Excavations at Tobacco Dock and Babe Ruth Restaurant, The Highway, London*, A. Douglas, J. Gerrard and B. Sudds (eds.). London: 103–118.

Sudds, B. (in press) 'Excavations at Crispin St, Spitalfields', *Transactions of the London and Middlesex Archaeological Society.*

Sunter, N. and Brown, D. (1988) 'Metal vessels', in *The Temple of Sulis Minerva, Bath Volume 2: The Finds*, B. Cunliffe (ed.). Oxford: 9–21.

Suzuki, S. (2000) *The Quoit Brooch Style and Anglo-Saxon Settlement*. Woodbridge.

Suzuki, S. (2006) *Anglo-Saxon Button Brooches: Typology, Genealogy, Chronology*. Woodbridge.

Swan, V. (1984) *The Pottery Kilns of Roman Britain*. London.

Swan, V., McBride, R. and Hartley, K. (2009) 'The coarse pottery', in *The Carlisle Millennium Project. Excavations in Carlisle 1998–2001. Volume 2: The Finds*, C. Howard-Davis (ed.). Oxford: 566–677.

Swift, E. (2000) *Regionality in Dress Accessories in the Late Roman West*. Montagnac.

Swift, E. (2003) 'Late Roman bead necklaces and bracelets', *JRA* 16: 336–349.

Swift, E. (2009) *Style and Function in Roman Decoration: Living with Objects and Interiors*. Farnham.

Swift, E. (2010) 'Identifying migrant communities: a contextual analysis of grave assemblages from Continental Late Roman cemeteries', *Britannia* 41: 237–282.

Symonds, R. and Tomber, R. (1991) 'Late Roman London: an assessment of the ceramic evidence from the City of London', *Transactions of the London and Middlesex Archaeological Society* 42: 59–100.

Tabor, R. and Johnson, P. (2000) 'Sigwells, Somerset, England: regional application and interpretation of geophysical survey', *Antiquity* 74: 319–325.

Taylor, J. (2001) 'Rural society in Roman Britain', in *Britons and Romans: Advancing an Archaeological Agenda*, S. James and M. Millett (eds.). London: 46–59.

Taylor, J. (2004) 'The distribution and exchange of pink, grog-tempered pottery in the East Midlands', *Journal of Roman Pottery Studies* 11: 60–66.

Taylor, J. (2007) *An Atlas of Roman Rural Settlement in England*. London.

Taylor, J. and Yonge, D. (1981) 'The ruined church at Stone-by-Faversham: a reassessment', *AJ* 138: 118–145.

Teague, S. (2005) 'Manor Farm, Monk Sherborne, Hampshire: archaeological investigation in 1996', *Proceedings of the Hampshire Field Club and Archaeological Society* 60: 64–135.

Thomas, C. (1993) *Tintagel: Arthur and Archaeology*. London.

Thomas, M., Stumpf, M. and Härke, H. (2006) 'Evidence for an apartheid-like social structure in early Anglo-Saxon England', *Proceedings of the Royal Society B* 273: 2651–2657.

Thompson, E. (1952) 'Peasant revolts in Late Roman Gaul and Spain', *P&P* 2: 11–23.

Thompson, E. (1977) 'Britain AD 406–410', *Britannia* 8: 303–318.

Thompson, E. (1984) *Saint Germanus of Auxerre and the End of Roman Britain*. Woodbridge.

Tilley, C. (1994) *A Phenomenology of Landscape*. Oxford.

Timby, J. (1990) 'Severn Valley Ware: a reassessment', *Britannia* 21: 243–251.

Timby, J. (1996) *The Anglo-Saxon Cemetery at Empingham II, Rutland*. Oxford.

Timby, J. (1998) *Excavations at Kingscote and Wycomb, Gloucestershire: A Roman Estate Centre and Small Town in the Cotswolds*. Cirencester.

Tipper, J. (2004) *The Grubenhaus in Anglo-Saxon England: An Analysis and Interpretation of the Evidence from a Most Distinctive Building Type*. Yeddingham.

Todd, M. (1977) 'Famosa pestis and Britain in the fifth century', *Britannia* 8: 319–325.

Todd, M. (1987) *The Northern Barbarians 100 BC–AD 300*. Oxford.

Todd, M. (1988) 'Villa and fundus', in *The Economies of Romano-British Villas*, K. Branigan and D. Miles (eds.). Sheffield: 14–20.

Tomalin, D. (1987) *Roman Wight: A Guide Catalogue*. Newport.

Tomlin, R. (1974) 'The date of the barbarian conspiracy', *Britannia* 5: 303–309.

Tomlin, R. (1987) 'Was ancient British Celtic ever a written language? Two texts from Roman Bath', *Bulletin of the Board of Celtic Studies* 34: 18–25.

Tomlin, R. (1996) 'A five-acre wood in Roman Kent', in *Interpreting Roman London: Papers in Honour of Hugh Chapman*, J. Bird, M. Hassall and H. Sheldon (eds.). Oxford: 209–215.

Toynbee, J. (1983) 'Mosaicists' sources', *Mosaic* 7: 15–17.

Trigger, B. (1989) *A History of Archaeological Thought*. Cambridge.

Tristram, H. (2007) 'Why don't the English speak Welsh?', in *Britons in Anglo-Saxon England*, N. Higham (ed.). Woodbridge: 192–214.

Turner, E. (1956) 'A Roman writing tablet from Somerset', *JRS* 46: 115–118.

Turner, S. and Gerrard, J. (2004) 'Imported and local pottery from Mothecombe: some new finds amongst old material at Totnes Museum', *Proceedings of the Devon Archaeological Society* 62: 171–175.

Turner, S. and Roskams, S. (2005) 'Excavation and survey at Mothecombe, September 2004', *Devon Archaeological Society Newsletter* 90: 4.

Tyers, I., Hillam, J. and Groves, C. (1994) 'Trees and woodland in the Saxon period: the dendrochronological evidence', in *Environment and Economy in Anglo-Saxon England*, J. Rackham (ed.). London: 12–22.

Tyers, P. (1996) *Roman Pottery in Britain*. London.

Ulmschneider, K. (2011) 'Settlement hierarchy', in *The Oxford Handbook of Anglo-Saxon Archaeology*, H. Hamerow, D. Hinton and S. Crawford (eds.). Oxford: 156–171.

Upex, S. (2001) 'The Roman villa at Cotterstock, Northamptonshire', *Britannia* 32: 57–91.

Upex, S. (2002) 'Landscape continuity and fossilization of Roman fields', *AJ* 159: 77–108.

Van Dam, R. (1985) *Leadership and Community in Late Antique Gaul*. Berkeley.

Van der Veen, M. (1989) 'Charred grain assemblages from Roman-period corn driers in Britain', *AJ* 146: 302–319.

Van der Veen, M. (1992) *Crop Husbandry Regimes: An Archaeobotanical Study of Farming in Northern England: 1000 BC–AD 500*. Sheffield.

Van der Veen, M., Lavarda, A. and Hill, A. (2007) 'The archaeobotany of Roman Britain: current state and identification of research priorities', *Britannia* 38: 181–210.

Von Petrikovits, H. (1971) 'Fortifications in the North-Western Roman Empire from the third to the fifth centuries AD', *JRS* 61: 178–218.

Von Schnurbein, S. and Köhler, H. (1989) 'Der neue Plan des valentinianischen Kastells Alta Ripa (Altrip)', *BRGK* 70: 507–526.

Wacher, J. (1964) 'A survey of Romano-British town defences of the early and middle second century', *AJ* 119: 101–113.

Wacher, J. (1975) *The Towns of Roman Britain.* London.

Wacher, J. (1990) *The Towns of Roman Britain.* London.

Wacher, J. (1998) 'The dating of town walls in Roman Britain', in *Form and Fabric: Studies in Rome's Material Past in Honour of B. R. Hartley*, J. Bird (ed.). Oxford: 41–50.

Wallace-Hadrill, A. (ed.) (1989) *Patronage in Ancient Society.* London.

Walters, B. (1985) 'A gold ring from Littlecote Park', *Britannia* 16: 247–248.

Walton, P. (2011) 'Rethinking Roman Britain: an applied numismatic analysis of the coins recorded by the Portable Antiquities Scheme'. Unpublished PhD thesis, University College London.

Walton Rogers, P. (2002) 'Dye tests on textile fragments from the lead coffin', in *Excavations at Alington Avenue, Fordington, Dorchester, Dorset, 1984–87*, S. Davies, P. Bellamy, M. Heaton and P. Woodward (eds.). Dorchester: 159.

Walton Rogers, P. (2007) *Cloth and Clothing in Early Anglo-Saxon England AD 450–750.* London.

Wamers, E. (1983) 'Some ecclesiastical and secular Insular metalwork found in Norwegian Viking graves', *Peritia* 2: 277–306.

Ward-Perkins, B. (2005) *The Fall of Rome and the End of Civilization.* Oxford.

Ward-Perkins, B. (2009) 'Call this a recession? At least it isn't the Dark Ages'. *Financial Times Online.* www.ft.com/cms/s/0/0dfee138-ef69-11de–86c4-00144feab49a.html#axzz2Q9WNEea1 (accessed 11/4/2013).

Watson, B. (1992) 'The excavation of a Norman fortress on Ludgate Hill', *London Archaeologist* 6(14): 371–377.

Watson, B. (1998) 'Dark earth and urban decline in late Roman London', in *Roman London: Recent Archaeological Research*, B. Watson (ed.). Portsmouth, Rhode Island: 100–112.

Watts, L. and Leach, P. (1996) *Henley Wood, Temples and Cemetery: Excavations 1962–69 by the Late Ernest Greenfield and Others.* London.

Weber, E. (1976) *Peasants into Frenchmen: The Modernization of France 1870–1914.* Stanford.

Weber, M. (2004) 'Politics as a vocation', in *The Vocation Lectures*, D. Owen, T. Strong and R. Livingstone (eds. and trans.). Indianapolis: 32–94.

Webster, C. (2000) 'The Dark Ages', in *Somerset Archaeology: Papers to Mark 150 Years of the Somerset Archaeological and Natural History Society*, C. Webster (ed.). Taunton: 79–84.

Webster, C. and Brunning, R. (2004) 'A seventh-century AD cemetery at Stoneage Barton Farm, Bishop's Lydeard, Somerset and square ditched burials in post-Roman Britain', *AJ* 161: 54–81.

Webster, G. (1980) *The Roman Invasion of Britain*. London.

Webster, G. (1983) 'The function and organisation of late Roman civil defences in Britain', in *Roman Urban Defences in the West*, J. Maloney and B. Hobley (eds.). London: 118–120.

Webster, G. (1996) *Roman Samian Pottery in Britain*. York.

Webster, J. (2001) 'Creolizing the Roman provinces', *AJA* 105(2): 209–225.

Webster, P. (1976) 'Severn Valley Ware: a preliminary study', *Transactions of the Bristol and Gloucester Archaeological Society* 94: 18–46.

Weddell, P. (2000) 'The excavation of a post-Roman cemetery near Kenn', *Proceedings of the Devon Archaeological Society* 58: 93–126.

Wedlake, W. (1958) *Excavations at Camerton, Somerset*. Camerton.

Wedlake, W. (1982) *The Excavation of the Shrine of Apollo at Nettleton, Wiltshire, 1956–1971*. London.

Welch, M. (1989) 'The Kingdom of the South Saxons', in *The Origins of Anglo-Saxon Kingdoms*, S. Bassett (ed.). Leicester: 75–83.

Welch, M. (1993) 'The archaeological evidence for federate settlement in Britain within the fifth century', in *L'Armée Romaine et les Barbares du IIIe au VIIe Siècle*, F. Vallet and M. Kazanski (eds.). Paris.

Wenham, J. (1989) 'Anatomical interpretation of Anglo-Saxon weapon injuries', in *Weapons and Warfare in Anglo-Saxon England*, S. Chadwick-Hawkes (ed.). Oxford: 123–139.

Wenham, L. (1968) *The Romano-British Cemetery at Trentholme Drive, York*. London.

Wenskus, R. (1961) *Stammesbildung und Verfassung: das Werden der frühmittelalterlichen gentes*. Cologne.

Werff, J. van der (2003) 'The third and second lives of amphoras in Alphen aan den Rijn, The Netherlands', *Journal of Roman Pottery Studies* 10: 109–116.

Wessex Archaeology (2006) *Excavations at the Former East Hill House, Sterndale Road, Dartford, Kent*. Salisbury, Unpublished Wessex Archaeology Report No. 62240.01.

Wessex Archaeology (2009) *Further Work on a Detached Roman Bath House and Earlier Building at Truckle Hill, North Wraxall, Wiltshire*. Salisbury, Wessex Archaeology Unpublished Report No. 58522.01.

West, S. (1985) *West Stow: The Anglo-Saxon Village Volume I: Text*. Ipswich.

Whitby, M. (2004) 'Emperors and armies, AD 235–395', in *Approaching Late Anti-quity: Transformation from Early to Late Empire*, S. Swain and M. Edwards (eds.). Oxford: 156–186.

White, R. (1988) *Roman and Celtic Objects from Anglo-Saxon Graves*. Oxford.

White, R. (2007) *Britannia Prima: Roman Britain's Last Province*. Stroud.

White, S., Manley, J., Jones, R., Orna-Ornstein, J., Johns, C. and Webster, J. (1999) 'A mid-fifth century hoard of Roman and pseudo-Roman material from Patch-ing, West Sussex', *Britannia* 30: 301–315.

Whittaker, C. (1983) 'Late Roman trade and traders', in *Trade in the Ancient Economy*, P. Garnsey, K. Hopkins and C. Whittaker (eds.). London: 163–180.

Whittaker, D. (1993) 'What happens when frontiers come to an end?' in *Frontières d'empire: Nature et signification des frontières romaines*, P. Brun, S. van der Leeuw and D. Whittaker (eds.). Nemours: 121–132.

Whittaker, D. (1998) 'Landlords and warlords in the later Roman Empire', in *War and Society in the Roman World*, J. Rich and G. Shipley (eds.). London: 277–302.

Whyman, M. (2001) 'Late Roman Britain in transition: a ceramic perspective from East Yorkshire'. Unpublished DPhil thesis, University of York.

Wickenden, N. (1988) *Excavations at Great Dunmow, Essex*. Chelmsford.

Wickham, C. (1984) 'The other transition: from ancient world to feudalism', *P&P* 103: 3–36.

Wickham, C. (2005) *Framing the Early Middle Ages: Europe and the Mediterranean, 400–800*. Oxford.

Wilcox, M. (2010) 'Marketing conquest and the vanishing Indian: an indigenous response to Jared Diamond's archaeology of the American Southwest', in *Questioning Collapse: Human Resilience, Ecological Vulnerability and the Aftermath of Empire*, P. McAnany and N. Yoffee (eds.). Cambridge: 113–141.

Wild, J. (1973) 'Roman textiles from the Walbrook', *Germania* 53: 138–143.

Wild, J. (2002) 'The textile industries of Roman Britain', *Britannia* 33: 1–42.

Williams, H. (1997) 'Ancient landscapes and the dead: the reuse of prehistoric and Roman monuments as early Anglo-Saxon burial sites', *Medieval Archaeology* 41: 1–32.

Williams, H. (1998) 'Monuments and the past in Early Anglo-Saxon England', *World Archaeology* 30(1): 90–108.

Williams, H. (2002) 'Cemeteries as central places – place and identity in Migration Period eastern England', in *Central Places in the Migration and Merovingian Periods. Papers from the 52nd Sachsensymposium*, B. Hardh and L. Larsson (eds.). Lund: 341–362.

Williams, H. (2004) 'Artefacts in early medieval graves – a new perspective', in *Debating Late Antiquity in Britain AD 300–700*, R. Collins and J. Gerrard (eds.). Oxford: 89–102.

Williams, H. (2005) 'Keeping the dead at arm's length: memory, weaponry and early medieval mortuary technologies', *Journal of Social Archaeology* 5(2): 253–275.

Williams, M. (2003) 'Growing metaphors: the agricultural cycle as metaphor in the later prehistoric period of Britain and North-West Europe', *Journal of Social Archaeology* 3(2): 223–255.

Williams, P. and Newman, R. (2006) *Market Lavington, Wiltshire: An Anglo-Saxon Cemetery and Settlement.* Salisbury.

Williams, R. and Zeepvat, R. (1994) *Bancroft: A Late Bronze Age/Iron Age Settlement, Roman Villa and Temple-Mausoleum Volume 2.* Aylesbury.

Williams, T. (1993) *The Archaeology of Roman London Volume 3: Public Buildings in the South-West Quarter.* London.

Wilmott, T. (1997) *Birdoswald: Excavations of a Roman Fort on Hadrian's Wall and its Successor Settlements: 1987–1992.* London.

Wilson, A. (2002) 'Machines, power and the ancient economy', *JRS* 92: 1–32.

Wilson, P. (1991) 'Aspects of Roman signal stations', in *Roman Frontier Studies 1989: Proceedings of the 15th International Congress of Roman Frontier Studies,* V. Maxfield and M. Dobson (eds.). Exeter: 142–147.

Wilson, P. (2002) *Cataractonium: Roman Catterick and its Hinterland, Excavations and Research 1958–1997.* London: 203–395.

Wilson, R. (2006) 'Urban defences and civic status in Early Roman Britain', in *Romanitas: Essays on Roman Archaeology in Honour of Shepherd Frere on the Occasion of his Ninetieth Birthday,* R. Wilson (ed.). Oxford: 1–47.

Winterbottom, M. (1978) *Gildas: The Ruin of Britain and Other Works.* Chichester.

Wolfram, H. (1988) *History of the Goths.* Berkeley.

Wolfram, H. (1997) *The Roman Empire and its Germanic Peoples.* Berkeley.

Wood, I. (1984) 'The end of Roman Britain: continental evidence and parallels', in *Gildas: New Approaches,* M. Lapidge and D. Dumville (eds.). Woodbridge: 1–25.

Wood, I. (1987) 'The fall of the western Empire and the end of Roman Britain', *Britannia* 18: 251–262.

Woodward, A. and Hill, J. (2002) *Prehistoric Britain: The Ceramic Basis.* Oxford.

Woodward, A. and Leach, P. (1993) *The Uley Shrines: Excavations of a Ritual Complex on West Hill, Uley, Gloucestershire 1977–1979.* London.

Woodward, P., Davies, S. and Graham, A. (1993) *Excavations at Greyhound Yard, Dorchester, Dorset 1981–4.* Dorset.

Woolf, A. (2000) 'Community, identity and kingship in early England', in *Social Identity in Early Medieval Britain,* W. Frazer and O. Tyrell (eds.). Leicester: 91–110.

Woolf, A. (2003) 'The Britons: from Romans to Barbarians', in *Regna and Gentes: The Relationship between Late Antique and Early Medieval Peoples and Kingdoms in the Transformation of the Roman World,* H.-W. Goetz, J. Jarnut and W. Pohl (eds.). Leiden: 345–380.

Woolf, G. (1998) *Becoming Roman: The Origins of Provincial Civilization in Gaul.* Cambridge.

Wright, J., Powell, A. and Barclay, A. (2009) *Excavation of Prehistoric and Romano-British Rural Sites at Marnel Park and Merton Rise (Popley), Basingstoke, 2004–2008.* Salisbury.

Yorke, B. (1990) *Kings and Kingdoms of Early Anglo-Saxon England.* London.

Yorke, B. (1995) *Wessex in the Early Middle Ages.* Leicester.

Yorke, B. (2003) 'Anglo-Saxon Gentes and Regna', in *Regna and Gentes: The Relationship between Late Antique and Early Medieval Peoples and Kingdoms in the Transformation of the Roman World*, H.-W. Goetz, J. Jarnut and W. Pohl (eds.). Leiden: 381–407.

Young, C. (1977) *The Oxfordshire Roman Potteries.* Oxford.

Youngs, S. (1995) 'A penannular brooch from Calne, Wiltshire', *Wiltshire Archaeological and Natural History Magazine* 88: 127–131.

Yule, B. (1990) 'The "dark earth" and Late Roman London', *Antiquity* 64: 620–628.

Zant, J. (2009) *The Carlisle Millennium Project: Excavations in Carlisle 1998–2001. Volume I: The Stratigraphy.* Lancaster.

Zeepvat, R. (1994) *Bancroft: The Late Bronze Age and Iron Age Settlement and Roman Temple Mausoleum.* Aylesbury.

Zimmerman, W. (1992) 'Die Siedlungen des 1. bis 6. Jahrhunderts nach Christum von Flögeln-Eekhotjnen, Niedersachsen: Die Bauformen und ihre Funktionen', *Probleme der Küstenforschung im Südlichen Nordseegebiet* 19: 1–360.

Zimmerman, W. (1999) 'Favourable conditions for cattle farming, one reason for the Anglo-Saxon migration over the North Sea?', in *Discussions with the Past: Archaeological Studies Presented to W. A. van Es*, H. Sarfatij, W. Verwers and P. Woltering (eds.). Amersfoort: 129–144.

Index

Page numbers in italics are illustrations; those with 't' are tables.

Made in United States
North Haven, CT
15 July 2022

21443987R00200